A
HISTORY
of
PSYCHOLOGY

ERWIN A. ESPER
Professor Emeritus of Psychology
University of Washington

W. B. SAUNDERS COMPANY, *Philadelphia & London 1964*

To the Memory of my Teachers

GEORGE MELVILLE BOLLING

and

ALBERT PAUL WEISS

αἰὲν ἀριστεύειν καὶ ὑπείροχον ἔμμεναι ἄλλων

PREFACE

In his *History of Psychology* (1914), Otto Klemm remarked: "The continuity of psychological thought has often been broken. How often a pre-Raphaelite return to long-forgotten forms of thought has followed a period of the keenest hopes and anticipations!" Such discontinuities and atavisms are of course sources of confusion for young psychologists, the more so because it is often uncertain whether a given tide is still flowing or is beginning to ebb. In the five decades since Klemm wrote the above words, the confusion has been magnified by a growing preoccupation with methodology and with practical—particularly social—applications and a decreasing interest in and knowledge of history.

In the first decade of our century psychology still defended its position as an independent science by defining itself as the study of "consciousness." By 1913 John B. Watson had begun his campaign to substitute "behavior" for "consciousness." Watson (1924, p. xi) claimed that behavior psychology "is purely an American production and the attempts of Titchener to tie it up with past 'revolts' in psychology and of Miss Washburn to link it with the so-called objectivism of Beer, Bethe, von Uexküll, Nuel and other continental writers are based upon an insufficient knowledge of its tenets." This seems an extraordinary statement to have been made by a pupil of Jacques Loeb. To understand it, we must remember that Watson's historical background, like that of other psychologists of his generation, had been obtained from philosophers, and that the only German psychologist whom he seems to have studied with any attention was Wundt. His biological orientation he picked up

personally from Loeb, Jennings, Donaldson, and Howell, and no
doubt from the famous lectures at Yale of Sherrington and Ver-
worn. His chief experimental method he adopted from Pavlov and
Bechterev, whose ancestor was Sechenov, the pupil of Ludwig,
Helmholtz, and du Bois-Reymond. Watson did not realize that he
himself represented a phase in a historical development—a phase,
moreover, which had in its essentials been anticipated—and the
myth of the immaculate conception of American behaviorism has
been accepted by many others.

The introductory sentence of Ebbinghaus's *Abriss*—"Psychology has a long past, but only a short history"—has been much
quoted. But Ebbinghaus then goes on to attribute the rapid development of modern psychology to the developments in natural science and particularly in biology. It has seemed to me that it might
be fruitful to propose the thesis that psychology's long past is also
its history, and that this history is that of the study of man as a
biological organism. A corollary of this thesis is the proposition that
the mentalistic psychology brought to America by the pupils of the
German philosopher-psychologists was a "pre-Raphaelite return
to long-forgotten forms of thought"; an interruption in the development of a natural science of man. It is this thesis and its corollary
which I have sought to document in this book, which is therefore
a history and not *the* history of psychology; in other words, my
history is *selective,* as are of course all histories. The kind of selection which I have made has seemed to me to be timely for four
reasons: (1) the tendency of American psychologists in the recent
past to neglect the history of their science; (2) the controversy as
to the relation of psychology to physiology ("reductionism"); (3)
the frequent recurrence in contemporary literature—both of psychology and of physiology—of ancient ways of talking which are
incompatible with naturalistic science; and (4) the anomalous contemporary situation of psychology amid a welter of "social" or
"behavioral" sciences and paramedical concerns.

If the attention I have given to the ancient writers seems excessive, I hope that the reader will note that in each case I have sought
to trace to modern times the subsequent history of the ideas which
they started. I have accepted Carr's (1962) thesis that "History
acquires meaning and objectivity only when it establishes a coherent relation between past and future." The historian, says Carr, is
"an individual human being," and history is "a dialogue between
the historian in the present and the facts of the past." This dialogue

involves inevitably an extrapolation into the future, concerning which judgments of validity will vary with the history of the reader and with the future course of science. Moreover, it is very commonly the case that what is presented as a historical extrapolation is actually a hope or a recommendation—an assertion, not that things will go in a certain way, but that it would be well if they did. If this is true of my book, perhaps I can still claim some historical justification in that my suggestions are the outcome of my reflection on our history.

George Bolling would have been amused to see the words of "the glorious son of Hippolochus" applied to himself and his colleague Weiss. But "Always to be best, and distinguished above the rest" seems to me to express the lofty and uncompromising dignity and dedication, the high seriousness, of their attitude toward scholarship and science, while the warmth of their personality cast a glamor over the subjects which they taught.

My academic colleagues will understand that in the production of this book, the dedication of my wife, while different in expression, was no less onerous than my own. Moreover, it was her persuasion, joined to warm encouragement from members of the Saunders Company, that initiated the conversion of my lectures into this book.

I gratefully acknowledge a grant received from the Graduate School of the University of Washington for typing service and for the purchase of books.

E   A   E

Index, Washington

ACKNOWLEDGMENTS

The author and publisher gratefully acknowledge the courtesy of the following copyright owners in granting permission to reprint quotations from their books:

Appleton-Century-Crofts, Inc. *A History of Experimental Psychology,* by Edwin G. Boring. Copyright 1950.

Cambridge University Press. *Man on His Nature,* by Sir Charles Sherrington. Copyright 1950.

Columbia University Press. *Aristotle,* by John Herman Randall, Jr. Copyright 1960.

William Barrett. *Irrational Man,* by William Barrett. Copyright 1958. Reprinted by permission of Doubleday & Company, Inc.

Dover Publications, Inc. *Primitive Man as Philosopher,* by Paul Radin. Copyright 1957.

Holt, Rinehart and Winston, Inc. *Language,* by Leonard Bloomfield. Copyright 1933.

W. Kneale and M. Kneale. *The Development of Logic,* by William Kneale and Martha Kneale. Oxford University Press. Copyright 1962.

Alfred A. Knopf, Incorporated. *A History of Medicine,* by A. Castiglioni. Trans. and ed. by E. B. Krumbhaar. Copyright 1947.

Longmans, Green & Co. Limited. *The Scientific Revolution 1500–1800,* by A. R. Hall. Copyright 1954.

The Macmillan Company. *A History of Modern Philosophy,* by Harald Höffding. Transl. by B. E. Meyer. Vol. II. Copyright 1920.

Oxford University Press, Inc. *A History of Medicine,* by Henry E. Sigerist. Vol. I. Copyright 1951. *Greek Biology and Greek Medicine,* by Charles Singer. Copyright 1922.

University of North Carolina Press. *Cell and Psyche,* by Edmund W. Sinnott. Copyright 1950.

Stanford University Press. *Disease, Life, and Man,* by Rudolf
    Virchow. Transl. by Lelland J. Rather. Copyright 1958.
University of Minnesota Press. *Minnesota Studies in the Philoso-
    phy of Science, Vol. I,* edited by Herbert Feigl and Michael
    Scriven. Copyright 1956.
University of Pittsburgh Press. *Current Trends in Psychological
    Theory,* by Wayne Dennis, Dorwin Cartwright, E. Lowell
    Kelly, et al. Copyright 1961.
University of Washington Press. *Portraits from Memory,* by Rich-
    ard B. Goldschmidt. Copyright 1956.
Yale University Press. *The Growth of Scientific Ideas,* by William
    P. D. Wightman. Copyright 1951.
The Free Press. *A Short History of Science,* by H. Lindsey, H. But-
    terfield, H. Dingle, et al. Copyright 1959.
McGraw-Hill Book Company, Inc. *Psychology: A Study of a Sci-
    ence,* Vol. 4, edited by Sigmund Koch. Copyright 1962. *Social
    Psychology,* 2nd ed., by Richard T. LaPiere and Paul R. Farns-
    worth. Copyright 1942.

CONTENTS

CONTENTS

1

Introduction:
The Uses of History

Es ist immer etwas höchst Bedenkliches, das Bestehende ohne
Kenntnis seiner Vergangenheit erklären zu wollen.—Lazarus Geiger,
Der Ursprung der Sprache. 1869.

This introductory chapter might perhaps have borne the title,
"An Apology for the Study of the History of Psychology," although
I would then have needed to explain that "apology" was used in its
primary sense of "something said or written in defense or justification of what appears to others to be wrong." For that the study of
the history of psychology is regarded as "wrong" by influential contemporary psychologists is evidenced by the inhospitality of journal
editors, one of whom has arrestingly characterized historical writings as "the hashing over of old theories." In one of our oldest universities the subject disappeared from the curriculum a few years
ago amid expressions of distaste for historical studies by eminent
experimentalists. But the era of ahistoricism in American psychology may perhaps in future history be temporally delimited as *circa*
1920-1960; for, as we shall see, there is much evidence of its passing. It has, of course, been a parochial American, not a universal,
phenomenon.

In medicine, it is a common observation that there are differences
not only of skills but also of personality between two classes of practitioners, the surgeons and the internists; these two classes might

1

perhaps be characterized as the doers and the verbalizers, respectively. It is not always recognized that there is an analogous dichotomy of scientists. We live in an age of rapid expansion of experimental techniques, and it is not surprising that men selected for aptitudes in electronics, mathematics, or industrial and clinical applications should have little motivation to acquire a background in the history of science. To such men it may seem inconceivable that anything of relevance to contemporary research could have been done more than twenty years ago. In her witty presidential address to the International Society for Cell Biology, Fell (1960) * remarked:

> In science, as in the world of dress, fashions recur. . . . There is one form of recurrence that is wholly regrettable, and which is one of the unfortunate consequences of the vast expansion of research and the monstrous and unwieldy literature that it now produces. I will mention a small example of the sort of thing that I have in mind. In the 1920's some of my colleagues did a rather extensive series of experiments which they duly published. A few years ago, an account of an almost identical research with the same results appeared in one of the journals, but with no mention of the earlier study. One of my colleagues wrote and pointed this out to the author, who replied that he never quoted any literature prior to 1946 [p. 1625 f.].

A first basic reason, then, for studying the history of any science is to know what has been done, in order both to avoid stupid repetition and to take advantage of research possibilities that may have been suggested long ago but have lain dormant. Here two further quotations from Fell's address are pertinent:

> Sometimes information or an idea has been available for years before some astute and enterprising person realizes its significance and places it in the public eye. The history of research on the nucleic acids is an interesting example of this. According to Hughes's *History of Cytology,* nucleic acid was first discovered by Miescher in 1871. Work then proceeded steadily but without attracting very wide interest until the 1930's, when the subject rapidly became extremely popular [p. 1625].
> The motives that prompt us to follow fashions in research are vari-

---

* The reference dates are those of the editions which I used; they are therefore merely code numbers which will enable the reader, if he wishes, to identify quotations in their contexts by page number. The reader need therefore not be startled by such a reference as "Kant (1951)." However, in the List of References I have added, where it seemed desirable, the dates of first and other editions.

ous and not always estimable. . . . In general, the waves of interest in something fresh that constantly sweep through our world are vital to its well-being, and without them research would indeed be stagnant and dreary. But rushing after new things merely because they are new (or what is more commonly termed "jumping on the band wagon") is another matter; it leads to the abandonment of existing lines of work that ought to be carried much farther, and even to contempt for the realities of nature, as in the disdain for structure that was such a regrettable fashion in cell biology a few years ago [p. 1627].

In psychology, too, we have had fashions in research; e.g., there really is no good reason why psycholinguistics should not have burgeoned in the 1920's as it did in the 1950's, nor why it should now be so extensively taken up by psychologists ignorant of linguistic science; one technique in this area, that of word-association, has been turned on and off like a tap during the past eighty years. If a young psychologist were to read the history of his science he would be very likely to come upon a problem which, were he to begin exploiting it now, would bring him into prominence a decade or two hence.

In the last of the passages quoted above, Fell referred to "the disdain for structure that was such a regrettable fashion in cell biology a few years ago." In psychology, we have been passing through a period of similar disdain for biological structure. Skinner, with his concept of the "empty organism," has been a chief representative of this attitude. The attempt to analyze behavior in terms of biological structures has been stigmatized as "physiologizing" or as "reductionism." Two historical reasons for this posture may be mentioned: first, the neurophysiology available to psychologists in the early decades of our century was so inadequate to behavioral theorizing as to bring physiological speculations by psychologists into disrepute; and secondly, experimental psychology from its birth has felt a compulsion to demonstrate to others and to reassure itself that it is an independent science, with its own subject matter and laws. But history suggests that it was a historical accident that the founding of experimental psychology was credited to professors of philosophy, and that these founders and their successors therefore felt it necessary to assert their independence from philosophy on the one hand and from the ancient disciplines of medicine and biology on the other. Actually, when we survey the great names of the early days of modern psychology—Weber, Fechner, Helmholtz, Hering, J. Mueller, Donders, Exner, von Kries, Koenig, Preyer—we find that these men were either biologists or physicists with an interest in physiology; others, whom we think of as primarily biologists, made contributions which have had greater influence on psychology than those of most psychologists: von Haller, Galvani, Bell, Whytt, Marshall Hall, Pflueger, Sechenov, Gall, Flourens, Broca, Munk, Goltz, Fritsch, Hitzig, Bechterev, Pavlov, Loeb, Sherrington. And of course many of the men whom we reckon as psychologists received training as biologists and not a few entered psychology with a medical degree: e.g., Locke, Hartley, Cabanis, Lotze, Wundt, James, McDougall. Moreover, in the last decade of the nineteenth century a group of German biologists—Beer, Bethe, Uexküll, Ziegler, and Loeb—formulated a program for an objective physiology that anticipated everything of importance in American behaviorism, which has usually been regarded as a brilliant (or crassly sansculottic) innovation of John B. Watson. The term "objective psychology" was applied to the program by Arnhart (1899), and the program was outlined by Bethe (1898), Beer, Bethe, and Uexküll (1899), and Ziegler (1900). I regard it as an unfortunate historical accident that what we now call "behavioristics" did not develop from this beginning and under biological auspices.

Most of the history of what is nowadays called clinical psychology is to be found in the history of medicine, beginning with Hippocrates, and there is little in current therapy, other than the nonrational use of lobotomy and tranquilizing drugs, which does not have a medical history of at least several centuries. As for diagnostic tools, Meehl (1960) warns the "fledgling clinical psychologist" that if his "self-concept is mainly 'I am a (test oriented) psychodiagnostician' [he] may have to maintain his professional security over the next few years by not reading the professional literature" (p. 26). Meehl further expresses the opinion that clinical psychology has neither a theory from which to predict behavior nor measuring instruments adequate for specifying it. A reading of such a history as that of Zilboorg (1941) might prompt a clinical student to ask the sobering question: what great advances have been made by psychologists in diagnosis or therapy in the last century? Particularly striking in this history from ancient to recent times are the alternating cycles of theological, organic, and functional interpretations, and of kind and punitive treatment. Very apposite is Zilboorg's quotation of Del Greco: *L'histoire nous rend modestes.*

In two areas, those of animal psychology and of behavioral correlates of brain damage, it seems possible that there might have been some advantage had the development occurred within biology and in continuity with the history of biology. Concerning animal psychology, Bitterman (1960) remarks:

> It is interesting to note . . . that the acceptance of the Darwinian hypothesis was accompanied by a growing disregard for the facts of brain structure. After giving up their inquiry into animal consciousness, the early comparative psychologists were at some pains to establish that there still remained to them an area of investigation different from that of the zoologists, and that their methods and findings were as important as those of the zoologists. If some primitive experiments with a maze or a problem box suggested that the process of learning was the same in monkey and sparrow, why then perhaps the difference in brain development had no fundamental significance [p. 706].

And concerning the literature on the rat, Bitterman observes:

> It is significant, I think, that nothing much in the way of well-defined functional relations has been forthcoming even from those who have rejected the traditional questions and advocated a vacant empiricism; in the hands of the Skinnerians, for example, batteries of expensive automatic equipment have yielded little more than an idiosyncratic assortment of kymograph tracings scarcely capable of quantitative analysis [p. 708].

Concerning the behavioral correlates of experimental brain lesions, some psychologists have come to conclusions which practically deny any significance to the elaborate cytoarchitecture of the brain. Hebb (1949, p. xvii) quotes an anonymous anatomist "who claimed that psychologists think of the brain as having all the finer structure of a bowlful of porridge." It may be questioned whether the neglect of histology and physiology which has resulted from the separation of psychology from biology has not delayed the discovery of basic behavioral explanations in general. Hebb (1949, 1955) has pointed out the failure of psychological theorists to exploit recent physiological research in its possible applications to unsolved behavioral problems. For example, he states that "When the detailed evidence of neurophysiology and histology are considered, the conclusion becomes inevitable that the nonsensory factor in cerebral action must be more consistently present and of more dominating importance than reluctant psychological theory has ever recognized" (1949, p. 7). And elsewhere Hebb (1958, p. vii) has described psychology as "fundamentally a biological science"; even its applied fields "demand a solid understanding of the mechanisms of behavior in the individual subject"; the theories of learning, perception, emotion, etc. "are biological because they have always been profoundly influenced by neurophysiology, neuroanatomy, and evolutionary and genetic theory." A similar view has been expressed by Pratt (1939, p. ix f.):

> The principal task of theoretical psychology in making a scientific portrait of human nature is to discover the immediate antecedents of initial descriptive data. These antecedent conditions are located within the biological organism. All psychological explanation must therefore move in the direction of physiology. The theoretical importance of psychological descriptions, as contrasted with any practical significance they may conceivably possess, derives almost exclusively from the light they throw on physiological mechanisms.

From such opinions Mandler and Kessen (1959) demur. They express the view that "A theory of dreams, or of thinking, or of animal learning which makes confirmed predictions and which is the basis for the design of informative research is a good theory, regardless of whether it is possible to re-interpret its premises into statements consistent with current physiological theory" (p. 268). Their argument is the familiar one that on the one hand there is "a set of protocol sentences about behavior," and a theory which permits its deduction, and on the other hand there is "a set of statements about physiological functions," and a corresponding theory, and that it is a mistake in strategy to attempt to "reduce" the one to the other. They also state that

> It is well to recall . . . that the criteria for a scientific vocabulary do not demand that "actual existence" underlie terms in the sense that tables and dogs exist. Rather, the basic requirements turn on the reliable usage of terms in particular observational circumstances and in the sentences of a theory. On the first criterion, there may be in the language of physiology a group of terms which, for reasons of their systematic history, have a high level of reliability of usage, but there seem to be no defensible reasons why "drive" may not come to be as reliably applied as "synapse," or "libido" as reliably applied as "association area" [p. 264].

But it should be observed that many of those who are most assiduously investigating "drive" are striving to "reduce" their behavioral sentences to the thing-language of reticular system, hypothalamus, and limbic lobe, or to that of blood composition, gastric conditions, etc. Moreover, in the convergent results of research on human isolation, early sensory deprivation in dogs and monkeys, and autistic children, on the one hand, and on the functions of neocortex, rhinencephalon, and brain stem reticular formation and lemnisci, on the other (cf., e.g., Sprague et al., 1961), physiological meaning and, it would seem, increased reliability of usage are being given to the ancient and nebulous concepts of "attention" and "affect." And though Mandler and Kessen express the hope that "in the rational scientific community . . . considerations of historical sources . . . would have little to do with research strategy and tactics" (p. 263), it seems legitimate to ask what history has to tell us about the sources and nature of our "protocol sentences." The language of conditioning comes to us from the physiologists Sechenov, Bechterev, and Pavlov. The language of animal psychology comes to us from the Darwinians, and contemporary animal psychologists are much preoccupied with neural and glandular structures. The language of sensation and perception was largely developed by physiologists and physiologically trained psychologists. Much of the history of personality analysis and most of the history of clinical diagnosis and therapy are to be found in the histories of medicine. What is there left? Social psychology? Or Freudian theory? It will hardly be argued that here are to be found the best examples of reliable protocol sentences or powerfully predictive theories. The hypothesis might be entertained that reliability of sentences is a decreasing function of distance from biological tissue.

The above discussion may suggest a second basic reason for studying the history of psychology; namely, that a knowledge of our historical roots may be relevant to charting our future course. It may then appear that the negative attitude of many contemporary psychologists toward physiological interpretations represents a passing phase, which increasing physiological knowledge will make untenable. Moreover, there has been a great deal of emphasis recently on the necessity of basic science research and theory; most psychologists, surveying the vast output of low-level data and high-level theories in their contemporary literature, probably share an uncomfortable feeling that psychology is still an immature science awaiting some future "break-through." It is hard to imagine a fundamental "break-through" in other than biological terms; so, for example, the researchers seem to think who are working so actively on computer models of the thinking process. In recent times, two interests, that in testing and that in social phenomena, have attracted relatively large numbers of psychologists with little or no training in biology. This phenomenon may turn out to have been a temporary perturbation of the curve of growth of our science, which will have been corrected perhaps by some future administrative reclassification.

Boring (1959) has denied the validity of the first two reasons which I have given for studying the history of science. He tells us that we should not study history with the expectation of projecting the future. "Specific prediction . . . almost always fails, or is right by mere chance, because the efficient antecedents are too numerous and too complexly related to be correctly understood." And, "The other wrong reason for studying the past of science is to protect oneself from rediscovering something already known." Scientific literature, Boring says, is so vast that it is hopeless for the investigator to catch possible anticipations of his projected work. There is left only one good reason for studying the history of science: "One finds that he needs to know about the past, not in order to predict the future, but in order to understand the present."

My comment on these views would be that in scientific research, as elsewhere in life, we are under the continual necessity of planning for the future, and there is no other basis for doing this than our knowledge of the past. And, as elsewhere in life, we do what we can; things are always too complex for perfectly reliable prediction, and yet we must predict, if not explicitly then implicitly. As for "understanding the present," what functional significance would this have if not to provide some preparation for the future? In the view of an eminent contemporary historian, "It is at once the justification and the explanation of history that the past throws light on the future, and the future throws light on the past" (Carr, 1962, p. 163).

Actually, the main point I would like to make is expressed very well by Boring in this same article: "Each individual effort is an eddy in the total stream of science; and we shall become much wiser, get much nearer the truth, if we remember to look at the stream as a whole and notice the eddies only as they contribute to the sweep of the main current." But I would apply this wise saying to the examples from the history of psychology which Boring gives as illustrations of the impossibility of predicting future trends in science. Karl Lashley, he says, "spent his life 'in search of the engram.'" "At one time it looked as if Lashley's skillful, ingenious, and indefatigable labor was destined to dissolve in failure." Then Boring goes on to say:

> But the face of nature was then changing under the combined attacks of physicists and psychologists. "Field theory" came into

physics, the realization that causality often does not work between little bits of stuff, but only between large patterns of activity. The Gestalt psychologists, who were rebels against conventional psychological atomism, made comparable discoveries for human perception; they found that one can understand an optical illusion only by considering it as a whole. And that is just what Lashley had also been proving for the pattern of communal excitation in the brain: one can get useful laws for the brain only by considering the whole and ignoring the parts of which it is made up.

First, as to the "field theory" of physics: the history of psychology reveals over and over again the pathetic eagerness of psychologists to adopt *analogically* the current fashion in physics or chemistry; well-known historical examples are the psychical mechanics of Herbart and the mental mechanics and mental chemistry of the Mills. Unfortunately, psychologists, practitioners of an adolescent science, come in either of two dispositional varieties: mentalistic-vitalistic or physicalistic-objectivistic, and they are therefore predisposed to hail with enthusiasm any development in the physical or biological sciences which, however misunderstood, seems to bolster their postulates, by whatever analogical stretch. Notoriously, quantum theory was seized upon by some as an argument for free will or vitalism, an argument which has been cogently refuted, e.g., by Frank (1950, pp. 158-171). In the light of our history, psychologists might well have raised the question whether the field theory of the physicists had any relevance whatever to psychological theory or research; this matter has been well put by Spence (1941), in a review of Köhler's *Dynamics in Psychology*. As Köhler (1947, p. 42) himself said:

> If we wish to imitate the physical sciences, we must not imitate them in their highly developed contemporary form. Rather, we must imitate them in their historical youth, when their state of development was comparable to our own at the present time. Otherwise we should behave like boys who try to copy the imposing manners of full-grown men without understanding their *raison d'être,* also without seeing that intermediate phases of development cannot be skipped. In this respect, a survey of the history of physics is most illuminating. If we are to emulate the natural sciences, let us do so intelligently.

A sobering *reductio ad absurdum* of band wagon jumping is to be found in Scripture's (1936, pp. 258 ff.) account of his "four stages of mental development"; he was, he says, successively a Cartesian, a Wundtian, and a Freudian. And then—"The fourth stage began with a shock. Everything that I had ever believed in was swept

away as soon as I managed to get some understanding of relativity.
. . . I am now trying to revise my psychological and phonetic
notions to accord with the new mode of thought." This traumatic
shock, he tells us, resulted from his confrontation of the equations
in Eddington's *Nature of the Physical World*. He foresees a "new
psychology," in which an important role will be played by "the
entropy clocks of the Great Unknown."

Secondly, as to gestalt theory: it has repeatedly been pointed out
that this sectarian school produced neither a great innovation nor
an acceptable general theory. For example, Commins (1932) listed
the precursors of gestalt psychology: Herbart's theory of apperception, Wundt's principle of creative synthesis, Külpe's central factors,
J. S. Mill's "mental chemistry," James's figured consciousness, conscious continuum, and experienced relations, and Dewey's organic
wholeness. Wheeler (1936) wrote: "Scientific theory has had a
strikingly cyclic history. At 1250, 1650, and 1820 and now at 1935
it is organismic in intent. . . . Between these peaks, the thought
pattern swerved to an opposite extreme, that of mechanism, whose
peaks fall at about 1400, 1775, and 1860." And Wheeler expressed
the opinion that the cycles of emphasis have been shortening, that
the peak of the then current organismic emphasis would be reached
by 1940, and that a later swing to atomism, reaching a peak
between 1950 and 1960, could be predicted. Line (1931), after
tracing the historical antecedents of gestalt psychology and evaluating its contributions, concluded that it had made few positive
accomplishments on which a distinctive general theory could be
based. These were critiques written when gestalt psychology was
young, and they used history both to evaluate the present and to
guess the future. How reliable were the predictions? The statements that one finds in current literature are mostly to the effect
that gestalt psychology had certain stimulating effects but that its
doctrines about learning, neural functioning, and even perception
are dubious or at least in need of a great deal of correction. Remarks
of this sort are to be found, e.g., in the volume edited by Marx
(1951). Thus Bergmann and Spence (p. 272) observe: "The extensive use of the term 'perception,' which the Gestalters advocate,
makes it a weasel word that covers the whole of psychology only
at the price of emptying it of any specific content. Historically
speaking, this verbal preference is probably grounded in the intui-
tionistic philosophical background of the Gestalters." And Spence
(1960), in his discussion of discrimination behavior, remarks: "The

Gestalt theories have failed to furnish either a satisfactory explanation of these phenomena or an adequate experimental formulation of the problem" (p. 306).

As we have seen, such dubiety had already been expressed by historically sophisticated psychologists in the 1920's and 30's. As it happened, however, the Titchenerians were at this very time desperately defending themselves against the attempts of the behaviorists to deprive them of both their subject matter and their methodology. Many of them were therefore ready to sacrifice their mental atoms as the price of admission to a vigorous "new" school which practiced introspection and, although it did indeed reject "analysis," nevertheless made up for this by damning behaviorism. The gestalt school was thus a home away from home for those who could not tolerate behaviorism. These included the vitalists. As Lund (1929, p. 307) wrote:

> But the very intangibility of the gestalt concept is doubtless responsible for the sympathetic if not enthusiastic response received from the mystics, the vitalists, and those who feel that there *is*, or at least *ought* to be something the matter with certain mechanistic and naturalistic interpretations of today. Hence, the chorus of approval from the purposivists, the Bergsons, the McDougalls, and the Driesches. Indeed, with Koffka's insistence that "the universal Gestalt" is an original property of experience . . . and Köhler's affirmation that "no experience is needed for a first formation of units in the visual field," we again feel ourselves in the atmosphere of the Hegelian Universals and the Platonic Forms.

Thus gestalt psychology became another in the long line of "new" psychologies whose enthusiastic reception has not been wholly rational nor historically justified. From the point of view of the sociology of science, the gestalt "movement" was an importation into America of the German-style academic warfare between Berlin and Leipzig, and between the nativists and the empiricists. Boring (1929) has given a classic description of such a controversy, that between Stumpf and Wundt on "tonal distances." Since the American Wundtians collaborated with the invaders, the native behaviorists became substitute objects of aggression. The reception of gestalt psychology was no doubt facilitated by the well-known American hospitality to visitors from distant and more ancient shores; as the general populace cheered Einstein, so perhaps many psychologists hailed gestalt psychology as a scientific revelation which, like the theory of relativity in physics, was to usher in a new, if dimly seen, era in psychology. "New" psychologies are of course very stimulating and great fun for the young in heart, but they can lead to a great deal of wasteful effort; proponents and opponents tend, so to speak, to conduct a dialogue in falsetto, and to perform research in the same register. Perhaps the study of history might be recommended as a moderating influence in such situations.

And what about Lashley, the engram, and the doctrines of equipotentiality and mass action? Lashley's (1929) own review of the history of brain localization could, I think, have suggested the possibility that his conclusions represented another swing of the pendulum rather than a final approach to reality. This was all the more true because of the relative crudity, for his purpose, of the method —extirpation—which was then available to him, and also because of his reliance on rat material. Adrian (1932, p. 79 f.) expressed the view that the anti-reflex movement inspired by the work of Coghill and of Lashley was a pendular swing in physiological history; physiologists as teachers (rather than as specialists) emphasize whatever principles are in fashion at the moment, and then over-correct in the opposite direction. Hunter (1931, p. 233) pointed out that "the integrative action of the nervous system is a well-established fact," and declared, *"Lashley is now presenting no new theory of neural action,* unless he can show that integration is equipotential and that such a conception has meaning." Thus, at the time of Lashley's basic contribution, there were historical reasons for reserve in accepting his conclusions and for questioning whether his proposed doctrines represented any marked advance over the views expressed over the years between 1842 and 1906 by Flourens, Goltz, Loeb, and Sherrington. It is to be noted that Lashley himself later carried out ingenious research whose results he regarded as incompatible with Köhler's "electrical field theory" of cerebral integration; the weakness of this theory, he said, "is that it has been elaborated without sufficient attention to details of structure, and that it has stopped with the subjective phenomena of perception without following out the implications for the translation of perception into actions" (Lashley, Chow, and Semmes, 1951, p. 123). Or one might say, it has preferred physical analogy to biological correlation.

Thus, to the historically sophisticated psychologist in the 1930's and to us in retrospect it could hardly appear that the gestalt psychologists had made revolutionary discoveries without historical antecedents, nor could they in any meaningful sense be said to have applied physical field theory to psychology. Lashley did not discover the engram, which is still undiscovered: "The detailed natures of the electric oscillations constituting consciousness and ephemeral memory, of the molecular patterns constituting permanent memory, and of the mechanism of their interaction are not known" (Pauling, 1961, p. 15). Nor was Lashley's view of neural function without precedent; it is not necessary to assert his historical unpredictability in order to pay proper homage to his contributions. Lashley himself, in summarizing his work (1960), said that "Innumerable studies have defined conditions under which learning is facilitated or retarded, but, in spite of such progress, we seem little nearer to an understanding of the nature of the memory trace than was Descartes." His own series of experiments "has yielded a good bit of information about what and where the memory trace is not. It has discovered nothing directly of the real nature of the engram. I sometimes feel, in reviewing the evidence on the localization of the memory trace, that the necessary conclusion is that learning just is not possible" (p. 500 f.). Here Lashley expresses very succinctly the impression left on a reader by the piling up of negative evidence. Lashley himself deprecated physiological inferences from anatomical data; it has seemed to me that similar difficulties arise from the functional interpretation of the results of extirpation procedures. Hebb (1949, pp. 38-59), after a most judicious review of the issues raised by Köhler and Lashley, remarks, "It is important as psychology comes of age to avoid, if possible, the extreme positions that have often been adopted in the discussions of the past," and he likens the debate between gestalt and learning theory to "the running battle between the Left and the Right in governmental policy." Here again history shows us alternating cycles of thesis and antithesis, with overlapping periods of conflict. There has no doubt, as Hebb says, been some progress, stimulated in part by the configurationists, but basically I think the situation is this: Köhler and Lashley have rejected one physiological theory and proposed another on the basis of correlations between behavioral or introspective data on the one hand and anatomical (extirpation) procedures or physical analogies on the other; learning theorists have sought to construct theories based on correlations between external energy patterns and physical displacements (as of levers). If, as seems reasonable to suppose, learning and perception are functions of the central nervous system, then true progress toward explanation of these phenomena will have to be in terms of neurophysiological processes. It is my impression that the necessary techniques are in process of being developed in electron microscopy, electrophysiology, and biochemistry; the historical analogies which at once come to mind are the events which followed the invention of the microscope and the discovery by Galvani. That is, cycles of scientific controversy end when adequate techniques are invented; controversies which *never* end are "metaphysical"! For these reasons I think that Boring (1960, p. xvi) is speaking as a partisan rather than as a historian when he says that "The major movement is from mechanism to field theory, from *Undverbindungen* to *Gestalten*, from atomism to emergent wholes," and when he goes on to suggest an analogy between "the new physics" and "the latest psychology," which "would seem to have pulled neuropsychology along with them." Boring, it seems to me, has mistaken an eddy for the total stream.

And finally, a third basic justification for the study of the history of science—and of history in general—is related to the anxiety expressed by many writers lately about the state of American education in general and of the education of scientists in particular. It has been felt that our education has been lacking in the communication of cultural values and of the historical background necessary for critical judgments in important areas of contemporary life. For scientists this has been thought a particularly serious matter because of their greatly increased influence on the course of affairs in our times. We are all familiar with the opprobrious epithets which have been applied to the graduates of engineering colleges and military academies, derisively called "trade schools"; according to the semi-humorous stereotype, they are practitioners of the slide rule—culturally deficient, technological robots. There has been some question whether we in psychology have not been turning out a good many technicians of a similar stripe: persons skilled in mental testing, Rorschach interpretation, scale construction, analysis of variance, factor analysis, electronics, polygraph reading, etc., who neither know nor have any interest in the history or philosophy of science and who are also lacking in general cultural background. Beardslee and O'Dowd (1961) have reported that in the college student's image of the scientist, cultural deficiency is a prominent trait. The lack of interest of pupils can of course be attributed in large degree to the lack of interest on the part of their professors. Barzun (1945, p. 101), after quoting a professor who said, "You don't have to teach the history of science to make a man understand that water is H_2O," remarks, "It is precisely what you have to teach, unless you are willing to barter understanding for mere voodoo formulas." His remark is truer for psychology than it is for chemistry, for voodoo is more pervasive in psychology; as can be seen in the olla-podrida of the *Psychological Abstracts,* precise experiment and painful logic are intermixed with fantasies and autonomous verbalisms worthy of Pythagoras, Empedocles, and Plato, and with the Protagorean formulae of the "psychology of adjustment." A writer in the *American Scholar* (Hyman, 1960) has described psychologists as provincial, ignorant of the humanities and of the history of their own discipline, philosophically shallow, and possessed of "an amazing tolerance and even respect" for "necromancers" such as the parapsychologists.

The first American psychological laboratories were founded, in the last three decades of the nineteenth century, by men who had been trained in German universities, and who therefore had knowledge of the history both of philosophy in general and of psychology as—at that time—a branch of philosophy; they usually had training also in biology and in other natural sciences. In the second and third decades of the twentieth century, behaviorism burst upon the scene as what seemed to many at the time a rootless bolshevism of a philosophically backward America. The Titchenerians especially, disregarding their own very special and limited origins and purview, as well as the French and German origins of objective psychology, issued dire warnings that should this movement triumph, American psychology would lose its historical heritage and its international affiliations. It did in fact happen, as behaviorism evolved into behavioral science, that American psychology, preoccupied with techniques and with practical concerns, entered upon an ahistorical period, in which history courses disappeared from curricula and many psychologists expressed impatience with historical studies. Characteristic was the coldness with which the directors of the American Psychological Association received the proposal for the fourth volume of the *History of Psychology in Autobiography.* This attitude was reinforced by the anti-genetic movement led by Lewin.

In the past few years evidence has appeared of an awakening of interest in the history of psychology and of the behavioral sciences in general. Swartz (1958) urged that psychologists should encourage graduate dissertations in the history of psychology. "To insist upon an experimental type of dissertation . . . is a manifestation of our lack of a historical sense." R. I. Watson (1960) suggested that the lack of historical interest on the part of American psychologists may be due to immaturity and youthful exuberance, and very cogently pointed out that history is not written once for all time; that "each generation rewrites the history in terms of its own values"; that "we have not [as yet] looked back upon the past from the perspective of today"; and that "in the past writing of our history, material either ignored as irrelevant or simply not known at that time now can be utilized." Or, as Croce (1921, p. 12) said, "Every true history is contemporary history."

In July 1960 appeared the first number of the *History of the Behavioral Sciences Newsletter,* sponsored by several psychiatrists of the Payne Whitney Clinic. It notes that "Although the history of the development of the behavioral sciences is a relatively new research area, within recent years this study has attracted numerous workers throughout the world." It remarks that "As far as we know, the American Psychiatric Association is the only organization in the behavioral sciences to have a formal committee on history."

At the 1960 convention of the American Psychological Association a meeting was held "for informal discussion about work and interest in the history of psychology." Many projects, in considerable variety, were presented at this meeting. A letter was sent to the Board of Editors of the Association pointing out that the journals published by the Association do not adequately provide for articles on the history of psychology. Concern was expressed at the refusal of university psychology departments to accept doctoral dissertations on historical subjects. It was suggested that the Association appoint an archivist such as the British Association has, "to collect official archives and to encourage eminent psychologists to see that their personal papers go to a responsible archives." These interests were continued, and further meetings were held, under the chairmanship of Robert I. Watson, in 1961 and 1962.*

Thus it appears that ahistoricism in American psychology was another passing phase in the history of science. It is interesting to note the influence of psychology's biological and medical affilia-

---

* Since this was written there have appeared Robert I. Watson's *The Great Psychologists* (Philadelphia: Lippincott, 1963), and J. R. Kantor's *The Scientific Evolution of Psychology,* Vol. I (Chicago: Principia Press, 1963). The June 1963 (No. 6) issue of the *History of the Behavioral Sciences Newsletter* contains an extensive list of books and articles published in 1961; additional publications for 1961-1962 are listed in the "History & Biography" section of the *Psychological Abstracts.* Leo Postman has edited *Psychology in the Making: Histories of Selected Research Problems* (New York: Knopf, 1962), with more than 1100 references, which should be valuable in giving students the sense of historical continuity in research.

tions in the revival of historical interest, and to speculate that those psychologists who decry "physiologizing" tend also to disparage the study of history. In the history of the history of medicine we may note interesting parallels to that of psychology. Sigerist (1951, pp. 4-6) tells us that "until about a hundred years ago the history of medicine was primarily medicine . . . part of the theory of medicine, the experience of the preceding generations that had to be assimilated if progress was to be achieved." But, "This attitude towards the past of medicine changed radically in the second half of the nineteenth century when a new medical science developed and progress was achieved such as never before. The past seemed dead. . . . Nothing could be learned from [the history of medicine]; to study it, to read the ancient writers, was a waste of time." But presently, collaborative work shared by historians, philologists, philosophers, and physicians began, and this eventuated in 1905 at Leipzig in the first research institute for the study of the history of medicine. The first such institute in America was founded at the Johns Hopkins University in 1929. Today the history of medicine is a generally recognized department of research and instruction. This development seems to be beginning in psychology, which might therefore, in this respect, be said to be following medicine at an interval of about fifty years.

But though the historical specialty has been much better recognized in medicine than in psychology, some medical writers have remarked upon a certain neglect in recent times. Dr. Fred A. Mettler, in his editorial preface to Cecilia Mettler's (1947) *History of Medicine*, attributes this neglect in large part to the losses in war:

> It is one of the functions of the historian to preserve and explain the continuity of the present with the past. The greatest obstacle to medical progress, and indeed to all cultures, is the loss of this continuity with the past. The most fertile source of such discontinuities is war. War destroys scholars directly, it destroys their opportunity to work . . . and it destroys historical perspective.
>
> In the Editorial Preface of the supplementary volume [of the *Encyclopaedia Britannica*, 1922] Hugh Chisholm pointed out that a completely new twelfth edition "could not be made today so as to have anything like the scholarly value of the work produced before the war. . . ." He said that neither the minds nor wills were any longer obtainable, nor would they be for years to come. Pre-war authorities had died without leaving lineal successors, and a shifting of interest had occurred "among writers of the academic type, so that there is a disinclination to make the exertion needed for entering anew into old subjects—a necessary condition for just that stimulating, vital presen-

tation of old issues in the light of all the accumulated knowledge about them, which was so valuable. . . ." (p. vii).

In a review of a recent book which is a "quite sophisticated exposition of biology," by an author whose "knowledge of the vast subject matter he covers is thorough and intimate," Graubard (1962, p. 276) wonders whether "so much precooked and ready-to-serve material can be consumed and digested by the beginning student," and continues:

> Moreover, should science be taught in this manner, without providing any historical perspective for the questions raised, the theories offered, discarded, accepted, modified, and challenged, or the controversies stirred up between such giants as Pasteur and Liebig, for example, which reveal the very essence and drama of growth and evolution in science as well as the meaning of theory and truth? Should the student memorize these thousands of facts with no motive, no evidence, no challenge, and above all, with no knowledge of how they came to be established and upon what foundations they rest?

It seems likely that the two world wars, and the threatened third, have had much to do with the neglect of history by psychologists, both because of the entrance of large numbers of young psychologists into applied fields, and because of the vast post-war increase in governmental and foundationary subvention of research which conforms to the patterns of "experimental design" or "statistical analysis" favored by selection committees. In recent times, a young psychologist without a numerically designated "project" and the "support" and prestige which this symbolizes has been at a grave professional disadvantage. Moreover, there have been the insistent demands of the military and of practical social problems arising from rapid social and political changes and from moral, intellectual, and artistic confusion. The times, in short, have not been favorable for quiet scholarship—for that historical scholarship which, as Mettler (1947) has observed, provides scientists with "a sense of perspective" and "a feeling of proportion among the component fields" of their sciences. One might be inclined to see the ahistoricism of recent psychology as a manifestation of the disenchantment with tradition which is characteristic of contemporary culture in general. As Bradbury (1962) says:

> Certainly one of the distinguishing features of what we like to call the modern dilemma is the degree to which we feel ourselves separated from the past, and the frenzy and energy with which we seek to annihilate the past. . . . There are scant signs that the creative artists

of the twentieth century, at least in the West, are concerned for the cultural tradition to which they are the heirs. Indeed their sense is rather that this is a meaningless heritage.

There is perhaps this difference: that whereas the revolt of the artists is a reaction of revulsion, disillusionment, and pessimism, the neglect of history by psychologists is a result of the limitations imposed by their education and prevailing professional motivations; one cannot revolt against that of which one is not aware, although one is likely to avoid that in which one is unversed.

2

Origins of
Magic and Animism

Altogether, the Soul is an outbirth of that sort of philosophizing whose great maxim, according to Dr. Hodgson, is: "Whatever you are *totally* ignorant of, assert to be the explanation of everything else."—William James, *Principles*, I, p. 347.

Psychology, like all other sciences, has emerged from the folk customs, interests, and beliefs of a prescientific age. Of the various types of behavior evolved by primitive peoples, magic and religion are of particular importance for an understanding not only of the antecedents of science but also of its subsequent history and of the difficulties which it has encountered. This is particularly true of the soul-body linguistic pattern whose origins we are about to discuss.

The anthropologist Marett (1912) has suggested that the world of men is a two-fold world. On the one hand there is the workaday world in relation to which every community has well-established routine behavior. Primitive man has more or less adequate practical ways of dealing with many things in his environment, so long as the environment remains "normal": how to obtain, prepare, and store food, how to obtain shelter and clothing, etc. Much of this behavior is adequate because it results from learning based on relationships inherent in the nature of things; e.g., the relationships between the sight, sound, or odor of fire, plants, or animals on the one hand and

20

the sensations of heat, taste, or pain which they produce on the other. But a great deal of man's routine behavior is "adequate" only because it conforms to social convention and hence has been socially "reinforced"; it would not be adequate in an unrelated social environment. Thus language, attitudes and responses to other members of the family and tribe, and the etiquette of eating and of performing other daily acts are traditional, arbitrary and conventional; the only "law of nature" on which they rest is that on which all socially significant human behavior rests: the law of the conditioned response.

On the other hand, Marett points out, there is the world of incalculable extraordinary events, of crises such as disease, death, famine, tornadoes, volcanic eruptions. And, we might add, there are innumerable sources of vague anxiety such as are described in the *Census of India* for 1901 as "the shifting and shadowy company of unknown powers or influences . . . which resides in the primeval forest, in the crumbling hills, in the rushing river, in the spreading tree, which gives its spring to the tiger, its venom to the snake, which generates jungle fever, and walks abroad in the terrible guise of cholera." Fear of the ghosts of the dead, and of spirits and demons, is almost universal among primitive peoples. It is obvious that in the presence of situations arousing fear or anxiety highly motivated behavior will occur but that this behavior in most cases cannot be rational, from a scientific point of view, because the situations are too complex. For example, an enormous cumulative development of highly specialized attitudes and behavior under highly special and favorable historical, economic, and political conditions was necessary before a rational method of dealing with such a disease as cholera was possible.

In fear-arousing situations which he cannot understand or in which highly motivated tendencies are blocked, prescientific man is likely to act in ways which we class as magical, animistic, or religious. *Magical* acts may result from fortuitous associations: someone may spit and "cause" a landslide, or urinate against a certain tree and "cause" a flood, or see a bird on his left and then break a leg; cats or pigeons learn to perform "superstitious" acts, such as rubbing against a certain post (Guthrie and Horton, 1946) or pecking at a spot on the wall (Hilgard, 1957, p. 239 f.; cf. Skinner, 1948) as a means of obtaining food; the central Australians used to rub a bull-roarer on the stomach in order to become strong; human sexual intercourse in the fields was regarded by some peoples as necessary to insure good food crops. Associative mechanisms are illustrated also in the magical prehistory of medicine, as observed among primitive peoples, where we encounter the two principles of "sympathetic magic" (Frazer, 1947, pp. 11-48): those namely of "contagion" and of "similarity." According to the principle of "contagion," anything which has been in contact with a person or with some source of "power" such as the sun, moon, an animal, or the dead, has thereby acquired some potency; thus operations on a man's nail parings, extracted teeth, excrement, etc. may inflict injury or disease upon him, and appropriate treatment of a weapon will cure the wound that has been made by it. According to the principle of "similarity," things which resemble one another are related, so that, e.g., yellow flowers might cure jaundice and bloodstone might stop hemorrhages; in medieval times this principle became the "doctrine of signatures." The principle of "similarity" also finds expression in the infliction of injuries or disease upon a person by operations on an image of him, or the causing or averting of calamities by imitative rites. By both of these associative principles of "sympathetic magic," the shaman acquired an armamentarium of objects and rites through the agency of which he could direct good or bad influences on others. Diseases and other misfortunes, unless their causes and courses seemed very obvious, usual, and "natural," were attributed to such manipulations by malignant men—"magic"—or, by generalization of this personifying tendency, to the hostility of ghosts, demons, or gods—"religion." The therapist therefore might proceed in one of three ways, according to his interpretation of the circumstances: he might apply "empirical" remedies, such as massage, splints, and herbal preparations; or magical countermeasures through the agency of potent objects or rites; or religious ceremonies placating or enlisting the help of supernatural persons (cf. Sigerist, 1951, pp. 125 ff.; Rivers, 1924). Procedures of either beneficent or maleficent intent of course owe many or all of their effects to "suggestion"; individuals in suitably indoctrinated groups have been known to die when they became aware that a "fatal" magic had been directed against them. In modern medicine, sophisticated methods are necessary to differentiate "placebo" from physiological effects. The modern practitioner, when "empirical" remedies fail, may refer the patient to a psychiatrist, or the patient in desperation may seek a "faith healer." That is to say, the behavioral tendencies which we have just been discussing are not merely curious aberrations of primitive peoples which were long ago sloughed off in the advance of civilization; they have merely been disguised by more sophisticated language.

A great variety of irrational and accidentally learned habits may thus accumulate, some consisting in performing certain acts so as to produce certain desired effects, others consisting in avoiding certain acts, places, or persons so as to avoid unpleasant consequences ("taboo"). Frazer (1947) gives numerous examples of such behavior. Moreover, as Malinowski (1954) has pointed out, when the practical expression of motivated behavior is blocked, fragments—particularly verbal and gestural fragments—of the relevant behavioral complex may nevertheless be released. Thus, the man whose enemy is inaccessible may shake his fists and utter imprecations, or the lover may in gesture and speech embrace and cajole the absent object of his passion. Such activity relieves tension and readily acquires functional reality; i.e., the verbal expression of desires, purposes, and anticipated ends becomes a magical substitute means of their realization. Word magic—the identification of verbal operations with operations on things—has been characteristic of man throughout the world and throughout history. Malinowski, describing magic spells, calls attention to "the use of words which invoke, state, or command the desired aim. Thus the sorcerer will mention all the symptoms of the disease which he is inflicting, or in the lethal formula he will describe the end of his victim" (p. 74). The primitive medicine man drives out pathogenic demons by exorcism. Skinner (1957) has analyzed verbal magic as a form of "mand," a term which he has invented to refer to "a verbal operant in which the response is reinforced by a characteristic consequence and is therefore under the functional control of relevant conditions of deprivation or aversive stimulation" (p. 35 f.).

The operation of the generalizing tendency of conditioned responses results, as mentioned above, in another type of irrational behavior known as *animism*: man reacts to an emotion-arousing situation as though in or behind it and capriciously "causing" it were a being with some human properties (cf. Weiss, 1919). This personifying attitude and behavior is aroused not only by cataclysms and crises but also by many other phenomena which attract attention and which for some reason or other suggest human action and motivation. Thus stars and planets, the sky, waterfalls, trees, the sea, animals, and countless other things may be treated as though each contained a "spirit" or man-like being whose "will" controls its actions. For example, we are told that the Omaha Indians regarded "all animate and inanimate forms, all phenomena, as pervaded by a common life which was continuous and similar to the will power they were conscious of in themselves" (A. C. Fletcher, quoted by Cornford, 1957, p. 85). Animism may thus serve as a general theory of nature which provides attitudes and patterns of behavior for all things and events. The propitiatory behavior—grovelling, prayers, gifts of food, etc.—previously learned in the presence of human authority is available as a tension-reducing form of adjustment; it is also, like magic, a method of controlling events. Moreover, as contrasted with a "general-alarm" reaction of the visceral nervous system, animistic behavior may have the advantage of permitting some sort of perceptual analysis of the situation: the terrible sounds are the hidden man's voice; the visual phenomena are missiles thrown by him, or the flashing of his eyes, or fires kindled by him. Dickinson (1904) has pointed out how the Greek gods represented an analysis, on the one hand, of external nature (sky, ocean, the various winds, etc.), and on the other, of coercive forces of human personality (love, aggression, etc.). Thus both external and internal forces, by being embodied in familiar human forms, became more tolerable, because they could be verbalized, interpreted, anticipated, and propitiated in human terms. Moreover, the projection of internal forces served as a defense against a sense of shame or guilt. In Homer, when a person acted in a way that was socially outrageous or beyond the normal range, this behavior could be attributed to a temporary insanity sent by a god or by "fate" *(moira)*, so that nonrational impulses and otherwise unaccountable behavior could be dissociated from the individual (cf. Dodds, 1957, p. 1 ff.). In a similar fashion, Freudian doctrine has assuaged feelings of guilt and made socially acceptable, and interesting, behavioral dispositions which had hitherto been considered shameful.

It may perhaps be convenient to regard the differences between the terms "magic," "animism," and "religion" as representing differences in degree of personification. In the performance of acts of magic, there may be only very vague personification of powers which are being manipulated, or no personification at all; in animism, there is such personification, though it may be vague and may include animal-like forms; in religion, the personification has usually arrived at idealized supermen or "gods." But the rites, sacrifices, and prayers of animism and religion can still be called magic, since they are irrational methods of controlling events; and some degree of animism is present in much magic and in all religion.

It should be pointed out that the twofold world suggested by Marett can hardly be taken as a strict dichotomy in the life of man. Animistic, magical, and religious behavior and attitudes on the one hand and practical, rational, and scientific behavior and attitudes on the other coexist and interpenetrate one another. Procedures of animistic and magical origin become part of the routine of life and may seem to their practitioners just as practical and sensible as any other behavior transmitted and sanctioned by tradition, although, to be sure, many of these procedures are fraught with much emotion. Moreover, as Radin (1957b) has emphasized, magical and religious behavior may be very practical as a means of control by the shamans, medicine men, or priests, who thus gain advantageous positions economically and socially.

It is important, I think, for us to have some notion of the conditions of life and the attitudes of prescientific man, from which only at a few times and places and under extremely favorable circumstances scientific attitudes and behavior have been able to emerge—to emerge, moreover, in only a quite limited portion of the population. For the prehistoric and pre-Homeric Greeks, the ancestors of those Greeks of the sixth century B.C. with whom our Western intellectual history begins, Gilbert Murray (1955) has provided a vivid description. Life was precarious. A failure of the food crop meant starvation. Wild beasts, human enemies, epidemic diseases, the ghosts of the dead, and all sorts of vague and only dimly personified daemons were continual sources of anxiety. As a defense against or propitiation of these dangers and forces, magical or religious rites developed through the centuries, especially in relation to the dead and to the vital renewal of life in the spring. Some of these practices were of an overwhelming emotional quality; e.g., the religious dances and the animal sacrifices; the latter might involve the smearing or drinking of blood, the eating of body organs, the touching of or getting inside the flayed animal's skin—all in the interest of gaining magical powers associated with the animal. There were all sorts of "sympathetic magic": men croaking like frogs to induce rain and engaging in innumerable other practices which were based on false associations. It may seem remarkable, perhaps even appalling, that the same human brain, with its vast capacity for conditioning, generalization, and abstraction, which has created science and art, has, by virtue of these same properties of the nervous system, created these irrational kinds of behavior based on the principles of analogy and of *post hoc ergo propter hoc*.

Very striking is the description given by Sigerist (1951, p. 442) of the magico-religious beliefs of the Babylonians:

> Like the Egyptian, and even more so, the Babylonian lived in a world that was haunted by evil spirits. They were everywhere, in the dark corners of the house, in the attic, in ruins, and on waste lands; they roamed the streets of the city at night, hid behind rocks and trees on the open land ready to attack you when you passed by; they rode howling with the stormwind. There was not a place where you could feel safe. Yet, it would be a great mistake to assume that the life of the Babylonian was one of perpetual terror, far from it. If you led a righteous life, worshiping the gods, keeping the ghosts of your ancestors in the Underworld by feeding them with regular offerings, if you respected taboos and possessed the necessary amulets and charms, there was no reason why you should be afraid of spirits. They were kept in check and had no power over you, although it happened here and there that they attacked a man without apparent reason.

In our own age, which in optimistic moods we think of as rational and scientific, cataclysmic events, overpowering situations, and anxieties of many kinds, which seem to be not amenable to rational analysis or intelligent control—death, incurable disease, human inhumanity, the not improbable destruction of all life by the products of science—still elicit either disorganized behavior or behavior in accordance with the ancient principle: "When in doubt, act as though there were a person or 'spirit' behind the phenomena," and behavior in accordance with this principle still has powerful social sanction. Even among scientists animism and magic have their exponents. Thus the eminent psychologist William McDougall (1871-1938) issued, in successive editions from 1911 to 1923, his *Body and Mind: A History and a Defense of Animism,* and under his sponsorship the magical arts of clairvoyance and of the control of inanimate objects by "will power" were revived on a large scale. Another eminent psychologist, Gardner Murphy (1949, p. 440 f.) appears to believe that the lack of acceptance of these phenomena by most psychologists is due to emotional prejudice. Other scientists (e.g., Price, 1955) have justified the rejection of the alleged phenomena by pointing out their incompatibility with the basic principles of science, and Rogosin (1939) suggested that such acceptance as they have enjoyed has been due in part to a tendency in present-day culture to return to mysticism, a tendency shared and reinforced by such eminent physicists and amateur philosophers as Eddington, Jeans, Millikan, and Compton.

On the other hand, Rhine (1957), the chief American representative of "parapsychology," attributes non-acceptance to the conformity imposed by our education and warns that our national defense may be endangered by failure to apply clairvoyance to the elimination of secrecy and surprise from military activities. We have here our first illustration of the continuity of ideas and of the persistence of motivations from prescientific to contemporary times, and our first demonstration that the history of a science is not a mere collection of obsolete curiosities but an essential propaedeutic for the understanding of what would otherwise appear to be novel aberrations or even plausible inventions of current science.

It is interesting to note that Price (1955) dates his disbelief in "extrasensory perception" from his reading, in David Hume's *An Inquiry Concerning Human Understanding*, of the chapter "Of Miracles," in which Hume describes a miracle as a violation of the laws of nature which have been established by experience. Price also refers to similar statements by Lucian, who wrote in the second century of our era. Thus, having some knowledge of historical precedents and of the historically evolved nature of science as contrasted with magic, Price is able, as some contemporary psychologists have not been, to see that "parapsychology, although well camouflaged with some of the paraphernalia of science, still bears in abundance the markings of magic." He points out that in "extrasensory perception," "The special linkage that seems to exist between a percipient and the proper target card or telepathic sender is the sort of linkage that is characteristic of magic." Moreover, being a biologist, he can give us an excellent example of physiological correlation as a test of alleged behavioral protocols: he asks, " . . . how does the information get into a brain? How is it converted into electrochemical changes within neurons? . . . can anyone describe a conceivable nerve network for interpreting the raw data of ESP?" A survey of the opinions of psychologists concerning "extrasensory perception" (Warner, 1952) showed that 16 per cent considered it either "an established fact" or "a likely possibility," and 34 per cent regarded it as "merely an unknown." Psychologists, that is, like other people, are subject to what might be called the "Hamlet fallacy." To the statement, "There are more things in heaven and earth than are dreamt of in your philosophy," which is undoubtedly true, most persons respond as reliably as they do to favorable statements about motherhood. In a general sort of way scientists regard "open-mindedness" as virtuous and scientifically necessary, but there is, as Dunham (1947) has said, a "kind of open-mindedness in which the mind is so open that everything falls through"; particular theories are fallible, and novel phenomena are to be expected, but phenomena which cannot be caught in any conceivable way in the total "nomological net" of physical and biological science might well be classed as magical.

Magical and religious behavior may, as has been suggested above, have adaptive value. It may serve as an alternative to intolerable conflict and completely disorganized emotional behavior. It may develop into socialized traditional forms which provide group coherence, moral sanctions, and mental defense or therapy. It may under exceptional circumstances promote a keenness of observation and an accumulation of knowledge from which professional scientific attitudes and work can emerge, as when in ancient Greece the magical and religious practices of the priests of Aesculapius gradually developed, with the accumulation of clinical experience, into diagnostic and therapeutic knowledge and skills.

There have been differences of opinion as to the criteria for the application of the term "science." Malinowski (1954) thinks that the "scientific attitude" is not wholly lacking in the savage; this is, of course, as he recognizes, a matter of definition. Malinowski means "patient and painstaking observation" of phenomena of interest to the observer, plus generalization and ability to connect long chains of events. However, he remarks:

> Science is founded on the conviction that experience, effort, and reason are valid; magic on the belief that hope cannot fail nor desire deceive. . . . As a matter of empirical fact the body of rational knowledge and the body of magical lore are incorporated each in a different tradition, in a different social setting and in a different type of activity, and all these differences are clearly recognized by the savages [p. 87].

Malinowski perhaps exaggerates the separation of the rational and the irrational modes of discourse. The mixture of careful observation and irrational inference to be expected of primitive thinkers is well illustrated in a discourse of a Dakota Indian informant quoted from Densmore by Radin (1957a, pp. 281 ff.):

> From my boyhood I have observed leaves, trees, and grass, and I have never found two alike. They may have a general likeness, but on examination I have found that they differ slightly. Plants are of different families, each being adapted to growth in a certain locality. It is the same with animals; they are widely scattered, and yet each

will be found in the environment to which it is best adapted. . . . It is significant that certain stones are not found buried in the earth, but are on top of high buttes. They are round, like the sun and moon, and we know that all things which are round are related to each other. Things which are alike in their nature grow to look like each other, and these stones have lain there a long time, looking at the sun. . . . In all my life I have been faithful to the sacred stones. . . . I make my request of the stones and they are my intercessors.

Even the adoption of the criterion of the experimental method has not insured uniformity in the use of the term "science." Thus Lynn Thorndike explains the title of his monumental *A History of Magic and Experimental Science* by the statement that he had begun with the intention of writing a history of magic but that an unexpected by-product, experimental science, had forced itself increasingly on his attention, and he emphasizes the role of experiment in magic. A reviewer (Multhauf, 1959) remarks: "But this experimentation not only arose in simple experience but seems, from this account, to have remained there. That is to say, it was very frequently the result of a single experiment and even more often simply the testimony of a group of 'eye witnesses.'"

Since magic and religion are based on attitudes inconsistent with those of science, attitudes which are dogmatic, irrational, emotionally reinforced, and sanctioned by compulsive tradition, much of the energy and genius of the creators of science has had to be expended on overcoming such attitudes, in themselves as well as in others, and nowhere has this been more true than in psychology, where the concept of the "soul" for centuries dominated thought and action concerning human beings. Among primitive peoples the phenomena of emotional seizures, disease, narcosis, dreams, after-images, hallucinations, and death gave rise to the notion of a "detachable soul" or "man-within" (Tylor, 1888; Weiss, 1919a), a vaporous or shadowy (human breath and shadow played a role here), impalpable but not immaterial something, normally residing within the body but capable of leaving it; this something was regarded as the cause of the life and mental activities of the individual whom it animated. Life or soul was also readily identified with the blood. As the author of the Hippocratic treatise on the *Nature of Man* says, "Seeing men whose throat had been cut bleeding from the body, they think that this blood is the soul of a man." Hemorrhage is often fatal and leaves the body cold and motionless; the observation of the loss of heat and motion in death was influential in the development of the concepts of vital heat and of animation, respectively. For many primitive peoples, anything that moved without obvious external force—stars, planets, rivers—was, by generalization, alive or animate; this categorization is perhaps found fossilized, e.g., in the animate-inanimate genders of the Algonquian Indian languages (Bloomfield, 1933, p. 272). The belief was widespread that disease or death could be caused by loss of the soul, e.g., by capturing or injuring a man's shadow; a number of primitive peoples have techniques whereby a medicine man can recapture a purloined soul and restore it to a patient's body.

Two modes of physiological functioning in human beings are of prime importance in understanding the development of the concepts of soul and of a spirit world; namely, memory encoding and "false" perception. Even for modern civilized man the fact that past environments and dead friends exist only—though often very vividly —as encodings in an individual brain is hard to digest, and an illusory, hallucinatory, or oneiric experience of "hearing" a voice or "seeing" a face—particularly of a dead person—may be unnerving.

Thus it is understandable that the human being came to be regarded as being composed of two parts: his body, which could be seen and felt under ordinary conditions, and a something which makes that body behave as it does and which leaves it temporarily in trances and in unconscious states and permanently in death. This something is not immaterial; it has many physical properties; under certain conditions it may be seen; even after the death of the body it eats, uses weapons, may help or injure the living. The Trobriand Islanders, e.g., distinguish between the *kosi*, the ghost which lingers around the village for a few days after death, and the *baloma*, the spirit which returns to the underworld; the former is like a shadow, the latter like a reflection in water (Malinowski, 1954, pp. 149 ff.). Radin (1957a, pp. 257 ff.) describes the concepts of the soul of various primitive peoples, and in the course of another survey (1957b, pp. 268-288) he very perspicaciously remarks, concerning the distinction between human "corporeal" and "non-corporeal" activity: "It has always been the welcome and happy hunting ground for mystics of all ages and all races, from primitive times to the psychoanalysts. It has not infrequently enabled tired intellectuals to spend the evening of their life in tragic solace and in romantic expiation for the sin of having attempted to think logically and realistically in their more robust years." Outstanding examples of this involutional phenomenon are to be found among contemporary physicists, biologists, philosophers, and, of course, psychologists.

In the development of religion, philosophy, and science, language has been all-important. In my *Psychology of Language* (unpublished lectures) I have included in a list of the "Uses of Language" a type described as "Literary, Religious, Philosophical, and Scientific Language." In such language the initiating processes represent various degrees of remoteness from practical environmental situations, and the responses are not practical or directly adaptive. ("Practical" is here meant to designate nonlinguistic external stimulus complexes and nonlinguistic, characteristically manual, adaptive responses to them.) There may be some external practical stimulus, but the eventual overt linguistic response is the product of the internal organization of individuals and of series of linguistic stimuli-and-responses (or alternatively, of series of processes in the brain). Moreover, the place even of the practical stimulus may have been taken by internal factors, as in hallucinations, dreams, and other "imaginal" processes. The products of the internal ("subjective") operations of each individual in a group can be transmitted to the mnemic organizations of other members; here of course the role of unusual individuals—whether geniuses or psychotics—will be particularly important. (See Radin, 1957b, on the "neurotic-epileptoid" type, and Radin, 1957a, on "intellectuals" among primitive peoples.) An artificial environment can thus be created and cumulatively transmitted whose features and objects are linguistically represented but which correspond only abstractly or remotely, or not at all, to the practical environment. Thus arise the worlds of myth, sacred scriptures, literary fiction, metaphysics, and science. Scientific language differs from the other forms of the type in that it is related to a methodology which includes systematic comparisons with practical situations and responses; if the linguistic processes eventuate in a practical response which is adaptive to, or a linguistic response which predicts, a practical situation, then the processes are considered to have been validated—provided, of course, that certain statistical requirements have been met. The other forms of the type, on the other hand, are controlled by no such systematic technique of objective check; they approach the limit of almost exclusively linguistic behavior in an almost exclusively linguistic environment—though usually reinforced by other institutional, traditional, and social objects, symbols, and behavior. The linguistic stimulus-response systems thus built up may be adaptive; e.g., myths may provide social sanction for socially integrating beliefs and for moral conduct. On the other hand, they may be not merely irrelevant to practical dealing with the practical environment but actually preclusive of such dealing; they may lead to behavior which historians will evaluate as maladaptive. Our times being what they are, the reader will perhaps wish to point out that the symbolic sequences of *science* may lead to behavior so maladaptive that in the end there will be no historians left to evaluate it.

Body and Soul in Ancient Greece

Cornford (1957) warns us that we must not be misled by the rationality of the early Greek philosophers into "imagining that Thales or Anaximander was like Adam on the day of his creation, with no tradition behind him, no inherited scheme of things, opening his innocent eyes on a world of pure sense impressions not as yet co-ordinated into any conceptual structure" (p. 3). Rather, it appears that " . . . in accounting for the dogmatic systems of the first philosophers, who had nothing but theology behind them, the two main causes are to be found in two opposed schemes of religious representation, and in the temperaments of the individual philosophers, which made one or other of those schemes the more congenial to them" (p. 138). These two theological schemes were the *Olympian* and the *Dionysiac-Orphic* or mystical.

The religion of the Olympian gods as it is presented in the Homeric poems is a religion created by poets for a nobility. It was an artistic creation by and for the upper classes of a heroic age of wealth and colonial expansion. The members of these privileged classes enjoyed a pleasant leisured life in which intellectual and artistic interests could grow. Their relative freedom from many of the anxieties of ordinary men was shown by the religion which they developed—gentlemanly, amoral, sometimes irascible gods, living a life much like that of the nobility. For human beings there was no personal life after death, except for a few great heroes who by special favor of the gods might be permitted to enjoy a life of endless bliss in the beautiful Elysian Fields somewhere in the Far West. All other human beings at death entered the gloomy underworld of Hades as pale shadows without consciousness or personality, and without distinction as to conduct during life. The body was regarded as an essential part of personality, and the will and

mental powers were supposed to reside in the region of the breast—
especially in the heart—or diaphragm, and to be annihilated at the
death of the body. There was thus an immortal breath-soul, the
psyche, a pale phantom which issued from the mouth of a dying
man and existed without memory, will, or other personality traits
in Hades, a "second self," which became active only when the
bodily self was unconscious, in sleep or death, and played no role
in waking life. There was also a mortal blood-soul, the *thymus,*
whose vehicle was the blood, with which it gushed out in violent
death, and which was the principle of emotion and volition, or more
generally of life. The innocuous life after death encouraged enjoyment of life in the flesh and attenuated a common source of human
anxiety. Much of the disquieting capriciousness associated with a
cult of the dead and of daemons was replaced by an orderliness
and rationality personified by intelligible man-like gods. In a context of prosperity such beliefs—or rather, artistic fancies—offered
few inhibitions to free-ranging thought, and imposed few dogmatic
aberrations.

But with the transition from the age of the kings and nobles to
that of the commercial and colonial expansion of the sixth and fifth
centuries B.C., the easy life and intellectual freedom of the upper
classes rested upon large submerged classes of peasants, day laborers,
and slaves, many of whom were foreigners of oriental origin. While
the favored upper classes could, if they wished, spend their days in
philosophical thought and discourse—though most of them were
more interested in sports, gossip, and politics—a large population
of laborers, slaves, and foreigners lived in various degrees of economic and political insecurity. Among the latter the more primitive magical and religious practices continued, and were much
influenced by oriental religions. Of particular appeal to the poor
and uneducated classes were the "mystery" religions, such as the
Orphic, based on legends of Dionysus, the god of vegetation, and
of his representative, Orpheus.

In fifth-century Athens, the extreme extension of democracy
brought in its train increasing disorder, corruption, and calamity,
and with these, a loss of prestige of the Olympian gods. Moreover,
there appeared a new type of private teachers, the "Sophists"—
"learned men" or "professors"—who wandered from city to city and
aroused the enthusiasm of some of the brighter young men; they
inculcated a sceptical attitude, particularly toward social institutions. This scepticism extended to religion, and the religion of the

Olympian gods was no more proof against logical inquiry than it was a bulwark of morals. Thus political, economic, and religious insecurity combined to cause increasing numbers of people—at first mostly the more ignorant, later even some of the philosophers —to turn to the mystery religions. The participants in the rites sought to attain, by means of fasting, dramatic ritual, and techniques of crowd suggestion, an ecstatic freeing of the soul from its "prison" or "tomb," the body. The Orphics introduced the mystical notion of the transmigration of souls: the immortal soul had during its divine existence committed some sin for which it was doomed to enter into a succession of plant, animal, and human bodies, a "circle of births," from which it could be freed by following the Orphic rules of a "pure" life. For what we think of as the typical Greek view that the true and happy life is life here on earth—the view, to be sure, of favored classes and of heroic and prosperous times—was substituted for the view that life on earth is really death. Thus in these "poor men's religions" the notion of a soul, the bearer of all the mental faculties, degraded by its temporary association with the unclean and contemptible body but separable from that body and immortal, was launched upon the stream of philosophical tradition, to be developed by Pythagoras and Plato into those abstractions which ever since have been the bane of psychological science.

The notion that the human soul has fallen from a heavenly state because of some "original sin" which must be expiated by life on earth and by purgation in the underworld (cf. Cornford, 1957, p. 178 ff.) was transmitted by Judeo-Christian theology to find an interesting echo in an article by the eminent contemporary psychologist Mowrer (1960, and, *in extenso*, 1961), who, rejecting the psychoanalytic doctrine that neurosis is a sickness, urges that the neurotic can be "redeemed" only by acknowledging his "worthlessness" and "expiating" his "sin." "Hell," he says, "is still very much with us in those states of mind and being which we call neurosis and psychosis; and I have come increasingly, at least in my own mind, to identify anything that carries us toward these forms of perdition as *sin*." "Sin," in ethnological terms, is the violation of a taboo, and taboos are under the sanction of a spirit or deity who punishes such violations. And so, quite appropriately, Mowrer suggests that "In this process of moving away from our erstwhile medical 'entanglements,' it would be a very natural thing for us to form a closer and friendlier relationship than we have previously had with religion and theology.

And something of this sort is unquestionably occurring." If this is true, psychotherapy has retraced three thousand years of human history. While Mowrer's strictures on psychoanalytic psychiatry are no doubt justified, they are so because of this profession's lack of a natural science (biological) basis. It is difficult to see how this situation can be rectified by substituting one mythology for another. But, as Sigerist (1951) observes, "The moral interpretation of disease . . . seems to satisfy a primitive atavistic need that is still alive in our societies" (p. 157), and we inherit from ancient religion the view that "The sin resides, so to say, in the patient and must be driven out by ritual of which confession is the initial step" (p. 196).

3

Origins of Naturalism

To attempt to explain the origin and process of the world by having recourse to gods and spirits endowed with special powers, is merely to beg the question, since the existence of such beings can never be proved (nor of course disproved) by the means wherewith we know the world. In a word, it was Thales who first attempted to explain the variety of nature as the modifications of something *in nature.*—Wightman, 1953, p. 10 f.

If the universe is a mingling of probability clouds spread through a cosmic eternity of space-time, how is there as much order, persistence, and coherent transformation as there is?—Whyte, 1961, p. 27.

Linguistic and Cognitive Limitations of the Greek Philosophers

Among the Greeks of the coastal cities of Asia Minor in the sixth century B.C., conditions seem to have been unusually favorable for free intellectual activity. In these Ionian cities the poems of Homer first appeared, and with them the Olympian gods; there was a continuity with the prehistoric Aegean civilization; there was close contact with the civilization of Egypt and with that of Lydia and Persia. There was commercial prosperity and colonial expansion. As a result perhaps of all of these there was an absence of religious dogmatism and a great degree of freedom and liveliness of thought.

But while the intellectual climate of ancient Greece—at least at certain times and places and among certain classes—was favorable to philosophy, the available knowledge and techniques were grotesquely inadequate to what the philosophers tried to do. They wished to describe the "ultimate nature of the universe" in terms of a "first principle," without having any of the knowledge of the structure and properties of matter—or energy—which physics and chemistry have since attained, nor any of the techniques and habits of thought whereby modern science frames hypotheses with a view to their experimental testing. Their intellectual baggage moreover consisted of the implicit assumptions and categories inherited from religious tradition. The Greek philosophers thus began the historical development of *metaphysics*, in which philosophers assumed that, utilizing whatever data were available to them—data derived from the unaided and uncontrolled sense organs and from introspection—they could, by the powers of human thought, work out the "ultimate" nature, composition, and plan of the universe. "They drew no definite line," says Nordenskiöld (1928, p. 23), "between objective facts and subjective opinions; they had no idea whatever of hypothesis." The ancient magical view had been that such phenomena as the movements of the heavenly bodies were the work of capricious daemons. Hence, as Karl Pearson (1949) has pointed out, the discovery in Babylonia that eclipses of the sun and moon recur in definite cycles, so that the dates of their occurrence could, at least sometimes, be predicted, must have had a remarkable impact upon those "who looked upon eclipses as an arbitrary interference with their perceptions, and prayed and drummed vigorously for a restoration of the light of sun or moon." As a result of such discoveries, it had come to be assumed that the "plan" of the universe was orderly and rational, and it was often assumed that it was rational because it was the creation of a wise Maker; the philosophers projected their own rationality into the universe, as they have been doing ever since. On the assumption of a universe operated according to a rational plan, it was thought that wise men should be able to puzzle out its reasonable structure and relations. "Common sense" and certain simple rules of "logic"—i.e., of linguistic usage—were relied upon to guarantee the correctness of thought about the universe: a thing cannot both be and not be; what is inconceivable cannot be; linguistic opposites are dichotomies of nature; etc.

In the organization of any language there are two kinds of categories: the linguistic and the (merely) associative. *Linguistic* categories are marked by morphologically similar features (e.g., masculine and feminine gender endings), or by similarities of syntactic usage (e.g., occurrence in certain positions in sentence constructions). *Associative* categories are revealed in the high-frequency responses of free-association experiments, e.g., the opposites, subordinates, and coordinates. Categories of both kinds—both derived by the processes of association, abstraction, and generalization from the common experiences of human physiological, social, and economic life—are applied by priests, poets, and philosophers to the world in general. Thus ethnologists report from widely separated regions the notion that the sky is masculine and the earth feminine, and that the rest of the world was generated by their intercourse. As late as the seventeenth century, scientists spoke of the sun and the moon as "the male and the female principle." Very common also is the notion of nature dying and being reborn every year, and of man at death going below the earth and being subsequently reincarnated; here there was associative generalization of the opposites of life and death, waking and sleep, growth and decay, light and dark, heaven and earth, warm and cold; and the languages of agriculture and of human physiology were assimilated to each other. Moreover, verbal opposites played a dominant role in Greek philosophy.

It is obvious that the development of science has been dependent upon the development of metalinguistic sophistication. As Leonard Bloomfield (1933, p. 270) has said:

> The categories of a language, especially those which affect morphology (book:books, he:she), are so pervasive that anyone who reflects upon his language at all is sure to notice them. In the ordinary case, this person, knowing only his native language, or perhaps some others closely akin to it, may mistake his categories for universal forms of speech, or of "human thought," or of the universe itself. This is why a good deal of what passes for "logic" or "metaphysics" is merely an incompetent restating of the chief categories of the philosopher's language.

The development of science has involved also a growing awareness of the futility—for science—of such questions as "What is the nature of reality?" and "What is the ultimate principle of the universe?" Scientists had to learn to set themselves limited problems which could be empirically investigated; to regard common sense and intuition as scientifically without significance *unless* they could be formulated in propositions to be empirically tested by accepted scientific methods; to regard all hypotheses as tentative and instrumental, and all knowledge as limited and relative; to recognize language as an instrument whose properties are as important to know as are those of any other instruments upon which science depends. In all of these respects ancient Greek naturalistic philosophy was deficient—at least until the linguistic and biological studies of Aristotle. Dampier-Whetham (1930, p. 24) very instructively compares the atomic theory of Leucippus and Democritus with that developed in modern times by Dalton, Avogadro, and Cannizzaro:

> The Greeks had neither definite experimental facts to suggest an exact and limited theory in the first place, nor the power of testing by experience the consequences of the theory when deduced. The Greek theory was founded on and incorporated in a cosmic scheme of philosophy and it remained a doctrine, like the metaphysical systems in ancient and modern times, dependent on the mental attitude of its originators and their followers, and liable to be upset and replaced from the very foundations by a new system of a rival philosopher. And this indeed is what happened.

In a historical succession of *scientific* theories, on the other hand, we do not usually find it appropriate to say that one stage is "upset and replaced from the very foundations" by a later stage; rather, it is usually said that the successive formulations describe more and more exactly and economically a wider and wider range of phenomena; earlier schemata become "special cases" of the more generalized formulae. From this usual statement, however, there has recently been an interesting dissent; Kuhn (1962) sees science as an evolutionary process in which phases of "normal science," each dominated by a "paradigm"—a corpus of theory, rules, and standards—alternate with creative phases of revolution which are reactions to anomalies or counter-instances that resist assimilation to the prevailing paradigm and demand a new paradigm; the new paradigm is not a more general theory from which the old paradigm can be derived as a special case; it is a revolutionary innovation of which only "new men" are capable, not those who have been indoctrinated in the old paradigm. Kuhn's conception has of course been inspired chiefly by the developments in modern physics, and the "anomalies" there have arisen from systematic and highly sophisticated techniques of experimental research; it was the absence of systematic correlations between such techniques and the "paradigms" of the ancient Greek philosophers that made the difference to which I have referred.

The Ionian Physicists

The philosophy of the "Ionian physicists"—they are called "physicists" because they sought to determine the *physis*, the basic nature and constitution of things—consisted largely in an attempt to formulate a set of postulates whereby the seeming heterogeneity of the sensible world might be reduced to some basic substance or "ultimate stuff." This substance was, in a sense, material in nature, although the "matter" was living rather than dead. The concept had in fact been inherited from religion; *physis* was a soul-substance which pervaded the universe, including men and animals, and constituted the principle of life and motion. For the early Greek philosophers *all* of nature was animate; matter and life were inseparable. This is the view called "hylozoism." Thus Thales, according to Aristotle, said that "all things are full of gods," i.e., that the world is interpenetrated by life. Many things exhibit "motive power" which seems analogous to that of animals; thus Thales was said to have attributed "soul" to the magnet because it moves iron. When the Milesian philosophers said that *physis* was air or water or fire, they probably did not mean to identify it with any of these things but meant rather to suggest that it was embodied in them or somewhat like them; actually it was a metaphysical intangible substance. But since it was after all an extended quasi-material substance, it lent itself well to that philosophical transition, which began with the Ionian physicists and culminated in the atomists, whereby the concepts of god, soul, and life became attenuated and the universe was conceived as a material continuum whose activity consisted of mechanical motion or change of position in space. The philosophers still spoke of a soul in man, but this was merely one mode of manifestation of the power which activates everything in the universe; the soul of man is immortal therefore only in the sense that it is a part of the universal life principle, not in the sense of a surviving individual personality. Thus man becomes merely an infinitesimal bit of the universe; what A. P. Weiss (1929) called a "locus in the movement continuum."

The first of the Ionian physicists of the sixth century B.C. were inhabitants of the ancient city of Miletus on the coast of Asia Minor. The first of these was Thales, and after him came Anaximander and Anaximenes. As we have seen, these men attempted an economical description of the universe in terms of a basic substance. Burnet

(1924, 1957) has suggested that their analysis was in terms of their observations of the three states of aggregation of matter—solid, liquid, and gaseous. Since water becomes solid when it freezes and vaporous when it evaporates, it was conjectured that earth and stones represent a solidification, that air is a purer form of vapor, and that the *aether*, "which is properly the bright blue of the Mediterranean sky," is a still purer form, "fed by vapor rising from the sea," and identified with fire. It was on the basis of this scheme, Burnet suggested, that Thales chose water as the basic substance and Anaximenes chose air. Anaximenes introduced the processes of rarefaction and condensation to explain how air becomes fire or water and earth, so that we might consider this as the earliest attempt to explain qualitative by quantitative changes. Air was, of course, an obvious choice for the basic substance, since it surrounded the universe, was essential to life, and was the substance of the soul, which, said Anaximenes, "being air, holds us together." Anaximander, the immediate successor of Thales, called the basic substance "the boundless," a neutral infinite substance—perhaps "a kind of mist or cloud," as Jones (1931) suggests—in eternal motion. From it, in the formation of the world, opposites—hot and cold, wet and dry, etc.—separate out; in infinite time and space successions of worlds are created and destroyed, although primary matter is eternal.

Burnet's scheme is conjectural and perhaps over-intellectualized; it will be recalled that Cornford (1957) has emphasized the view that these earliest Greek philosophers did not begin their labors with an analysis of their own world of sense perception. (No more, of course, do we, who as a prerequisite to the doctorate must learn to see the world in terms of the current "paradigm.") Rather, their concepts of "nature," "soul," and "gods" were taken over from a long religious tradition, in which the notion that there is a moral order in nature was basic. This moral order, personified by *moira* ("one's portion in life, lot, fate, destiny, justice, necessity"), was held to govern the distribution of everything not only in human life but also in nature generally. For anything whatever to trespass on the allotted sphere of anything else is an "injustice"; this concept, which according to Cornford (but cf. Dodds, 1957, p. 6 f.) was derived from the Olympian scheme in which each god was allotted his sphere—the heavens, earth, ocean, etc.—was extended by the philosophers as the principle governing the proportions of things in the universe; e.g., the proportions of fire, air, earth, water, the excess of any of which would therefore be said to be an "injustice" for which a compensatory "penalty" must be paid by way of restoring equilibrium. Behind the religious concept, in turn, Cornford suggests, was the structure of tribal, e.g., totemistic, society. Thus the religious constructions were projections into the universe of human social arrangements, and constituted the material whose reworking under special historical—particularly economic—conditions was the beginning of science. In the beginning, "man was the measure of all things"; the development of science depended on the progressive freeing of a small company of intellectuals from the anthropocentric —religious and moral—bias. What Anaximander did was to adopt the prescientific classification, retain the concept of *moira,* but eliminate the gods. According to this account, therefore, not only the mystical tradition of Pythagoras and Plato but also the "scientific" tradition stemming from Thales and Anaximander grew out of earlier religious beliefs, and we have here at the beginning an impressive example of how men bent upon rational analysis inescapably and unconsciously follow pre-existing models, which may be of irrational and extra-scientific origin, and of how Western philosophy and science have developed by a series of historical accidents and their accompanying semantic shifts. *Moira,* the moral law of the Greeks, becomes the "natural law" of modern thought.

What I have said thus far might easily give the impression that the Milesian physicists were purely theoretical verbalizers, like modern metaphysicians. Their ancient reputation however was that of men with an active interest in practical affairs, as illustrated by the legend that Thales made a fortune by cornering the olive oil market and thus demonstrated that an intellectual can become rich if he cares to direct his intelligence to that end. Various practical inventions were credited to Thales: prediction of eclipses, methods of celestial navigation, and the application of geometrical propositions to the measurement of the height of buildings and of the distance of ships from the shore. Miletus was a bustling seaport trading with all parts of the ancient world; the ruling class was a commercial aristocracy. Many of the things which Butterfield (1951, Chap. 10) attributes to seventeenth century Europe—the century of Newton—could be attributed to the sixth century B.C. seaport cities of Ionia: commercialization, colonial and trade expansion, the secularization of thought, the cultural and moral relativism resulting from growing acquaintance with other lands, the interest in practical applications of science.

Anaximander conjectured that animal life arose from the sun-heated mud which once covered the earth—a notion perhaps suggested by the "insects which issue from marine larvae" (Sarton, 1960, p. 176)—and that man arose from a fish-like form. Because of man's requirement of a lengthy period of suckling, he cannot represent an original type of animal, for he would have been incapable of survival. Anaximander suggested the shark as an ancestor, since it seemed an intermediate form in which, as he observed, the embryos are retained for a prolonged period within the oviduct. Anaximander's speculations on this subject seem quite reasonable, and when we read the warnings of a number of authors against regarding him as a precursor of Darwin, we might well remind ourselves that the basic notion of man's evolutionary origin was still a very strange one in Darwin's time. Moreover, in the history of philosophy and of science the functionally important question often is not why a man said something, or what justification he had for saying it, or even what he said, but rather what he is traditionally or subsequently thought to have said and meant. The historical role which the Milesian philosophers have played is that of the first men to offer a non-mythological description of the universe as an orderly system of which human beings are infinitesimal components. In the long view, the hylozoistic tinge does not seem important, nor does the probably mythological and certainly inadequate background of the statements about the origin of life and of man. The important thing, it might be suggested, is that when such seeds of thought as the notion of the world as a physical movement continuum and of man as derived from more primitive animal ancestors are cast into the stream of history, they become part of the cultural heritage of later men who have much more knowledge at their disposal.

As for the contrasting accounts of Burnet and of Cornford, we are probably justified in assuming that both are right. Religious preconceptions *were* operative, but within the conceptual limits which they imposed these highly intelligent philosophers did observe natural phenomena, and their formulations were inevitably influenced by their perceptions. As evidence of the habits of observation of the Greeks, Burnet (1957, p. 26) points to the anatomical accuracy of their sculpture and to the "models of scientific observation at its best" contained in the Hippocratic writings. Habits and techniques of objective and accurate observation must have been very well developed if Thales, as tradition tells us, was able not only to make contributions to mathematics, astronomy, and meteorology, but also to solve problems in navigation, husbandry, politics, and business. On the other hand, Burnet's (p. 14) complete rejection of Cornford's suggestions, and his statement that "Ionia was a country without a past" seem to me less convincing than Cornford's assertion that the early Greek philosophers had a tradition behind them; it would be difficult to imagine what the pre-philosophical tradition could be if not religious. That the language used by the philosophers was borrowed from religion does not lose its historical significance because of the fact that the philosophers used religious words in non-religious ways.

Heraclitus

Heraclitus (c.535-c.475 B.C.) was a native of Ephesus, a city near Miletus in Asia Minor, and it is natural that his world-scheme, in the light of subsequent history, should appear to us to be of the same general sort as those of the Milesian philosophers. The difficulty is that, on the one hand, Heraclitus expressed the greatest contempt for all other philosophers, including the Milesians, and spoke in the language of the mysteries, but, on the other hand, seems to have felt an equal contempt for the Orphic mystery religion, to which he has been thought to have referred by the epithets "night-walkers, magicians, priests of Bacchus and priestesses of the wine-vat, mystery-mongers." The fact seems to be that Heraclitus was a brilliant and arrogant aristocrat and intellectual who felt that he had a divine mission to promulgate his "Word"; in this he reminds us of Kepler and Fechner, both of whom did important scientific work in fulfillment of mystical motivation; as Fechner cried to a sleeping public, "Steh' auf!" so, Patrick (1889, p. 59) tells us, Heraclitus called "to men everywhere to *wake up*, to purify their [barbarous souls], and to see things in their reality."

Whereas Anaximander's fundamental process was the "separating out" of opposites from the "boundless," and that of Anaximenes was the rarefaction and condensation of air, Heraclitus fixed on the process of combustion. The world is "an eternal living Fire, kindled and extinguished measure for measure." Heraclitus probably selected fire as his primary substance for the same reason that Anaximenes selected air—because its apparent insubstantiality made it particularly appropriate to represent the soul-substance, and its mobility made it seem fitted to represent the pervasive moving force of life. It seems likely that the warmth of the animal body in life as compared with its coldness in death favored these selections; there was perhaps not very much distinction between the soul-substance as fire and the psyche as warm breath.

In Heraclitus' scheme, two opposite and balanced processes are endlessly going on: an "upward path" whereby earth changes into water and water into fire, and a "downward path" in which the reverse changes occur. Here as with the Milesians the perceptual basis was probably the observation of the processes of evaporation and liquefaction; as Jones (1931, p. 454) says, "symbolically or actually, fire is a good example of physical transformation. Fuel is supplied from below, the flames quickly alter its nature, and finally it rises as smoke and fumes." Thus there is nothing permanent in the world; change, like time, is a continuum, and "everything flows," but things appear to remain the same because the opposite processes are in equilibrium. Where Heraclitus says that the two opposites of a pair are "the same thing," we would say that they are polarities, and hence relative to one another. The dynamic relation between the polarities—the opposite tensions as between bow and cord or harp and strings—is the principle of nature; "all things are born through strife"; "war is the father of all"; as we might say, "absence of dynamic tension between polarities would be a state of total entropy." The "opposites" which Heraclitus emphasized were, in the macrocosm, night and day, summer and winter; in the microcosm or soul, sleeping and waking, life and death. Life, sleep, and death correspond to fire, water, and earth; sleep is a stage between life and death. Sleep, disease, and death result from an increase of moisture, as is demonstrated in alcoholic intoxication: "It is death to a soul to become water." Waking and life correspond to an increase of warmth and fire: "The dry soul is the wisest and best." All of these states are reversible; just as day follows night, so does life follow death, so that the soul is immortal—but immortal only as a part of the eternal fire. There is no individual or personal immortality; both soul and body are in constant flux; just as we cannot step twice into the same river, so we ourselves cannot be the same for two successive instants. During life, the soul-fire is constantly renewed from the external light and air through the senses and the breath. In Heraclitus we find the first reference to the distinction which we, in terms of recent neurophysiology, may interpret as that between afferently and intrinsically dominated cortical activity: "The waking have one common world, but the sleeping turn aside each into a world of his own." "For in sleep, when the channels of perception are shut, our mind is sundered from its kinship with the surrounding, and breathing is the only point of attachment to be preserved, like a kind of root . . . ." (Sextus, quoted by Kirk and Raven, 1957, p. 207).

On first acquaintance the schemes of the Milesians and of Heraclitus may appear nonsensical and irrelevant to the history of science, and this impression may have been strengthened by Cornford's arguments for their religious and mystical background. Hence it may be well to pause at this point to note the status assigned to them by writers who have been particularly concerned with the history of scientific conceptions. Of Thales and his concept of water as the primary substance, Wightman (1953, p. 10 f.) says:

> His dictum then, though certainly not wholly true, was, at its face value, very far from being nonsense. The greater part of the earth's surface is water; water pervades every region of our atmosphere; life as we know it is impossible without water; water is the nearest approach to the alchemists' dream of a universal solvent. . . . All these facts . . . gave Thales good grounds for thinking that *if there is any one thing at the basis of all nature,* that thing must be water. If there is any one thing! This supposition, that is to say, the asking as it were of this question, constitutes Thales' claim to immortality.

Farrington (1944, p. 36 f.) quotes Brunet and Mieli:

> [The Ionian philosophers] observe the phenomena which present themselves to their eyes, and, putting aside all supernatural or mystical intervention, they endeavor to give strictly natural explanations of them. It is in this sense, and by their rejection of all magical intervention, that they make the decisive step towards science and mark the beginning, at least the conscious and systematic beginning, of a positive method applied to the interpretation of the facts of nature.

But Farrington thinks it necessary to supplement this judgment by recognition of the fact that the Milesians "were observers of nature whose eyes had been quickened, whose attention directed, and whose selection of phenomena to be observed had been conditioned, by familiarity with a certain range of techniques"—the techniques whose invention was motivated by an active interest in practical affairs.

The above will not persuade us that the Milesians anticipated modern science, but it may make us less ready to describe their speculations as mere nonsense, without influence on the subsequent history of thought.

The intellect of Heraclitus seems to have been one of the greatest and most independent of ancient Greece. He sharply criticized popular religion and pointed out its symbolic character. He recognized the relativity both of human knowledge and of human ethical values. As for his metaphysics, though it was certainly not "a great scientific generalization," as Burnet (1924) asserts, since it was entirely speculative and dogmatic, nevertheless it might be well to remember that it was part of the cultural background of those who centuries later formulated the concepts of physical and chemical equilibria and of metabolism, nor can a psychologist fail to be reminded by the analogy between the ever-changing river and the ever-changing soul of the "stream of consciousness" of William James. In his assertion that the only permanent feature of the ceaseless flux of things is the orderliness of succession—which he attributed to a rational principle or *logos* which pervades the universe—he foreshadowed the modern conception of the uniformity of natural law.

In these days of scientific interest in the nature of language, particular mention should be made of Heraclitus' role in the history of this subject. He was the first explicitly to describe words as embodying the nature of things, and to regard the structure of language as reflecting the structure of the world. He considered language to be an expression of the common wisdom of the human race, and as the most nearly constant thing in a universe of ceaseless change. The distinction between the problems of physics and those of linguistics and psychology had however not yet become explicit in Heraclitus; his doctrine of opposites was inspired at least as much by linguistic associations as by polarities of nature. This domination by linguistic "opposites" was pervasive in Greek philosophy, notoriously so in Pythagorean schemes. Heraclitus says that justice is known only through injustice, and that health, satiety, rest, and goodness are pleasant only in contrast to disease, hunger, toil and evil. Heraclitus' philosophy of language received further development—or as some think, debasement (Kirk and Raven, 1957, p. 165)—at the hands of his disciple Cratylus, who was Plato's first teacher. In the opening of Plato's dialogue *Cratylus*, Hermogenes says (Fowler's translation),

> Cratylus, whom you see here, Socrates, says that everything has a right name of its own, which comes by nature, and that a name is not whatever people call a thing by agreement, just a piece of their own voice applied to the thing, but that there is a kind of inherent correct-

ness in names, which is the same for all men, both Greeks and
barbarians.

In the course of the dialogue, Socrates discusses

the theory advanced by Hermogenes and many others, who claim
that names are conventional and represent things to those who established the convention and knew the things beforehand, and that
convention is the sole principle of correctness in names, and it makes
no difference whether we accept the existing convention or adopt an
opposite one according to which small would be called great and
great small.

Socrates, perhaps somewhat playfully, suggests that the separate
sounds of words have symbolic value; in modern linguistics this
doctrine is known as "phonetic symbolism," to which a great deal
of discussion and research have been devoted in recent times
by psychologists and others; the literature has been extensively
reviewed by Brown (1958, Ch. IV).

Democritus

Democritus (c.460-c.370 B.C.) was born at Abdera, a Greek colony on the Thracian (northern) coast of the Aegean Sea. Of his
teacher Leucippus we know almost nothing, but there is some evidence that it was Leucippus who was the founder of the atomic
theory which has historically been associated with the name of
Democritus. This theory assumed an infinite number of indivisible
(*atomos*, "uncut") atoms, so small as to be invisible, of countless
shapes and sizes, whose eternal motions in all directions result in
collisions and impacts, which impacts result in vortex motions and
the formation of aggregations of atoms in definite arrangements
according to shape and size. Thus arise worlds, only again to perish,
and thus arise the things which we perceive with our senses; the
variety of these things is a consequence of the variety of their
atoms in shape, number, size, position, and arrangement. Out of
nothing arises nothing; nothing that is can be destroyed, for though
aggregations of atoms—perceived things—are ephemeral, the atoms
themselves are eternal. All change is only combination and separation of atoms. The mechanical processes of impact and pressure are
the only means by which things can produce effects on other things.
Thus Democritus foreshadows two doctrines of classical modern
physics: the indestructibility of matter and the conservation of

energy. Moreover, "nothing happens by chance, but everything for some reason and of necessity." The "cause" of anything is merely the mathematico-mechanical law followed by the atoms in their motions. This is a negation not only of chance but also of teleology; Aristotle, for whom "final cause" or purpose was an important explanatory principle, ascribed chance as the Democritean principle of atomic combination, but the atomists themselves "emphasized the other aspect of non-planned mechanical sequences, i.e. as necessity" (Kirk and Raven, 1957, p. 413). Not divinities but a purely impersonal necessity governs the universe.

The soul consists of the smallest and most mobile atoms, like those of fire; they permeate the body and give it life; life and soul are the same thing. This notion may have had a perceptual origin: Aristotle says that Democritus compared the soul-atoms to the motes in the air seen "in shafts of light coming through windows." Through inhalation the body receives a fresh supply of these fine atoms, and thus life depends on respiration. Man is a microcosm in which every kind of atom is represented. The brain is the organ of thought, the heart is that of anger, and the liver that of desire. Democritus seems to have performed dissections on animals, and on this basis to have arrived at a number of ideas which Aristotle rejected but which modern research has shown to be correct, e.g., the significance of the brain and the view that even the lower and the most minute animals have complex structures.

Sensation consists in the impact of atoms from without on the atoms of the soul. When the impact is immediate, as in the sense of touch, the qualities (e.g., weight, density, hardness) can most reliably be taken as properties of things themselves, but when stimulus transmission involves a medium as in hearing and vision, this medium may introduce distortions, and in any case perception involves an interaction between the emanations ("images") thrown off by objects and the variable organs of sense. "By the senses," said Democritus, "we in truth know nothing sure, but only something that changes according to the disposition of the body and of the things that enter into it or resist it." Sweet, bitter, warm, cold, red, green—all these are so called by usage or convention, "but in sooth there are atoms and the void." But in spite of the unreliability and subjectivity of the senses, Democritus holds that true knowledge of reality is possible. He distinguishes between "bastard" knowledge derived from the special senses and "true-born" knowledge which results from the fact that the atoms outside us can affect the atoms of our soul directly, without the intervention of the organs of sense. Democritus thus introduced two distinctions which were destined to have a long history in psychology: that between primary and secondary qualities which was to be popularized by John Locke in the seventeenth century, and that between perception and reason or thought for which we are only now beginning to see some hope of a naturalistic (physiological) interpretation.

Democritus was also the author of an ethical doctrine, which Vlastos (1945, 1946) has called "the first rigorously naturalistic ethics in Greek thought." It has commonly been supposed that a materialistic, mechanistic, or naturalistic theory of the universe—and of man as a part of the universe—is incompatible with lofty moral principles and with a high regard for human worth and dignity. Thus Dewey (1944) cites contemporary writers who "identify naturalism with 'materialism' and then employ the identification to charge naturalists with reduction of all distinctively human values . . . to blind mechanical conjunctions of material entities—a reduction which is in effect their complete destruction." It is interesting therefore to observe how in ancient as in modern times some of the most thoroughgoing naturalists have given expression to and exemplified the greatest humanity and moral idealism. Lange (1925, I, p. 47) clothes this observation in eloquence: "Nay, we may say that the sober earnest which marks the great Materialistic systems of antiquity is perhaps more suited than an enthusiastic Idealism, which only too easily results in its own bewilderment, to keep the soul clear of all that is low and vulgar, and to lend it a lasting effort after worthy objects." The chief fragments of Democritus' writings on this subject are from his treatise *On Cheerfulness*. He shared with most of the ancient ethical theorists the principle of "eudaemonism," according to which the aim of right action is happiness. But this is not hedonism. Just as thought is superior to sense perception, so knowledge of the good and tranquillity of the spirit are superior to sensual pleasures. What we should strive for is a state of the soul; we must apply the test of judgment to pleasures, so that we may attain calm of the body—health—and of the soul—cheerfulness. In his definition of the conditions of happiness Democritus arrived at a principle which Zeller (1955, p. 85) has described as "the moral autonomy of reason, in virtue of which nothing is so much to be avoided as an action of which one would be ashamed in one's own eyes." "By temperament one of the greatest idealists of all time, this materialist devoted his whole life to research and thought it a greater gain to discover a causal connection than to receive the crown of Persia" (ibid., p. 81).

4

Origins of Antinaturalism

> What is amiss, even in the best philosophy after Democritus, is an
> undue emphasis on man as compared with the universe. First comes
> scepticism, with the Sophists, leading to a study of *how* we know
> rather than to the attempt to acquire fresh knowledge. Then comes,
> with Socrates, the emphasis on ethics; with Plato, the rejection of
> the world of sense in favour of the self-created world of pure
> thought; with Aristotle, the belief in purpose as the fundamental
> concept in science. In spite of the genius of Plato and Aristotle,
> their thought has vices which proved infinitely harmful.—Bertrand
> Russell, 1945, p. 73.

We have seen that the intellectual atmosphere which made possible the origins of naturalistic philosophy had as its theological source the religion of the Olympian gods. The theological background of the mystical tradition, on the other hand, was the religion of Dionysus. Its key concept was that of a group bound together in a common life which transcended every individual and was therefore immortal. The spatial scheme of the Olympian-scientific tradition was replaced in the Dionysiac-mystic tradition by a scheme of temporal continuity characterized by cycles of birth, death, and rebirth, the model for which was on the one hand the cycle of seasons and of vegetative growth and decay, and on the other the cycles of the heavenly bodies. The spatial ("physical") model lent itself well to an analysis of the universe into material substances occupying space and undergoing changes of position in space, and

51

lent itself well also to quantitative conceptualization. The temporal ("vitalistic") model, on the other hand, did not lend itself to such analysis. As Cornford (1957, p. 150) observes, " . . . in the spontaneous, procreant movement of life there is something which defies analysis in mechanical terms, something gratuitous and unaccountable, of supreme importance to the mystical temperament, and correspondingly abhorrent to a science that is bent upon making physics conform to the perfect lucidity of geometry." Throughout the subsequent history of biological and psychological science we shall find a similar dichotomy between the "vitalistic" and the "naturalistic-mechanistic" temperaments. Lashley, in 1923, reviewing the issues between behaviorism and the psychologies of consciousness, observed, "Adherence to mechanism or finalism seems to be wholly a matter of temperament; the choice is made upon an emotional and not a rational basis" (Lashley, 1923, p. 345). The choice is not one which could be made by a computer.

Pythagoras

When we come to Pythagoras (c.582-c.500 B.C.) and his school, we come to a great muddle of religious mysticism, music, mathematics, medicine, and cosmology. Pythagoras was a native of Samos, an island town not far from Miletus, and seems to have begun his philosophical thought under the influence of the Milesian philosophers. He left Samos about 530 B.C. to found a religious and philosophical community at Croton in southern Italy. Apparently he and his associates attempted to rule Croton and some neighboring towns according to the tenets of their religious order, an undertaking which was so unpopular with the inhabitants that Pythagoras had to flee, and some eighty years after his death most of the brotherhood were massacred and their establishment destroyed. Pythagoras himself is said to have written nothing, and there is no way of distinguishing his dicta from those of his disciples of the period ending with the destruction of the order at Croton ("earlier Pythagoreans"). In the fourth century B.C. there were philosophers, especially at Tarentum in southern Italy, who are referred to as "later Pythagoreans," and who greatly influenced Plato.

There is also no way of distinguishing between the doctrines and practices of the early Pythagoreans and those of the Orphic cult-societies, though they seem to have been very similar. Prominent in Orphic ritual was the spectacle *(theoria)* of the suffering god. Cornford (1957, p. 200) tells us that

> Pythagoras gave a new meaning to *theoria*; he reinterpreted it as the passionless contemplation of rational, unchanging truth, and converted the way of life into a "pursuit of wisdom" *(philosophia)*. The way of life is still also a way of death; but now it means death to the emotions and lusts of this vile body, and a release of the intellect to soar into the untroubled empyrean of *theory*.

The mysticism which the Pythagoreans introduced into the Western philosophical tradition included the notions of the transmigration of souls and of the release from the "circle of births" by purification. This purification included, as among the Orphics, various rituals and taboos (e.g., abstinence from flesh and beans), but it also involved the purification of the soul by mental work and music, and of the body by gymnastics and medicine. It was said that the Pythagoreans used medicine to purge the body and music to purge the soul; philosophy and mathematics were also "purges for the soul." The doctrine of transmigration was related to the idea of the universal kinship of all living things—both plant and animal— which found expression, e.g., in the admission of women to the order, in humane treatment of slaves, and in a general spirit of friendship and self-sacrifice. But just as in the transmigration of souls there was a gradation according to the previous life of each soul, so in society the Pythagoreans favored a social order in which men were not equal but enjoyed rights according to their merits— not "arithmetical" but "geometrical" (proportional) equality. With the great development of statistical methods in our own times, it has been possible for a contemporary psychologist to propose a more sophisticated version of this scheme (Horst, 1951).

Music was important to the Pythagoreans not only, so to speak, as a therapeutic method, a "purgation of the soul," but also as the starting point of their mathematics and hence of their cosmological doctrine that "all things are numbers." They discovered that the pitch of tones is a function of the length of strings, and that the relative lengths of the strings which give the consonant intervals are expressed by simple numerical ratios between the first four integers (2:1, 3:2, 4:3). The four fixed notes of the lyre could be expressed by the numbers 6 8 9 12. Here 9 was found to be the arithmetic mean of the extreme values 6 and 12, and 8 the harmonic mean. For what must seem to us incredibly inadequate reasons these discoveries were thought to provide the key to the secret of the universe. The Milesian philosophers had been preoccupied by the problem of "opposites"—wet and dry, warm and cold, etc. Anaximander had sought to handle this problem by means of his concept of the "boundless," a neutral substance from which the opposites arise and into which they are reabsorbed. The Pythagoreans now assumed that there was an ideal blend of the opposites whose numerical value might be discovered. The "boundless" became the "unlimited," for which number was the "limit" which determined its form.

The problems involved in making informed guesses as to what the "Pythagoreans" of various times and places in the fifth and fourth centuries B.C. said and meant are far beyond the scope of this survey; moreover, very different guesses have been made by various competent scholars. However, since what might be called the Pythagorean view of the role of mathematics in science is a matter of concern in contemporary science, some further account seems desirable. I have found most helpful for this purpose the recent explication by Kirk and Raven (1957, pp. 217-262), who give relevant Greek texts with translations.

The Pythagoreans, says Aristotle, having devoted themselves to mathematics, "thought its principles were the principles of all things"; "they supposed the elements of numbers to be the elements of all things." Basic in their "ten principles" or scheme of "opposites" were the pairs limit-unlimited and odd-even. As a result of the fact that numbers were expressed as geometrical patterns like those on our dominoes or dice (e.g., the "sacred" number 10 by ten dots arranged in an equilateral triangle whose rows of 1, 2, 3, 4 corresponded to the integers containing the "secret" of the musical scale), the arithmetical "odd" was equated with the geometrical "limit," and similarly "even" with "unlimited." Now when the Pythagoreans said that "all things are numbers," they identified numbers with real things; their mathematical unit-points were a primitive form of atom, and each concrete object was an aggregation of such unit-point atoms. "The unfortunate consequence of their diagrammatic representation of numbers was that the Pythagoreans, thinking of numbers as spatially extended and confusing the point of geometry with the unit of arithmetic, tended to imagine both alike as possessing magnitude" (Kirk and Raven, p. 246 f.). Thus numbers took the place of the elements and atoms of the other Greek philosophers. But it was not only concrete objects which could be "equated" with numbers; such an abstraction as "justice" was equated with the first square number, 4, and similarly "soul," "reason," and "opinion" each had its numerical equation, which perhaps represented its "ratio of opposites."

It has become a commonplace of modern science that observed relationships are most economically expressed in mathematical form. In our more rational moments we recognize that both the observations and the numerical values which are based upon them are functions of human beings, their history, biological and social properties, and techniques; that these numerical values are statistical and not absolute; and that any apparently "absolute" numbers are the results of "ideal" calculations—e.g., the fitting of lines and equations—by human scientists, and cannot in any but a mystical sense be said to express the "design of the universe." But we not infrequently find a persistence of the old Pythagorean notion that certain *particular* numbers correspond to ultimate realities of life or of the universe. It is often difficult to draw the line between numerology and science. Kepler, whose discoveries were so important in the history of astronomy, was motivated by a search for the musical ratios in planetary motions which would fill the ether with celestial music; following Plato, he attributed his ability to express mathematically the motions of the planets to the fact that God was a geometer. "In our own day," says Dampier-Whetham (1930, p. 20), "Aston with his integral atomic weights, Mosely with his atomic numbers, Planck with his quantum theory, and Einstein with his claim that physical facts such as gravitation are exhibitions of local space-time properties, are reviving ideas that, in older, cruder forms, appear in Pythagorean philosophy." In the presidential address of Sir George Thomson before the British Association for the Advancement of Science in 1960, we find the following:

> It is one of the strangest facts of nature that she is so fond of whole numbers. The mere existence of large classes of individuals identical in each class, such as electrons, protons, atoms of fluorine, molecules of ethyl alcohol, and many more, is surprising enough. One might expect a continuous gradation of sizes, weights, and charges. But it is not so. On the smallest scale only certain types of particles exist. The next most complicated things, atoms, are built of integral numbers of electrons, protons, and neutrons. . . . Further, the details of the pattern made by the electrons depend on another set of small integers, the quantum numbers. . . . We are getting back to one of the earliest scientific ideas. Pythagoras taught that whole numbers are supreme. . . . Rather the same can be said of the concept of the cell. Living matter is, generally speaking, cellular, and the cells that com-

pose a given kind of tissue are mostly pretty much alike in size and shape. Even the organisms that they form tend, at least, to fall into species each containing very many similar individuals . . . [Thomson, 1960, p. 999].

Examples are not difficult to find in contemporary psychology. Thus Zipf, whose work has been much esteemed by some psychologists, made frequency counts of words in Chinese, English, and Latin texts, and found that the relationship between frequency of occurrence of words (b) and the number of different words of a given frequency (a) could be approximately expressed by the formula $ab^2 = k$, where k is a constant. Of this discovery Zipf exclaims, "But the overwhelming disclosure is this, that the formula for abbreviation is $ab^2 = k$, a formula exactly identical to that of gravitation" (Zipf, 1932, p. 24). As Joos (1936, p. 199) observes, "For Zipf this nearness of [the exponent of b] to 2 is a discovery of cosmic import. . . . And so he is ready to disregard the possibly significant differences among the three languages, and to find that in all three the exponent equals exactly 2. . . ." It is interesting to note that Zipf's notion of causality is also quite Pythagorean: " . . . all speech-elements or language-patterns are impelled and directed in their behavior by a fundamental law of economy in which is the desire to maintain an equilibrium between form and behavior" (Zipf, 1935, p. 19). "Psychophysics" has often been regarded as a field in which true constants might be discovered. Swets (1960) has analyzed the factors which make doubtful the existence of a "sensory threshold." Many psychologists will sadly remember the eager search for "the" Weber-Fechner constant, and for "the" equation of the learning curve; the "constant I.Q." is another recent memory. Large numbers of psychologists are still busily occupied in "measuring" and expressing by numbers the "intelligence," "personality," and "interests" of individuals. The hum of electronic computers is the new "music of the spheres."

Alcmaeon

There was a medical school in Croton which, though not a part of the Pythagorean community—it had been founded before the arrival of Pythagoras—was influenced by its doctrines. Most famous of this school was Alcmaeon (c. 450 B.C.), who has been called the first physiologist; he may also be regarded as the first physician to influence the history of psychology (cf. Jones, 1946, pp. 3-6). On the basis of dissection of animals he is said to have recognized that the brain integrates sensations and stores memories. He described the nerves as canals leading from sense organs to brain. He distinguished between sense perception and thinking, the latter occurring in man only. He seems to have been the source of Aristotle's view that knowledge arises from sensation after it has been stored in memory and undergone organization—as we would say, by the processes of generalization and abstraction. He expressed the mystical notion that man is related to the universe as microcosm to macrocosm; man's body reproduces in miniature the structure of the world, and his soul is a harmony of number. To the Pythagorean doctrine of harmony in music corresponded a doctrine of physiological equilibrium. Health consisted in an ideal balance among the various pairs of opposite qualities, and disease was a disturbance of this balance—the old idea of "injustice." This ancient doctrine may well have been reinforced by observation: as Jones (1946, p. 4) says, "To an observer, handicapped as were the early Greeks, fever appears to be caused by excess of heat, biliousness by an excess of 'the bitter,'" etc. The physician's task was to restore an "isonomy of substances," an equilibrium of the qualities or "powers." He did this by supervising the patient's regimen, his way of life, surroundings, and diet. This was the basic idea developed by Hippocratic medicine, which was also influenced by the Pythagorean doctrine of the magical significance of number: "critical days" in the course of diseases, for which malaria furnished an empirical model; and the number seven in, e.g., menstruation (4 x 7) and human gestation (40 x 7). The works of Alcmaeon are lost, but he exercised great influence on the development of medical theory. He illustrates for us the fact that just as a patient needs the support of a physician, so the physician needs the support of a theory; the theory serves to rationalize diagnosis and treatment, but need not correspond to underlying physiology and pathology, in so far as the therapeutic effect is of the "psychosomatic" sort, as it still is in a great deal of modern medical practice.

Parmenides and Zeno

Parmenides, who flourished in the first half of the fifth century B.C., was a native of Elea in southern Italy, and the chief representative of the Eleatic school of philosophy. The intellectual atmosphere of southern Italy favored Pythagorean mysticism and mathematical abstractions rather than the naturalism of the Ionian philosophers. Parmenides perhaps began his philosophical career as a Pythagorean, and if so, he would have been indoctrinated with the Pythagorean mathematical approach. As Burnet (1924, p. 67) observes:

> To the mathematician of all men it is the same thing that can be thought . . . and that can be . . . and this is the principle from which Parmenides starts. It is impossible to think what is not, and it is impossible for what cannot be thought to be. The great question, *Is it or is it not?* is therefore equivalent to the question, *Can it be thought or not?*

By this method Parmenides sought to prove that change, motion, diversity and multiplicity, time and space are illusions of the senses. There is only one reality, a finite, uniform, spherical, motionless, continuous plenum, and this can be apprehended only by thought; sensory experience is pure illusion. To illustrate Parmenides' reasoning, I shall quote Burnet's (1924, p. 67 f.) paraphrase of the "proof" that real being can neither have an origin nor move:

> In the first place, it cannot have come into being. If it had, it must have arisen from nothing or from something. It cannot have arisen from nothing; for there is no nothing. It cannot have arisen from something; for there is nothing else than what *is*. Nor can anything else besides itself come into being; for there can be no empty space in which it could do so. . . . Further, it is immoveable. If it moved, it must move into empty space, and empty space is nothing, and there is no nothing.

Parmenides identified both thought and language with reality. As W. K. C. Guthrie (1960, p. 47) says, "One idea which the Greeks at this stage found it difficult to absorb was that a word might have more than one meaning. Their difficulty no doubt had something to do with the proximity of the primitive magical stage at which a word and its object formed a single unity." Bertrand Russell (1945, p. 49) states the essence of Parmenides' argument as follows:

> When you think, you think of something; when you use a name, it must be the name *of* something. Therefore both thought and language require objects outside themselves. And since you can think of a thing or speak of it at one time as well as at another, whatever can be thought of or spoken of must exist at all times. Consequently there can be no change, since change consists in things coming into being or ceasing to be.

Zeno of Elea, the famous disciple of Parmenides, who was called the father of dialectics and sophistry—as Parmenides himself has been called the father of metaphysics—invented a number of famous "proofs" of the impossibility of multiplicity and of motion. His arguments were directed not only against Heraclitus but also against the Pythagorean doctrine that all things consist of integral numbers. His reasoning is illustrated by the following: a continuity, such as a line, can be bisected, the resulting halves can be bisected, and so on; an ultimate unit or point is never reached. If a given terminated straight line is composed of unit-points, it must be composed of an infinite number of such points; if these points have magnitude, every line will be of infinite length; if they have no magnitude, every line will be infinitely small. Similarly, motion is inconceivable: "If a thing moves from one point to another, it must first traverse half the distance. Before it can do that, it must traverse half of the half, and so on *ad infinitum*. It must, therefore, pass through an infinite number of points, and that is impossible in a finite time" (Burnet, 1924, p. 84).

This sort of mare's-nest has been repeatedly created throughout the history of philosophy and of science; it is not a special naïvety of the ancient Greeks; it was from just such products of the autonomous use of language that Ernst Mach and Karl Pearson, near the end of the nineteenth century, sought to disencumber science; more recently still, the logical positivists and the operationalists have addressed themselves to the same task—a task which will not end while men can talk. The fundamental difficulty arises from the fact that sensory experience results in mnemic patterns in the brain which can undergo endless repatterning in the course of overt or implicit symbolic activity or of intrinsic activity of the brain—the processes, i.e., which we summarize as *thinking*. Pearson (1949) contrasted *perceptual* with *conceptual* processes, and pointed out that processes which begin in the perceptual realm may be continued to a limit which lies in the conceptual realm. For example, we can bisect a one-inch line with dividers, again bisect the halves, and continue thus several times more; when we are unable to perform a further bisection perceptually or physically, we can nevertheless *imagine* making further bisections endlessly, the more so that, being talking animals, we can, having successively said, "*Another* bisection, and *another* bisection. . . . ," suiting actions to words, continue to say these words after the actions are no longer possible; we can do this even more easily when we have invented convenient abbre-

viations, such as " . . . to infinity." But when our perceptual or practical series has reached its limit while our verbal or imaginal series
continues, we can expect nothing but mystification if we demand
that the perceptual world shall continue to show point-for-point
correspondence with the conceptual. The history of science has
shown that conceptual devices such as geometrical points, lines, and
surfaces, infinite series, and the various constructs of physics are
extremely valuable or rather indispensable in developing economical formulae which summarize and predict systems of perceptual
relationships. But the conceptual formulae are not photographs of
nature or "mirrors of reality" (see the elegant discussions of Quine
[1953]; e.g., " . . . it is meaningless . . . to inquire into the absolute
correctness of a conceptual scheme as a mirror of reality" [p. 79]);
they are symbolic shorthand. Whether and by virtue of what interpretations this shorthand summarizes perceptual relationships must
be determined by perceptual tests.

Moreover, we have had to learn that our ordinary language habits
are not reliable guides to scientific analysis. The use in various traditional senses of such words as *matter, force, space,* etc. caused
great confusion in physics and biology, as did such words as *soul,
mind, consciousness, will, ego,* etc. in psychology. When Parmenides argues that "Being cannot have arisen from something, for
there is nothing else than what *is,*" he is merely engaging in an exercise in verbal habits, as though he were to say, "What is up is not
down, what is here is not there," etc. The notion that the philosopher can determine in his thought what is and what is not perceptually possible, and what perceptual relations exist, is of course the
basic dogma of metaphysics, and the antithesis of science. But it still
reappears in science. McVittie (1961) finds explicit or implicit in
four recent books on astronomy, intended for educated laymen and
written by eminent scientists, "the dictum that what is logically
possible is also physically possible," and observes, "Assuredly one of
the remarkable features of science is that logical possibility is by
itself insufficient; one may even say that three or four hundred years
ago the founders of modern science were struggling to establish this
insufficiency." And finally, the notion that the senses give illusory
information gave rise to the endless exercises of "epistemology"; so
far as science is concerned, we have had to learn to extend, refine,
and control our sense organs instrumentally, to apply the criteria of
consistency, repeatability, and statistical probability, and also to
reconcile ourselves to the incommensurability of the conceptual

world of science and the perceptual world of everyday life. The homely kitchen table is not the atomic dance of the physicist, although to be sure the machinery of the modern kitchen has been arrived at by way of esoteric conceptual operations, perceptually confirmed.

Protagoras

Protagoras (c.500-c.410 B.C.) of Abdera was the greatest of the Sophists. His famous saying, that "man is the measure of all things," gives expression to the great change in attitude and interest that occurred among fifth century intellectuals. Men seem to have wearied of the conflicting metaphysical systems which sought to explain the origin and nature of the universe; this reaction began at about the middle of the century. Scepticism arose as to human ability to attain such ultimate knowledge, and this scepticism was reinforced by doubts concerning the reliability of sense perception. As Burnet (1924, p. 101) says, " . . . there was a revolt against science which proceeded from men whose chief interest was in practical life. How do you know these things are true, they said, and even if they are, what does it matter to us?" The application of this scepticism to religion and morals, particularly in the teaching of youths, aroused great hostility among the older generation, with such results as the burning of books and the imprisoning or exiling of philosophers and artists. These events have a grim interest for us who, like the Athenians of the last third of the fifth century, live with a sense of doom and witness the tensions generated between a sophisticated intellectual elite and a frightened democracy in times of cumulative disaster. In Athens, the major disasters were the plague of 430 B.C., which carried off a third of the population, the destruction of the navy and a large army at Syracuse in 413, and the final defeat in 404 in the war with Sparta. Following this defeat there was a harrowing period in which traitorous oligarchs and rebellious mobs alternated in power and brutality. The Athenian empire had been lost and the farmlands laid waste. Recovery involved the growth of a new capitalistic class, with such characteristic features as bank loans, usury, mortgages, slavery for debt, factories manned by slave labor, and loss of peasant landholdings by foreclosure. The ensuing fourth century was an era of political chaos in which Sparta, Thebes, and Macedonia struggled for supremacy in Greece. The self-made millionaire, lacking in civic intelligence and virtue, but quite capable of obtruding his ignorance into public affairs, became a typical figure. We will thus not find it hard to understand why many intellectuals turned their attention to morals and ethics and sought either mystical religious sanctions for their principles or rational grounds for the authority of customs and laws.

With colonial expansion the Greeks had come in contact with foreign peoples and had observed the great variety of their institutions and customs, political, social, and religious. Even in the Greek motherland and its colonies a great diversity of communal forms—oligarchies, aristocracies, democracies, tyrannies—existed side by side or superseded one another in the same city-state. The result was the growth of an interest in and a critical and relativistic attitude toward social forms and moral laws, which gradually displaced the older view that they were products of "nature" and also divinely sanctioned. Politically, relativism appears as "cosmopolitanism," which the masters of present-day Russia regard as a crime, no doubt for the reason mentioned by Lange (1925, p. 49) in his discussion of the Sophists, that "it destroys the interest of the citizens in their country, and in consequence cripples the country's vital force." While the Russians have whole-heartedly adopted the sophistic technique of "making the worse appear the better argument," they have rejected the doctrine of "world-citizenship" advocated by such Sophists as Hippias and Antiphon; this doctrine has similarly been rejected by American "patrioteers."

Moreover, in Athens the political and economic developments had resulted in an aristocratic and educated minority—upon whom wealth was having a corrupting influence—confronting a large, increasingly powerful, and intellectually reactionary majority, whose hostility toward "eggheads" has for us a melancholy interest. A frequently practiced "racket" consisted in a citizen lodging accusations against a wealthy man, who then had to stand trial before five hundred poor and ignorant jurors, whose pay often depended upon the fine which they assessed. The Sophists, who naturally taught those who could pay their fees (teaching for pay was regarded by the gentlemanly conservative members of Athenian society as was being "in trade" by eighteenth century British aristocrats), had as their main specialty the teaching of rhetoric, oratory, and legalistic reasoning to those who might thus be obliged to defend themselves. But this situation also reinforced the interest in social questions: the individual versus society, the origin and sanction of institutions and laws, the relative potencies of nature and of nurture. Thus the earlier philosophy of nature gave way to a philosophy of civilization, in which man is no longer an incident in the universe but the main focus of interest. The sophistic approach, in contrast with the previous philosophy, was similar to that of Dewey's "instrumentalistic" doctrine of education and of our contemporary "psychology of adjustment." Plato (1924, p. 125) makes Protagoras say that a young man who comes to him will not be "maltreated" by being taught arithmetic, astronomy, geometry, and music, but "will learn precisely and solely that for which he has come. That learning consists of good judgment in his own affairs, showing how best to order his own home; and in the affairs of his city, showing how he may have most influence on public affairs both in speech and in action." Windelband (1958, p. 66 ff.) points out that "science," which had been an esoteric pursuit, by small schools, of knowledge for its own sake, rose in the fifth century in popular interest. "In the feverish emulation of intellectual forces which this greatest period in the world's history brought with it, the thought everywhere gained recognition that in every walk of life the man of knowledge is the most capable, the most useful, and the most successful." We, in a similarly dynamic period of social disintegration, have been experiencing a similar public clamor for "science" applied to practical affairs, and the result has similarly been that science has come "into a state of *dependence upon the demands of practical, and in particular, of political life.*" The "science" in greatest demand in Athens was the art of persuasion—"public relations" or "applied psychology." Possibly another similarity of the classical Greek era to our own is that as the publicity of "science" increased, the faith in it of its practitioners decreased.

Thus the Sophists did not seek knowledge for its own sake; their attitude was practical rather than theoretical; the purpose was to teach people how to be good citizens, and how to control their lives and to be successful, efficient, and happy. (The Sophist Antiphon wrote the first "peace of mind" book.) These somewhat disparaging remarks however are least applicable to Protagoras, who in Zeller's words (1955, p. 98) was "the most gifted and original brain among the sophists," and who, as Lange (1925, I, p. 41) says, "marks a great and decisive turning-point in the history of Greek philosophy." It is perhaps not irrelevant to point out that Protagoras, in contrast with the later Sophists, lived most of his life in the Periclean age of colonial, commercial, and artistic vigor; it was only in his later years that cumulative disaster and mob rule led both to his own—legendary?—exile and death, and to the anti-scientific excesses of the later Sophists and the Socratics.

It is unfortunately true that we possess no works of Protagoras, and that interpretations of his doctrine depend chiefly upon judgments of the reliability of the presentations by Plato in his *Protagoras* and in his *Theaetetus*, judgments which are complicated by Plato's animus against the Sophists. Such judgments are products of technical scholarship, and the data permit of controversy among experts. We see all of the pre-Socratic philosophers through two lens systems: the distorting lenses of Plato and Aristotle (both of whom had ends to serve other than those of critical scholarship, and both of whom have enjoyed overwhelming prestige among philosophers), and the various correcting lenses offered by modern scholars. It would be absurd for us as philological laymen to review the evidence; it will be more profitable, I think, for us to select those interpretations or those putative Protagorean principles which have influenced the subsequent history of psychology or which have reappeared in modern writers. That the influence of Protagoras has been largely indirect is suggested by the scanty references to him in works which deal with questions which he was the first to raise; this is notably true of histories of psychology. In histories of philosophy (e.g., Lange, 1925, I, pp. 37 ff.) we may find Protagoras described as a founder of sensationalism and hence of "antimaterialism" regarded as a reaction against the "materialism" of Democritus, for whom "the atom was a 'thing in itself.'" For philosophers, of course, such terms bear a heavy semantic and emotive burden. From the vantage point of a modern philosophy of science, the issues can more profitably be restated as the following postulates: (1) In scientific research it is useful to assume (on an "as if" basis) an "independent" or "objective" external world. (2) Nevertheless, scientists must deal with this assumed external world in a "coded" form; that is, as it has been "processed" by individual human nervous systems, conditioned as they are physiologically, historically, and socially. (This proposition may be stated alternatively, as by Protagoras, in the language of "phenomenalism." Whether the language of biology or that of phenomenalism is preferable can, I would suggest, most profitably be treated by scientists as a methodological rather than a "philosophical" question.) (3) The coded information of individuals is validated, or "objectified," by social

confirmation: by confirmation, that is, by other individuals competent in the relevant area. Protagoras was the first to adumbrate the
second and third of the above postulates, whose restatements under
such names as "anti-metaphysics," humanism, pragmatism, positivism, operationalism, and the "Whorfian hypothesis" are a familiar
feature of our modern "frame of reference" in psychology.

The basic teaching of Protagoras was the relativity or contingency of experience, knowledge, and values. Three propositions
have been traditionally attributed to him:

1. "Concerning every subject opposite statements are possible."

2. "Man is the measure of all things: of those that are that they
are; of those that are not that they are not."

3. "The wise man causes the good instead of that which is evil to
be and seem right."

Untersteiner (1954, pp. 19-26) derives the *first* of these propositions from an intellectual movement which had been developing
during the sixth century and in which were involved the following
influences and components: the contact with contrasting cultures;
the increasing sense of the precariousness and the dilemmas of life
as expressed in the subjectivism of lyric poetry and the moral conflicts of tragic drama; the conflicts which arose concerning the
concept of "justice" in religion and law; the Pythagorean doctrine
"that things are compounded of opposite qualities" and that hence
"nothing in existence is simple and unmixed"; the Heraclitean doctrine of the co-existence of opposites. Protagoras seems to have
found exemplifications of his doctrine of opposite alternative propositions in religion; in metaphysics—the ultimate nature of the universe and of "reality"; in the adverse or ambivalent arguments of
rhetoric, law, and morals; and in art. In each of these what is "true"
or "right" depends upon point of view and hence upon the individual who makes the judgment; this "rule of opinion," this anti-abso-
lutism, was also thought to apply to mathematics, which served as
the symbolic model in the mystical philosophies of the Pythagoreans and Plato.

Protagoras' *second* proposition, "Man is the measure" etc., has
received various interpretations, particularly with respect to the
meanings of the words usually translated as "man" and "measure."
I find persuasive Untersteiner's (1954, pp. 41 ff.) interpretation, that
"having completed the description of the negative aspect of reality
defined [in the first proposition]," Protagoras embarks on the inquiry
into the positive aspect implicit in this discovery, and which he

formulates in the [second proposition]." I take this to mean that
Protagoras did what many others (e.g., Descartes) have done when
driven into scepticism about the relation of propositions to "reality"; he retreated into the "immediate experience" of the individual, i.e., into phenomenalism, and from this bastion attempted to
reconstruct relations with reality or "values." For Protagoras this
reconstruction is represented by his third proposition. Untersteiner
(1954, p. 48) quotes with approval Rensi's (1921, p. 171) statement
that for Protagoras

> . . . we cannot know anything except that which perception offers
> us to know; that thought cannot create by itself . . . or rather (to
> apply a Kantian principle) our thought does not function except by
> means of experiences, outside of and without which we cannot have
> knowledge . . . moreover . . . the mode of existence of the sense-
> faculty impresses itself upon the mode of existence of the intellect.
> It is therefore a considerable absurdity to say in opposition to
> Protagoras that his relativity does not touch the principles of knowl-
> edge properly understood, that is as purely intellectual principles
> which should be exalted above the relativity of sense-perception as
> something absolute and universal.

In Plato's *Theaetetus*, Socrates, in presenting Protagoras' views,
says that Protagoras, Heraclitus, and Empedocles all agree that
everything is in continual flux. Since for Protagoras this is true both
of the external world and of man, perception must be an interaction between two continuously changing systems. As for the changing individual, his perceptions (and memories) will vary with his
organization (e.g., whether he is this man or that man, a man or a
pig) and with his states (no man is ever exactly the same from one
moment to the next). What is sweet to me may be bitter to you, or
to me in ill health. Hence, "I am the judge of the existence of the
things that are to me and of the non-existence of those that are not
to me." "Each person differs immeasurably from every other in just
this, that to one person some things appear and are, and to another
person other things."

But if each individual man is thus "the measure," and if a given
man may be well or ill, dreaming or waking, and different men may
be baboons or philosophers, and if on every subject contradictory
statements are possible, what becomes of *values*? Protagoras' solution of this problem was contained in the third of the propositions
listed above, according to which some men are wiser than others
and, being wise, can cause others to see good things as better than
bad things. "Things" offer different possibilities of perception or

knowledge, but of these possibilities some are "better" than others, and accordingly one proposition may be, not "truer," but "better" than another. To effect a change for the better in a man's perception or opinion there must be brought about a change in his state or attitude; this the physician does with drugs and the teacher with words. But wise men belong to various classes, according to their fields of competence: physicians, farmers, teachers, statesmen, etc., and the "better" opinion seems, in the view of Protagoras, to represent a consensus of the wise men of the relevant class. Thus the individuality of experience and the existence of obvious individual differences are reconciled with socially sanctioned values. The comment of Menzel (quoted by Untersteiner, 1954, p. 71) that "The experience of the individual constitutes merely the point of departure for science" seems to me a reasonable resolution of the question of whether science must be public (as affirmed by the writers of the *Encyclopedia of Unified Science*) or whether it may be private (as affirmed by Bridgman [1940]).

"Socrates" in the *Theaetetus* suggests that when "better" is interpreted as "advantageous," this implies *confirmation in the future,* and here it is not "man" in general but the specialized expert who is the most reliable "measure." This interpretation Plato treats as an argument against Protagoras, but for F. C. S. Schiller (1908, p. 24) "the appeal to the future leads to a triumphant vindication of the Humanist interpretation. For *how* does the future decide between two rival theories of truth? By the value of the consequences to which they severally lead. That is precisely the meaning of the pragmatic testing of truth by its consequences." Thus Schiller (1911) saw here the historical germ of pragmatism (C. S. Peirce, William James), humanism (Schiller), instrumentalism (John Dewey), and the tendencies represented by Mach and Poincaré (positivism). All of these have of course been influential in the shaping of modern psychology. The general principle introduced by Protagoras is that human experience and behavior are functions of individual (biological, genetic, physiological) organization and states as modified by social environment. The general tendencies are antimetaphysical and relativistic; the emphasis is on individual and social experience and evolution; as we would say, on "learning." In so far as we can regard the implied confirmation by future consequences as authentic Protagorean doctrine, we can speak also of an anticipation of the experimental attitude, and hence be justified in rejecting the characterization of Protagoras as anti-scientific (as by Burnet, 1924, p. 109 ff.). The "science" which he might be said to have opposed was the metaphysical speculation and logic-chopping of such philosophers as Parmenides and Zeno; he was not anti-scientific with regard to such existing professional fields of knowledge as medicine and agriculture.

In Plato's *Protagoras*, an evolutionary account is given, in the form of a myth, of human development: when man and the other animals were created, the various species of animals were provided with various means of survival; only as an after-thought were men provided with manual skills and with language. But these gifts favored only *individual* survival; the state of affairs was that of scattered groups, like the family troops of apes or primitive men of modern descriptions, in which such social behavior as language, religion, and the production of food, clothing, and shelter were already present. When men congregated in cities to escape the perils of wild animals, they lacked the political art necessary to prevent them from injuring one another. Mankind was therefore granted the final gifts of respect for the rights of others and a sense of justice, whereby social order and solidarity became possible. Thus an earlier biological stage of "nature" *(physis)* was superseded by a later distinctively human and social stage of both unwritten and written "law" or convention *(nomos)*. As Untersteiner (1954, p. 62) points out, there is a parallelism between this evolution from individual survival to social cohesion of the *Protagoras* and the reconciliation between individual perception and social consensus represented by the three propositions of the *Theaetetus*.

But, says Protagoras—changing his form of discourse from myth to empirical argument—while man has by nature social tendencies, social behavior is not inborn but must be acquired by instruction. This instruction is in the first place administered not through special lessons, as for manual and artistic skills, but by the collective social environment—parents, teachers of various subjects, fellow citizens—as in the learning of one's native language. This social environment administers punishment for errors, not by way of vengeance but as a training device. (Protagoras' interpretation of punishment as corrective and deterrent was something of an innovation; more prevalent in his time was the old religious doctrine of expiation.) But the success of the training varies with native endowment, and because of the vagaries of heredity a virtuous father may have a wicked son, just as the son of a good flute-player may or may not turn out to be a good flute-player. Those who have had the basic social training can benefit by advanced instruction given by specialists in civic virtue such as Protagoras himself.

It should be noted that of the two opposed views of human social evolution found among the Greeks, that of a decline from a golden age to present misery versus that of a progression from savagery to civilization, Protagoras adopted the latter. The pedagogical aim of the Sophists, based on the assumption that social behavior—language, religion, morality, the state—are not "natural" but learned and conventional, favored an emphasis upon nurture as opposed to nature which may remind us of the anti-instinct movement of the 1920's; in both cases an optimistic faith in individual and social change and improvement was encouraged. Also encouraged in both cases was the doctrine of social relativity: all morals, laws, religion, art, etc. have been created by human communities and are valid only for those communities which accept them.

It is obvious, I think, that Protagoras stated in evolutionary terms a principle which many modern psychologists have struggled to express: e.g., Weiss (1929) when he described man as both a biophysical and a biosocial organism. As Loenen (1940) has emphasized, Protagoras, probably influenced by Anaxagoras, makes man a part of nature, a biological organism, but an organism that has the *capability* of social organization. The biological and the social factors do not oppose but rather limit and interact with each other. In particular, social organization, as Weiss also emphasized, makes possible not only mutual protection but also division of labor and the utilization of individual differences in skills and knowledge.

Protagoras' principle that perception is an interaction between a continuously changing individual organism and a continuously changing environment has had echoes throughout the subsequent history of psychology. One thinks at once of the "process theory of mind" shared, e.g., by William James, Wundt, and Titchener. This is expressed by James (1890, I, p. 225) in the propositions: "1) Every thought tends to be part of a personal consciousness. 2) Within each personal consciousness thought is always changing." Neglect of the principle James attributes to "the whole organization of speech, which . . . was not made by psychologists, but by men who were as a rule only interested in the facts their mental states revealed" (p. 236). Perhaps it was no more than a *déjà entendu* when I thought I heard the voices of Protagoras and James in Bergmann's (1957, p. 45) discussion of the properties of an "ideal language" which would permit philosophical analysis of scientific theories: the lobster which was green is now (after boiling) red, and hence the sentence which was true is now false.

> This [Bergmann says] contradicts the fundamental insight that no sentence is both true and false. To safeguard it, an atomic sentence of a "realistic" schema must in addition to a predicate and its subject or subjects contain a temporal determination, which destroys the desired syntactical form. The things named by the proper names of a "phenomenalistic" language are "momentary". . . . Such a language therefore does not encounter this particular difficulty.

But Bergmann is discussing scientific *language*, which is a social affair, whereas "phenomenalistic" refers to the data of (necessarily) private experience; when he says that "In a properly functioning language an undefined descriptive term . . . occurs only if the speaker is directly acquainted with what it names," we might argue that this criterion is insufficient, and wish to add that of Mandler and Kessen (1959, p. 45), that the words of a scientific vocabulary "must show a high consistency of usage from user to user and from occasion to occasion"; that is, the *consensus of experts* criterion which seems to have been implied by Protagoras' third proposition and which finds expression in the remark by Menzel, quoted above, that "The experience of the individual constitutes merely the point of departure for science."

In recent times a number of psychologists, under the tutelage and with the collaboration of philosophers, linguists, and philosophically inclined natural scientists, have concerned themselves with the "logic" or "philosophy" or "language" of science (e.g., Pratt, 1939; Feigl and Brodbeck, 1953, pp. 523-659; Frank, 1956; Mandler and Kessen, 1959; influential allies among linguists and philosophers have been Bloomfield, 1939, and the other authors of the *International Encyclopedia of Unified Science;* Morris, 1946; Ogden and Richards, 1947; Bergmann, 1957). The writings of these authors might be regarded as representing the modern phase of the long tradition which began with Protagoras. Of contemporary "Protagoreans," though some are more coherent, none has been more single-minded than Kantor. In the first place, Protagoras' principle that perception is an interaction between a particular individual and a particular object on a particular occasion is echoed in Kantor's specificity doctrine of "interbehavioral psychology," according to which "Psychological data . . . are the interbehavioral events taking place between organisms and the objects and proc-

esses with which they are in contact in definite behavioral fields"
(1945, p. 123). Further, Protagoras' relativism and denial of the
absolute truth or falsity of propositions is reflected by Kantor's
extended attacks on "absolutistic" and "universalistic" logic, and his
insistence that "logical processes are acts of persons" (p. 109). He
does not seem, however, to have adopted Protagoras' third proposition, to judge from his apparently disparaging reference to "objectivity guaranteed by public knowledge or what is sometimes called
intersubjective belief." "Such views," he says, "have obviously arisen
because of the prevailing notion that psychological actions are intangible processes or at least private and not objective interbehavior"
(p. 154). To Kantor, privacy, especially of processes in the brain,
smells of mentalism. It is interesting to note that Kantor has, like
Protagoras, attempted to apply his "interbehavioral" principle not
only to logic (1945) but also to language in general (1936),
although his endeavors in both works have been dissipated by his
preoccupation with the errors of predecessors and contemporaries,
so that he hardly gets beyond the programmatic statement of his
(Protagorean!) doctrine. It is amusing to note that "Protagoras"
does not occur in the indexes of Kantor's two books cited above,
although "Plato," his bête noire of essences, absolutes, and psychophysical dualism, occurs twelve times.

Protagoras has been called the founder of the science of grammar among the Greeks (Zeller, 1955, p. 100 f.), and credited with a
classification of linguistic categories and sentence types. Burnet
(1924, p. 118) says that he "called attention to the arbitrary character of certain grammatical genders, no doubt in illustration of the
reign of Law or convention, and his classification of sentences into
command, wish, etc. prepared the way for the distinction of the
moods." Language naturally—in view of their concern with rhetoric
and logical analysis—attracted the attention of other Sophists,
among whom the most notable was *Gorgias* (c.485-c.380 B.C.).
Strongly influenced by the Eleatic Zeno, Gorgias pointed out the
difficulties which arise from the assumption of the correspondence
of concepts to referents and of signs to concepts. His famous three
propositions were: (1) nothing exists; (2) if anything existed it
could not be known; (3) if anything could be known it could not
be communicated. In terms of logic, synthetic propositions are
impossible; all propositions are tautologies. (Cf. Pratt, 1939, p. 154:
"Science is a vast and impressive tautology.") Of these difficulties
we have heard a great deal in modern times; the relations among

referents, signs, and concepts have been argued influentially and at length, e.g., by Ogden and Richards (1947) and by Morris (1946), the latter availing himself of Hullian theory. Modern operationalism (and for that matter, all "antimetaphysics") has been concerned with identifying and eliminating signs which lack demonstrable referents. Formerly these difficulties were discussed under the heading of "the privacy of consciousness": Brett (1953, p. 60) paraphrases Gorgias, "As the condition of an object cannot be at the same time a condition of the perceiving or knowing subject, we can know nothing; as the condition of the speaker cannot be at the same time the condition of the hearer, we can impart nothing." This, he suggests, represents a progression toward "a recognition of the significance of consciousness," for it raises the question of how a state of one consciousness can be transferred to another. Brett's implication that the problem so stated has since been solved would probably not meet with general acceptance today; many psychologists would incline rather to H. M. Johnson's (1945) conclusion: "The so-called problems of psychophysics, namely, of deducing or inferring what other individuals than ourselves may sense and feel, are not genuine, but spurious. In other words, they are forever insoluble."

Socrates

Socrates (470-399 B.C.) left no writings, and we know his teachings chiefly through the writings of his pupils Plato and Xenophon. Xenophon was a soldier and a practical man, an admirer of Socrates as a martyr to a social mission, but not a reliable historian nor a philosopher. As for the dialogues of Plato, some thirty in number, in most of which Socrates appears as the leader of the conversation, it is usually supposed that the earlier dialogues, especially the *Apology* and the *Crito*, more nearly represent the actual teachings of Socrates than do the later ones. However, in the sorting out of doctrines between Socrates and Plato, the experts disagree. Burnet (1924, p. 153) suggests that Socrates became "the head of the Pythagoreans" in Athens and "revived the mystical side of Pythagoreanism"; he ascribes to Socrates the doctrines of the *Phaedo*: the "theory of ideas" and the doctrines of the immortality of the soul, rebirth, and "reminiscence." Others maintain that in most of his dialogues Plato merely uses Socrates as a mouthpiece for his own views. Since it was Plato who transmitted this complex of notions, we may perhaps be content to let "Plato" stand for "Plato or Socrates or both," in most matters. As we have seen, specialist scholars also disagree in their attribution of doctrines to Protagoras and Plato. The interested bystander, observing these perhaps emotionally reinforced differences among experts, may quote Protagoras' dictum: it is to each man as it seems to him. For the student of the history of ideas it almost becomes a matter of using the names of the various philosophers as convenient pegs for the various influential ideas current in classical Greece.

As for the actual Socrates, a good deal of probability would seem to attach to the following account. Socrates, at least in his later life, rejected natural science and concerned himself wholly with practical problems of human conduct. He devoted himself to the moral education of his fellow-citizens, whom wealth and easy living had corrupted; he lived, we recall, in times when the aristocrats and the democrats of Athens were vying with one another in the stupidity and treachery which led to their city's downfall. In the pursuit of this objective he gave to philosophy, says Zeller (1955, p. 122) such a powerful impulse "that until the end of the ancient world it never left the path he pointed out, and from now on epistemology and ethics occupied the centre of interest in a way that was fatal to natural philosophy and science." The philosophers (Empedocles, Anaxagoras, the Ionians) "explained everything mechanically, whereas Socrates wished to be shown that everything is as it is because it is best for it to be so" (Burnet, 1924, p. 133).

In contrast with the moral relativism of the Sophists, Socrates sought to attain universally valid knowledge of the nature of virtue which should serve as motivation and guide to moral conduct, most particularly in those who were to conduct public business. Knowledge of virtue, he thought, will make men both virtuous and happy; evil conduct is due to ignorance, to lack of insight. Knowledge is valued only as a prerequisite to morality and hence is confined to anthropocentric concerns, excluding natural science. The imparting of knowledge by verbal teaching operates upon the intellect and provides rational grounds for moral behavior, whereas "habit," acquired by ordinary "experience," gives only an unreliable basis of "goodness"; hence "true goodness" is identified with knowledge.

The Greek model for *arete* (virtue, goodness) was excellence in some art or skill, which obviously depends on special knowledge.

Socrates sought to define an analogous generalized knowledge which could serve as a basis of ethical and political excellence. His ethical criterion remained pragmatic: those actions are good which are suited to the end in view, which are "good for something" (Windelband, 1958, p. 79). This is the general and traditional Greek view: goodness was *effectiveness,* the ability so to act as to secure profit, personal happiness, and social approval (cf. Snell, 1960, p. 153 ff.). Thus the association of virtue with knowledge was natural for the Greeks, whereas for Christianity virtue is more negative, consisting of the avoidance of certain actions, and being thus possible for the ignorant. The term and concept of *arete* have recently reappeared: Frumkin (1959) tells us: "If an individual is endowed with those qualities, situations, and things that his society holds dear, then that individual is said to have arete. To achieve American arete one strives to become wealthy and powerful, and/or famous. . . . A study of the identification models of students at a teachers' college showed that actors, entertainers, professional athletes, military leaders, and industrial magnates rated highest as models."

Socrates, whose teachings appear to have been a mixture of common sense and mysticism, exercised a profound influence on his followers while antagonizing many others by his criticisms of institutions and practices, criticisms which took the frequently annoying form of question and answer (dialectic). The Socratic method of "analysis" (borrowed from Parmenides and Zeno) was to set up a postulate and then to examine its propositional consequences; judgments as to whether these were "true" or absurd were ostensibly reached in seminar fashion by group agreement, although the professor in charge guided the process in its predetermined course. The consensus thus "inductively" arrived at was, as Russell (1945, p. 93) points out, a consensus concerning linguistic usage. Some (e.g., Sarton, 1960, p. 272; Windelband, 1958, p. 99 ff.) give Socrates great credit for influencing subsequent philosophy and science in the direction of linguistic precision and the definition of concepts by the inductive method, but Russell (1945, p. 78) points out that Plato's Socratic method was vitiated by the fact that he thought he knew the answer before he began his questions, and "twisted the discussion so as to lead to a virtuous result." Tendentious "logic" without empirical checks has been the Platonic heritage, a bane to science, and, where morally motivated, a danger to society. The "idealistic" dialectic of Socrates leads to results for science and society not dissimilar from those which follow from the "materialistic" dialectic of modern communism; as Stephen Spender (1958) has said, the communist "uses his philosophy as a stick to beat his perceptions with." "The truth observed, the particular experience, has to be submitted to the doctrinal propaganda of the side supposed to be inevitably, unalterably, eternally right, automatically benefiting humanity!" (p. 127).

Logical and semantic analysis, when practiced by morally neutral persons such as some of the Sophists, can be annoying enough, for it is very likely to disturb irrational and emotionally involved beliefs and prejudices; it is likely to become intolerable when it is performed with moral and religious certitude. Like Kant, Socrates sought a moral absolute; like Fechner, he felt that he had a divine mission to awaken men to their moral duty. In the end, he was condemned to death on charges of corrupting the young and subverting the national religion. In catastrophic times, hostility tends to be directed against the teachers of youth, and this tendency was reinforced in the case of Socrates by the unfortunate fact that some of the leading traitors who brought disaster on their city were his pupils, a fact to be borne in mind by those who place hope in verbal indoctrination in otherwise uncontrolled social contexts. Moreover, Socrates' teachings had an anti-democratic tendency at a time when the Athenian democracy was insecure; any suggestion that public offices should be held by men of education and intelligence—in our vernacular, by "eggheads"—has of course an anti-democratic tendency and is likely to be highly unpopular.

Two minor schools of the fourth century, founded by disciples of Socrates, illustrate combinations of Socratic and sophistic doctrines, as well as the intellectual climate of the times. *Antisthenes* (c.445-c.365 B.C.), founder of the *Cynic* (precursor of the *Stoic*) school, despised art, learning, mathematics, and natural science; only "virtue" is important. His view that scientific research is of value only in so far as it is directly applicable to the life of action has reappeared in our own times in a widely held interpretation of pragmatism and instrumentalism, and seems to be the principle governing public support and management of science and education in the United States. Virtue and true happiness consist in self-sufficiency, freedom from needs and passions; this is favored by poverty and by rejection of society and of all its conventions which limit "nature." This is therefore a doctrine of adjustment by disengagement or by "retreat from reality." Credit must be given, it appears (Windelband, 1958, p. 96), to Antisthenes for the distinction between "undefined" and "defined" terms which Bergmann (1957) has recently been at such pains to elucidate for psychologists. Diogenes the tub-dweller was a Cynic.

Aristippus (c.435-c.355 B.C.), founder of the *Cyrenaic* (precursor of the *Epicurean*) school, also despised mathematics and science, and valued knowledge only in so far as it had practical utility. He held that our perceptions give us knowledge only of our own states and hence are always true; they give us no information about the nature of an external world or about the sensations of other men; moreover, "common nomenclature is no guarantee of similarity in the content of the thought" (Windelband, 1956, p. 147). Aristippus therefore derived the laws of conduct only from subjective sensation. All sensation consists in movement; i.e., in the collisions of the respective movements of the perceived object and the perceiving subject; as in some modern theories of sensory physiology, the difference between pleasure and pain is made a quantitative difference in intensity of stimulation; gentle movement produces pleasure, violent movement pain, and absence of motion corresponds to indifference. Pleasure, which is identified with the good and with happiness, is thus the sensation of a natural process in the body (cf. the James-Lange theory of emotion), and it is the chief end of life. Only the present moment can bring happiness. However, philosophy teaches men to judge the relative values of pleasures and to free themselves from desires and fancies—violent motions—which disturb happiness. Aristippus was an exponent of "permissiveness"; nothing "natural" is blameable. Both the Cynic and the Cyrenaic schools stood for an isolation of the individual from society. They strove in opposite ways to make good the failure of Socrates to arrive at an adequate definition of "the good"; for the one, virtue is freedom from wants; for the other, it is ability to enjoy. In both schools sophistic relativism ended in social disengagement, a "philosophy of parasites," expressed by the Cyrenaic Theodorus in the declaration that sacrifice for others, patriotism, and devotion to a general object are foolishness, unworthy of a wise man (Windelband, 1958, p. 86). One may perhaps be reminded of our contemporary "beatniks," and reflect that if the world proceeds upon its present course to the final catastrophe which science has made possible we shall, if we are capable of any philosophy at all, have a choice between the Cynic and the Cyrenaic, which were also adaptations to social disintegration. We may likewise experience a distaste for science.

Plato

Plato (427-347 B.C.) elaborated the doctrines of psychophysical dualism and teleology in a fashion which has profoundly influenced the whole subsequent history of philosophy and of science. It is difficult for a modern, scientifically educated reader to understand this influence; as Sarton (1960, p. 426) says, "The history of Platonism is the history of a long series of ambiguities, misunderstandings, prevarications." The Platonic legend "is largely due to literary prejudice. The language of Plato was so beautiful and so difficult to understand that the contents were overlooked, beauty was mistaken for justice, and obscurity for depth." For Socrates we can feel a good deal of sympathy; for his aims were practical and modest, and found expression in a courageous resistance to arrogance and injustice. In Plato we are more likely to find a combination of mysticism and ruthless inhumanity presented in the guise of intellectual analysis and moral principle. Plato illustrates that approach to the problems of nature and of man which is ethical and anthropocentric rather than scientific. His absolutistic philosophy was an attempt to counter the relativism of the Sophists and to furnish a theoretical justification, reinforced by religious mysticism, for a totalitarian political organization which would, in his opinion, cure the social ills of the fourth century.

Plato's philosophy was determined chiefly by the following influences: the fact that he was born a well-to-do aristocrat in times when political disaster and social corruption could be attributed to democratic government; his teachers: first Cratylus, a disciple of Heraclitus, and then Socrates; the later Pythagoreans, whom he visited at Tarentum, their headquarters in Italy; and the Eleatics, especially Parmenides and Zeno.

Plato's school, the *Academy*, was opened in 387; here, in a garden which he had purchased near Athens, he lectured to his pupils, who lived in small houses on the Academy grounds after the fashion of a religious guild. In something like fifty years of teaching and writing Plato's views changed greatly, so that a careful account would have to differentiate between different periods; such an account would also have to enter into verbal subtleties which are of no significance for the history of science. I shall summarize only the main features of his philosophy as they appear more particularly in his later dialogues and as they have exercised an influence

—almost wholly deleterious—on the historical development of science. It should be mentioned that Plato's Academy in Athens lasted for nine centuries, until closed by the Emperor Justinian in 529 A.D., undergoing various changes in doctrine, and that in the third century A.D. *Plotinus* founded *neo-platonism,* whose modification of Platonic dualism and mysticism determined much of Christian doctrine in the first twelve centuries A.D.

Plato, in opposition to Ionic monism, adopted the Orphic-Pythagorean psychophysical dualism. The individual human soul consists of three parts: the rational or thinking soul has its seat in the head and is immortal and divine, whereas courage and sensual desires reside in the chest and in the belly, respectively, and are mortal. (Cf. the "cognitive, volitional, and affective" classification of nineteenth century psychology, and the categories of "thinking, motivation, and drive" of twentieth century psychology.) Different types of individual characters and of political states result from the predominance of one or other of these kinds of soul; in the ideal case, "justice" (cf. *moira*) keeps them in balance.

Platonic dualism found more general expression in the "theory of ideas." (The Greek word usually translated "idea" in Plato more nearly means "archetype," "model," or "ideal form.") This doctrine had two sources: the mystical Orphic-Pythagorean notion of the body as the "prison" or "tomb" from which the soul may escape at death to return to its divine home in heaven, and the Parmenidean-Heraclitean dilemma: reality is eternal and unchangeable, or reality is ceaseless change. The world of matter and of sensory experience is, as Heraclitus said, in perpetual flux, and this, in Plato's view, meant that it cannot be an object of knowledge. The real and permanent world, corresponding to the unchangeable "Being" of Parmenides, is the world of thought, in which reside the only realities, the *forms*; this world is accessible only to the soul; the bodily senses are only a hindrance to the acquisition of true wisdom. By *forms* are meant all possible generic concepts; i.e., all possible verbal generalizations and abstractions. "We suppose an idea to exist when we give the same name to many separate things" (*Republic*, X, 596A). Every noun designates an idea. (Cf. Locke, 1959, I, p. 121: "Every man being conscious to himself that he thinks; and that which his mind is applied about whilst thinking being the *ideas* that are there, it is past doubt that men have in their minds several ideas,—such as are those expressed by the words *whiteness, hardness, sweetness, thinking, motion, man, ele-*

phant, army, drunkenness, and others. . . .") As Russell (1945, p. 121) puts it, the word *cat* "means something which is not this or that cat, but some kind of universal cattyness." Pythagorean mathematics furnished a model for this notion; e.g., there are many circles, but the *form* of a circle exists apart from all particular circles *(Gestaltqualität?).* Moreover, there are in sensory experience no "perfect" circles; particular figures which exemplify circularity are merely approximations to the "upper limit" of the geometrically "ideal" circle. Plato applied this mathematical model to aesthetics and ethics; beside ideal circularity he placed the ideally beautiful and the ideally good. The world of forms is eternal, changeless, and perfect; the physical world of sense perception—the particularities of individual experience—is an imperfect and evanescent copy of the ideal world which can be comprehended only by thought. Cornford points out that Plato's contemporary, Democritus, explained visual perception by the entrance of "images which flow off continually from the objects seen, are of like form with them, and impinge upon the eye."

> [These images] were nothing but soul-phantoms or wraiths, reduced, as Atomism demanded, to filmy tissues of atoms. At this stage of thought, images and concepts could still be credited with the properties ascribed to phantoms or souls—objective reality, existence in time, extension and localization in space, and even bodily properties such as resistance. . . . Plato still conceives Ideas as soul-substances, and assigns to them the same properties he now assigns to souls: both alike are immutable, uniform, incomposite, immortal, divine [Cornford, 1957, p. 250].

Plato's theory of knowledge supposes that the soul brings with it from the realm of pure being, in which it existed before incarnation, an innate knowledge of the forms, which also have their abode in the super-celestial realm. Reason, the immediate apprehension of a priori ideas, is the only source of true knowledge. The copies of the forms furnished by sensation, though imperfect and unreliable, may arouse memories of the forms which are their originals and which exist in a latent state in the soul (doctrine of reminiscence). Education is the process of reviving the latent ideas. Here we have the origin of the philosophical notion of "innate ideas," which in modern times became associated with the name of Descartes and which in the 17th and 18th centuries was rejected by the British empiricists: Hobbes, Locke, Hume.

The theory of forms finds application also in Plato's teleology.

The forms are the ideal patterns, the ends or aims toward which all cosmic and human processes tend. They are like the ideal image in the mind of the artist who strives to realize it in material form. They are thus "final causes" which determine the "becoming" or development of things. The entire universe is created, after the patterns of the world of forms, by an anthropomorphic being in a rational manner; that is, in the way that we would expect it to be done by a very wise man who had good reasons for everything he did. Hence those who are wise enough may discover these reasons and thus arrive at a "rational" explanation of the world. Plato, being such a wise man, was able to rethink the thoughts of the Creator; rejecting the naturalistic approach of the Ionian physicists, he described the creation of the universe in accordance with mathematical proportions and geometrical figures. In biology, this method, freed of the crudities of observation, produced the doctrine that women and the lower animals are degenerated forms of men.

In the *Republic* the doctrine of forms is thus exemplified: there are many perceptually experienced beds, all of which we recognize as examples of 'bed'; there are innumerable individual beds, the "same" bed is perceptually different when seen from different points of view, and we may also see a 'bed' in a painting. Moreover, the maker of a particular bed makes it according to a pre-existing "ideational" model.

As for the relation between perceptual particulars and conceptual universals or "forms," Plato's thought, according to Cornford (1957, p. 254 ff.) underwent a change. The forms began by being group-souls, each of which dwells within each of a class of things of which it is the "cause"; later the relationship tended toward a reduction to the relation of logical subject to universal predicate. The predicate of a proposition is always a "form," but each perceptual particular has a number of possible predicates and thus "participates in" a number of forms; the mystical "forms" thus tended toward a transformation into concepts, logical predicates, verbal generalizations. So Cornford, and also Stenzel (1940); but the direction of development is reversed by Kapp (1942, p. 32 ff.), who holds that Plato in the *Meno* was dealing with concepts and only later, in the *Phaedo*, transformed these into "forms" which are something apart and different from sensible things; he began the transformation by seeking the essential meaning—the criteria—of moral qualities such as piety, justice, virtue, etc., and ended by talking of the eternal "ideas" of such sensible things as 'man' and 'bull.'

It must be remembered that the life of the intellectuals among the leisured gentlemen of Athens was a verbal life; they were, like modern philosophers, preeminently talkers. Unlike the medical practitioners, they had no laboratories or clinics in which to submit hypotheses to empirical tests, nor would such tests, in the opinion of Plato, have comported with the dignity of a philosopher. They had lost interest in the simple sort of observations on which Anaximenes, Empedocles, Anaxagoras, and Democritus had based their hypotheses. These naturalistic philosophers the Platonic Socrates found unsatisfactory because they gave no teleological explanations nor value judgments. There was a good deal of justification for his dissatisfaction, as we can understand from his example in the *Phaedo* of the explanation which, he says, the "scientists" would give of Socrates' sitting in prison, in terms of his bones and postural muscles, whereas the "true causes" were his having been condemned and having refused to escape. This is the same objection which has been raised in our own times against a "muscle-twitch" psychology, a psychology, i.e., which was alleged to attempt the explanation of "molar" behavior in "mechanistic," "non-purposive," or "reflex" terms. Since the analysis of the correlates of complex behavior, both environmental and physiological, is even now in its infancy, the objection, so far as psychology is concerned, can only be countered "in principle" and by generalization from the successes of "natural" science. The principle is however not unimportant as a postulate for a developing natural science of behavior, and its rejection by Plato has not been favorable to that development.

The world of words—particularly of such high-level abstractions as "virtue," "knowledge," "beauty"—became for Plato the world of true reality. In the history of science the mystical embellishments of the Platonic analysis have of course been a nuisance; if it were possible to abstract from these embellishments we might agree with Russell (1945, p. 126 f.) that Plato's analysis was a milestone in the history of logic. The distinction between "particulars" and "universals" has become in modern logic the distinction between "proper names" and "character" or "property" words (e.g., Bergmann, 1957, p. 12 f.). The statement that "a particular sensible thing is nothing else but the common meeting-place of a number of predicates" (Burnet, 1924, p. 165) becomes in modern logic the statement that "one and the same subject term can occur in different singular propositions" (Copi, 1953, p. 279), and on the other hand, the statement that each form may be "participated in" by a number of sensible things becomes the statement that "one and the same

predicate term can occur in a number of singular propositions."
Cornford (1957, p. 257 f.) asserts that Plato's whole conception is
manifestly mythical, but,

> The logical interpretation is struggling to get clear of the mythical;
> the Idea threatens to pass from being an indwelling group-soul to
> being a mere universal concept, which does not exist at all, and, if it
> did, could not cause the existence or becoming of particular things.
> Plato did not realize that he was only making an important discovery
> in logic; he thought he was discovering the causes—the sole, true
> causes—of the existence of the world.

What began as mysticism has become linguistic analysis, except of
course in those areas of psychology which have been affected by
psychoanalysis, where such an intuited being as "the ego" is still
taken as the "cause" of phenomena.

The problem with which Plato sought to deal in his theory of
"forms" arose from the same phenomena which gave rise to the
soul-ideas of primitive peoples and to dualistic conceptions down
to our own times. In modern terms, the problem arises from the
fact that an individual's cumulative experience is stored in coded
form in his brain. On the one hand, passing individual experiences
—objects, persons, scenes—can live on apparently unchanged into
old age, having thus a seeming existence of their own which may
appear uncanny. On the other hand, the coding involves generalizations (concepts), and these cortical patterns are represented by
linguistic symbols. This coded interior world may readily come to
seem not only more permanent but also more "real"—especially in
old age—than the external world of successively and momentarily
perceived objects and scenes. Moreover, as the organization of the
coded brain processes proceeds, these processes are more and more
readily triggered by symbolic or organic cues, or even by autonomous neural activity, so that individuals experience such phenomena as dreams, hallucinations, and fantasies. The upshot of all this
may be the notion of an interior mental world which is independent
of and more permanent and "real" than the world of sense experience. Socrates, for example, was guided by a "voice," and was subject to ecstatic trances: "He would stand still for hours together
buried in thought, and quite forgetful of the outer world" (Burnet,
1924, p. 130). For Plato, this notion offered a solution of the
Parmenidean-Heraclitean dilemma in terms of the Pythagorean
dualism of soul and body, thought and the senses, the mathematical forms of things and their perceptible appearances.

Ethics at Plato's hands received a transcendental basis. Life on earth and all corporeal things are evil and worthless. Whereas at first Plato accepted Socrates' view that evil is error which can be removed by instruction, later he described it as a disease of the soul which can be cured only by punishment; if a man is not punished for his misdeeds he is deprived of the only possibility of improvement (cf. Mowrer's [1960] conception of psychopathology as "sin"). The source of evil is of course the body with its earthly needs and lusts. The basic drives in man are hunger, thirst, and sex. In his discussions of the struggle between the spirit and the flesh, Plato developed the concept which came to be known as "Platonic love," described by Sarton (1960, p. 425) as "the sublimation of pederasty." Heterosexual activity was justified only in terms of stockbreeding. True bliss can be attained only when the soul after the death of the body enters the next world and there receives a favorable judgment on its conduct during its earthly existence; an unfavorable judgment may consign the soul to an animal body. True philosophy is "practice in dying and death."

The practical consequences which Plato drew from his idealistic philosophy included an anti-democratic totalitarian government in which a ruling and a military elite of "supermen" were to rule a lower class which constituted at least four-fifths of the population. This lower-class majority was described as naturally inferior and as motivated by gross appetites, whereas the elite ruling and military classes corresponded, respectively, to the "rational" and the "courageous" souls of individual life. The function of the lower class was to be the economic support for the elite. All personal rights and individual freedom were to be subordinated to the supreme state; every man was to be an "organization man," who had been taught to do nothing without orders or apart from others. There was to be censorship of literature, art, and music, and communality of women, children, and property. In Plato's *Laws,* "Free thought, criticism of political institutions, teaching new ideas to the young, attempts to introduce new religious practices or even opinions, are all pronounced capital crimes" (Popper, 1945, I, p. 171). Official lies (what we call propaganda) were endorsed as a method of social control. This Utopia was not wholly a theoretical construction of Plato's; a contemporary model existed in Sparta, which influenced not only Plato, but, through both Plato and Plutarch, the doctrines of Rousseau, Nietzsche, the educators of the aristocratic youth of England, and the German Nazis. There was also the Oriental pattern, and more than one intellectual took refuge from Athenian political chaos at the courts of Oriental autocrats. And finally, there were the Pythagorean principles of "geometrical equality," of the three classes of men (lovers of wisdom, lovers of honor, lovers of gain), and of government by an intellectual aristocracy, and the sophistic doctrine of "supermen" and "might is right." The vastest realization of totalitarian political and social organization has of course occurred in our own time in the communist states.

The judgments which have been passed on Plato's ethical and political views have been severe. Thus Sarton (1960, p. 418): "It is paradoxical that the writer who hated individualism was canonized as a master of humanism, and some enthusiasts went so far as to consider him a kind of proto-Christian." Zeller (1955, p. 156) points out that "Plato's theory of values, conditioned as it was by his un-Greek dualistic metaphysics, brought him into a position of antagonism to the essential and basic values of Greek culture." And Russell (1950, p. 7) remarks, "That Plato's *Republic* should have been admired, on its political side, by decent people is perhaps the most astonishing example of literary snobbery in all history." It is also an example of what might happen if the management of affairs were to be turned over to philosophers or other professors. The pitfalls in the way of the application of philosophical and scientific theory to problems of human conduct and welfare are of great concern at the present time. There has been a division of opinion among psychologists; on the one hand, the organizers of the *Society for the Psychological Study of Social Issues* have felt that psychologists should make direct contributions to the solution of social and political problems; on the other hand there are those who see in such intervention a danger both to society and to psychology. Skinner (1948b, 1955) seems convinced that the time is ripe for the "planned improvement of cultural practices"; Viteles (1955) demurs, quoting A. V. Hill: "Scientists should be implored to remember that, however accurate their scientific facts, their moral judgments may conceivably be wrong." The question has been argued by Rogers and Skinner (1956), Rogers emphasizing the danger that Skinner's "scientific control" of human behavior would neglect values. Some psychologists have been contending that psychotherapy deals with "sin," or at least with moral problems (Mowrer, 1960, 1961; London, 1961), and that there should be a synthesis of psychology and religion (Feifel et al., 1958); others vigorously reject these contentions and defend the concepts of "mental illness" and "maladjustment" (Ellis et al., 1960). The disquiet among psychologists has been shared by other behavioral scientists; e.g., Opler (1961) remarks, "Probably as a reaction to the charge that the comparative data of their discipline have fostered cultural relativism and thus have contributed to unsettling the foundations of Western morality, anthropologists have lately been addressing themselves to a search for universal values or at least, for universal value categories." If, as seems probable, the human world is to continue to become more threatening, increasing numbers both of the general population and of scientists will undoubtedly seek to return to the "ancient verities," or, alternatively, to institute mass applications of scientific principles and inventions.

In Plato's Athens there were democratic chaos and sophistic relativism within and a disciplined enemy without; today we face a "monolithic" enemy without while we seek to integrate a pluralistic democracy within. Russian psychology has the task of contributing to the production of the "new man" (Bauer, 1952) by means of the Pavlovian "second signal system"; Wolfe (1952) has conjectured "that the Soviet rulers have set themselves in the Fifties to the final psychological task for the total state, namely the conditioning of man to react to slogans, formulas, symbols, rather than to the real world within him and around him." There are many who urge that our survival requires that we imitate the discipline of our enemy and suppress the relativistic and individualistic elements in our society. Russell (1945, p. 115) remarks that all that Plato's Republic would achieve would be "skill in war and enough to eat"; it is perhaps to these ultimates that the peoples of the modern world are being driven.

As for natural science, this was rejected by Plato on the ground that true knowledge is attainable only by thought, aided by divine inspiration and intuition, while sense-perception yields only opinions and probabilities. (Dewey [1944] mentions a modern critic of naturalism who remarked "somewhat naively" that without supranatural absolute and final truths "there would be in morals merely the kind of certainty that exists in physics and chemistry.") The true philosopher, the seeker after true knowledge, ignores sight and hearing and turns his mind inward. (The reader will recognize this notion as similar to recent importations from the Orient; in disordered times the navel seems a desirable substitute for the outward scene.) Scientific research is nothing but "a game and a recreation," or else a "presumptuous prying of man into the divine order of nature" (Zeller, 1955, p. 163). Experiment is either impious or a base mechanical art. Plato thus challenged the materialistic and monistic theory of Democritus which had been gaining currency and which interpreted all things in mechanistic terms.

Of particular interest to us is Plato's attitude toward biology. In a discussion of the *Timaeus,* Jones (1946, p. 20) remarks:

> Anatomy, physiology and pathology are not congenial to Plato's mentality, and yet they comprise a great part of the treatise. We are amazed at his apparent ignorance of his own ignorance. . . . The answer to this puzzle seems to be that Plato could not understand any method of procedure, any "scientific method," that did not start with a postulate. In the *Phaedo* he blames Anaxagoras for not working out his doctrine of Mind, for not showing that an intelligent Creator must in all things work for the best.

Plato's remarks, in the *Timaeus,* on Anaximander's theory of evolution, were similar in spirit to those of Bishop Wilberforce attacking Darwin (cf. Irvine, 1955, ch. 1); whereas Anaximander had suggested that man was descended from a fish, Plato declared that fish were descended from "mindless men," and that while such a one as Anaximander may have become a fish, other "light-witted men who paid attention to the things in the heavens but in their simplicity supposed that the surest evidence in these matters is that of the eye" were turned into birds. Singer (1922, p. 17), after describing the remarkable development of Greek biology up to the early part of the fourth century B.C., says that we must seek some external cause for its subsequent failure, and continues,

> Nor have we far to seek. This period saw the rise of a movement that had the most profound influence on every department of thought. We see the advent into the Greek world of a great intellectual movement as a result of which that department of philosophy that dealt with nature receded before Ethics. Of that intellectual revolution— perhaps the greatest the world has seen—Athens was the site and Socrates . . . the protagonist. With the movement itself and its characteristic fruit we are not concerned. But the great successor and pupil of its founder gives us in the *Timaeus* a picture of the depth to which natural science can be degraded in the effort to give a specific teleological meaning to all parts of the visible Universe. The book and the picture which it draws, dark and repulsive to the mind trained in modern scientific method, enthralled the imagination of a large part of mankind for wellnigh two thousand years. Organic nature appears in this work of Plato . . . as the degeneration of man whom the Creator has made most perfect. The school that held this view ultimately decayed as a result of its failure to advance positive knowledge. As the centuries went by its views became further and further divorced

from phenomena, and the bizarre developments of later Neoplatonism stand to this day as a warning against any system which shall neglect the investigation of nature. But in its decay Platonism dragged science down and destroyed by neglect nearly all earlier biological material.

The attempt to burden science with teleology and spiritualism or dualism is not something which ended long ago; it has continued into our own times at the hands of physicists such as Jeans (1930, 1933) and Eddington (1929), of biologists such as Sinnott (1950, 1960) and Driesch (1928, 1944), and of the practitioners of "parabiology," "parapsychology," and psychoanalysis. Spiritualism in modern physics is discussed by Frank (1950, pp. 122-137); as he points out, the technical mathematical perplexities of the physicists, which should properly be regarded as temporarily unresolved problems of specialists, have been seized upon, both by physicists and by others, to justify a spiritualistic reaction to "a crisis in human society arising from quite different processes." "Parabiology" is discussed by Mainx (1955, pp. 58-81); whatever may be the *extra-*scientific value of such tendencies as vitalism, purposiveness, "wholeness," and indeterminacy, he says, "For the progress of biological science . . . they seem to be useless, or even harmful in so far as they mislead non-biologists about the real character of scientific biology and divert the expert from a correct formulation of his problems." Whatever may be the case in philosophy, the canons of scientific method do not permit its practitioners to introduce into scientific discourse, or pretend to emerge from their laboratories with, propositions responsive to their own personal anxieties.

5

Origins of
Biological Analysis

For the biologist, Anaxagoras and Empedocles are at once the most interesting and the most frustrating of early Greek philosophers—frustrating, because, of their works, only a few fragments remain, together with accounts, of uncertain reliability, by later writers. The tradition has been confused by the credence historians have given to Aristotle's reports, which seem to have been governed, not by ideals of scholarly accuracy, but by Aristotle's own preconceptions.

Anaxagoras

Anaxagoras has especially suffered in this way, and the literature dealing with him is contradictory and confusing. Cleve (1949) has most thoroughly reviewed the ancient sources and attempted a reconstruction freed of Aristotle's misconceptions; for the main outlines of Anaxagoras' system I follow his account.

Anaxagoras was born about 500 B.C., or perhaps earlier, in the Ionian city of Clazomenae, which was some sixty miles north of Miletus on the coast of Asia Minor. His intellectual background was that of the Milesian physicists; that is, naturalistic rather than mystical. His presuppositions, says Burnet (1924, p. 77), "were . . . derived from medical sources. Medicine was the great interest of the time." Anaxagoras spent much of his life in Athens; he stood at the beginning of that city's intellectual tradition. While his friend Pericles was in power, Anaxagoras enjoyed his protection, but when the opposition "business men's" party came into power at the beginning of the Peloponnesian War (431-404 B.C.), Anaxagoras, accused under the law against people "who do not accept the religion and who spread astronomical doctrines," had to leave Athens. As in our own times, intellectuals who could endure rationality were far outnumbered by the ignorant and bigoted; these latter, it seemed, regarded as particularly reprehensible Anaxagoras' statement that the sun is a glowing mass of stone rather than a god, and they therefore attacked him as a convenient scapegoat in their anti-Pericles campaign. One thinks of the modern American animus against "brain-trusters" and "eggheads," who also serve as convenient political targets. As for the judgment of history, Zeller (1955, p. 76), e.g., describes him as "consciously and deliberately the first pure contemplative thinker, who saw in knowledge of the world the task and end of life and was fully convinced of its incidental ethical effects. His nature presented a happy combination of a capacity for knowledge founded on experience and observation with a power of speculation."

Anaxagoras' predecessors had derived everything from air, water, fire, or a neutral stuff; Empedocles made fire, air, water, and earth his elementary substances. These substances seemed to Anaxagoras to be themselves compounds, and he therefore started from a finer analysis into the perceptual qualities represented by the familiar linguistically classified opposites: moist-dry, warm-cold, bright-dark, large-small, etc. This analysis reminds us of the "attributes of sensation" of "structural psychology"; however, the elements of Anaxagoras were not, for him, psychical qualities but *things* having spatial extension. ". . . to Anaxagoras not only was a particle of 'the bright' a part of space thoroughly filled with color, to put it in modern terms, but to him also a particle of 'the warm,' e.g., was a part of space thoroughly filled with warmth" (Cleve, 1949, p. 7). Since stimulus objects can act on various sense organs, they must all be *mixtures* of the various elements, the actually perceived qualities being determined by the predominance in each opposite-ratio of one member of the pair (e.g., an object is perceived to be warm if the warm-element quantitatively exceeds the cold-element in its composition). Thus snow appears white and cold because particles of these qualities predominate in its composition, although particles of black and warm are also present. (The modern reader will here think of color-mixture involving complementary colors, or perhaps of the phenomena of "masking.") All the quality-quanta exist in molecular unions in each of which all the elements are represented; a substance like snow consists of an aggregation of molecules in all of which the element-pairs (quality-opposites) exist in ratios characteristic of the substance; snow is black as well as white, for when it melts it may become black water.

Just as sensory analysis provided Anaxagoras with his elements, so *nous* ("mind") provided him with a model for cosmic *organization*. Anaxagoras has therefore been reckoned by some as the inventor of mind-body dualism; actually, his *nous* is an element which, like the other elements, has spatial extension. It is unique among the elements in being pure and homogeneous, not mixed with any of the others, and in having the power to move itself and those others. It is a sort of pervasive fluid which, being in contact with everything, can "know" and move everything. ". . . since everywhere and at any time every [molecule] is being flowed around and touched and thereby known by Nous as the infinite embedding medium, the [element-particles] and their [molecules] are always an actual *Bewusstseinsinhalt* in the infinite divine 'consciousness' of Nous" (Cleve, 1949, p. 90). This is of course a development of the hylozoistic notion of an animating principle, pervading the universe, which was characteristic of early Greek naturalistic philosophy; it cannot therefore be properly regarded as a mind-body dualism; it is, rather, a mechanistic monism. (Although, of course, if we are to attach labels, we can say that its assumption of numerous elements makes it, like modern chemistry, a pluralism, and its distinction between intellect and perception—i.e., between *nous* and the other elements—makes it *in that sense* a dualism.) For *nous* imparts motion to elements and bodies not by "command" but by mechanical pushing and pulling. (One thinks of the "fine, smooth, and round" atoms of Democritus, or even of the "imponderable fluids" hypothesized in the eighteenth century to account for the phenomena of heat, electricity, and magnetism.) And yet *nous* is spoken of in personifying language, as if it were a god; it has knowledge of all possibilities, and in molding the world chooses those possibilities which will give the most beautiful and variegated results. Hence Anaxagoras has been called a teleologist, but Cleve points out that *nous* is not a creator, like the God of the Bible, who creates the world by fiat out of nothing; *nous* organizes the world within the limitations of the properties inherent in the eternal elements. The point is, of course, that Anaxagoras was trying to account for order and organization—and beauty—and was using the obvious model of human planning, which too must operate within the limitations of available materials.

The original state of the world was that of an undifferentiated and therefore qualityless continuum of molecules of identical composition, each containing equal quanta of all the elements. *Nous*, the non-molecularized medium in which the molecules were embedded, somehow initiated a differentiation whereby molecules containing unequal quanta of the different elements were produced and sorted out, in accordance with their specific gravities, into (initially) earth, water, air, and aether. Further differentiation and organization resulted from a rotary motion, with resulting centrifugal force, which *nous* imparted to the world.

But still further intervention by *nous* was necessary not only for the initial formation of biological organisms but also for their maintenance; for without such intervention the various constituents of organisms would simply be deposited in layers according to their specific gravities. There are three kinds of intervention which counterbalance the stratification tendencies of inorganic nature; namely, breathing, digestion, and perception. In digestion, the elements in foodstuffs have to be reorganized into the characteristic combining-ratios of the various organic parts. Perception too is an equilibratory function; *nous* corrects the derangements in the normal combining-ratios of the elements in the organic molecules by replacing deficits from, or eliminating surpluses into, the environment. Death ensues when *nous* ceases these operations and the organism becomes subject to the stratification of its components.

Cleve (1949, Chap. IX) conjectures that in Anaxagoras' theory the formation of biological organisms involved a separating off of bits of the world-*nous* within the individual integuments (perhaps within the lateral ventricles of the brain, which Anaxagoras observed in his animal dissections), so that individual minds were constituted which were in contact with the outer world only through the limited channels of the senses. Anaxagoras is said to have offered a demonstration of sensory limitation: if we take two vessels, containing respectively a white and a black fluid, and transfer the one to the other, drop by drop, the change in color will be imperceptible until a certain number of drops have been transferred. Sensation depends upon the quantitative relations between, on the one hand, the size of the sense organs and the continual perturbations of the combining-ratios of their organic molecules, and on the other, the excesses of any of the quality-elements in the environment. If the environmental surpluses are insufficient, there is no sensation; if they are excessive, pain is experienced; pain thus results from overloading of any of the sense channels. The individual *nous* responds to pain by causing movement of the organism whereby the normal combining-ratios of the sense organs are restored to a harmony which constitutes physical delight. Plants too are organisms with individual shares of *nous* and vital maintenance functions similar to those of animals.

We have quoted Burnet to the effect that Anaxagoras' presuppositions were in large part derived from medical sources. What is the justification for this statement? (1) In the first place, his postulate that all molecules contain all of the quality-elements seems to have been suggested, at least in part, by the physiological fact that ingested food is transformed into the various tissues of the body, so that food-stuffs must contain innumerable elements which become sorted out according to different ratios in the processes of assimilation. (2) His postulate of an organizing principle was on the model of organic nature. This may seem more respectable to a modern reader if it is pointed out, in terms of modern physics, that living things are the prime examples of local regions in which entropy can be decreased and order increased by rearrangement of molecules. This process is however, as Anaxagoras saw, a dynamic equilibration dependent upon continued metabolic activity which eventually ceases. (3) His (conjectured) postulate of individually isolated bits of *nous* was perhaps based on his animal dissections, in the course of which he discovered the lateral ventricles of the brain and concluded that the sense organs meet in the brain as their central organ. (4) His doctrine of perception was a metabolic hypothesis which empirically and logically was of the same order of validity as, e.g., the nineteenth-century physiologist Hering's theory of color vision; the latter was suggested by a more developed general doctrine of metabolism, but was, as respects the actual sensory processes, just as analogical as the former.

The relations between biology and the beginnings of scientific thought have been described by Castiglioni (1947, p. 130 f.) in the following words:

> There is no doubt that some of the great philosophers of the pre-Socratic school were also physicians; and that indirectly the fertility of the most ancient philosophic thought proceeded from medical

knowledge and from the accumulated wisdom of the Orient. It is from the observation of nature and the vicissitudes of human life and its accompanying phenomena that the first philosophic speculations arose. These first philosophers were in fact naturalists and biologists who passed from the study of the individual to that of the cosmos; and regarding the cosmos as a unit, returned to the study of the individual and thus established that line of philosophic thought that will never again be abandoned.

Empedocles

Empedocles (c.495-c.435 B.C.) was a citizen of Acragas (Agrigento) in Sicily, a city famed in his time for its beauty, wealth, and sophistication. He was influential in subsequent scientific history as the founder of the Sicilian school of medicine. But he was also a poet, a religious and political reformer, and a philosopher. With his philosophy he combined a mystical religion of the Orphic-Pythagorean type which included the doctrines of earthly existence as a punishment for sin and of the transmigration of souls. The individual soul persists throughout its thirty thousand years' cycle of reincarnations, during which it passes through all the shapes of life, and finally returns to God. "For I have been ere now a boy and a girl, a bush and a bird and a dumb fish in the sea." The soul's fate depends upon its own free choice. This doctrine of an earthly life devoted to redemption whereby the soul ascends from a world of sorrow to incorporeal blessedness in heaven was taken over from Pythagoras and Empedocles by Plato and, through Neoplatonism, by Christianity. "Dass wir 'von Gott stammen' und 'zu Gott gehen,' ist heute der Glaube und der Trost unzähliger Millionen Menschen. Zu ihm hat auch Empedokles beigetragen" (Kranz, 1949, p. 77).

Like Anaxagoras, Empedocles offered a compromise between Heraclitus and Parmenides based on medical analogies—but in the Pythagorean rather than the Milesian tradition. He accepted the doctrine of Parmenides that "what is"—the real—is without beginning or end, but he sought to avoid the results of the assumption that "all that *is* is one"—the assumption which had for Parmenides eliminated the possibility of motion—by asserting that the world of our experience results from the mixture and separation of a number of primary "roots" or elements (which represent the old opposites of warm and cold, wet and dry): namely, fire, air, water, earth.

(He demonstrated that atmospheric air is neither empty space nor vapor by means of a water-clock, a *clepsydra*, a brass vessel with openings at top and bottom; he showed that when it was immersed, water could not enter the bottom openings when the top opening was occluded, but only when air was allowed to escape.) Thus the elements are uncreated and indestructible, but the things which are mixtures of them are evanescent. Differences among things— e.g., among body tissues—are expressions of differences in ratios of mixture.

Empedocles made a second main assumption: he attributed the origin of motion to "love," a centripetal force by which the different elements attract each other and become mixed, and "strife," a centrifugal force by which they become separated. The mixing and separating processes are reversible. In an initial phase the sphere of the world consists of the four elements in a perfect mixture because of the predominance of "love"; in a second phase, "strife" enters the sphere from the outside and progressively separates them; in a third phase they are completely separated because of the predominance of "strife"; in a fourth phase, "love" becomes increasingly predominant and they are recombined. As these phases recur in continuous cycles, new worlds arise and are again dissolved; the world of individual things appears always in the second and fourth phases, by the interaction of "love" and "strife," mixture and differentiation.

A scheme which pictures the world as consisting of a limited number of elements whose organization results from the opposed actions of attraction and repulsion inevitably tempts us to call it an anticipation of modern chemistry; at least, it was, like other Greek hypotheses, such as Empedocles' theory of disease and theory of evolution, an intelligent guess which became part of the heritage of modern thought; the hypothesis of cosmic cycles certainly anticipates, e.g., Herbert Spencer's notion of alternate cosmic rhythms, "in which as motion is dissipated, so matter cleaves from the dispersed and homogeneous into more coherent and more segregated shapes; until in the turn of the great wheel, a new redistribution of matter and motion takes place, and evolution is inevitably followed by dissolution at its heels" (Thompson, 1913, p. 7). As we review the natural science and also the linguistic analysis of the Greek philosophers and physicians, our impressions may well be expressed in the words of a well-known song: "They went about as far as they could go," and it is difficult to believe that, had not the political deterioration of Greek civilization supervened, the limitations both of scientific technology and of linguistics would have been surmounted. Moreover, we must not forget that the great founders of modern science and philosophy in the nineteenth century shared a classical education.

To us it may appear that for the hylozoism of the Milesians, in which matter contained its own principle of motion, Empedocles substitutes a dualism of matter and force, apparently for two reasons: starting from Parmenides, he cannot regard matter as self-moving; and starting from ethico-religious prepossessions, he attributes to "love" and "strife" the causes of goodness and evil respectively, and thus in the words of Cornford (1957, p. 241) "does not entangle himself in the difficulties which beset those who have to make out that a world, half good and half bad, was designed by pure benevolence united with omnipotence." And yet the dualism is not a Cartesian psychophysical dualism; for the distinction between corporeal and non-corporeal is still not sharply drawn; the "material" elements are personified as gods and the "forces" are also listed as elements. Everything in the world is *both* physical *and* psychical, or rather, everything is "animate." But in the further development of this tradition, chiefly by Plato, dualism became explicit.

What were the sources of Empedocles' scheme? Here, as with the Milesians and Heraclitus, we can emphasize either religious influences or observations of nature. On the one hand he was undoubtedly a mystic who travelled about with the paraphernalia of a magician, attracting thousands in the cities through which he passed, prayed to and sought as a guide to salvation, a sort of medical missionary. Had he been a member of a modern medical association, he would have been in difficulties with the Committee on Professional Ethics, for he claimed to be able not only to heal the sick but also to raise the dead, cure the infirmity of old age, and control wind, rain, and sunshine; in fact, he claimed to be a god. However, a good deal of empirical knowledge and skill was probably mixed with the magic. Galen, in the second century A.D., cited Empedocles and Hippocrates as exemplars of the medical profession who chose their calling not for fame or money but for love of mankind. On the other hand, one of the Hippocratic physicians, perhaps a younger contemporary of Empedocles, speaks contemptuously of "the magicians, purifiers, charlatans, and quacks of our own day, men who claim great piety and superior knowledge."

Cornford (1957) emphasizes the religious influence, pointing out that the recurring cycles of cosmic creation and destruction parallel the cyclic movement of the soul in Orphic religion. On the other hand, others have emphasized the fact that Empedocles was a physician and have argued that his conceptions were influenced by both physical and biological observations. In the first place, his demonstration with the water-clock has been regarded as important both methodologically, as an early example of experimental observation, and in its conceptual consequences, in that the demonstration that "Nature works by unseen bodies" was basic to the theory of the Atomists, as appears from the emphasis placed upon atmospheric phenomena by Lucretius. Empedocles "had revealed the existence of an imperceptible physical universe by examining its effects on the perceptible world" (Farrington, 1944, p. 56). In the second place, his water-clock demonstration had some analogy both to his physiology and to his cosmology. He formulated a theory of circulation and respiration: blood, the carrier of "innate heat," issues from the heart and flows back to it; like the water in the clock, it drives the air out as it rises, and lets it in again as it sinks; thus respiration depends upon the systole and diastole of the heart. This was an anticipation of the "tidal theory" which was developed some six centuries later by Galen and which persisted altogether some 2000 years until the time of Harvey (1628). Moreover, Empedocles describes the attractive force of "love" as analogous to the impulse to union "implanted in the frame of mortals," and this perhaps places his love-hate scheme in a more modern light; it might possibly be taken as an anticipation of Freud.

Both the water-clock and the physiology may be related to the cosmological scheme; as Burnet (1924, p. 73) says: "Love expands and Strife is driven outwards, passing out of the Sphere once more in proportion as Love occupies more and more of it, just as air is expelled from the *klepsydra* when water enters it. In fact, Love and Strife are to the world what blood and air are to the body." The notion that the cosmos "breathes" had already appeared in Anaximenes, who said, "Just as our soul, being air, holds us together, so do breath and air encompass the whole world"; the world "inhales" air from the mass outside it. There were probably other sources of perceptual suggestion. Dampier-Whetham (1930, p. 23) refers to the ancient interpretation of combustion as a resolving of a substance into its elements, "the first great guiding idea of chemistry." In Greek painting there were four basic colors: white, black, red, and yellow; and Empedocles, after describing how "trees and men and women, beasts and birds and the fishes that dwell in the waters, yea and the gods" all spring from mixtures of the four elements, uses these same words in a simile describing how the painter mixes his colors to produce the forms of these things (Burnet, 1957, p. 209; Kranz, 1949, pp. 61, 70).

Burnet (1957, p. 250) has pointed out the strange fact that Empedocles' cosmological system, according to which all things, including men, are eventually resolved into the elements, leaves no room for the immortal soul of his religion. "All through this period there seems to have been a gulf between men's religious beliefs, if they had any, and their cosmological views." This state of affairs may vaguely remind us of the conflict between new science and old religion in the intellectuals of 18th and 19th century Germany, from Leibnitz to Fechner.

As a physician, Empedocles was particularly interested in biology, and here his speculations are of great historical interest. He offered a *theory of evolution* which was an elaboration of Anaximander's conjecture. Living creatures arose out of the earth. The evolution of animals began with undifferentiated living masses which formed themselves into limbs and other parts—"heads without necks, arms without shoulders," etc.—which were presently conjoined in various chance unions. Most of these unions resulted in non-viable monsters (a notion usually thought to have been suggested by the part-man, part-animal creatures of Greek and Egyptian mythology—sphinxes, bull-gods, centaurs, etc.—but which may also have been suggested by malformed fetuses; e.g., "compound monsters," made up of parts of more than one individual). Only those unions survived whose several parts proved to be adapted or complementary to one another; there was thus a sort of natural selection by survival of the fittest. The embryo receives some parts of its body from the father's and some from the mother's seed. The heart is the nucleus of embryonic development; it is the source of "inborn heat." Growth and senescence are due to increase and decrease, respectively, of body heat. Human males originated in a southern climate and are therefore of a warmer temperament; women, created in a colder climate, are more cold-blooded; in Empedocles' researches on this matter, there was perhaps a bias in his sample populations.

Empedocles' medical rationale was based on the assumption that health depends on the equilibrium of the four elements in the

body; disease results from a disequilibrium. The therapies inspired
by this notion, transmitted through Hippocrates, Aristotle, and
Galen, dominated medicine for hundreds of years; particularly
prominent was the emphasis on diet, which was reinforced by
Pythagorean religious prescriptions. "The precepts of morality,"
remarked Wallace (1910), "are with Empedocles largely dietetic."

It has been suggested by Kranz (1949, p. 24 f.) that the Pythagorean-Empedoclean (Italian-Sicilian) and the Hippocratic (Ionian)
schools represented two contrasting fifth-century approaches to
medicine. Empedocles started from the Pythagorean and oriental notion of a mystic relation between cosmos and human being,
between macrocosm and microcosm, and made a basic philosophy
of nature a propaedeutic to medicine. The Hippocratic school
started with man himself, and not only sought to derive its therapy
from an understanding of his nature but also regarded such understanding as the most reliable source of knowledge of nature in general. The Empedoclean approach and, one might even say, the
Empedoclean personality, reappeared in the Renaissance physician
Paracelsus (1493-1541), who, like Empedocles, combined philosophy, medicine, and magic. "It is an impertinence," said Paracelsus,
"for a doctor who is ignorant of philosophy to call himself a
doctor."

We encountered in Alcmaeon the notion of health as dependent
on an "isonomy" of constituents in the human body. As we shall see,
not only nosology and therapy but also a theory of personality
could be based on this Pythagorean-Empedoclean concept of a
"chemical" balance in the human body, and in fact the oldest char-
acterological theory, which has persisted into our own times and
textbooks, was later developed in this manner by Theophrastus and
Galen.

Underlying Empedocles' theory of *sensation* were two postulates:
(1) All action of one body on another requires contact, whereby
small parts or emanations of the one enter "pores" of the other. (2)
"Like can only act on like." This latter doctrine is derived, not from
experience, but from the old magical principle of sympathetic
magic, according to which causal interaction occurs among things,
persons, or animals who are linked in kinship. Sensation thus results
when emanations from objects enter sensory pores (which they
selectively fit) and unite themselves to corresponding components
in the sense organs. The heart is the central sensorium. (It will be
recalled that Alcmaeon, who had also spoken of canals—the nerves

—leading from the sense organs, had made the *brain* the seat of mental life; there were to be several later reversals of this sort; e.g., from Plato to Aristotle.) Among the sense organs the eye and ear are special cases. Certain (fiery?) particles go forth through pores in the membranes of the eye to meet similar particles given off by objects, and the resultant contact constitutes vision; this formulation was perhaps a compromise between two ancient notions: the Pythagorean view that light is something emitted by luminous bodies, and the rival view that the eye actively scans objects by sending out rays of light. (A good antidote for the smile of superiority which may be elicited by these notions is the discussion of "hypothetical constructs" in psychology by MacCorquodale and Meehl [1948].) In audition, the impact of air currents on the cartilage of the ear sets up a gong-like ringing which is what we hear. Brett (1953, p. 41) has suggested that these notions were derived from observations of the "flashing" of the eyes and the "ringing" of the ears, respectively. Empedocles is said to have been the first to assign the auditory function to the labyrinth of the ear. He was the first to list five senses; Alcmaeon had not mentioned the tactile sense, but Empedocles made tactile contact the model for all modalities. And finally, Empedocles was the first to reason that light has a finite velocity, a fact which was confirmed by Roemer in 1676; in the intervening centuries, the tradition that the transmission of light was instantaneous was generally accepted; e.g., by Kepler.

Thinking is described as a function of the blood; "the blood round the heart is the thought of man." Each of the four elements in the thinker and in the thought seeks its like element. Since the blood contains the most complete mixture of the elements, it is the seat of intelligence. Desire and aversion, like sensory pleasure and pain, are evoked by that which is akin or repellent, respectively, to something in us.

Empedocles' emphasis on the heart and the flux and reflux of the blood was influential in the development of the doctrine of *pneuma*. The notion of pneuma, identified with air and breath, as a principle which interpenetrates and gives life both to man and the universe, was introduced by Anaximenes, but has traditionally been associated with Empedocles in accounts of the historical antecedents of the "Pneumatic School" of medicine of the first century A.D. It was mentioned above that Empedocles considered the respiratory air and the blood in the heart and vessels to be functionally interrelated. This idea was taken up by Aristotle, who taught that sensation is conveyed to the heart by the flow of pneuma through the arteries, and that muscular movement is produced by a flow from the heart to the muscles. In the second century A.D., Galen, who made the brain the seat of the soul and of intelligence, held that the pneuma was produced in the cerebral ventricles and that it circulated through the nervous system. Thus originated the notion of "animal spirits," a mysterious substance distilled in the brain ventricles from the "vital spirits" of the blood (whereby the breath and the blood theories of the vital principle were united); this substance was, for many centuries thereafter, supposed to flow through the nerves (thought of as hollow tubes) to produce the phenomena of sensation and of movement. The notion received its classical development in the hydraulic neurophysiology of Descartes in the 17th century. It reappeared in the attempt of William James (1890, II, pp. 580-592) to explain learning as the formation of new neural pathways by the action of a process called "drainage." James described the process, in emphatic italics, as follows:

> *Each discharge from a sensory cell in the forward direction tends to drain the cells lying behind the discharging one of whatever tension they may possess. The drainage from the rearward cells is what for the first time makes the fibres pervious. The result is a new-formed "path," running from the cells which were "rearward" to the cell which was "forward" on that occasion; which path, if on future occasions the rearward cells are independently excited, will tend to carry off their activity in the same direction so as to excite the forward cell, and will deepen itself more and more every time it is used . . . the deepest paths are formed from the most drainable to the most draining cells . . . the most drainable cells are those which have just been discharging . . . the most draining cells are those which are now discharging or in which the tension is rising towards the point of discharge [p. 584 f.].*

The notion of the "drainage" of "neural currents" was developed by von Uexküll (1909, p. 185) as an explanation of inhibition; from him, and probably also from James, Max Meyer (1911, 1921) adopted it as his basic mechanism of learning, illustrated by his conventionalized "reflex arch" diagrams; A. P. Weiss (in his oral teaching rather than in his publications), a pupil of Meyer, made extensive use of the notion of "neural flux" whose "drainage" resulted in "reduction of resistance" at synapses; both Meyer and Weiss spoke in frankly hydraulic terms, and used the analogy of the jet pump. And finally, McDougall (1903) employed the concept of a "stream of energy," which he called *neurin*, to explain reciprocal inhibition of reflexes; the mechanism here too was that of "drainage" of less by more strongly stimulated neurons; this scheme was rather favorably reviewed by Sherrington (1906, pp. 200-203).

By all of these avenues the ancient doctrine of pneuma extended its history into the first two decades of the present century, although the increase of neurophysiological knowledge had by then made it quite untenable. How was this possible? Bayliss (1931, p. 424 f.), in his amusing review of "drainage" theories, remarks: "It must be admitted that von Uexküll defends himself from the imputation of using a misleading image, in speaking of a liquid flowing about in the nervous system, on the ground that the object of science is not 'truth' but 'order,' so that we must accept his assurance that he uses such expressions as 'quantity' and 'pressure' of excitation and 'varying capacities of reservoirs' merely to facilitate the description of experimental facts." A somewhat similar argument has been used by Mandler and Kessen (1959, p. 267 f.) to justify Freud's "quasi-hydraulic theory of libido." MacCorquodale and Meehl (1948), in their well-known essay on "Hypothetical Constructs and Intervening Variables," had remarked that, "Even admitting the immature state of neurophysiology in terms of its relation to complex behavior, it must be clear that the central nervous-system does not in fact contain pipes or tubes with fluid in them, and there are no known properties of nervous tissue to which the hydraulic properties of libido could correspond" (p. 106). To this Mandler and Kessen (p. 268) reply:

> This reinterpretative device misses the function of explanatory systems. Freud's theory has as its range of intent certain responses of human beings, e.g., reports of fantasies and dreams, sexual behavior, and so on. If the libido explanation leads to testable and confirmed statements about such behavior, then it has met the central requirement of a good theory. If it achieves this function at a very high level, then discussions of the "reality" of libido in pipes becomes as irrelevant as discussions of the "reality" of electrons in orbits.

Irrelevant, that is, if we disregard the fact that human beings are biological organisms, ignore what is known about the nervous system, and attach no importance to the unity of science. The intuitive speculations of Empedocles and the other ancients, by which they made the most of their scanty data, seem incongruous in Freud,

trained in 19th century physiology. The acceptability of the pneu-
matic-hydraulic "model" became steadily less as neurophysiological
discoveries accumulated which were incompatible with it, and as,
on the other hand, it became increasingly obvious, as Marquis summarized the matter in 1951, that "There is at present no satisfactory
theory of the nature of the relatively permanent synaptic changes
that would account for learning. The nature of the excitation process itself is a matter of controversy, and extensions of electrical,
chemical, or growth theories to the phenomenon of learning are
without any basis in fact" (Marquis, 1951, p. 303). On the other
hand, there *has* been an accumulation of neurophysiological knowledge which has not been assimilated nor exploited by psychology;
the animus of some contemporary psychologists, notably Skinner
(1938), against "physiologizing" is beginning to seem more relevant
to the neurology of the 1920's than to that of the 1960's. Or so it has
seemed, e.g., to Hebb (1949, 1955, 1958), who has attempted to
bring the new knowledge to bear upon the central problems of psychology; in particular, substituting a hypothetical "growth of synaptic knobs" for "drainage" as a basic mechanism of learning.

Well! The preceding must have seemed to the reader an uncon-
scionable chain of historical free association. Is there really a historical thread running from Empedocles to Hebb? I think there is,
and a very instructive one. The "drainage" of James, von Uexküll,
and McDougall could hardly be understood otherwise than in the
tradition of "a liquid flowing about in the nervous system"; the
hydraulic notion having finally to be abandoned, the "drainage" of
these writers becomes the "growth of synaptic knobs" of Hebb,
which at least has more physiological plausibility and greater prospect of experimental test. I have seemed to see the ancestry of
Hebb's neural diagrams (e.g., Hebb, 1949, p. 71) in those of James
(1890, II, pp. 582-592). The history of science *is* in large part a
series of unanalyzed free associations.

Zeller (1955, p. 75) says: "Empedocles had enormous influence
in after times. By his reduction of the material world to a limited
number of elements and their combination in fixed mathematical
proportions, he became the founder of modern chemistry, while his
theory of elements was accepted until the beginning of the 18th
century. His attempt to explain the creation of organic beings on a
mechanistic basis places him with Anaximander among the precursors of Darwin." And we have made him a precursor of Freud
and of Hebb!

The Origins of Medicine

When we come to the history of medicine, we come to perhaps the most ancient and continuous tradition of attentive observation and practice, from which emerged, after early entanglements with magic, religion, and philosophy, both the basic biological sciences and the healing arts. Among primitive peoples, wounds, fractures, disease, and death were, like other disasters and calamities, of compelling interest; the alleviation of pain and the postponement of death are urgent and universal concerns of mankind. The evolution of verbal and manual behavior, thus motivated, varied from the practical and rational to the magical and religious, in accordance with the degree of obviousness of the situation. Thus treatments of superficial wounds and of fractures and dislocations were early learned, as illustrated, e.g., in Egyptian records of practices going back to at least 3000 B.C. Sigerist (1951, p. 201 ff.) points out that minor ailments of everyday life—colds, stomach-ache—as well as more serious diseases which are common in a country—malaria, tuberculosis, skin eruptions—may be considered "natural" by primitives and treated by palliative empirically discovered methods—poultices, massage, vapor baths, herbal remedies; for the people involved, however, these methods may also have the magical significance of driving out evil spirits. Sigerist's distinction between "natural" diseases which are treated "rationally" and those diseases which require magico-religious intervention will remind us of Marett's distinction between the world of everyday life and the world of crises. Internal diseases and psychoses, being causally occult, were treated by magical methods, although even here, in the applications of primitive pharmacology and physical therapy there was a certain admixture of empiricism. In general, the magical and the rational were threads of the same fabric.

Quite common was the notion that disease was a punishment inflicted by supernatural beings, or caused by the entry into the human body of foreign objects or demons; in the simpler societies, Radin (1957b, p. 68) tells us, a human enemy is almost always thought to be the mediating agent. Thus the remedies suggested were religious appeals, magical rites, or techniques for driving out demons. For the latter procedure there were analogies: superficially observed foreign bodies could be removed, superficial abscesses drained, and "peccant substances" evacuated; similarly, it seemed, morbific agents magically implanted could be extracted or expelled. This notion sometimes led to the cultivation of sleight-of-hand by which medicine men could palm and then exhibit the causative object, or the practitioner might suck the site of pain and spit out the foreign object. The notion of pathogenesis by object intrusion could also arise from the observation of worms leaving the body. In Hippocratic-Galenic humoral medicine, which persisted into the seventeenth century, the substance to be expelled became the *materia peccans* or *materia morbi,* the pathogenic substance which was to be eliminated with the phlegm, stool, urine, or blood. A striking figure of speech is Garrison's (1929, p. 44) description of psychotherapy as "removing the splinter of worry or misery from the brain." Garrison's introductory chapter will repay reading; he offers many parallels between primitive and modern folk medicine, and some also between these and modern scientific medicine.

A very ancient and wide-spread surgical technique was that of trephination, the removal of a disk of bone from the skull, an operation which in Neolithic times was done with sharpened flints. There have been differences of opinion as to the purpose of this operation; it may have originated in the treatment of skull injuries or fractures, but it seems very probable that it was or became also a technique for permitting the escape of a demon, especially in cases of headache, epilepsy, and insanity. Widespread in South America was the technique of bleeding by venesection or scarification; the demon was supposed to escape with the blood. But practices which are magical among some peoples may have acquired practical motivations among others; thus Sigerist (1951, p. 202) points out that "Bleeding . . . is practiced by most primitive peoples in the treatment of pneumonia, pleurisy, and other diseases, particularly those that are combined with fever. It brings a certain relief by decongesting the system, as primitives found out empirically."

Mental illness especially excited religious or magical attitudes. Thus in Homeric Greece, madness was a condition visited on man by a god as punishment for impiety. Similarly, in the Old Testament, the Lord may smite a man "with madness and blindness and astonishment of heart" (*Deuteronomy* 28:28). Hostility toward the mentally ill found expression in the notion of possession by evil spirits, and the scriptural injunction that "A man also or woman that hath a familiar spirit, or that is a wizard, shall surely be put to death: they shall stone them with stones: their blood shall be upon them" (*Leviticus* 20:27) was taken as justification for atrocious cruelty to the mentally ill in later centuries. Yet even in the treatment of the psychoses there was, at least in prehistoric Greece, an admixture of practical procedures; thus the legendary demigod-priest-physician Melampus cured the daughters of Proetus, King of Tiryns, of mania, which had been visited upon them for impiety, by driving them to exhaustion with violent exercise and administering hellebore, a violent cathartic, emetic, and emmenagogue. This treatment would hardly be considered rational today, and yet the driving to exhaustion was perhaps as rational as "shock therapy," and the use of hellebore in insanity was transmitted by the Hippocratics to find an echo in a medical dictionary of the 1940's which said that hellebore "is sometimes used in mania." The question of the relative rationality of trephination and lobotomy may give us at least a moment's pause. From ancient to modern times, the choices of therapy in psychoses have been the same: purges, kind treatment, sedation, physical therapy, restraint, shock. Emphasis has varied from one to another of these in something like recurring cycles, and it is only very recently that there has appeared a prospect of a rational therapy, based on neurophysiology and biochemistry.

"Scientific" medicine has traditionally been said to have had its beginnings in the Greek world of the fifth century B.C. The Greek interest in a rational interpretation of nature began, as we have seen, in the coastal cities of Asia Minor, and it was in this region too, on the Aegean islands of Rhodes and Cos and in the peninsular city of Cnidus, that Greek medicine had its origin. In the intellectually freer atmosphere of these Greek colonies, the astronomical and medical lore which had been accumulated by the priests and magicians of the adjacent oriental empires could be selectively utilized in the development of more rational cosmologies and medical doctrines. The early Greek physicians, as part of their education, sojourned in Egypt and western Asia, and there became acquainted with priestly lore, which was a mixture of magic, religion, accumulated observations of the courses of various diseases, and accumulated experience with trial-and-error manipulations, drug administration, etc.

Here I must pause to discuss views put forward by the eminent historian of medicine Sigerist, views which are incongruent with those of the present book. Sigerist (1951) has argued strongly against the view that science and rational medicine began in sixth and fifth century Greece, and in support of his opinion has presented detailed descriptions of the processes of diagnosis and of physical and mental therapy in ancient Egypt and Mesopotamia in the three millennia before our era. In Egypt there was some differentiation of priests, magicians, and "physicians" in terms of both diagnosis and therapy. The priest diagnosed the voluntary or involuntary "sin" which had been committed by the patient and performed the prayers, sacrifices, and other rites necessary to placate the gods. The magician diagnosed the demon, ghost, or other magical agent who was causing the trouble and performed the incantations and manual operations necessary to expel this agent. The "physician" diagnosed the physical "cause" or "seat" of the trouble and applied such procedures as bone-setting, reduction of dislocations, treatment of wounds, massage, application of poultices, ointments, or fumigations, and administration of drugs (especially cathartics, emetics, expectorants, astringents, and enemas). With priests and magicians we have no further concern, except to note that they undoubtedly had and still have a psychotherapeutic function, especially for persons suffering from neuroses, or too ignorant or too poor to seek help from medicine, or whose illness is beyond medical help. Our concern is with the "physicians," whom Sigerist considers to have practiced much rational medicine and whose speculative theories he describes as representing "the beginning of medical science" and as having "anticipated the views and methods of the pre-Socratic philosophers of Greece" (Sigerist, 1951, p. 355). Sigerist shows that these practitioners carefully examined their patients, observing visually and by palpation, auscultation, smell, and even taste, many details which a modern physician also notes, such as facies, posture, anaesthesias and paralyses, skin color, temperature, pulse, excretions and secretions; he shows also that some of the therapeutic procedures and remedies, such as bone-setting and the treatment of injuries, and of disorders which can be relieved by purges or emetics, were effective or at least palliative, especially in a psychotherapeutic sense.

The question is one of definition—of "science" and "medicine" and "rational." The "science" with which we are here concerned is biological science, the science of living organisms in all of their manifestations, including the states of health and of disease. Is medicine a biological science? Here as in psychology differences of viewpoint arise because of the distinction which we make between the biophysical and the biosocial aspects of man. Sigerist (1951, p. 14) states that

We must always keep in mind that medicine is not a natural science, either pure or applied. Methods of science are used all the time in combating disease, but medicine belongs much more to the realm of the social sciences because the goal is social. Medicine, by promoting health and preventing illness, endeavors to keep individuals adjusted to their environment as useful and contented members of society . . . medicine actually is but one link in a chain of social-welfare institutions.

This view led Sigerist to include in his *History of Medicine* (1951, 1961) a vast array of material on folk "medicine" and on religious and magical practices of prehistoric and ancient peoples. "Our approach to the history of medicine," he says, "cannot be broad enough."

Now it is undoubtedly part of the task of the historian of science to show how certain terms, concepts, and practices of science are survivals or transformations of ancient notions and practices. But it seems unwise to apply to such notions and practices the term *science,* or to say, as Sigerist does (1951, p. 272), that "Magic in all early civilizations was a perfectly legitimate science in its own way. . . ." We discussed the modern concept of science in Chapter 2; here let me quote Nagel's (1961, p. 12) statement, in the course of his chapter on "Science and Common Sense," that "Implicit in the contrasts between modern science and common sense already noted is the important difference that derives from the deliberate policy of science to expose its cognitive claims to the repeated challenge of critically probative observational data, procured under carefully controlled conditions." By such a criterion it seems inappropriate to describe the activities of the ancient practitioners of Egypt and Mesopotamia as the "beginnings of medical science." If we make the criterion less severe but demand some use of the experimental method in physiology, we can hardly speak of medical science before Erasistratus (310-250 B.C.). If finally we require only that there be careful and "objective" observation, "naturalistic" explanations free of religious and magical implications, and procedures based upon such observations and explanations, we cannot go further back than the Hippocratic physicians of the fifth century B.C. Sigerist (1951, p. 209) himself remarks that "From the Greek period on, a system of medicine developed that was based on experience and excluded the transcendental. It became our scientific medicine of today. . . ." Sigerist's descriptions of the notions and practices of Egyptian and Mesopotamian practitioners seem to me to lead inescapably to the view that the so-called "rational ele-

ments" were so imbedded in religion and magic that they cannot
possibly be brought under the most attenuated definition of medical or biological science (or of their "beginnings"). They were not,
as far as I can see, essentially different from the practices of the
"Stone Age" North American Indians, who, though their theory was
demonistic, "were especially skilled in surgery, practising great
cleanliness of wounds, and using sutures, cautery styptics, and poultices. They splinted fractures and reduced dislocations" (Castiglioni, 1947, p. 24). This conclusion is not altered by the fact that the
Egyptian and Mesopotamian beliefs and practices often had psychotherapeutic effects (as do modern quackeries), or that modern
physiology and biochemistry have demonstrated the potency of
certain ancient drugs. The attitude of the practitioner is an essential factor in our judgment of whether a procedure is "scientific"; in
Egyptian and Mesopotamian "medicine" the attitude is pervasively
religious and magical. Thus the potency of a drug seems to have
depended usually upon the reciting of an incantation, and diagnosis was hardly to be differentiated from divination. Even in what
might seem the obvious situation of a fractured bone, for which a
practical technique was available, the question of why this particular patient should have suffered the accident might arise and find
a supernatural answer. The development of the attitude necessary
for the origins of scientific medicine was begun in Greece by the
Milesian philosophers and the atomists. Alcmaeon, Anaxagoras, and
Empedocles represent transitional applications of this attitude to
biological phenomena, in which applications however the older
religious and prescientific linguistic categories are still perceptible.

It is for the above reasons that I find myself unmoved by Sarton's
(1960, p. ix) assertion that "It is childish to assume that science
began in Greece; the Greek 'miracle' was prepared by millennia of
work in Egypt, Mesopotamia and possibly in other regions. Greek
science was less an invention than a revival." The Greeks utilized
the Egyptian and Mesopotamian practices, and the Greeks, as Sarton points out, also had their own religious and magical background; the difference is that the Milesian philosophers introduced
a naturalistic attitude divorced from religion and magic. To speak
of Egyptian "science" is like speaking of "Christian Science"; religiously or magically motivated behavior does not become nor give
rise to science merely by an accretion of practical—e.g., therapeutically efficacious—devices. I find overwrought also Sigerist's
(1961, p. 4) emotive statement that "It goes without saying that

such an approach to history is utterly naïve and viciously wrong"
[the approach is that in which "We glorify the Greeks . . . as our
precursors and true ancestors who first developed the scientific
method"]. The modern historian of science, it seems to me, needs to
have in mind some approximation to a definition of the terms *science* and *scientific method,* and should not use these terms as
honorifics to express his admiration for the complexities or practical
utilities of prescientific beliefs and practices. The notion that Western science has much to learn from the "Wisdom of the East," is, I
think, an expression of the mystical tendency of our troubled times
to which I have referred elsewhere. I find more congenial Sigerist's
(1961, p. 111) statement that "Greek science and medicine . . . laid
the foundations upon which our modern systems of medicine and
science are erected."

Is it justifiable or useful to classify medicine as a social science?
We had better dispose first of the term *medical science.* Few physicians in either ancient or modern times have practiced research or
have been trained in the disciplines of experimental and statistical
controls; if modern physicians were so trained, it would be impossible for drug firms to distribute a continuous stream of "miracle"
drugs, of which many are presently found to be therapeutically
ineffectual and some allergenic or even fatal. Most physicians, in
modern as in ancient times, follow recipes and clinical demonstrations of manual and instrumental techniques. This situation is
described by calling the practice of medicine an *art,* and speaking
of anatomy, physiology, biochemistry, pharmacology, etc. as *sup-
porting* or *basic medical sciences.* Clinical research, the observation
and classification of symptoms, syndromes, and courses of diseases
and of the effects of treatments, varies in its position between the
poles of art and science in accordance with the degree of experimental and statistical control, but such controls are in turn dependent upon the state of the "basic" sciences. The extreme technical
sophistication required for a scientific pharmacology is described
by Irwin (1962), according to whom it has by no means been generally attained even today.

The state of the basic medical sciences of anatomy and physiology in ancient Egypt and Mesopotamia was such as to give little
or no support to medicine, which might therefore with some justice
be described as a "social" art; the psychotherapeutic or psychosomatic effects of the practitioner's speech, actions, and "bedside
manner," based on ancient and esoteric traditions, were undoubt-

edly as great, or perhaps greater than, those of modern practice (one thinks of such disorders as "mucous colitis" and "psychogenic constipation"). It was formerly thought that the Egyptian practice of embalming resulted in anatomical knowledge; Sigerist (1951, p. 44) however points out that embalming involved a crude evisceration by uneducated craftsmen which could have led only to "the kind of knowledge that the butchers or cooks had." The priests sacrificed animals and examined their entrails for purposes of divination; this art developed a complex and esoteric tradition in which the various organs received names and were assigned augural meanings; the heart, liver, and spleen, the "bloody organs," were especially noted. Egyptian "physiological" theory was to the effect that a system of vessels radiated from the heart to all the organs and parts of the body, "carrying air and liquids such as blood, urine, tears, sperm, and solid matters such as feces" (ibid., p. 349). There was a recognition of an interrelation between air, food, blood, and excretions. The heart was the seat of mental and emotional functions. Since such "knowledge" could not support a rational pathology or therapy, internal diseases could be treated only by irrational empirical remedies or in accordance with speculative and particularly magico-religious notions. In Mesopotamia, the healing arts were even more primitively magico-religious. They were practiced by priests, and disease was attributed primarily to demons, ghosts, and evil spirits, and was commonly considered a punishment for sin, a view which was transmitted by the Old Testament and which from ancient times has been rationalized by the axiom that the ways of God are beyond human understanding and hence need not conform to human ideals of justice and compassion. Dreams were analyzed in divinatory diagnosis; from ancient Babylon to modern Vienna dreams have been taken to have meanings beyond their manifest content. Therapy was predominantly magico-religious (and hence psychotherapeutic), but with an admixture of primitive practical procedures: the use of suppositories, enemas, emetics, heat, massage, and the administration of "drugs," a few of which had physiological potency. As for "mental" functions, ". . . the heart was believed to be the seat of the intellect, the liver of affectivity, the stomach of cunning, the uterus of compassion, ears and eyes of attention" (Sigerist, 1951, p. 491). The physician-priests practiced some primitive surgery, and here we may note an interesting equivalent of modern malpractice penalties: when an operation ended fatally, the surgeon was to suffer cheirotomy.

Medicine as an art is undoubtedly a "social" profession (as is "clinical psychology") in so far as it involves the physician-patient relationship and in so far also as it is institutionalized, whether by guilds or by public employment—both of which occurred in the ancient world. This reason for calling medicine a social profession, and, rather surprisingly, thereby justifying the study of its history, finds interesting expression in the following remarks of Sigerist (1951, p. 32), which are perhaps not unrelated to the fact that he himself had been active in military and social medicine:

> It is obvious that a doctor can treat a patient suffering from pneumonia or syphilis or any other disease successfully without any knowledge of general or medical history. The only history he must know is that of his patient. The moment, however, when we plan an anti-venereal disease or anti-tuberculosis campaign, or medical services for rural districts, or whatever it may be—the moment, in other words, when we address our efforts not to a single individual but to a group —we need more historical knowledge. The success or failure of our efforts may well depend on whether we have a correct appreciation of the many social, economic, political, religious, philosophical, and other non-medical factors that determine the situation, an appreciation that we may acquire only as the result of historical analysis.

The objection to classifying medicine as a social science is, I think, the same as the objection to so classifying psychology: it encourages a neglect of the properties of biological tissues and organs, in which are to be found the ultimate explanations of all human functions, in health and disease, "social" as well as "biological." Human social behavior is learned behavior, and learning is a function of the nervous system as determined or modified by hereditary mechanisms, biochemical factors, and stimulus combinations and sequences. The study of social interactions and institutions is of course essential, and it is entirely appropriate to describe medicine and psychology as taking account of the interaction of biosocial with biophysical factors. But as soon as they or any of their specialties are classed as social sciences—as soon, that is, as they lose contact with biological tissues—there develop such conceptual systems and arts as those of psychoanalysis, clinical psychology, depth psychology, individual psychology, parapsychology, and—at least until recent years—psychiatry, in which connections with or references to biological structures and functions are neglected or mythicized, not only in theory and practice but also in the education of practitioners. Clinical psychology is, of course, also in the peculiar position of standing outside the medical profession, thereby continuing the ancient distinction between priests and philosophers (who deal with the "soul" or "mind") on the one hand and physicians on the other.

In Greece, both physical and medical science emerged from a magico-religious background. The first healers of serious ills were the gods and their priests, especially Apollo and later Asclepius (better known to us by his Roman name of Aesculapius). The prehistoric origins of such cults is suggested by the symbolic role of serpents, the representatives, agents, or even embodiments of gods or demons of the underworld. Magical practices—incantations, divination, administering of miraculous potions and ointments— were components of these cults. At a number of places temples were erected where priests ministered to the sick. The techniques of the priests, in addition to magical and ritualistic practices, seem to have included hypnotism and suggestion. Dreams were utilized both for diagnosis and for suggestion; as in Freudian practice, they were a means by which the priest might surmise the patient's problems and needs, and their narration and interpretation afforded opportunity for catharsis, rationalization, and reassurance. Dreams and visions were encouraged by the practice of "incubation"— sleeping in the temple after preparatory baths, fasting, purgation, massage, anointing, and impressive rites. These temples were typically built near mineral springs, and in their neighborhood were built theaters (one of which seated 10,000 persons), gymnasia, stadia, concert halls, baths, and hostels, so that the environment must have been more inspiriting than that, e.g., of Rochester, Minnesota. To these places the sick repaired in large numbers to try the curative powers of religious rites reinforced by fine air, medicinal springs, exhilarating scenery, rest, drama, games, social amusements, diet, and gymnastics. These were obviously highly favorable situations for the practice of "psychosomatic medicine," similar in their therapeutic effects—especially in hysteria and other neurotic disorders—to those of modern religious shrines such as that of Lourdes, and probably more effective than such techniques as that of modern psychoanalysis, which though it speaks in a mythological language, lacks supernatural reinforcement. There was also an economic aspect; poor people, who could not afford to pay a physician, and who were uneducated and superstitious, could, by a modest gift, receive help in a temple; in our days they go to chiropractors, naturopaths, and faith healers, whose education and overhead are less expensive and who more nearly talk the language of their patients.

Already in Homeric times, although diseases were believed to be sent by the gods, we hear of men who were not priests nor magicians but physicians skilled in the treatment of wounds, fractures, and dislocations, and who were knowing also in the use of medicinal herbs. There must have been an evolution of practical techniques and, above all, of a naturalistic attitude toward life and disease between the ninth and the fifth centuries, but the curtain of medical history rises for us as suddenly in the fifth century as does that of general science in the sixth. And even so, what we have is a miscellaneous collection of writings—the "Hippocratic Corpus"—obviously by different hands, from different times and places, of very uneven quality, and showing many inconsistencies of doctrine. Moreover, these writings have been transmitted to us by manuscripts of the tenth and later centuries A.D. There seems actually to have been a famous physician named Hippocrates who was born on the island of Cos about 460 B.C. and who died about 380; he and his immediate predecessors and successors were probably the authors of some of the best of the "Hippocratic" works. The physicians of ancient Greece seem to have been mostly itinerant practitioners, travelling from town to town in Greece, Italy, and Asia, although some of the most eminent were retained on salaries by municipalities or monarchs. Thus we should probably take in a very limited sense such expressions as the "school" of Cos, or of Cnidus, and "guilds" of physicians. There certainly were cumulative traditions; medical education was by apprenticeship, and medical treatises and clinical notes were transmitted and progressively annotated.

While Greek medicine undoubtedly had an ancient magico-religious background, its immediate sources were naturalistic philosophy and the experience of gymnasium trainers. Physical training was very important in Greek education. Health, beauty, and physical vigor were part of the gentlemanly ideal. The ideal of *mens sana in corpore sano* had also been dominant in the program of the Pythagoreans, who therefore, like the Hippocratics, paid much attention to diet and regimen. What we call "preventive medicine" —the preservation rather than the restoring of health—was more emphasized by the Greeks than by us. Although we attempt—verbally—to redress the balance by speaking of "health sciences" rather than of "medicine," our athletic trainers are occupied predominantly with "spectator sports," and our physicians with treating diseases.

The *surgery* of the Hippocratic school, in so far as applied to bone fractures, articular dislocations, and treatment of wounds, other superficial conditions, and disorders observable in body orifices such as the anus (an ancient focus of trouble; at the Egyptian court there was a specialist called the "Guardian of the Anus"), was very skillful. A modern reader may well be astonished at the anatomical knowledge and surgical techniques of the Hippocratic treatises *On Fractures* and *On Joints;* as Garrison (1929, p. 97) says, modern commentators have considered that "these treatises, given the limitations under which they were written, are not surpassed by any similar works of recent times"; their spirit and style are those of modern orthopedics. *Internal medicine* was based on close observation and classification of the combinations and sequences of external symptoms of disease (which in the dominant disease, malaria, showed regular rhythms and "crises"), and upon the study of constitutional dispositions. The Coan school placed great emphasis on prognosis; in the *Prognostics* we read:

> It appears to me a most excellent thing for the physician to cultivate Prognosis; for by foreseeing and foretelling, in the presence of the sick, the present, the past, and the future, and explaining the omissions which patients have been guilty of, he will be the more readily believed to be acquainted with the circumstances of the sick; so that men will have confidence to intrust themselves to such a physician. And he will manage the cure best who has foreseen what is to happen from the present state of matters. For it is impossible to make all the sick well. . . . Thus a man will be the more esteemed to be a good physician, for he will be the better able to treat those aright who can be saved, from having long anticipated everything; and by seeing and announcing beforehand those who will live and those who will die, he will thus escape censure [Adams, n.d., p. 194 f.].

The precaution against attempting to treat a patient who will die is given a social justification by Plato (Republic, III, 407):

> And therefore our politic Asclepius may be supposed to have exhibited the power of his art only to persons who, being generally of healthy constitution and habits of life, had a definite ailment; such as these he cured by purges and operations, and bade them live as usual, herein consulting the interests of the State; but bodies which disease had penetrated through and through he would not have attempted to cure by gradual processes of evacuation and infusion: he did not want to lengthen out good-for-nothing lives, or to have weak fathers begetting weaker sons;—if a man was not able to live in the ordinary way he had no business to cure him; for such a cure would have been of no use either to himself, or to the State [Jowett, 1908].

The social criterion of eligibility for medical attention has undergone further refinement in our own atomic age: the technique of *triage* is described as a culling of casualties so that limited supplies of blood plasma, etc. can be apportioned to those who are of the greatest value to the survival of society. "It will not be enough to decide whether or not a life can be saved" (DuShane, 1957). No doubt psychologists will have the task of providing criterion measures.

Hippocratic internal medicine could not, of course, be based on a knowledge of underlying pathology, for the anatomy and physiology then available were quite inadequate for such purposes. (It must be remembered that pathological anatomy was a development of the eighteenth century, and bacteriology of the nineteenth.) The only systems fairly well known were the skeleton and the muscles. The basic physiological doctrine was that of the four humors—blood, phlegm, yellow bile, and black bile—to which we referred in our discussion of Empedocles' doctrine of the four elements. As a theory of pathology, the humoral doctrine lasted into the seventeenth century and might be regarded as a foreshadowing of the concepts of endocrinology and biochemistry; after Theophrastus and Galen, it became also a dominant theory of temperaments. The emphasis on body fluids is understandable in view of the symptomatic significance, especially in the most prevalent diseases—chest troubles and malaria—of liquid excretions, expectorations, hemorrhages, vomiting, diarrhetic stools, etc., in which blood, phlegm, yellow bile, and "black bile" (i.e., black stools, urine, or vomit) are recognizable. The Pythagorean doctrine of an equilibrium or "isonomy" of body constituents which we encountered in Alcmaeon was applied by the Hippocratics to the humors: health depends upon the maintenance of the proper proportions of these juices, and disease results from various imbalances, such as might be caused by costiveness, plethora, fatigue, atmospheric conditions, improper diet, etc. The gastroetiologic explanation of disorders had been prominent in Egyptian medicine and is of course a very natural one; patients today are very likely to attribute their trouble to "something I ate"; hence the universality of purges (which are among the very few "specifics" observable in their physiological action by the layman). The notion that digestion was analogous to the cooking of foods whereby they were converted into a semifluid state was part of the background of the humoral theory. In Hippocratic medicine, recovery from a disease involved a "pepsis" (Latin

"coction"), a "cooking," digestion, or ripening of a morbid substance or excessive body constituent, which could then be eliminated, as by evacuation or abscession, so that the proper mixture
and balance of body humors could be restored; this process was
thought to be observable, e.g., in the progressive change in the
nature of phlegm—thickening and decrease in acridity—in the
course of a common cold, from onset to recovery.

The healing power of nature strives to restore a disturbed balance; the physician's task is mainly to provide a supportive therapy.
Therapeutics followed a policy of watchful waiting upon nature;
diet, waters, fresh air, purgation, massage, and supervised exercise
were favored over more radical interventions; the influence of
climate on health and personality was emphasized. If the physician
could not help nature he was at least to avoid doing injury; this
cautious and conservative approach was very wise in view of the
scanty knowledge of the time. There was emphasis on the observation and treatment of the total and individual patient. In areas of
modern medicine where there has been a comparable lack of knowledge, this same policy of watchful waiting has been considered
most judicious. Thus Clancy (1950, p. 50), describing the influenza
pandemic of 1918 as he saw it in a naval hospital, writes, "We could
only give general hygienic care, careful observation for complica-
tions, antipyretics, fluids, and be on the lookout for pneumonia."
"Watchful waiting" might also describe the so-called "non-direc-
tive therapy" of contemporary clinical psychology. In modern
medicine and psychology there has also been much emphasis on
the therapeutic value of paying attention to the patient as a whole
and as an individual; e.g., Powers (1957, p. 753) writes, "We have
observed repeatedly that if a boy or girl afflicted with acne is shown
that someone is genuinely interested, not only in his skin ailment,
but in him as a whole person, he will eagerly discuss his anxieties
and concerns. Through this process one can almost see the tension
disappear and the individual become more comfortable." Probably
a large percentage of the "cures" effected both by the Hippocratic
physicians and by modern general practitioners are attributable to
this general policy and approach, rather than to any specific treatments; the physiological operation of this therapy has been classically illustrated by Wolf and Wolff (1943). In Hippocratic writings
there was much emphasis on "psychological" factors: a kind and
understanding attitude of the physician; trust, hope, and cheerfulness on the part of the patient. Two passages have frequently been

quoted to illustrate the Hippocratic ethical attitude; from the *Aphorisms* (Adams, n.d., II, p. 192):

> Life is short, and the Art long; the occasion fleeting; experience fallacious, and judgment difficult. The physician must not only be prepared to do what is right himself, but also to make the patient, the attendants, and externals cooperate.

And from the *Precepts* (Jones, 1923, I, p. 319):

> Sometimes give your services for nothing, calling to mind a previous benefaction or present satisfaction. And if there be an opportunity of serving one who is a stranger in financial straits, give full assistance to all such. For where there is love of man, there is also love of the art. For some patients, though conscious that their condition is perilous, recover their health simply through their contentment with the goodness of the physician.

However, in admiring Hippocratic deontology we must not forget a qualification that applies equally to modern medicine: the individualized treatment, the careful supervision of diet and other regimen, the daily house calls, the expensive medicaments, the detailed patient-physician communications, were available to the wealthy minority, not to the poor majority; the physician, then as now, had to "meet his overhead," and only the rich could devote themselves to lengthy diagnosis and treatment. The aim of the physician's art, says Aristotle, is health, "but some men turn every quality or art into a means of getting wealth" (*Politics*, 1258a 10). (It is tempting, though of course quite unjustified, to see an unconscious symbolism in the caduceus, which is properly the attribute, not of the god of healing, but of Hermes, the god of business.) In Plato (*Republic*, III, 406D) we read:

> When a carpenter is ill he asks the physician for a rough and ready cure; an emetic or a purge or a cautery or the knife,—these are his remedies. And if someone prescribes for him a course of dietetics, and tells him that he must swathe and swaddle his head, and all that sort of thing, he replies at once that he has no time to be ill, and that he sees no good in a life which is spent in nursing his disease to the neglect of his customary employment; and therefore bidding goodbye to this sort of physician, he resumes his ordinary habits, and either gets well and lives, or, if his constitution fails, he dies and has no more trouble [Jowett, 1908].

As Sigerist (1951, p. 336) remarks, "Dietetics is a difficult art, even today when we possess the scientific foundation for it, because more than any other treatment it requires far-reaching adaptation to the individual's constitution and condition. All our norms and standards are based on average figures, and what may be good for one patient may have a totally different effect on another." It is doubtful whether most physicians today find it practicable to do more than to hand a diet sheet to the average patient. And as for indigent patients, Sigerist (1961, p. 72) points out that neither the physicians nor society in ancient Greece felt any responsibility for them. These are problems with which we today are, rather confusedly, struggling. And yet, with the above qualifications, it is perhaps just to say that, in comparison at least with modern "professional ethics," Hippocratic etiquette was more concerned with the welfare of the patients than with the fees and prestige of the doctors, although the most eloquent and most quoted deontological works —the *Oath*, *Precepts*, and *Laws*—are probably late, and expressive, respectively, of Pythagorean, Epicurean, and Stoic influences.

In modern medicine, after the triumphs of cellular pathology, bacteriology, and other laboratory research techniques, there have been reactions, often termed "Hippocratic revivals," toward renewed attention to clinical examination and the individual constitution—"the whole patient." This dilemma, which the individual practitioner must solve according to his own personality and training, is present also in contemporary clinical psychology, where a similar choice of emphasis must be made between "client-centered" and "test-oriented" procedures. An interaction between individualized medicine and technology may be in the making; Ledley (1959) in speaking of a suggested national health computer network "as a means for accumulating and recalling desired aspects of individual total medical records," remarks, ". . . . just the availability of the biochemical and physiological indices of an *individual's* normal state of health, which in general deviate from the *population* norms now used, may serve as an invaluable tool in instituting preventive measures *before* diseases occur, as well as in diagnosing disease states." The Hippocratic ideal would thus—ostensibly—be built into an electronic computer.

The quality of case-histories (objectivity, accuracy of observation) can be taken as one indicator of the state of medical science; those of the Hippocratic Collection were not equalled until modern times, so that here again we have evidence of the great waste of two millennia between the promising beginnings of science in ancient Greece and the resumption of progress in modern times. Such progress, we are reminded, is specific to times and places; it is not a universal characteristic of either man in general nor of certain races. Hence too extrapolation is unreliable, particularly now, when it begins to appear that scientific progress may be self-limiting.

The rational approach of Hippocratic medicine is illustrated in the essay on epilepsy, which is described as a disease of the brain, although it had traditionally been called "sacred" because it was thought to be inflicted by the gods. The author says,

> I am about to discuss the disease called "sacred." It is not, in my opinion, any more divine or more sacred than other diseases, but has a natural cause, and its supposed divine origin is due to men's inexperience, and to their wonder at its peculiar character. . . . My own view is that those who first attributed a sacred character to this malady were like the magicians, purifiers, charlatans, and quacks of our own day, men who claim great piety and superior knowledge. Being at a loss, and having no treatment which would help, they concealed and sheltered themselves behind superstition, and called this illness sacred, in order that their utter ignorance might not be manifest [Jones, 1923, II, pp. 139, 141].

By this insistence on natural causes the doctrine of the uniformity of nature was introduced into medicine, an achievement which in the opinion of at least one medical historian "marks the greatest revolution in the history of medicine" (Robinson, 1943, p. 51). This was in fact the great contribution of Hippocratic medicine to biological and hence to behavioral science: the introduction of the empirical, naturalistic, objectivistic attitude in the study of human beings. The attempt to hold to or to recapture this attitude seems to me to run through the entire varied history of naturalism, mechanism, materialism, determinism, positivism, anti-metaphysics, pragmatism, behaviorism, physicalism, the "unity of science" movement, etc. The contrasts have been mysticism, metaphysics, vitalism, animism, idealism, dualism, mentalism, supernaturalism, spiritualism, etc. For the progress of biological and psychological science the attitude has been far more important than any particular tenets (dependent as the latter are on the linguistic and instrumental techniques of a particular time), although controversy has been concerned chiefly with the latter.

The attitude is remarkably expressed in the Hippocratic treatise *On Ancient Medicine*. It consists, in the first place, of a polemic against "hypotheses" in medicine, by which the writer means unverifiable assumptions. We met in Alcmaeon the notion of man being related—structurally analogous—to the universe as microcosm to macrocosm. Some ancient philosophers held that understanding of man, the microcosm, could be attained only through knowledge of the universe, the macrocosm. To us, accustomed to the existence of the basic medical sciences, this may seem a not unreasonable point of view, but in the time of the Hippocratic writer there were no basic sciences but only inspired guesses about "elements" and assumed cosmic processes; i.e., metaphysical postulates. The method of philosophy consisted in deduction from such postulates. Not unjustifiably, therefore, the writer declared that these speculations had nothing to contribute to medicine; that, on the contrary, knowledge, not only of medicine but also of nature in general, was more likely to be gained from empirical study of the constitution of man. We may be reminded of the contrast in modern times between theoretical and clinical medicine; the difference is that modern theoretical medicine is "empirical" in that it is based on and tested by experiment, whereas the "empiricism" of the Hippocratic clinical approach consisted not in controlled but merely in "careful" observation. As for the biological and medical approach to the problems of nature in general, it will be recalled that we found this extensively exemplified by Anaxagoras, and characteristic of the fifth century.

The particular "hypothesis" attacked by the Hippocratic writer is that the causes of disease can be reduced to one or two, such as "heat" and "cold," in accordance with the old philosophical schemes of a primal substance and of "opposites." He treats heat and cold as symptoms rather than causes of disease; his discussion of body temperature suggests to us our concept of homeostatic regulation. The physician, he declares, must build upon the empirically accumulated knowledge of the medical art—upon a knowledge therefore of its historical development—which took its origin from human experience with dietetics; medicine began with trial-and-error experiences with foodstuffs and with methods of their preparation and compounding, and medicine must continue with research into the adjustment of dietary regimen to individual constitutions, visceral habits, and states of health or disease. Many constituents, not just one or two, must be blended in foods to match corresponding constituents in the human body. (Since there was available no chemical means of analysis, the "constituents" had of course to be discriminated in sensory terms: salt, bitter, sweet, acid, astringent, etc.) Here accuracy of measurement must be striven for, so as to minimize errors. Bad physicians are like bad steersmen, who do well enough in a calm:

> In the same way, bad physicians—and most of them are bad—so long as they treat patients with no serious illness, so that no great harm could be done by the worst blunders—such illnesses are common, occurring much more frequently among men than serious ones—under these circumstances do not manifest their blunders to laymen; but when they are faced with a severe, violent and dangerous illness, then their blunders and want of skill are obvious to everybody [*On Ancient Medicine,* Jones, 1946, p. 72].

This statement obviously also applies to modern medical practice, with the difference that the modern physician, having more medications and techniques at his disposal, can blunder in a greater variety of ways.

Moreover, says our author, the physician must strive for communication with his patient, which he cannot do if he talks metaphysics (or, we might add, if he talks scientific jargon). While the author himself makes use of "hypotheses" for which techniques of verification were not yet (and in some degree are not now) available, and was innocent of the modern concept of experimental test of theories, he was nevertheless a pioneer in scientific medicine. As Jones (1946, p. 47) says, ". . . he outlines and defends a scientific method which, we moderns are tempted to think, ought to have revolutionized Greek thought. That it did not do so was due to the power and influence of Greek philosophy, and especially to the persuasive dialectic and artistic skill of Plato." Most important was the positivistic attitude: everything necessary for the practice of medicine can be discovered if research continues on empirical lines. The author emphasizes what we would describe as the importance of discovering the physiological mechanisms underlying human reactions. "[The physician] must not be content with the unqualified statement that 'cheese is a bad food, for it gives a pain to the man who has eaten his fill of it.' We must know what the pain is, the reason for the pain and to what constituent of the man cheese is unsuitable" (*On Ancient Medicine,* Jones, 1946, p. 85). Without such knowledge the physician may confuse *post hoc* with *propter hoc.*

Similar views are expressed in the late Hippocratic treatise on the *Nature of Man,* where the belief that man is blended of various constituents is supported by the arguments that both diseases and their cures are various, that there must be a blending of constituents in sexual generation, that constituents are separated after death, that there are medicines whose specific effects are the elimination, respectively, of phlegm, yellow bile, and black bile, while a wound results in the flow of blood. These four humors, as they are properly blended or present in excess or deficiency, determine health or disease, and seasonal variations in the predominance of certain humors determine the incidence of various types of diseases. "The clearest proof is that if you will give the same man to drink the same drug four times in the year, he will vomit, you will find, the most phlegmatic matter in the winter, the moistest in the spring, the most bilious in the summer, and the blackest in the autumn" (Jones, 1931, p. 23). These observations are of course related to the predominance of respiratory and malarial diseases.

This is the treatise which translated the Empedoclean doctrine of the four elements into the medical doctrine of the four humors. In the treatise on *The Sacred Disease* there is a foreshadowing of the Galenic doctrine that excess of any of the humors produces the respective *temperaments*: sanguine, phlegmatic, choleric, and melancholic. The Hippocratic treatise speaks of hereditary phlegmatic, bilious, consumptive, and splenetic constitutions, and explains depressive and manic psychoses as resulting from excess of phlegm and of bile, respectively. In Book III of the pseudo-Aristotelian *Problems*, the first section discusses the influence of black bile on mood, temperament, and disease. (This work is a miscellaneous collection of questions and possible answers—probably lecture notes—of which the section here in question is thought to be genuinely Aristotelian [Hett, 1953, p. vii], perhaps attributable to Aristotle's successor Theophrastus [Sigerist, 1961, p. 324].) The physiological effects of black bile are said to vary with its quantity and temperature. It is "naturally cold," and if this cold bile is present in excessive amount, it produces despondency or fear; suicides are thus accounted for. (The name *melancholia* [Greek *melas* = 'black' + *chole* = 'bile'] was "probably . . . given to any condition resembling the prostration, physical and mental, produced by malaria, one form of which (the quartan) was supposed to be caused by 'black bile'" [Jones, 1923, I, p. lviii]). But if the bile is overheated, it produces, according to degree, cheerfulness, frenzy, or madness. The physiological effects of bile thus vary as do those of wine. These conditions may be temporary, in which case they constitute moods which condition reactions to situations; thus arise daily despondencies and elations for which we are unable to account. In some persons, however, these conditions may be constitutional and thus determine temperaments. Individuals who by constitution have an excess of cold bile are sluggish and stupid, while those with excessive hot bile are "mad, clever, or amorous," and may be seized with frenzy, as are soothsayers and inspired persons. Those in whom this latter condition is less excessive "are melancholic, though more intelligent and less eccentric, but they are superior to the rest of the world in many ways." This is the answer to the question with which the section begins: "Why is it that all men who have become outstanding in philosophy, statesmanship, poetry or the arts are melancholic, and some to such an extent that they are infected by the diseases arising from black bile?" Empedocles, Plato, and Socrates are cited as examples. "All melancholic persons are abnormal, not owing to disease but by nature." (Quoted translations from Hett, 1957). The doctrine of temperaments was crystallized in the second century A.D. by Galen. As usually stated, he attributed four different temperaments to excess of blood, phlegm, yellow bile, or black bile, which originated in the heart, brain, liver, and spleen, respectively. Actually, Galen added four intermediate temperaments and one dependent upon a perfect balance of the humors, so that he reached a total of nine (cf. Smith, 1930, and Greenwood and Smith, 1934). (Note that *temperament* is Latin *temperamentum* = "a mixing in due proportion," corresponding to Greek *krasis* = "a mixing of things so that they are blended to form a compound.") In his discussion of Albrecht Dürer's famous engraving *Melencolia I* (dated 1514), Panofsky (1948, pp. 156-171) points out that Marsilio Ficino, a fifteenth century Florentine Neo-Platonist, himself of melancholy disposition, having found consolation in the Aristotelian discourse on "melancholy by nature" as contrasted with the extreme melancholy of insanity, popularized the idea that melancholy was an attribute of genius, not a handicap to be hated and feared as it had been. Thus, ". . . the Aristotelian tenet that all great men were melancholics was twisted into the assertion that all melancholics were great men." In the sixteenth century it became fashionable to be melancholy. In modern times there occurred another twist whereby intellectual superiority was associated with emotional instability and incapacity for social "adjustment"; Terman's studies of gifted children failed to confirm such a constitutional association, but it is understandable that the peculiarities of environment and life history which seem to produce artists, scholars, and scientists might suggest it; a proclivity to read books might well, in our society, be equated with "queerness," an anti-social nature, and even constitutional inferiority.

As Allport (1937, p. 63 f. says, the humoral theory of temperaments "has endured from the dawn of history down to the latest text-book in psychology." It has been "reworked by Kant, Wundt, Ribot, Fouillée, Ribéry, Azam, Malapert, Paulhan, by Höffding, Bahnsen, Herbart, Külpe, Ebbinghaus, Meumann, Spurzheim and Klages." Allport suggests two reasons for this long life:

> In the first place, the happy guess that temperament, the emotional groundwork of personality, is conditioned above all else by body-chemistry has been increasingly borne out in modern research. In the second place, the four-fold classification of temperament is still useful, because of certain fundamental dimensions of emotional response that it implies, a fact that Wundt, of all the writers on the subject, seems most clearly to have perceived.

Allport points out that such "quantitative dimensions" as quick-slow versus strong-weak or excited-calm versus pleasant-unpleasant yield four-fold tables which can be interpreted in terms of the Galenic temperaments. Wundt's attempts to correlate his introspective "dimensions" with physiological measures constitute one of those blind alleys in experimental psychology for which he was notable. Allport's first reason is more impressive; for endocrinology and biochemistry in general have increasingly been found to provide explanations of "temperament," defined as constitutional emotional reaction tendencies.

In various books of the Hippocratic Collection we find passages of great interest for neurology and psychiatry. In *The Sacred Disease* a physiological explanation is given of epilepsy. Vessels lead up to the brain from all parts of the body; through them the air which enters the mouth and nose is distributed, first to the brain and then to the rest of the body. The air which enters the brain causes intelligence and movement of the limbs. But if phlegm produced in the brain flows downward in the vessels so as to obstruct the distribution of air and blood to the rest of the body, convulsions ensue. Convulsions and syncope are thus explained as resulting from respiratory-circulatory stoppage, or as we would say, asphyxiation. (Suffocation was no doubt suggested by the symptoms which are mentioned: e.g., choking, frothing at the mouth, rolling of the eyes, clenching of hands, gnashing of teeth, etc.) Apparently, observed fetal asphyxia had something to do with this explanation, for it is said to "begin in the embryo," so that there is a constitutional predisposition; the disease "attacks the phlegmatic but not the bilious." A proof of the theory is "that should minor veins be so compressed, when a man is lying or seated, that the breath cannot pass through the vein, a numbness immediately seizes him"; local paralyses and anesthesias result from local circulatory stases. Moreover, if the head of a goat which has been attacked by the disease is opened, "you will find the brain moist, very full of dropsy and of an evil odour." Chronic sufferers from the disease have a presentiment of an imminent attack.

The brain is described as "the most powerful organ of the human body,"

> for when it is healthy it is an interpreter to us of the phenomena caused by the air, as it is the air that gives it intelligence. Eyes, ears, tongue, hands and feet act in accordance with the discernment of the brain; in fact the whole body participates in intelligence in proportion to its participation in air. To consciousness the brain is the messenger. For when a man draws breath into himself, the air first reaches the brain, and so is dispersed through the rest of the body, though it leaves in the brain its quintessence, and all that it has of intelligence and sense [Jones, 1923, II, p. 179].
>
> Men ought to know that from the brain, and from the brain only, arise our pleasures, joys, laughter and jests, as well as our sorrows, pains, griefs and tears. Through it, in particular, we think, see, hear, and distinguish the ugly from the beautiful, the bad from the good, the pleasant from the unpleasant. . . . It is the same thing which makes us mad or delirious, inspires us with dread and fear, whether by night or by day, brings sleeplessness, inopportune mistakes, aimless anxieties, absent-mindedness, and acts that are contrary to habit. These things that we suffer all come from the brain, when it is not healthy, but becomes abnormally hot, cold, moist, or dry, or suffers any other unnatural affection to which it is not accustomed [Jones, 1923, II, p. 175].

Depressive insanity and "causeless distress and anguish" are caused by the chilling effect of phlegm on the brain, while mania and night terrors result from heating of the brain by an accession of bile or hot blood.

From the above it will be apparent that the Hippocratics had arrived at the conception of the brain as serving the functions of perception, motor control, memory, thought, and emotion, and of abnormal states of the brain as the causes of temporary or persistent behavioral aberrations. This was a remarkable achievement, but it was as far as they could go, for it was not until Erasistratus, in the third century B.C., that arteries, veins, and nerves were clearly distinguished and a beginning made in working out the relationship between central nervous system and periphery; and it was not until the discoveries of Galvani in the eighteenth century and of Helmholtz and du Bois-Reymond in the nineteenth that the concept of neural transmission as an electrical surface phenomenon rather than a flow of air or "spirits" through hollow vessels could begin to be developed. The latter developments had, of course, to await technological inventions.

Some miscellaneous clinical observations are of psychological interest. In the *Aphorisms* we find the following: a greater pain in one part of the body obscures a lesser pain in another; brain damage has as sequelae fever, vomiting of bile, stertorous breathing, and aphasia. In the treatise *On Joints,* the symptomatology of damage to the spinal cord is said to include anesthesia and paralysis below the lesion, and retention of urine and feces.

In the famous treatise on *Airs, Waters, Places,* there is a discussion of the relation not only of diseases but also of racial differences to topography, climate, season, water, food, and cultural factors. Individual differences are also emphasized. These are ideas ("environmentalism") which were reintroduced by modern anthropologists and psychologists—e.g., Franz Boas, J. McKeen Cattell, J. B. Watson, and, much earlier and without historical effect, the forgotten Samuel Stanhope Smith (1750-1819), who in other respects echoed Hippocratic principles; e.g., "No law should be admitted on hypothesis but should rest solely on an induction of facts." (On Smith, see Fay, 1939, pp. 61-67; Roback, 1952, pp. 38-43.)

6

Aristotle: The Linguistics
of Science

The words, the aphorisms, the distinctions, and even the ideas of Aristotle have in many instances become commonplaces in our culture and in other instances have been made the familiar whipping horses by which we castigate old errors and so boast of our own advances. It is wise to profit by our limitations and to make the familiar vestiges of a philosopher's thoughts in present-day inquiries and interests the beginning point of the study of his philosophy.—Richard McKeon: *The Basic Works of Aristotle*, p. ix.

Aristotle (384-322 B.C.) was born in the Macedonian city of Stagira, a center of Ionian culture on the northwest coast of the Aegean. His father was a physician to the king, and, as was the custom of ancient Greek medical fraternities, no doubt instructed the son in medicine. Aristotle, though he did not become a physician, was thus, like Alcmaeon, Anaxagoras, and Empedocles, an example of what we may be tempted to set up as a historical generalization; namely, that the men who have been most influential in the history of psychology have been trained in medicine. In contrast to Plato, Aristotle represented the Hippocratic medical rather than the Pythagorean mathematical tradition; Plato and Aristotle may be regarded as archetypes, respectively, of the mathematical a priori and the biological empirical tendencies. According to legend, Aristotle at the age of eighteen went to Athens and entered Plato's Academy, with which he maintained some association until

127

the death of Plato twenty years later. Aristotle then spent some five years on the northwest coast of Asia Minor, where Hermias—eunuch, financial genius, and alumnus of Plato's Academy—was for a time, until he was captured and crucified by the Persian king, ruler of a large domain. Here, and on the adjacent island of Lesbos, Aristotle did much of his biological field work. He was recalled to Macedonia as tutor to the future king, Alexander the Great, who for a short time was to be ruler of the ancient world. After three years in this post and some five additional years in Macedonia, he returned to Athens, where, in 335 B.C., at the age of forty-eight, he founded his own school in a gymnasium called the Lyceum; this school came to be known as the "Peripatetic," from a Greek word meaning "walking about," presumably because the lectures were often given in the course of a stroll about the establishment. Here a large organization was developed, with numerous teachers, regular lectures, a large library, and extensive natural science collections; in short, the first university.

The works of Aristotle have come down to us mostly in the form of a large, though incomplete, collection of lecture notes, written in a systematic and pedestrian style, with heads and subheads, which has prompted Bertrand Russell to call Aristotle "the first to write like a professor"; few professors, however, would wish to have their literary style judged by their lecture notes, and there is evidence that Aristotle did better in his written work.

It was in Aristotle's time that the Greek city-states, after incessant civil wars and intrigues of "patriots"—or "collaborators"—with the two rival foreign powers, Persia and Macedonia, finally lost their independence. When the Athenians rebelled against the king of Macedonia—Aristotle's former pupil and patron—Aristotle, accused of "impiety," as Socrates had been, had to leave Athens, and shortly thereafter died.

Beginning with Francis Bacon and Galileo, the rise of modern science has commonly been described as a struggle against Aristotle. Thus Russell (1945, p. 160): "Ever since the beginning of the seventeenth century almost every serious intellectual advance has had to begin with an attack on some Aristotelian doctrine." Boring (1950, p. 158) assures us that "We may even dare almost to ignore Aristotle"—although he follows this statement with a list of Aristotelian influences: on Descartes, William James, Hobbes, Locke, and on both association and gestalt psychology. Peters (1953, pp. 90-92) declares that Aristotle's claim to the title of founder of scientific method "rests on a slight misconception of science which dies very hard—the view that science is a vast body of knowledge accumulated by a laborious and systematic process of classification and definition." On the other hand, a philosopher whose intellectual progenitors were Peirce, Mead, and Dewey describes Aristotle as "the outstanding functionalist in the Western tradition," who "in modern terms . . . can be viewed as a behaviorist, an operationalist, and a contextualist, with a thorough-going philosophy of process" (Randall, 1960, p. 31). In large part the unfavorable judgments are stereotyped reactions against the ossification and distortion of Aristotelian doctrines in their transmission by a long line of Greek, Latin, Arabic, and Christian philosophers and theologians during the intervening two thousand years. They are also, however, a result of an overemphasis on Aristotle's metaphysical, astronomical, and—in our sense—physical works, and a neglect of his biological works. In evaluating references to Aristotle in the literature of psychology, it is well to remember the implications of the definition of a classic as "a work often cited but seldom read," and that secondary, tertiary, etc., sources are likely to be very unreliable. Historically-minded psychologists who have been influenced in their judgment of Aristotle by Bertrand Russell's lively *History of Western Philosophy* should note that Russell makes no mention of Aristotle's biological works.

The Linguistics of Science

In the word-magic of primitive peoples, isolated words, particularly names, are treated as having intrinsic significance and potency. Among the Greek philosophers—the Pythagoreans, Heraclitus, Parmenides, Plato—names became shadow-souls, more perfect and more real than the world of sensory experience. Aristotle has been severely criticized by various writers from the first century A.D. to modern times for his "verbal approach" to philosophical problems. Thus Mauthner (quoted by Ogden and Richards, 1947, p. 35) declared, "Aristotle is dead because he was, more than perhaps any other notable writer in the whole history of Philosophy, superstitiously devoted to words. Even in his logic he is absolutely dependent on the accidents of language, on the accidents of his mother-tongue." In a previous chapter I quoted Bloomfield's remark that "a good deal of what passes for 'logic' or 'metaphysics' is merely an incompetent restating of the chief categories of the philosopher's language." The recent wave of sophistication with respect to language has found expression, e.g., in the "Whorfian hypothesis" (Whorf, 1956, p. 214), according to which "all observers are not led by the same physical evidence to the same picture of the universe, unless their linguistic backgrounds are similar, or can in some way be calibrated." Many writers have regarded Aristotle as the fountainhead of the confusion which results from lack of linguistic sophistication. Russell (1945, pp. 201 f.), for example, in criticizing the Aristotelian concept of "substance," describes it as "a metaphysical mistake, due to transference to the world-structure of the structure of sentences composed of a subject and a predicate."

These are matters which should be and recently have been of lively interest to psychologists, for whom the following remarks of Ogden and Richards (1947, p. viii) may have a familiar ring:

> Nothing is commoner in discussion than to hear some point of difference described as purely or largely "verbal." Sometimes the disputants are using the same words for different things, sometimes different words for the same things. So far as either is the case a freely mobilizable technique of definition meets the difficulty. But frequently the disputants are using the same (or different) words for nothing, and here greater modesty due to a livelier realization of the language situation is recommendable.

Psychologists might well bear such cautionary remarks in mind when they encounter such terms as *personality, anxiety, psychic energy, intelligence, the unconscious,* etc. Some forty years ago, while I was listening to a seminar report which, after the fashion of the investigation of "emotions" by James and by McDougall, sought to distil from the—chiefly non-experimental—literature a definition of "intelligence," there occurred to me the simile of a clerk who, bundle of labels in hand, takes each label as a guarantee for the existence of one particular box which *when found* will yield a unique set of properties. It has often happened that scientists, sharing only a label, have disputed about its "real meaning."

Aristotle's Linguistic Predecessors

Our judgment of Aristotle's contribution to the logic of science becomes less censorious when we consider, on the one hand, what he received from his predecessors, and on the other, the failure of his successors—except, as we shall see, for the Stoics of the third century B.C.—for two thousand years significantly to advance his analysis. His logical writings, says Russell (1945, p. 202) "show great ability, and would have been useful to mankind if they had appeared at a time when intellectual originality was still active." We have in modern times learned the convenience of analyzing the totality of events determinative of science into a number of non-identical but functionally interrelated trains, particularly those designated as *environmental* (events external to the scientist), *neural* ("sensory" and "cognitive" events), and *linguistic* (symbolic socially interchangable utterances). The early Greek philosophers began the long struggle toward these distinctions. They saw the problem as the need to find something permanent in a world of continuous change. This "something permanent" was in fact *conceptual*, i.e., a product of human thought expressed in language, but the Milesian philosophers defined it in physical terms, or at least as analogous to a primary material substance. The distinction between sensory experience and thought was implied by Pythagoras, who made numbers and their relations the permanent ordering principles, and by Heraclitus, who contrasted the ceaseless change perceived by the senses with the universally valid formula or law of change apprehended by reason. The contrast was sharpened by Parmenides, for whom sensory experience was pure illusion and only thought could apprehend reality. Parmenides started from the premiss "What is, is" and proceeded "in much the same way as Descartes started from the premise 'cogito' . . . by the sole use of reason unaided by the senses, to deduce all that can be known about Being" (Kirk and Raven, 1960, p. 266). Thought thus becomes the only reality; it will be remembered that Democritus distinguished between "obscure" or unreliable knowledge gained by the senses and "genuine" knowledge gained by thought. But the contrast for Parmenides is not only between illusory senses and rational thought, but also between the "true thought" of Parmenides and "opinions," either those of other philosophers or else those which he himself finds it necessary to adopt "if he is to give an account of phenomena" (Kirk and Raven, p. 281). In either case, the validity of any given product of "reason" becomes a matter for debate or "dialectic." Zeno, the disciple of Parmenides, was called by Aristotle "the inventor of dialectic," but it was dialectic in the special sense of argument to show that a certain proposition leads to contradictory conclusions. This is therefore a purely logical, i.e., verbal, exercise; for the argument is not from premisses assumed by the logician to be true but from a proposition attributed by him to an opponent, and the purpose is to confound the opponent and to win plaudits from others—the technique often exemplified in the sequences of critique-reply-rejoinder in our journals. In spite of the ulterior motive, Zeno thus originated the technique of dealing with propositions, i.e., linguistic utterances, *as such,* and in particular, with the implicative relations of propositions.

Protagoras made explicit the relativity of thought, its dependence not only on sensory experience but also on the organization and state of the individual. To reconcile this relativity with the possibility of knowledge, he introduced the principle of intersubjective confirmation, which is a basic principle of modern science, although it is but little emphasized by the philosophers of science, who seem to proceed implicitly—whatever their explicit statements—on the assumption that statements are confirmed when evidence for them is found acceptable by an individual intelligence.

Gorgias raised explicitly the problem of the relations between concepts, things, and linguistic terms, pointing out that difficulties arise in determining whether given concepts do or do not correspond to realities, and that linguistic terms must not be identified with things. The lesser Sophists, by their incessant hairsplitting and attention to such linguistic matters as synonymy, definition, grammatical categories, and orthology, prepared the way both for logic and for linguistics in general.

In the period from the fourth century B.C. through the second century A.D. the Greek grammarians arrived at generalizations about language which "were not improved upon until the eighteenth century" (Bloomfield, 1933, p. 5). Their limitation was that their study was confined to their own language, of which they discovered the parts of speech, syntactic constructions, and inflectional categories. This limitation resulted in their tendency to confuse the structure of language with the structure of the universe, as in the doctrine of "opposites," the Platonic technique of "investigation" by dialectic, and the Aristotelian analysis in terms of the— Greek—syntax of subject and predicate. It was not until the eighteenth century, when European grammarians discovered the work of the Hindu grammarians, that comparative and historical grammar began that development which in the nineteenth century put an end to linguistic parochialism and made possible the study of language structure and of the processes of linguistic change as a specialized discipline disentangled from logic and metaphysics, a development which has been much accelerated within the past thirty years but which, because of cultural lag, has only recently begun to influence scientists of other disciplines and some philosophers and logicians.

Aristotle said that

> when Socrates was occupying himself with the excellences of character . . . it was natural that [he] should be seeking the essence, for he was seeking to syllogize, and 'what a thing is' is the starting point of syllogisms; . . . for two things may be fairly ascribed to Socrates—inductive arguments and universal definition, both of which are connected with the starting-point of science [*Metaphysics*, XIII, 1078b; transl. Ross].

Aristotle's appreciation must be qualified by the observation that Socrates' purpose was ethical and practical rather than theoretical, and that in consequence his "inductive" method was selective and his "universal" definitions were based on agreement elicited from disciples by a master. Nevertheless, as against the persuasive rhetoric of the philosophic monologue, he introduced the practice of examining terms and of seeking—at least ostensibly—conventions of usage by means of a technique of questioning "informants"—to borrow a term from linguistics.

Gorgias had drawn from the Eleatic doctrine of identity the consequence that nothing can be said; the same consequence had been drawn by Cratylus from the Heraclitean doctrine that everything is continually changing. Antisthenes, the founder of the Cynic school, who before becoming a disciple of Socrates had been a pupil of Gorgias, denied the possibility of predication; only purely identical judgments are possible. "Definition is merely a circuitous method of stating an identity: 'a tree is a vegetable growth' is logically no more than 'a tree is a tree.'" Definition and predication are either false or tautological, and universals have only subjective existence. "A horse I can see, but horsehood I cannot see" (*Encycl. Brit.*, 1911, *s.v. Cynics*). Only the simple things of sensory perception have real existence, and these cannot be further known or defined but only named. This was therefore the first appearance of *nominalism*, which reappeared as a highly controversial doctrine of medieval scholastic philosophy, most familiarly associated with the name of William of Occam (1280-1349), and which reappeared again in the "undefinable words" or "primitive concepts" of modern logical positivism, words which can be "defined" only by pointing (e.g., Kraft, 1953, p. 30). According to Antisthenes, a composite can be accounted for by enumerating its simple constituents: the whole is the sum of its parts, as a syllable is constituted by its letters.

These then were the issues in Plato's time: the intuition that something is permanent amid universal change; the relations between assumed external reality and two means of human apprehension: sensation and reason; the relations between things, concepts, and names. To these were added, for Plato, his own reaction against the intellectual and ethical relativism and scepticism of the Sophists, the influence upon him of Orphic-Pythagorean mysticism and numerology, and the model provided by Socrates of dialectic and definition in the service of morality and political "virtue." This last factor was especially potent because of the continued political and moral disintegration of Athens and Plato's own aristocratic predilection for an oligarchy of the socially elite. There was another more personal source of emotional reinforcement for Plato: his animosity not only against the Sophists in general but also against Antisthenes in particular; the latter wrote a polemic against Plato entitled *Sathon,* which Zeller (1955, p. 125) decorously translates "Bigtail" (Liddell and Scott, "a coaxing word of nurses to a boy-baby," derived from *sathē, 'membrum virile');* Plato replied with the bitter caricature of his *Euthydemus.* Of all this tangle of problems, influences, and prejudices, the issues that are still discussed in our "philosophies of science" are those of (1) the nature and source of "intelligible principles" and of their status and role in empirical science (cf., e.g., Frank, 1957); and (2) the relations between things, concepts, and words (cf., e.g., Morris, 1946; Ogden and Richards, 1947; Mandler and Kessen, 1959).

Plato's solution of these problems was based on his theory of ideas. The model here, as in Pythagoreanism and in most of the philosophy of science ever since, was mathematics and especially geometry. It seems "intuitively" to be the case that the evanescent, "phenomenal," or sensorimotor triangles which can be constructed of rigid materials or drawn on surfaces are somehow copies of an ideal "conceptual" triangle the sum of whose angles is "really" and not merely approximately 180 degrees. It is usual for our contemporary philosophers of science to seek in physical theory, from Newton to Einstein, the principles of scientific theory in general, and the overwhelming influence of relativity theory, non-Euclidean geometry, etc., finds expression in a reliance on geometry as the main avenue of methodological pedagogy (cf. Frank, 1957;

Nagel, 1961). Plato, however, extended his doctrine of ideas from mathematics to other spheres, including esthetics, ethics, and psychology: all abstract nouns—"beauty," "justice," "virtue"—represent, not generalizations produced by human organisms (as Antisthenes declared) but the only "true realities." "The chain that links science with philosophy" (Frank) could not be forged by Plato, who, as Frank (1957, p. 27) says,

> severely criticized those scientists who confirmed theorems of pure mechanics or mathematics by individual tests. According to Plutarch, "Plato inveighed against them with great indignation, as corrupting and debasing the excellency of geometry, by making her descend from incorporeal and intellectual to corporeal and sensible things." Whoever applied mechanical instruments in geometry had to "make use of matter, which requires much manual labor and is the object of servile trade."

If however we seek to disentangle from his mystical, ethical, and political preoccupations Plato's contributions to the historical development of logic, as they emerged in his latest dialogues, especially in the *Sophist*, we may note the following:

(1) He approximated the statement of the relation of logical subject to universal predicate. We can, contrary to Antisthenes, say, not only that A is A, but that, on the one hand, A is C and D and E, etc., and on the other, that B is also C or D or E, etc.

(2) He distinguished the logical copula from the verb which affirms existence. This was necessary because Parmenides had confused the existential with the predicative use of the verb; he assumed that to say that a thing *is* must mean that it *exists*, and that to say that a thing *is not* must mean that it *does not exist*. Plato pointed out that these expressions have meaning only in predications. The statement that A is not B says nothing about the *existence* of A; it says only that A is something *other than B*. We can say, therefore, that Plato initiated the analysis of *propositions*; that is, of those types of linguistic utterances which are called logical *forms*. Also (and paradoxically, in view of his metaphysics), he thus initiated that development of syntactic-semantic sophistication which eventually counteracted the primitive tendency to identify the structure of a particular language with the structure of the universe.

(3) He pointed out that truth and falsehood are attributes of propositions, not of terms (*Sophist* 261d-263d). In the Indo-European languages we have syntactic patterns of noun-verb (subject-predicate) which, generally, correspond to perceptual patterns: we

can say "A is (at this moment) sitting." But when we have once acquired such patterns, it is quite possible for us to say "A is (at this very same moment) flying." However, this latter statement is not only perceptually false, but it belongs to a universe of discourse such that it is one of many statements which are excluded by the former statement. Nevertheless it is possible for us to make false statements, and also, since thought is internal speech, to make false judgments. Moreover, since perceptual appearance is a mixture of sensation and judgment, it too may be either true or false. Thus Plato was the first to call attention to the "autonomous" uses of language; to the fact, that is, that when syntactic patterns have once been established in relation to the environment, human beings can use—play with and ring the changes on—these patterns independently of the environment. The fact that many such utterances do not correspond to the perceptually experienced environment may be expressed by the judgment of falsehood. Plato however was not aiming at a technique of perceptual confirmation; rather, he sought to demonstrate that a logical analysis of the implicative relations between propositions was possible and necessary; e.g., that any given positive predication implied many negative predications.

(4) He developed the form of dialectical argument (e.g., in the *Theaetetus*) which was the starting point of Aristotle's logic. In this sort of argument, a proposition—called a "hypothesis"—which a respondent has been induced to accept is shown by the questioner to have unacceptable consequences which require the rejection of the hypothesis. This is a verbal game played according to rules: the questioner having proposed a problem and the respondent having chosen a position, the questioner tries to find and ask a series of questions the answers to which will force the respondent to accept a conclusion contradictory to his original position; the form of the argument is 'If P then Q; but not-Q; therefore not-P.' This was the technique formalized by Aristotle in his *Topics*, which Kapp (1942, p. 17) calls "the first textbook of logic" and regards as the origin from which Aristotle developed the formal demonstrative or "apodeictic" syllogistic of the *Analytics* made familiar to us by modern textbooks of logic. "Thus it happened," says Kapp, " . . . that the original subject matter of logic was the 'dialectical syllogism,' the syllogism that develops in conversation." Its original contexts were probably the law courts and the "language arts" pedagogy of the Sophists. Plato regarded it as a method for seeking philosophical truth, for arriving at "true" definitions of such terms

as "virtue," "knowledge," and "justice." It was because of this origin in verbal gymnastics, Kapp suggests, that Aristotle's syllogistic was presented as a formal logic and not as a science of the laws of thought; ". . . logic was originally conceived as a science of what happens, not when we are thinking for ourselves, but when we are talking and trying to convince one another" (Kapp, p. 19). It was in later times that "psychological" schools arose—such as the "Port Royal logic" of 1662—which defined logic as "the art of thinking," and it was against these schools that modern formal logic reacted by asserting that logic is concerned, not with thought processes, but with propositions and their implications.

(5) He developed the "method of division"; that is, the analysis of a concept into species and subspecies by successive dichotomies which proceed from the general to the progressively more specific, a method which was to influence not only Aristotle but much later Galileo and Francis Bacon, and still later Brentano—through whose influence Carl Stumpf, as he mentions with some complacency in his *Autobiography* (1930), adopted it as the method of his doctoral thesis. Thus in the *Statesman*, Plato begins his definition of a statesman or king by distinguishing between pure and applied knowledge; a king is to be classed under the latter, whose representatives are in turn divided into those who initiate and those who transmit directives, etc.

(6) In his description of the process of "combination" (*Statesman* 278), Plato suggested the inductive method which William James characterized as "dissociation by varying concomitants," the process which for psychologists was classically exemplified in Hull's (1920) experiments on generalization induced by training in abstraction; Plato uses the illustration of children who have learned to recognize letters in short and easy syllables but still boggle at more difficult combinations; the teacher sets the easy beside the more difficult combinations and thereby shows the children by the comparison that the same character is to be found in various combinations.

The Logic of Aristotle

Having thus sketched the state which linguistic analysis had attained by the last quarter of the fourth century B.C., we turn now to the structure which Aristotle erected on this foundation. By way of motivation, we may remind ourselves that the logic which he invented not only finds—though often in a distorted form—a large representation in modern textbooks of logic, where it commonly precedes the presentation of the "symbolic" logic which originated in the nineteenth century with Boole and Frege, but is also a subject of serious discussion, pro and con, in contemporary works on the philosophy and logic of science, including some written by psychologists. Thus Kantor (1945, p. 46 f.) asserts that Aristotelian logic "comports with an objective psychology according to which psychological events are exclusively actions of organisms," and "anticipates by many a century a behavioristic assimilation of thinking with language." Lewin (1935), on the other hand, declares that psychology can advance only by throwing off the fetters of Aristotelian methodology based on the concept of class-membership. On a less serious but more widely influential level, Korzybski (1933) makes Aristotle the archenemy not only of scientific thinking but of sanity in general. As for the recent literature produced by logicians and philosophers, this contains surprises for the layman in these fields. We have relatively extensive writings of Aristotle, and commentators have had more than two thousand years to digest them. Yet an eminent logician, Lukasiewicz (1951), has recently argued for a rather radical revision of traditional notions of Aristotle's logic; these notions, he believes, are not authentically Aristotelian but of later origin, and their continued acceptance he attributes to philosophers and philologists ignorant either of the Aristotelian texts or of modern logic. One philosopher whom Lukasiewicz has convinced is Randall (1960); on the other hand, Kneale and Kneale (1962, p. 80 f.), in their very judicious and sober review of the history of logic, seem less impressed: "The result," they say, "is something of great interest but something very different from Aristotle's own conception of his work." Thus in trying to gain some impression of Aristotle's contribution to the logic of science, we must remember that there are disagreements not only between contemporary philosophers, logicians, and philologists, but also between representatives of each of these disciplines. In Chapter 1 we pointed out that each epoch tends to rewrite history: thus Aristotle's logic can hardly fail to undergo a repatterning when read by a modern logician, philosopher, or experimental scientist. The tenor of any account of a writer's work will depend upon the relative emphases placed on (1) an examination of his actual writings, (2) the tradition which has transmitted them, (3) the persistence in his writings of older views, and (4) his anticipations of formulations and methods now accepted. In the case of Aristotle, it seems to me more useful to emphasize his positive contributions than to deprecate his Platonic inheritance. It was no minor achievement for a pupil of the author of the *Timaeus* to initiate a program of scientific research; that this program was soon ended by conditions and interests incompatible with science was not the fault of the program but of political and economic factors.

In this and the following two chapters I have given what may seem a somewhat detailed account of Aristotle's contributions. I have done so because it has not seemed to me that most American psychologists are aware of the wealth of these contributions and of their relevance—and the relevance of the objective scientific attitude which they represent—to modern psychology. References to Aristotle in psychological works are as ritualistic as references to God in political oratory, but Aristotle seems to be read, if at all, only in excerpts or at brief second-hand. And though my account may seem overlong, I have in writing it felt despair of conveying the richness, acuity of observation, and analytic ingenuity of Aristotle's scientific works. To this felt difficulty has been added the uneasiness occasioned by my awareness of trespass upon areas of scholarship other than my own; my justification must be that Aristotle has seemed to me to have things to say to contemporary psychologists which the representatives of those other areas are not, in their turn, in a position to recognize in their relations to the current situation within psychology.

Aristotle developed his logic in a group of treatises which later came to be known as the *Organon* ("Instrument"), a title which expressed the Aristotelian view that logic furnishes the general rules—as we might say, the linguistic tools—of scientific method. His distinctive contribution was the form of argument known as the *syllogism*. Thus, suppose that we wish to prove, or demonstrate, the proposition 'All S is P,' where S stands for the subject and P for the predicate of this proposition. We can show the *validity* of this proposition *as the conclusion of an argument* if we can find a *conjunction* of two other propositions (*premisses*) which will necessarily *imply* the proposition in question; the implication will depend upon the fact that the two premisses contain a common "middle term" M, whereby S and P are related or "linked" in certain required ways. For example, one of the valid argument forms is: 'If every M is P and every S is M, then every S is P.' Aristotle made a thorough analysis of the various types of syllogisms resulting from the possible combinations of the various kinds of propositions as premisses: *positive* ('All *A* is *B*' or 'Some *A* is *B*') versus *negative* ('No *A* is *B*' or 'Some *A* is not *B*'), and *universal* ('All *A* is *B*' or 'No *A* is *B*') versus *particular* ('Some *A* is *B*' or 'Some *A* is not *B*'). He examined the validity of the syllogisms yielded by the various possible pairs of premiss-forms and formulated rules for judging the validity of categorical arguments. He distinguished between demonstrative and dialectical argument: in the former, the premisses must be true and necessary; in the latter, they are assumed for the sake of argument. But in science Aristotle was concerned with proof and hence with demonstrative argument; not only must the argument be valid but its premisses must be true.

By his introduction of letters as *variables* in syllogistic arguments, Aristotle became the founder of formal logic. The relationship-pattern of letters represents the *form* of an argument, abstracted from any *content* or subject matter. The validity or invalidity of such an argument depends exclusively upon its form. Concrete general terms—words having definite meanings—may be substituted for the variables of the formal argument, provided the same term is always substituted for the same variable; the validity of the argument will then still be that of its form. Thus a system of abstract syntactic patterns of arguments of known validity or invalidity can be used to test the validity of arguments whose concrete terms might otherwise predispose to fallacies. Here as in mathematics, which served as the model for ancient logic and deductive system-building, formal relations can be clearly seen and expressed only by the use of symbols devoid of concrete reference. It seems just, therefore, to credit Aristotle with a major invention in the history of thought.

For Aristotle, the syllogistic demonstration of propositions is possible in a *perfected* science, for which the model is geometry, in which theorems are demonstrated from initial axioms and definitions. In such a science, an observed fact can be explained or given systematic status by deriving it in accordance with logical principles from basic or "ultimate" premisses which are intuitively true and are not themselves derived from more universal propositions. The ultimate premisses are axioms and not mere postulates; they are "first causes," which cannot themselves be logically demonstrated.

But while this method would be appropriate to a finished science, it is not the method of Aristotle as a practitioner of natural science, nor of Aristotle in his later, post-Platonic period, according to Jaeger (1962). The "ultimate premisses" of Aristotle's syllogistic become, in his works on natural science, hypotheses to be tested by the facts of observation. Whereas in logical demonstration we proceed from true premisses to valid conclusions, in empirical research we proceed in the reverse direction: from repeated observations of facts we capture, by acts of insight, laws or principles of relationship. Such acts of insight or "intuitive reason" might be regarded as examples of the "aha phenomenon" of modern gestalt psychology: a perceptual "snapping together" or "seeing the point." However, Aristotle seems less of a nativist than the gestalt psychologists; he does not regard knowledge of ultimate universal propositions as innate; such knowledge results rather from the fact that in man sense impressions leave memory traces, and "from memory, experience is produced in man; for the several memories of the same thing produce finally the capacity for a single experience" (*Metaphysics* A 980). "Thus it is clear that we must get to know the primary premisses by induction; for the method by which even sense-perception implants the universal is inductive" (*Post. Analytics* II, ch. 19, 100b). That is, "intuitive" principles are products of perceptual, mnemic, and generalizing operations. Very cogently, Randall (1960, p. 45) observes:

> Aristotle's formulation was taken over by the great scientific pioneers of the seventeenth century, from Galileo and Newton on. Their method was to take a few instances, like that of the ball rolling down an inclined plane, and to analyze those instances, in order to "see" the mathematical relations involved. . . . How, then, is the relation or law seen there in the instance to be proved to be true? By "experience"? No, experience can only "illustrate" the law, it cannot prove its truth. One or two crucial instances will suffice to "reveal" the law, and make us "recognize" its truth. No matter what their theory of method, scientists have always done something just like this. . . .

We find very similar descriptions of scientific method in the writings of contemporary experimental psychologists. Thus Hebb (1958, pp. 213, 217) distinguishes between "Two modes of thought: (1) *discovery* or invention, the attaining of new ideas, and (2) *verification*, the process of testing, clarifying and systematizing them."

> . . . scientific generalizations or laws are not arrived at by a slow process of accumulating cases and gradually formulating the idea, with increasing confidence in it as the number increases. Instead, the conclusion is likely to be formulated on the basis of one or two cases,

and the remaining cases are gathered *in the light of that idea,* as a means of testing it or of convincing others of its value.

One of the chief features of Aristotle's logic to which Lewin (1935) objected was the doctrine that the classification of an object defines its essential nature and consequently its behavior. The purpose of Aristotelian demonstrative science is to explain things by showing their position in the structure of the world, a structure characterized by certain essential properties. Thus we would account for man by classifying him in the genus which has the essential property of being *animate,* and in the species which has the essential property of being *rational*; all other properties of man would be said to follow from these classifications. Kneale and Kneale (1962, p. 94 f.) point out that for Aristotle a definition is not, as in modern usage, a linguistic convention, but is either correct or incorrect, and a correct definition is a true proposition which can serve as a premiss in demonstration; it is the predication of a universal or common nature. "Here, as in Plato's work, we have the picture of a chain of universals connected by definitions, and their necessary connexions are supposed to make possible the demonstrative, syllogistic reasoning of science." In addition to these essential properties inseparable from class membership, an individual thing has of course "accidental" qualities and relations. But these are not the concerns of science, which deals with regularities—"statistical averages"—in a world characterized also by contingency and "chance." As E. R. Guthrie used to say, "There can be no science of the unique." The writings of Guthrie (e.g., 1935), whose influence on recent psychological theory is well known, are of especial interest in this connection because they reflect an unusual training in the Greek texts of Aristotle and Plato, in modern formal logic, and in the philosophy of science, all of which were brought to bear on the great transformation of psychology of the 1920's and 1930's. Observation of a species, whether rats, monkeys, or men, can yield, he says, "a great deal of important information concerning what to expect of members of that species." It is true that Guthrie's main intent is to show that "there is a source of information still more important. *This source is the past history of the individual man.*" But as Guthrie pointed out, the principle of associative learning was invented by Aristotle, and the laws of learning "will constitute our explanation of learning, for all scientific explanations are nothing more than generalized laws or rules which cover the event needing explanation." That is, science can explain things only by referring them to classes. To all of this Lewin vigorously objected; for him, Aristotle's doctrine was the origin of what he regarded as the unfortunate habit of modern psychology to think in terms of classes and averages and to neglect individual cases and isolated events. Nagel (1961, p. 30, *note*) points out that among the laws which are tacitly assumed in scientific explanations are those which assert that there are various "distinct kinds of substances, each of which exhibits certain fixed concatenations of traits and modes of behavior." He states that ". . . the history of science repeatedly confirms the view that the noting and mutual ordering of various kinds—a stage of inquiry often called 'natural history'—is a prerequisite for the discovery of more commonly recognized types of laws and for the construction of far-reaching theories." ". . . some of the social sciences," he observes, "are still struggling to achieve usable and reliable formulations of kinds of human beings and of social institutions." On the other hand, Lewin's thesis might be thought equivalent to Nagel's statement that "general principles alone do not determine any individual case"; the explanation of such a case requires the statement also of "initial conditions," i.e., of particular circumstances. Nevertheless, a scientific explanation *must* include a universal law among its premises. It is interesting to note that Guthrie also emphasized the necessity of observing and specifying "particular circumstances," the particular sequences of stimuli and movements of given individuals on specified occasions (e.g., Guthrie and Horton, 1946), in explaining the performances of individuals.

Randall (1960, pp. 51-56) summarizes Aristotle's method of investigating any given subject matter: a preliminary survey to delimit the object to be investigated, a survey of previous hypotheses, a dialectical examination of these hypotheses for contradictions in logic or fact, an objective investigation of the relevant facts in order to discover their natural connections, and, finally, the formulation of principles which account for the observed facts in an intelligible, clear, and logically satisfactory manner, and which fit in with other principles. Until explanations satisfy these specifications, they must be regarded as tentative hypotheses. In view of this admirable methodology, Randall (pp. 56-58) asks why Aristotle failed to make some "obvious"—to us—discoveries and made some egregious errors: e.g., he accepted spontaneous generation, and stated that the back of the head of all animals is empty and hollow, that man has only eight ribs, and that the heart is the organ of intelligence. Randall's explanation, which may seem surprising in view of Aristotle's traditional reputation as the fountainhead of the deductive method in scientific explanation, is that "Aristotle was too much of an empiricist."

> All of Aristotle's errors of fact are due to his confidence in observation, in what "we see," combined with the lack of any instruments of observation, and consequently the lack even of any sense of the need of instruments, or of their very possibility. . . . Modern science represents the triumph of rationalism, of theory, over the mere observation of facts. As . . . James B. Conant . . . has put it, the advance of science means the reduction of the element of "empiricism" in the body of science, its replacement by rational theory, its "formalization," we say [p. 56].

The "facts" of a science, Randall says, are not actually "hard data"; they are continually being altered by improvement of instruments and evolution of theories. The methodological model which these statements imply is of course that of modern physical science, which has created a universe in equations; and historically behind this model is the geometric model of Pythagoras, Plato, and the Aristotle of the *Analytics*. But as for us, we must ask, What is the relevance of such a model, and of Randall's explanation, to biology and psychology? Some one hundred years before Aristotle, Alcmaeon had observed the relation of the sensory nerves to the brain and had concluded that the brain was the organ of sensory integration and storage; this discovery, it would seem, was a triumph not of rationalism but of observation. The errors concerning men's ribs and heads resulted from failures of observation. So far as biology and psychology are concerned, the lack of instrumentation was not a handicap because it prevented "mathematical formulations" but because it limited observation; moreover, the initial observations which launched these sciences were not mediated by what we call "instruments" in the modern sense: I refer to the researches of Alcmaeon, Herophilus, Erasistratus, Galen, and Vesalius. As far as I can see, the beautiful researches of Sherrington and his associates (e.g., Creed et al., 1932), in spite of their instrumentation, were closer to the methodology of Aristotle than to that of Einstein. In psychology there has been a vast effort to achieve formalism by means of quantification, but in the investigation of the basic principles of the behavior of animals as biological organisms the model of physical science seems hardly relevant; the techniques are complex, but the "rationalism," "formalization," and mathematics, so far as they are at present fruitful, are relatively simple.

Nagel (1961, pp. 42-46) discusses the epistemic (cognitive) requirements for explanations which were stipulated by Aristotle (*Post. Analytics,* Book 1, Ch. 2); namely, that the premisses of a deductive explanation must be true, must be known to be true, and must be better known than that which is to be explained. Nagel points out that "The truth of the premisses is undoubtedly a desirable condition for satisfactory explanations," since otherwise "only a moderate logical and mathematical ability would be required for explaining any fact in the universe without leaving one's armchair" (p. 43). Nevertheless, he says, there are "competent thinkers" who deny that universal statements which are part of a scientific theory can appropriately be characterized as either true or false. (Among these thinkers are presumably those psychologists who assert that it is inappropriate to raise the question of the biological truth or falsehood of Freudian pseudobiological and mythological figures of speech as premisses of behavioral explanations.)

Aristotle's requirement that the premisses must be *known* to be true, Nagel points out, is so strong that it would eliminate most explanations, and he therefore proposes the weaker stipulation that the explanatory premisses (a) must be compatible with established empirical facts, and (b) must be adequately supported by evidence other than that used to establish the explicandum. It might be observed that *in practice* Aristotle's "strong" stipulation would probably be equivalent to Nagel's weaker one, and that Aristotle was quite aware of the fallacies of circularity and of *post hoc*. It is most basically on these grounds that many psychologists reject the arguments for "parapsychological" phenomena; on the grounds, that is, that the premisses are incompatible with the facts of neurophysiology and of physics. The argument that at some future time the premisses may be confirmed by the discovery of some at present unknown form of energy does not satisfy this stipulation.

Aristotle's requirement that the premisses in a scientific explanation must be "better known" than the explicandum Nagel attributes to the model of geometry, where the premisses are (or once were thought to be) "self-evident" axioms. "This conception is true of nothing that can be identified as part of the asserted content of modern empirical science" (Nagel, p. 45). Nevertheless, many contemporary scientists would agree with Bridgman's (1936, p. 63) statement that an "Explanation consists merely in analyzing our complicated systems in such a way that we recognize in the complicated system the interplay of elements already so familiar to us that we accept them as not needing explanation." But this conception of explanation, says Nagel (p. 46) "is in patent disaccord with the fact that throughout the history of science explanatory hypotheses have frequently been introduced which postulate modes of interrelation between assumed elements, where the interrelations and elements are initially strange and occasionally even seemingly paradoxical." However, we must ask, strange when and to whom? Bridgman (1927, p. 42) remarked:

> Whenever experience takes us into new and unfamiliar realms . . . the only sensible course is . . . to wait until we have amassed so much experience of the new kind that it is perfectly familiar to us, and then to resume the process of explanation with elements from our new experience included in our list of axioms. Not only will observation show that this is what is now actually being done with respect to quantum and gravitational phenomena, but it is in harmony with the entire spirit of our outlook on nature. All our knowledge is in terms of experience; we should not expect or desire to erect an explanatory structure different in character from that of experience.

We might say that a *hypothesis* becomes an *explanation* when it has been so thoroughly grounded in evidence that its premisses have acquired axiomatic familiarity for those who are competent to offer or to accept the explanation; whether the premisses are still strange to laymen is quite irrelevant.

The interrelationships of language, thought, and reality were left unsettled by Plato and Aristotle. Plato sometimes seemed to identify thought with speech and to attribute truth or falsehood to *sentences,* defined as consisting of at least one noun and one verb, but he also spoke of truth or falsehood as characterizing *thought,* conceived as an activity of the soul; these two views, the linguistic and the "psychological," have been associated in the history of logic with the words 'sentence' and 'judgment,' respectively. Plato however also asserted that the true relationships studied by philosophy subsist between real entities, the Platonic 'forms,' existing independently of human thought, which may discover but cannot create them. "Plato seems to hold that a sentence is true if the arrangement of its parts reflects or corresponds to a connexion between Forms" (Kneale and Kneale, 1962, p. 20).

In what seems to be the earliest of Aristotle's logical works, the *Categories,* he attempts a basic classification (*substance, quantity, quality, relation, place, time,* etc.), but whether of linguistic symbols or of the "things" which they symbolize has ever since been debated; Kneale and Kneale (1962, p. 27) are of the opinion that

Aristotle himself would have asserted that he was dealing with things rather than with words, and that "he uses the differences between rules for different linguistic expressions as a clue to the differences between types of being." They suggest further (p. 29) that this analysis served Aristotle as a refutation of the Platonic doctrine of "forms." Whereas Plato treated the "forms" as substances capable of independent existence, Aristotle maintained that only "primary substances" (i.e., individual concrete things as contrasted with classes or properties) are capable of independent existence. That this was a necessary correction of a Platonic aberration seems none the less obvious because Aristotle himself did not succeed in freeing himself wholly from the Platonic doctrine, as in his classing species and genera as "secondary substances." And finally, Kneale and Kneale (p. 32) point out that "the *Categories* seems to be the first attempt at what has recently been called a theory of type-distinctions, that is to say a theory in which entities are classified according to what can be said about them significantly." Sentences may be grammatically correct without being "meaningful"; thus there is no meaningful way of completing the sentence: "The opposite of man is. . . ." Here again we have the problem which arises from the "autonomy" of language; having learned to talk in interaction with an environment, we can "play" with our language in accordance with all of the syntactic permutations and combinations which the evolved formal "rules"—the neurally built-in "computer instructions"—of our language permit; but these are linguistic, not logical nor empirical rules.

Linguistic matters are discussed by Aristotle in his *De Interpretatione*. Here he says that "Spoken words are the symbols of mental experience. . . . Just as all men have not the same writing, so all men have not the same speech sounds, but the mental experiences which these directly symbolize are the same for all. . . ." Here we have the "expressive" theory of language made familiar to psychologists by Wundt's *Voelkerpsychologie,* and we have also the problem of biosocial equivalence (Weiss, 1929, pp. 84 ff.). With this nest of problems—the relations between language, thought, and "things," the nature of concepts, generalizations, and abstractions, how the "same ideas" may be "expressed" by different utterances (in the same or different languages)—men have wrestled in the intervening centuries. Very recently such work as that of Penfield (e.g., Penfield and Roberts, 1959) has offered hope that we shall eventually have an objective physiological account of the relations among percepts, concepts, and speech mechanisms. But this will not obviate the necessity of a *modus operandi* in the linguistic methodology of science, which must be adapted to the facts that there is not available a practical technique of *identifying* "thoughts" and that biophysically different utterances may be biosocially equivalent. The practical result has been that logic has dealt not with thoughts but with utterances; it is a set of techniques of linguistic analysis. Aristotle's attempts to deal with these problems of semantics (and particularly with the criterion of "truth") led him to several other positions. (1) He repeated Plato's statement that truth or falsehood can be predicated only of syntactic combinations (noun-verb), not of words as such. (2) He settled the debate of the *Cratylus* by asserting that words are significant by convention and not by a "natural" relation between sound and meaning. (3) He anticipated modern logic in ascribing truth or falsehood only to declarative sentences (not to questions, commands, etc.). (4) He did not succeed in anticipating later logic with respect to the principle of "Excluded Middle," which asserts that every statement of the form "Either p or not-p" (where *p* symbolizes a declarative sentence) is true (is a tautology). Aristotle was troubled by the fact that such sentences as 'Man is beautiful' and 'Man is not beautiful' are both true, and he was particularly troubled by statements about the future, as appears in the following:

> A sea-fight must either take place tomorrow or not, but it is not necessary that it should take place tomorrow, neither is it necessary that it should not take place, yet it is necessary that it either should or should not take place tomorrow. . . . This is the case with regard to that which is not always existent or not always non-existent. One of the two propositions in such instances must be true and the other false, but we cannot say determinately that this or that is false, but must leave the alternative undecided. . . . It is therefore plain that it is not necessary that of an affirmation and a denial one should be true and the other false (*De Interpretatione*, 9, 19a30 ff.).

This quandary involved for Aristotle, and later for the Stoics and the Epicureans, the problem of determinism. For if a statement about the future is either true or false then "nothing is or takes place fortuitously . . . and there are no real alternatives; everything takes place of necessity and is fixed." Hence, "There would be no need to deliberate or to take trouble, on the supposition that if we should adopt a certain course, a certain result would follow. . . ." But this view, Aristotle says, "leads to an impossible conclusion; for we see that both deliberation and action are causative with regard to the future, and that, to speak more generally, in those things which are not continuously actual there is a potentiality in either direction. . . . It is therefore plain that it is not of necessity that everything is or takes place; but in some instances there are real alternatives, in which case the affirmation is no more true and no more false than the denial. . . ." (ibid., 9, 18b5 ff.). The problem here is one of semantics and pragmatics rather than of syntactics; it would not arise in a formal logic dealing only with the relationships among symbols, just as similar problems do not arise in mathematics nor in "structural" or "descriptive" linguistics; thus Harris (1951): "Descriptive linguistics . . . deals not with the whole of speech activities, but with the regularities in certain features of speech. These regularities are in the distributional relations among the features of speech in question, i.e., the occurrence of these features relatively to each other within utterances" (p. 5). "In principle, meaning need be involved only to the extent of determining what is repetition" (p. 7, note 4). But logic like linguistics has in addition to its formal also a semantic interest. Aristotle, and the Stoics after him, felt it necessary to deal with the lack of correlation between "sentences" and "meanings": e.g., 'I am at home' may be true at one time and not at another, or true when spoken by one person but not when spoken by another; it may or may not "mean the same thing" as 'I am here,' which may be said to "mean the same thing" as 'Ich bin hier' or 'Me voici.'

The solution of Aristotle's quandary adopted by modern logic is stated by Kneale and Kneale (1962, p. 51) thus:

> By introducing the phrase 'it is true that' we make no assumption about determinism which is not made by use of the simple sentence in the future tense. We mislead ourselves, however, when we speak, as Aristotle does, of its being true *now* that there will be a naval battle tomorrow, for we thereby induce ourselves to suppose that *this* will not be true tomorrow evening, when the battle is over, but something else will, i.e., 'There has been a naval battle today.' Two different *sentences* are plainly involved here, but they both express the same proposition in the sense that to convict any person who uttered either of error would also be to convict of error any person who uttered the other at the appropriate time.

Modern textbooks tell us that the concern of logic is not with sentences but with propositions, and a proposition is defined as "the content of meaning of a declarative sentence, i.e., a postulated abstract object common not only to different occurrences of the same declarative sentence but also to different sentences (whether of the same language or not) which are synonymous or, as we say, mean the same *thing*" (Church, in Runes, 1942, s.v.). The problems of meaning, translation, and synonymity have of course been debated for at least two and a half millennia, and recently have been making difficulties for the engineers of "machine translation." But operationally, at least in dealing with natural languages, the logician like the linguist must ask an "informant"—himself or others —the question, "Is this utterance the same or different?" It is a problem, that is, of biosocial equivalence, and the testing instruments are human nervous systems. Since a science is a social institution, there must be agreement among "calibrated"—relevantly competent—individuals. The esoteric quality of some writings on the philosophy of science perhaps results from the use of a single "informant"—the philosopher himself; philosophers perennially return to Descartes' *cogito* in the hope of gaining a fresh running start toward the goal of a soundly verbalized universe; like their Greek ancestors, they hope to build a universe out of symbols for personal, subjective intuitions, sense-data, images, "direct acquaintance," beliefs, judgments, and similar operations or affections of an "I." So far as science is concerned, it seems more useful to start from the principle stated by Urban (1939, p. 14): "All knowledge, including what we know as science, is, in the last analysis, discourse"; in which we can take "discourse" to imply that the statements of science describe, not the privately "experienced" worlds of individual philosophers, but the linguistically shared world of scientists. Hence I doubt the utility, for science, of an "ideal" or "improved" or "properly functioning" language (Bergmann, 1957; cf. Russell, e.g., 1921, 1940). Kapp (1942, p. 55 ff.), in his discussion of Plato's method in the *Sophist*, remarks that "you need a second person." Kapp has vigorously argued for the thesis that the logic of Plato and Aristotle owes its character to its origin in dialectic; that is, in the question-and-answer of a social teaching-and-learning situation; and that therefore "there are very few reflections on solitary thinking in the whole of Aristotle's logical writings" (p. 86). *Contra* J. S. Mill, Kapp observes,

> If logic really does not interest itself in the means of imparting knowledge to others, it should be on its guard in dealing with definitions, propositions, syllogisms, and induction; their immediate use for our own knowledge may be more limited than even the most cautious modern logician would suspect, as long as he ignores their history [p. 87].

The Stoic school, founded by Zeno of Citium (c.336-c.264 B.C.) and notably represented by Chrysippus (280-207 B.C.), was much concerned with the problems of meaning and truth. The Stoics introduced a number of important distinctions: (1) between "speech" as sound and "discourse" as meaningful utterance; (2) between speech' sounds and their written symbols (which we still find confused by the makers of "nonsense syllables" and other linguistically unsophisticated persons); (3) between what Ogden and Richards (1947, p. 11) diagrammed as (a) "symbol," (b) "thought or reference," and (c) "referent." Kneale and Kneale (1962, p. 140) quote Sextus:

> The Stoics say that three things are linked together, that which is signified, that which signifies, and the object; of these that which signifies is speech, as for example "Dion," that which is signified is the thing itself which is revealed by it and which we apprehend as subsisting with our thought but the barbarians do not understand, although they hear the spoken word, while the object is that which exists outside, as for example, Dion himself. Of these two are corporeal, that is, speech and the object, while one is incorporeal, that is, the thing which is signified, i.e., the *lekton*, which is true or false.

Kneale and Kneale (p. 141) point out that "In being incorporeal, *lekta* are exceptional in Stoic metaphysics; for in general the Stoics were materialists who believed that even the soul was corporeal." This is a linguistic paradox which we still find it difficult to avoid; it is built into our language almost as inescapably as are our grammatical genders and tenses, so that, just as Descartes (*Meditations* VI) speaks of processes in the brain which "give rise" to processes "in the mind," so a modern biochemist, in proposing a theory, based on detailed evidence, in which "anesthesia is attributed to the formation in the brain of minute hydrate crystals"—a theory and area of research which could scarcely be more "materialistic"—finds it natural to assume that consciousness "involves" electric oscillations in the brain (Pauling, 1961). The fact that objective criteria of anesthesia are available and used does not overcome the compulsions of language based on the traditional analogy of the self. It seems impossible not to say that the anesthetized subject "loses consciousness"; similarly, the rapid development of physical science in the nineteenth century did not prevent the intrusion of theological language into physical contexts. Joule (1847), in presenting the principle of the conservation of energy, which along with Wöhler's (1828) synthesis of an organic compound, was basic in establishing the physiochemical view of biological processes, wrote this sentence:

> And though, as in the awful vision of Ezekiel, "wheel may be in the middle of wheel," and everything may appear complicated and involved in the apparent confusion and intricacy of an almost endless variety of causes, effects, conversions, and arrangements, yet is the most perfect regularity preserved—the whole being governed by the sovereign will of God.

Like the early Greek philosophers, the early modern—and not a few contemporary—physicists were constrained by the traditional theological patterns of their language.

The Stoic *lekton* is translated by Kneale and Kneale (p. 140) as 'what is meant'; it is "to be distinguished from any spoken sounds, words, or sentences," but "can be identified only by use of a word or sentence which expresses it" (p. 143); it seems therefore to correspond to Ogden and Richards' "thought or reference," and, in terms of modern neurophysiology, to patterns of "electric oscillations in the brain." It is a special kind of *lekton,* the *axioma* ('assertion'), which is said to be true or false; being a *lekton* and therefore 'what is signified' rather than any particular sentence which signifies, it comes close to the modern "proposition," with which, however, it is not identical. "What a sentence means . . . [in the view of the Stoics] is what a person means when he utters it. And what a person means when he utters a sentence includes what he expresses by mood and tense" (Kneale and Kneale, 1962, p. 157). "A *lekton* is the result of abstraction from particular forms of linguistic expression. It is what remains constant in translation from one language to another. But a proposition is the result of a further abstraction from the time and circumstances of utterance" (ibid., p. 158). This seems to be the point of Bergmann's (1957, p. 45) chameleonic lobster, and of his assertion that the "ideal language" must be "phenomenalistic," an assertion whose language seems "philosophical" rather than logical.

Whereas Aristotle had dealt with the logic of general terms, the Stoics dealt with the logic of propositions; the latter is the more fundamental and has developed into the modern calculus of propositions. While an Aristotelian syllogism is exemplified by 'If every M is P and every S is M, then every S is P,' where the letters represent variables marking gaps to be filled by *general terms,* a Stoic argument is exemplified by 'If the first, then the second; but the first; therefore the second,' where the numerals represent variables marking gaps to be filled by *propositional signs*. The basic Stoic argument forms include the familiar 'modus ponens' and 'modus tollens.'

Kapp (1942, p. 74), commenting on "the historical fact that according to Aristotle's concept of a syllogism the syllogism itself and the preceding mental activity run in opposite directions," points out that in the third and second centuries B.C., when the Stoic logic was being formulated, the non-Aristotelian view had become current that a scientific syllogism was a means of proceeding from known facts to something previously unknown. It was in this context, says Kapp, that

> In competition with Aristotle the Stoic school developed a new system of syllogistical forms which probably culminated in a form intended to reproduce the way in which scientific discoveries are made. We know the following example: "If drops of sweat transpire through the skin, there must be invisible pores; now, drops of sweat do transpire through the skin; therefore there are invisible pores." No matter whether or no this is a description of how the scientist comes to new knowledge, the intention of following his mental ways directly by means of a simplified straight-forward syllogistic is clear, and the intention may be quite remarkable.

7

Aristotle: Man as a Biological Organism

We know that the history of biology harks back to Aristotle by a road that is straight and clear, but that beyond him the road is broken and the lights are dim. And we have seen that biology was no mere by-play of Aristotle's learned leisure, but was a large intrinsic part of the vast equipment of his mind.—Sir D'Arcy W. Thompson, 1913, p. 30.

Whence the comparison which Socrates the younger used to make in the case of "animal" is not good; for it leads away from the truth, and makes one suppose that man can possibly exist without his parts, as the circle can without the bronze.—Aristotle, *Metaphysics*, 1036B 25; transl. Ross.

A discussion within reasonable compass and relevance to our purpose in this chapter is possible only upon the basis of the following stipulations: (1) We shall discuss Aristotle's own works, not the tradition of "Aristotelianism" developed during the long history of ancient and modern scholasticism. (2) We shall select the statements of the "mature" rather than the "younger" or "Platonic" Aristotle. Many scholars have accepted, at least in a general way, the view most explicitly formulated by Jaeger (1962) that Aristotle progressed from an early philosophical Platonism toward a later biological empiricism. But even if we were to follow the inclination of scholars who have become critical of Jaeger's thesis to regard the Platonism and the empiricism as continuing strands

154

rather than developmental stages in Aristotle's thought, we would still find it more rewarding to emphasize the empirically based biological contributions rather than to deprecate again the scientifically sterile mysticism which Aristotle inherited from Plato and which at its worst was at the level of Plato's *Timaeus*. (3) We shall consider only the works relevant to biology and psychology, disregarding the physics, metaphysics, astronomy, theology, and other works of a more "Platonic," mystical, or speculative nature. There seems to be general agreement that in so far as Aristotle deserves respect as a scientist he deserves it as a biologist. It is odd to think that in Aristotle biology and psychology developed before physics.

When scientific research was being resumed in the sixteenth century, while Aristotle's philosophical, logical, and physical works were being assailed as false by the reformer Luther, the humanist Peter Ramus, the philosopher Francis Bacon, and the physicist Galileo, his zoological works were utilized—together with those of Pliny—as the basis for Conrad Gesner's four-volume work on the *History of Animals*, the first great encyclopedic textbook of zoology. As modern biology continued its development, Aristotle's biology fell into neglect and disrepute, but there was a second revival of interest in the late nineteenth century, illustrated by the oft-quoted letter written by Charles Darwin after reading the *Parts of Animals*, in which he said, "Linnaeus and Cuvier have been my two gods . . . but they were mere schoolboys to old Aristotle." A modern historian of biology (Singer, 1959, p. 45 f.) says that Aristotle's researches on living things "established his claim to be regarded as a man of science in the modern sense," and elsewhere (1957, p. 17) says that "on him all subsequent biological development, including that of modern times, is surely based." If, in reading Aristotle's biological works, we find ourselves appalled by his errors, the results variously of unfortunate prepossessions, of reliance on hearsay, or simply of careless observation, we must remember the vast scope of his labors, the fact that he was the pioneer in the systematic study of plants and animals, that he had at his disposal almost nothing in the way of effective instruments and techniques, and that he began as a Platonist. A mild analogy would be the development of "behavioristics" in recent decades by men who were trained by students of Wundt, whose doctrine made memory and learning inaccessible to experimental science, as Plato's doctrine made science itself impossible; the behavioristic pioneers of the 1920's and 1930's had to invent both theoretical systems and techniques. It might be

remarked that Wundt resembled Aristotle in his premature ency-
clopedism; in both men this propensity was inconsistent with their
view of themselves as pioneers in empirical science.

Let us begin with the work whose Latin title is *De Anima* and
which deals with *psyche* (see especially *P* II, 1-3).* If we follow
the usual practice of translating *psyche* as 'soul,' we immediately
activate in ourselves that welter of Pythagorean, Platonic, Judeo-
Christian, and philosophical associations which has perplexed psychology through most of its history. Because of this translation we
have even come to find the name of our science—"psychology"—
embarrassing, so that we have coined new names, such as "anthroponomy," "behaviorism," "behavioristics," and "behavioral science,"
which avoid the historical associations at the price perhaps of a
suggestion of faddishness and of a confusion with the "social sciences." We have seen that the primitive meaning of *psyche* is
'breath,' the inhaled and exhaled air which is the principle of life
and whose departure is death. In Aristotle, *psyche* is the principle
of life; it is that which makes the difference between "animate" and
"inanimate" bodies; it is to be defined in terms of what animate
bodies *do,* the functions or processes which they exhibit. Aristotle's
predecessors had recognized two criteria for the presence of *psyche*
in bodies: *movement* (especially respiratory movement), and *cognition* (sensation, perception, "knowing"). Aristotle described a
hierarchy of criteria, of which self-nutrition, growth, and reproduction are found in plants; the preceding plus sensory processes
and motor activity in animals; and all of the preceding plus the

---

* The works of Aristotle to which I shall refer, in the alphabetical order
of the abbreviations (in parentheses) by which I shall refer to them, are as
follows:

(D)	On Dreams	(Ph)	Physics
(G)	On Generation of Animals	(Poet)	Poetics
(H)	History of Animals	(Pol)	Politics
(L)	On the Locomotion of Animals	(PS)	On Prophecy in Sleep
(LD)	On Life and Death	(R)	On Respiration
(M)	On Memory and Reminiscence.	(Rh)	Rhetoric
(MA)	On the Motion of Animals	(S)	On Sense and the Objects of
(N)	Nicomachean Ethics		Sensation
(P)	On Psyche	(SW)	On Sleep and Waking
(PA)	On the Parts of Animals	(Y)	On Youth and Old Age

Quotations are from the Oxford translations (Ross, 1908-1931), except
that in a few cases I have substituted Randall's (1960) excellent translations
of certain passages, or, in a very few cases, words or phrases which seemed to
me to convey better the biological meaning of Aristotle's Greek than did the
traditional philosophical terminology of the Oxford translations.

"rational" processes of thinking, planning, and generalizing in man. Sensory capacity involves also appetite, desire, and aversion. *Psyche*, we might say, is a collective term for those processes occurring in plants, animals, and man which are studied by physiology; let us, avoiding the spiritualistic connotations of the translation "soul," disencumber "psyche" of its italics and naturalize it as our technical term for the Aristotelian concept. As Shute (1941, p. 128) says, "To sum up: with Aristotle's definition of the soul as the actuality of a natural body having organs, the usual problem of the relation of soul and body does not exist." If we could wipe out two thousand years of metaphysics, and return to this meaning of psyche, we would need to feel no embarrassment at calling our science "psychology"; as it is, the synonymous—in the Aristotelian sense—term "biology," or more specifically, "physiology," might seem preferable. For physiology, says Webster, "is the branch of biology dealing with the processes, activities, and phenomena incidental to and characteristic of life or of living organisms."

Ross (1955, pp. 5-18) presents the view that in Aristotle's "middle period," to which his biological works were assigned by D'Arcy Thompson, he held a "two-substance" view of the relation between psyche and body; psyche is described as "incorporate in some substance of a fiery character," whose seat is in the heart (*PA* II, 7:652b); whereas in a later period, that of the *De Anima*, he adopted a "one-substance" or "psychophysical" doctrine, according to which psyche is the "entelechy" or principle of organization of the whole body. With great diffidence I suggest that if this was a genuine change in Aristotle, it might be regarded as a refinement of biological language rather than an evolution in metaphysics, and that the adjective "psychophysical," with its modern philosophical connotations, distorts the functional concept which was Aristotle's apparent intention. It is reasonable to assume, I think, that throughout his career Aristotle, handicapped as have been many modern psychologists by his Platonic education, was struggling to develop a language and technique of biological analysis; this fact has been obscured for us by the tradition of arid intellectualistic and introspective mentalism which we inherited from the eighteenth and nineteenth century philosopher-psychologists—especially the British —for whom man was a "mind" rather than an organism and whose theater of operations was the study rather than the laboratory.

In Aristotle as in modern science, functional language easily slips over into reification. Psyche, "the activity" or "the function" of a living body (cf. Shute, 1941, pp. 122-129) and *nous,* commonly translated "mind" but more accurately "the capacity or process of thinking," are inevitably used in such locutions as "Psyche [or *nous*] does so and so," or "resides in such and such a place." Such locutions, in which, in accordance with linguistic habits, verbs masquerade as nouns, will persist until they can be replaced by statements about physiological mechanisms. (Cf. the very "Aristotelian" discussion by Mandler and Kessen, 1959, p. 76.) German "act psychology" and American "functional" or "dynamic" psychology were— not very fruitful—attempts to deal with these difficulties.

But in speaking of the point of view of "Aristotle" I have been referring to the Aristotle of Books I and II of the *De Anima.* In Book III we have a relapse into Platonism and into the language of psychophysical dualism (cf. Jaeger, 1962, p. 332 ff.). Here we find it stated that *nous,* that part of the psyche "whereby it thinks and judges," is "separable from the body" and, unlike the faculty of sensation, has no bodily organ; it is moreover immortal and eternal. Aristotle, like philosophers of all ages, was impressed by the apparent dichotomy between sensory experience in the presence of correlated external environment, and autonomous thought processes more or less independent of sensory input. "That is why a man can exercise his knowledge when he wishes, but his sensation does not depend upon himself—a sensible object must be there" (*P* II, 5:417b). Moreover, whereas sensation apprehends particular things, thought apprehends "universals," i.e., concepts. This view of thought processes is a characteristic product of specialization of mathematical thinking, from Pythagoras and Plato through Descartes and Leibnitz to Poincaré; thus we find Poincaré (1952, p. 46) saying that mathematical creation "is the activity in which the human mind seems to take least from the outside world, in which it acts or seems to act only of itself and on itself, so that in studying the procedure of geometric thought we may hope to reach what is most essential in man's mind." The "ideal" figures of geometry, mathematical equations and curves, abstractions and relations of all kinds seem somehow to be independent of sensory and even of neural physiology. That human thought can take off on "autonomous," highly symbolic flights which eventuate in such creative visions as that of the hydrogen bomb is of course impressive. Although Aristotle says that "no bodily activity has any connection with the activity of reason"(*G* II, 3:736b), he seems less certain of this in *De Anima* II (1:413a).

Whereas it was obvious that the sense organs were organs of sensory processes, it required the physiological research of modern times—foreshadowed to be sure by the observations and intuitions of early physiologists, even before Aristotle—to bring recognition of the fact that thought is no less physiological than perception. As for Aristotle—at least in his "biological period"—it was his view that the *heart* was the organ of sensory and emotional experience, whereas the brain served the purpose of producing mucus and cooling the blood. Some of Aristotle's arguments for the heart as the central organ of sensory and motor functions are similar to those of Descartes for the pineal gland: central location, and the assumed possibility that a very slight motion of the central organ could produce large peripheral effects, as in mechanical devices. In his ignorance of the nervous system, Aristotle saw the heart as the center of a system of vessels whereby the sensory and motor functions of the entire body could be integrated. He was influenced also by the fact that, in his observation, the heart was the first differentiated structure to appear in the embryo, and by the theoretical consideration that the growth of the embryo depended upon nourishment by the blood and hence upon the priority of blood, vessels, and heart (G II, 4:740a).

It is interesting—and puzzling—to note that Kantor (1947) is led by his concept of "interbehavioral psychology" to reject the "ancient dogma" that the brain, or more generally, the nervous system, is the main organ of behavioral organization and of mnemic and thought processes, and to assert that, "Were writers not so bound by the brain tradition they would not be so disturbed at Aristotle's reasons for making the heart more prominent than the brain as a locus of psychological processes" (p. 80). Kantor quotes from Ogle (1882) a summary of Aristotle's arguments for the heart and against the brain as the organ of psychological activities. For the fourth century B.C. some of these were "good" arguments, but they do not seem relevant to Kantor's depreciation, in 1947, of the views of such contemporary neurologists and neurophysiologists as Parker, Herrick, Tilney, Sherrington, and Fulton concerning the role of the brain in correlation, coordination, and, in general, integration. I join Kantor in deprecating Herrick's lapses into spiritualism, but when Herrick and those others describe the integrative functions of the nervous system they, far more than any psychologist, are speaking of what they have observed, and are, moreover, participating in the self-correcting processes of an empirical laboratory science. In these matters a psychologist, unless he is also a physiologist, speaks as, and with the limitations of, a philosopher, and, like the "philosophers of science," trespasses into the domain of pragmatics.

There was involved in Aristotle's psychology the old notion that things are composed of the "four elements" (earth, water, air, fire), and that sensation consists in an interaction of "like with like"—of the elements in things with the like elements in the sense organs; this is the ancient equivalent of the statement often found in modern textbooks that the various sense organs are "tuned" to the various kinds of environmental energy. Thought, since it can "think all things," must be—as Anaxagoras had said—"unmixed" with corporeal elements and structures. Randall (1960, p. 90 ff.) points out that Aristotle was concerned to show "that the human mind can grasp the structure of things directly," without distortion by human structure; this "logical realism" was the classic view which succumbed to the critical philosophy of Hume, Kant, and their successors. "That knowledge is not the passive reception of the structure of things, that it is an active process of interpretation and construction, is the biggest difference between our voluntaristic and biological conceptions of knowledge and that of Aristotle" (Randall, 1960, p. 92). The dichotomy between "animal" functions and a "rational" soul was of course adopted by the religiously dominated philosophy which was the heritage of modern psychology; it was this language, rather than the language of empirical biology spoken by Aristotle in his non-Platonic, natural science phases, which we have had transmitted to us in our histories. Of this strain in Aristotle, conditioned by religious tradition, philosophic verbalism, and a complete ignorance of neurology, we shall take only brief notice; it has been worked and reworked *ad taedium* in the philosophical tradition of psychology.

The Empirical Method

Aristotle was the first to state explicitly the methodological principle that research must begin with observation. Ascertainment of the facts should precede attempts at explanation (*P* III, 3:432a; *PA* I, 5:645b). In the study of animal structure, verbal description must be supplemented by dissection. The purpose of studying structures is to make possible inferences concerning organismic functions.

> We must therefore not recoil with childish aversion from the examination of the humbler animals. . . . If any person thinks the examination of the rest of the animal kingdom an unworthy task, he must hold in like disesteem the study of man. For no one can look at the primordia of the human frame—blood, flesh, bones, vessels, and the like—without much repugnance. Moreover, when any one of the parts or structures, be it what it may, is under discussion, it must not be supposed that it is its material composition to which attention is being directed or which is the object of the discussion, but the relation of such part to the total form [*PA* I, 5:645a].

But while Aristotle thus recognized the principle of empirical method and the fact that error is likely to arise in interpretation of the facts, he inevitably paid the price of being a pioneer. Nowadays we have a vast accumulation of reliable knowledge and an array of statistical and experimental tests and criteria, and we have a long tradition of restraint and caution acquired through the examples in the literature of observations and interpretations discredited by replication and critique. Aristotle, who lacked these sources of control and caution, and who sought to encompass in his research the whole of nature, made many errors because of insufficient observations, acceptance of hearsay—like Darwin!—and in particular because of insufficient verification of results. Moreover, contrary to his stated principle, he sometimes substituted a priori notions for observation: Lones (1912, p. 27) cites his conclusion that the blood of the right side of the body is hotter than that of the left side, which "followed from his idea that the right side is nobler or more honourable than the left." However, superior as we may feel in our methodological sophistication, we can hardly assert that errors of any of these kinds are unknown in our contemporary literature; we must marvel rather that Aristotle got so many things right and that he stated so correctly the principles of research. His view of the proper relation between theory and observation is very clearly stated in his discussion of animal movement: "And we must grasp this not only generally in theory, but also by reference to individuals in the world of sense, for with these in view we seek general theories, and with these we believe that general theories ought to harmonize" (*MA* I, 1:698a), a principle which we would have done well to remember when we were busily generating learning theories from "group learning curves."

Causation and Teleology

Here we have two topics which have been perennially debated, and which the philosophers of science—who of course have to take account of the vast strata of philosophical discourse which have been superimposed upon Aristotle's writings—are still attempting to analyze and define. When in our student days we first encountered Aristotle's doctrine of "causes" as traditionally presented, we found it strange, for we had been historically conditioned to use the term "cause" in the sense of "a sufficient antecedent." But the difficulty is a verbal one, and disappears if, instead of indiscriminately translating *aitia* by "cause," we say, as Aristotle did, that he uses this term to refer to the following four kinds of biological facts —the sorts of things which we need to know in order to "understand" something and which together constitute the answer to the question "why?":

(1) An organism consists of certain *materials*: (a) elements— earth, water, air, fire; (b) "homogeneous parts," which are compounds of the elements and are exemplified by flesh, fat, blood, bone, etc.; (c) "non-homogeneous parts"; e.g., face, eye, tongue, arm, heart, etc., which are combinations of various homogeneous parts and have definite forms and functions. The distinction between homogeneous and non-homogeneous parts corresponds to the distinction between tissues and organs introduced in the eighteenth century by Bichat, founder of histology, whose functional point of view is very reminiscent of Aristotle; the historian Buckle declared that "between Aristotle and Bichat I find no middle man." This aspect of biology has to do with the *structure* of organisms as studied nowadays by biochemistry, histology, and anatomy. *Aitia* in this sense is traditionally translated "material cause."

(2) An organism is so organized as to be capable of certain functions; it has a characteristic pattern or *form*. This is the aspect of organisms which has become the business of physiology. *Aitia* in this sense is traditionally translated "formal cause."

(3) An organism is initiated in growth or movement by an agent. Thus insemination initiates the development of an individual, and stimuli instigate his movements. In our science, this area is shared by experimental embryology, physiology, and psychology. *Aitia* in this sense is traditionally translated "efficient cause."

(4) The seed or fertilized ovum of an organism, barring accidents, grows in a predetermined manner into a typical adult organ-

ism. "For if a thing undergoes a continuous change and there is a stage which is last, this stage is the end or 'that for the sake of which'" (*Ph* II, 2:194a). *Aitia* in this sense is traditionally translated "final cause."

Perhaps much unnecessary controversy might have been avoided if it had been generally recognized by psychologists that all four of these modes of biological description are legitimate and necessary. Randall (1960, p. 66 f.) describes Aristotle as "a thoroughgoing behaviorist" because for him "life or *psyche* is the behavior of the organism as a whole in its environment"; he resembles the gestalt psychologists in holding "that there is a structure in the world that is grasped by 'insight'"; he differs however from the gestaltists in having "no objections to mechanism in itself: physical mechanisms of a determinate character are for him always involved in any function, and necessary for its understanding." He resembles the behaviorists and differs from the gestaltists also in his emphasis on genetic explanation: "He who considers things in their first growth and origin will obtain the clearest view of them" (*Pol* I, 1:125a).

Our tradition associates Aristotle with Plato as the fountainhead of "teleology," interpreted in terms of the medieval concept of the operation of divine providence in nature in general; whereas in fact, Aristotle attributes "purposes" or "intentions" only to human actions. Aristotle often uses the analogy of a carpenter building something according to a design preexisting "in his head," or similarly a sculptor creating a statue. But as a biologist he is dominated by the concept of ontogenetic development, and here his "teleology" is quite respectable when viewed from the point of view of modern genetics and embryology. His problems were the modern ones of how embryonic development is initiated and how the successive differentiation of structures is regulated. He was naturally wrong about many things—it must be remembered that he had no microscope and that it required centuries of research at the descriptive level before the experimental research of the last fifty years could lead to true theories instead of intuitive guesses (cf. Waddington, 1962, p. 17)—but he was the founder of embryology. He studied the development of the embryo in hens' eggs opened after various periods of incubation and made many excellent observations. But it is his central theoretical idea that is most interesting: the idea that animal organisms develop in a predetermined way toward a characteristic adult pattern; we are not likely to refer to this idea by the pejorative term "teleology"; the geneticists have

taught us to speak, in Aristotelian terms, of function-inseparable-
from-matter, of genetic codes carried by genes. Aristotle was correct in his opposition to the theory of "pangenesis" shared by
Democritus, Hippocrates, Darwin, and Lysenko, by which they
thought to account for the supposed inheritance of acquired characteristics; this was the theory that the germ plasm is determined
by something which comes from all parts of the parental body. Aristotle pointed out, among other arguments against this theory, that
children may resemble their more remote ancestors. Any approach
to a Mendelian theory of resemblances was precluded by Aristotle's
notion that the essential generative agency—the "code"—is contributed by the male, while the female contributes a passive formative material. But Aristotle (*G* II, 1:734b) foreshadowed modern
"epigenetic" theory, which holds "that the egg starts as a simple
structure which gradually changes into new structures according to
certain principles" (Barth, 1953), and opposed the "preformation"
theory, which held that the young animal already existed complete
in the germ and simply grew in size. The latter theory became
very influential in the late seventeenth century, when with the aid
of the newly invented microscope and a lively imagination, Hart-
soeker and others "saw" in the spermatozoon a "homunculus," a
tiny but complete human body which needed only to increase in
size to become an adult. The rivalry between the two theories has
continued to the present; for as Dobzhansky (1955) points out, the
genes were named for organs or characters and are now tied to
enzymes, so that they might be described as "preformistic." But
the enzymes might be regarded as a pluralistic modern version of
Aristotle's *pneuma*, which in the process of generation forms "a
sort of frothy bubble," like that which we now attribute to the
enzymatic action of yeast. Another "anticipation" in Aristotle is
that of "von Baer's law," the principle that in embryonic development more general characters appear before the more specific: "For
e.g. an animal does not become at the same time an animal and a
man or a horse or any other particular animal. For the end is developed last, and the peculiar character of the species is the end of
the generation in each individual" (*G* II, 3:736b).

The Functional Point of View

Aristotle describes the animal body as an organized whole consisting of structures at two levels of organization: tissues and

organs. The term *psyche* refers to the functional potentials of the whole body, as "sight" signifies the functional potential of the eye. "That is why we can wholly dismiss as unnecessary the question whether the [psyche] and the body are one: it is as meaningless as to ask whether the wax and the shape given to it by the stamp are one" (*P* II, 1:1412b). Or, we might add, as meaningless as to ask whether respiration and the lungs are one, or thinking and the brain.

"Life is an activity" (*N* X, 4:1175a), and all functional activities of an organism—"e.g. anger, courage, appetite, and sensation generally," probably "thinking" as well, involve bodily reactions. Reactions to stimuli depend on the state of the body at the time, and bodily states may eventuate in profound emotional reactions in the absence of relevant external situations (*P* I, 1:403ab). "It is doubtless better to avoid saying that the psyche pities or learns or thinks, and rather to say that it is the man who does this with his psyche" (*P* I, 4:408b).

The biological functions constitute a series. Thus plants have only the self-nutritive function while animals have the sensory function, but the sensory function presupposes—is never found apart from—the self-nutritive; and similarly, the additional capacity of man, thinking, is never found apart from perception. These functional capacities are defined by reference to the corresponding activities. Thus the definition of "psyche" must be in terms of the particular capacities found in each order of living things, and definition of these forms of psyche requires study of the *processes* involved; "for in the order of investigation the question of what an agent does precedes the question, what enables it to do what it does. If this is correct, we must on the same ground go yet another step farther back and have some clear view of the objects of each; thus we must *start* with these objects, e.g. with food, [with the thing perceived, or the thing thought]" (*P* II, 3-4:414b, 415a). As we would say, in order to describe the nature of an organism, we must study its types of behavior and the stimulus objects in relation to which the behavior occurs. While Aristotle's organism, like Leibnitz's monad, contained from the first the potentiality of its whole subsequent development, its activity, unlike that of the monad, was a causal function of an environment; as in modern psychology, behavior was for Aristotle a product of processes in the organism—sensory, mnemic, and motivational—and environmental factors. He was, as Randall says, a functionalist, a behaviorist, and an operationalist.

The Classification of Living Things

We have seen that Anaximander proposed a primitive theory of organic evolution, according to which living things originated from the mud which at one stage of cosmogenesis covered the earth; fish preceded land animals, the latter representing an adaptation to the drying of the land; and man too had developed from more primitive fish-like forms. This theory was perhaps, as Nordenskiöld (1928, p. 12) has suggested, derived in part from legends of autochthonism, but it was also based on observations: e.g., the viviparous dogfish seemed an intermediate form between fishes and land animals, and the long infancy of human beings seemed incompatible with the survival of early animal forms. And, as we have also seen, Empedocles proposed a primitive theory of variation and of "survival of the fittest."

Aristotle did not explicitly formulate an evolutionary theory of the origin of species. Like Anaximander he assumed that living forms were generated from inanimate matter, but he criticized Empedocles for assuming that forms whose structures fitted them for survival could have arisen by chance (*Ph* II, 8:198b). "It has been well said that for him nature is like an army forever marking time, but never marching anywhere" (Randall, 1960, p. 138). What Aristotle did was to describe living things as capable of being ordered in a classification in terms of their resemblances and differences in structure and function; this classification constituted a *scale*—not, as in modern evolutionary biology, a branching tree— of increasing complexity. "Nature proceeds little by little from things lifeless to animal life in such a way that it is impossible to determine the exact line of demarcation, nor on which side thereof an intermediate form should lie" (*H* VIII, 1:588b). There was a continuous gradation from inanimate matter through the various grades of complexity, first of plants and then of animals. We have spoken of the hierarchical relations of the vital functions in this series: nutrition and reproduction (plants); these plus sensation and movement (animals); these plus recollection and thinking (man). Aristotle did not make a formal presentation of a complete classification; his classification has been drawn up by modern writers by means of a collation of numerous passages. Since it was based on an insufficient accumulation of knowledge it naturally contains many defects, but it was not improved upon until the systematicians of the seventeenth and eighteenth centuries began their work —Ray, Cuvier, Linnaeus, etc. The general notion of classification by means of coordinate and superordinate terms had originated with Plato. Aristotle used the terms *eidos* and *genos*, of which the former corresponded fairly well to our "species," though often to our "genus," while the latter included all superordinate classes— those which we designate as classes, orders, or families; the two terms represented differences in the degree of sameness of structure and function. "By 'genus' I mean, for instance, Bird or Fish . . . and there are many species of fishes and of birds" (*H* I, 1:486a; cf. *PA* I, 4:644b). To gain an idea of the degree to which Aristotle was pioneering in the very fundamental matter of biological classification, one has only to read *PA* I, 1-4; e.g.:

> We must, then, have some clear understanding as to the manner in which our investigation is to be conducted; whether, I mean, we are first to deal with the common or generic characters, and afterwards to take into consideration special peculiarities; or whether we are to start straight off with the ultimate species. For as yet no definite rule has been laid down in this matter [*PA* I, 1:639b].

When we read that "Some animals share the properties of man and the quadrupeds, as the ape, the monkey, and the baboon," and "In all such creatures the internal organs are found under dissection to correspond to those of man" (*H* II, 8:502ab), we may be tempted, as some have been, to attribute a Darwinian meaning to these words. There seems however to be agreement among the historians of biology that while Aristotle's hierarchical classification was very influential in subsequent biology, including the eventual development of the theory of evolution, he himself went no further than a classification in terms of resemblances and differences. Singer (1950, p. 39) remarks, "It cannot be said that he ever definitely attained to the 'evolutionary' point of view. But it is evident that he was moving in that direction, and perhaps if he had lived another ten years he might have reached it." It is evident also that for Aristotle man was a biological organism. The temptation to "extrapolate" Aristotle's biology—and his psychology—is very great, because the curve of his development from Platonism toward natural science seems so evident, and also because the evolution in modern times from a religious to a scientific view of man presents itself as an analogy.

Sensory and Appetitive Processes

Sensation is defined by Aristotle as an interaction between a stimulus object and a sense organ.

> Sensation depends . . . on a process of movement or affection from without. . . . It is clear that what is sensitive is so only potentially, not actually. The power of sense is parallel to what is combustible, for that never ignites itself spontaneously, but requires an agent which has the power of starting ignition [*P* II, 5:416b].
>
> By a "sense" is meant what has the power of receiving into itself the sensible forms without the matter . . . the sense is affected by what is colored or flavored or sounding, but it is indifferent what in each case the *substance* is; what alone matters is what *quality* it has, i.e. in what ratio its constituents are combined. . . . What perceives is, of course, a spatial magnitude, but we must not admit that either the having the power to perceive or the sense itself is a magnitude; what they are is a certain ratio or power *in* a magnitude [*P* II, 12:424a].

In other words, sensation is a receptor *process functionally related* to certain stimulus variables. Randall (1960, p. 87 f.) states that for Aristotle "sensing and sense images . . . are not 'mental,' they are physical." And, he continues,

> In Aristotle . . . the line is drawn . . . between sensing the particular and knowing the universal, not between "body" and "mind." Descartes was thus introducing a genuine and fundamental revolution into the analysis of human nature and human knowledge, when he took sensing and all the other "passions" of the soul out of the physical world, now reduced to extension alone, and put them into "mind," a revolution from which we have hardly recovered yet. For Aristotle and the tradition that followed him, images, imagination, pains, and emotions are all particular and corporeal, not "mental" at all.

All animals have at least one sense: namely, touch, "and whatever has a sense has the capacity for pleasure and pain and therefore has pleasant and painful objects present to it, and wherever these are present, there is desire, for desire is just appetition of what is pleasant" (*P* II, 3:414b). Nowadays we speak of "positive and negative incentives" and of stimuli which elicit "appetitive" or "aversive" responses.

Aristotle rejected the ancient theory of vision according to which objects emit streams of corpuscles which enter the eyes or which are met by effluences from the eyes. Instead, he assumed a pervasive medium, "a translucent something," to which motion or activity can be communicated by something of the nature of fire; the absence of such activity is darkness (*P* II, 7:418b). The medium for sound transmission is air; the cause of sound is mechanical impact of a solid body on a mass of air which in turn sets in motion the air enclosed in the ear (*P* II, 8:419b f.).

Although Aristotle apparently saw the optic nerves of several vertebrates, spoke of "three ducts which go from the eye to the brain" (*H* I:16, 495a), and said that in the chameleon "The brain is situated a little above the eyes, but connected with them" (*H* II, 10:503b), he nevertheless declared, "That [the brain] has no continuity with the organs of sense is plain from simple inspection, and is still more clearly shown by the fact that, when it is touched, no sensation is produced" (*PA* II, 7:652b). The spinal cord he described as bone marrow, which, being "hot," is opposite in function to the "cold" brain in the homeostatic control of body heat. Considering Aristotle's extensive dissections, particularly of such "diagrammatic" vertebrates as the dogfish, we can only marvel at his retrogression from Alcmaeon, and we can appreciate all the more the work of Erasistratus and of Galen. Presumably, Aristotle's observation was dominated by his preconception of the heart as the sensorium, so that he was prepared to see the sense organs as connected, not with the brain, but by blood vessels with the heart (*Y* III:469a). He says, "The sense organ of the eyes is set upon certain passages, as are the other sense organs. Whereas those of touch and taste are simply the body itself or some part of the body of animals, those of smell and hearing are passages connecting with the external air and full themselves of innate pneuma; these passages end at the small blood vessels about the brain which run thither from the heart" (*G* II, 6:744a). The "pneuma" mentioned here is some sort of "vital air," not otherwise defined, which mediates mechanically between the external air and the blood; pneuma is also present in the blood, being generated in the heart, which receives air through the pulmonary vessels; thus, it appears, pneuma is the agency by which motion is transmitted from environment through blood vessels to the heart. (On pneuma, see Peck, 1943, pp. 576-593.) Heart and pneuma play the roles in Aristotle of pineal gland and "animal spirits" in Descartes: that of a locus of transition between what is not quite corporeal and the frankly corporeal; this is, like many subsequent dodges, a means of attenuating the embarrassment of "psychophysical interaction," although in Aristotle the pneuma, though refined, is not in the Cartesian sense "inextended" or "incorporeal." As we shall see, pneuma is also, like Descartes' animal spirits, the means by which movements of the body are produced.

We find in Aristotle (S VII) the beginning of the doctrine of fusion or "mental chemistry" which in modern associationistic psychology was utilized for the explanation of perceptual organization; i.e., the perception of "objects." Two simultaneous sensations which are not separate, i.e., incompatible, may combine into a resultant perceptual object by virtue of the unitary perceptual function, the "common sense." In this connection Aristotle touches upon some other characteristics of perception which were to receive much attention in modern psychology: "why persons do not perceive what is brought before their eyes, if they are at the time deep in thought or in a fright, or listening to some loud noise"; also, "it is easier to discern each object of sense when in its simple form than when an ingredient in a mixture"—e.g., a tone by itself alone than when sounded with its octave.

Aristotle makes a distinction which reappeared, with a different interpretation (see Shute, 1941, p. 94) in the seventeenth century in John Locke's "primary and secondary qualities"; Aristotle distinguishes between the "special objects" of the various senses—color, sound, taste—and the "common sensibles"—movement, number, figure, magnitude—which can be perceived by more than one sense. He also makes the distinction which in modern psychology became that between sensation and perception: e.g., between a "white patch" and the perception of the white patch as a particular person (P II:6). In emphasizing the new empiricism of the British philosopher-psychologists of the seventeenth and eighteenth centuries, our histories perhaps neglect to remind us that these men were educated in the Greek classics; much of their new empiricism was old Aristotle in revolt against the Aristotle which had been created by medieval tradition. The same was true at the beginning of modern psychology in Germany; there Trendelenburg (1802-1872) indoctrinated Brentano and G. E. Müller, among others, in the philosophy of Aristotle; the founders of experimental psychology were men thus trained. We shall see that associationism, the historical background of our psychology of learning, was also founded by Aristotle.

Motor Processes

The term "neuron" is frequently used by Aristotle, but it refers indifferently to tendons, ligaments, and nerves; it is not used of "nerves" in our sense until the time of Galen (second century A.D.). Of the nature of nerves and of the nervous control of movement Aristotle knew nothing; his contribution was rather an elegant analysis of movements in terms of the geometry and mechanics of levers, an analysis from which Fulton (1926, p. 3 f.) quotes a passage as being in its "wisdom and clarity . . . typical of Aristotle's biological writings." Aristotle has a good deal to say, in a manner which reminds one of the commonsensical verbosity of the nineteenth-century British psychologists, about the cognitive and appetitive causation of movement, but when he comes to a "physiological" explanation, he does what Descartes did—he employs the analogy of the automata of his day, the mechanical toys or puppets operated by strings (*MA* 7:701b; cf. notes, *loc. cit.*, by Farquharson, 1912). The motive power of these toys was apparently supplied by cylinders around which strings, under the tension of suspended weights, were wound. A "serial reaction" could be produced by means of pegs on the cylinders which could progressively release other cylinders. The principles involved were essentially the same as those utilized in some recent machine models, e.g., Stevenson Smith's (1936) "electrical rat," though the latter had the improvements of an electric motor and pegs which could be operated by "exteroceptive" impacts and which could thus mediate "correction of errors" and "learning." Such machines and others, such as those of Hull, as well as the more recent computer models, are, though more sophisticated, still, like Aristotle's, analogical rather than physiological. A maze-running trolley quite similar to Smith's is described by Deutsch (1960, pp. 124-133), who seems not to have known of Smith's model. Ever since my student days, when I was required to spend many hours in calculations based on hydraulic and electrical analogies of the nervous system, I have doubted whether such analogies serve any purpose in science beyond the very general pedagogical one of inculcating a predilection for "mechanistic" explanations. Deutsch appears to have constructed his electrical rat as a means of testing his theory of rat behavior, and he concludes that the results are "encouraging from the point of view of theoretical psychology" (p. 133). I incline rather to Chapanis' (1961) view that

Modeling is playing a kind of child's game—a grown-up sophisticated version of a child's game, to be sure, but a game nonetheless. The game is called "Make believe." Theory, on the other hand, is a conceptual system which attempts to describe the real thing. The basic elements, or pieces, of a theory are actually supposed to be there in the thing about which you are theorizing and they are supposed to behave the way the theory says [p. 118].

Whatever may be the heuristic requirements in the more esoteric reaches of *physical* theory, I think that this distinction between models and scientific theories has much to recommend it in biology and psychology. If we accept Aristotle's view that biological function is inseparable from biological structure, it would seem to follow that the explanation of biological function, including "behavior," must be in terms of biological structure; it must, that is, be "physiological," not analogical, and certainly not fictional nor mythological. Neurophysiology has made enormous progress in recent years, but on the evidence of recent machine models, behavioral science has, in its basic explanations, remained at the analogical stage where Aristotle left it. If it is argued that neurophysiology —as known, with cultural lag, to most psychologists—is still inadequate for the explanation of behavior, we might recommend Wittgenstein's *Woven man nicht sprechen kann, darüber muss man schweigen.*

As to how the "strings" attached to the bones are operated, Aristotle is necessarily vague. "The object we pursue or avoid in the field of action is . . . the original of movement." The perception or imagination of this object results in desire, and desire results in a change of body temperature and consequent expansion or contraction.

Blind courage and panic fears, [sexual emotions], and the rest of the corporeal affections, pleasant and painful, are all accompanied by a change of temperature, some in a particular member, others in the body generally. So, memories and anticipations, using as it were the reflected images of these pleasures and pains, are now more and now less causes of the same changes of temperature [MA 8:702a].

The heart, which is the sensory center, is also the origin of motion; for it, like the penis, responds in its motion to temperature changes. In the heart, which is the main seat of the "vital heat," there is generated from the blood the pneuma or "innate spirit," a refined fluid or gaseous something—it will be remembered that in the heart the blood was supposed to be mixed with air; in G II, 2:736a the pneuma in semen, which is concocted from the blood, is described as "hot air"—which, acting presumably through the blood vessels, is the means by which movement, "thrusting and pulling," is communicated to the moveable parts of the body. Farquharson (1912), in a note on *MA* 10:703a20, remarks,

> Aristotle seems to have conceived the contractions of the spirit as giving a pull, and its expansion as loosening the sinews, whereas Descartes thought the vital spirits blew up the muscles and so shortened them. Aristotle probably was thinking of such a similitude as that of an inflated wineskin or bladder, having in mind the familiar Greek mode of reducing a dislocation of the thigh by blowing up a wineskin.

The notion of pneuma or animal spirits was adopted by Galen in his explanation of muscular contraction; these spirits, passing from the brain through the nerves, caused a transverse swelling and longitudinal shortening of muscles. This notion began to be discredited in the seventeenth century when Swammerdam and Glisson showed that a muscle does not increase in volume when it contracts, and became increasingly untenable in the eighteenth century when von Haller demonstrated the irritability of muscle, Whytt demonstrated the reflex control of movement, and Galvani initiated electrophysiology. But as we have seen, the fluid-in-pipes theory, though it disappeared from neurophysiology, lingered on in psychology until the early decades of the twentieth century.

Aristotle distinguishes between voluntary actions preceded by thought and actions in which perception or imagination issues immediately in movement. But "appetite" is always the essential immediate instigator of movement, mediating between cognition and the bodily origin of movement. Not all objects of intellect initiate movements, but only those which have practical ends: "the movement of living creatures has a term"; it begins with a desire and ends at a goal. "For the object of desire causes motion, and the reason thought does so is that its starting-point is the object of desire" (*P* III, 10:433a). It is obvious that what we call motivation is basic in Aristotle's explanation of conduct. "Motion always implies that we are avoiding or pursuing something" (*P* III, 9:432b). "Thought by itself never moves anything, but only thought directed to some end, and concerned with action" (*N* VI, 2:1139a). Activity depends both upon initating motivation and upon attendant pleasure. Pleasure is described as a state which accompanies, intensifies, and completes an activity; there are various pleasures specific to various desires and activities. In Aristotle's discussion of pleasure

(*N* X, 1-5) there are involved the factors which in modern literature have been distinguished as instinct, drive, goal-object, and
drive-reduction.

> . . . when one is active about two things at once, the more pleasant
> activity drives out the other. . . . That is why when we enjoy anything
> very much we do not throw ourselves into anything else, and do one
> thing only when we are not much pleased by another; e.g. in the
> theatre the people who eat sweets do so most when the actors are
> poor [*N*, X, 5:1175b].

Pleasure has a homeostatic function: "It must therefore be pleasant
as a rule to move towards a natural state of being, particularly
when a natural process has achieved the complete recovery of that
natural state." Habits are pleasant, whereas

> all acts of concentration, strong effort, and strain are necessarily
> painful; they all involve compulsion and force, unless we are accus-
> tomed to them, in which case it is custom that makes them pleasant.
> The opposites to these are pleasant; and hence ease, freedom from
> toil, relaxation, amusement, rest, and sleep belong to the class of
> pleasant things; for these are all free from any element of compul-
> sion [*Rh* I, 11:1370a].

Life is a struggle in which animals seek an equilibrium free both of
external compulsions and of conflicts between incompatible motives.
Such conflicts are particularly likely to arise when there is opposition between the desires associated with more and less rational or
more distant and more immediate goals.

Perhaps Aristotle might be thought to have anticipated Mowrer
(1961) in declaring that wickedness is voluntary, that the sinner is
rightly held responsible for his acts, and that, even if wicked acts
are the irresistible expressions of a man's character, "it was open at
the beginning not to become a man of this kind" (*N* III, 5:1114a).
But, "The problem is for Aristotle not one of arbitrary 'freedom of
the will' but of motivation toward a more intelligent or remote or
socialized goal versus that toward a more stupid or immediate or
primitive goal" (Shute, 1941, pp. 80-82). "For while mind bids us
hold back because of what is future, desire is influenced by what is
just at hand" (*P* III, 10:433b).

Aristotle emphasizes the inevitability of change and consequent
variety in motives and behavior—and of variability in individual
habit formation—attributable to satiation and fatigue, conditions
which may be relieved by change of activity, play, or sleep (e.g.,
Rh I, 16:1371a; *Pol* VIII, 3:1337b).

In his work on animal locomotion, Aristotle analyzes the coordinated movements of locomotion of various kinds of animals: man, quadrupeds, birds, snakes, fishes, insects. He introduces some basic biological distinctions and relations: those for which we use the terms rostral and caudal, dorsal and ventral, right and left, bilaterality, flexion and extension, and contralateral coordination: "For since limbed creatures stand and take their weight alternately on one or other of the opposite legs, if one be thrust forward the other must of necessity be bent" (*L*, 9). He expresses the basic physiological principle of integration as follows:

> And the animal organism must be conceived after the similitude of a well-governed commonwealth. When order is once established in it there is no more need of a separate monarch to preside over each several task. The individuals each play their assigned part as it is ordered, and one thing follows another in its accustomed order. So in animals there is the same orderliness—nature taking the place of custom—and each part naturally doing his own work as nature has composed them. There is no need then of a psyche in each part, but she resides in a kind of central governing place of the body, and the remaining parts live by continuity of natural structure, and play the parts Nature would have them play [*MA* 10:703a].

Compare Child (1924): "... the physiological factor primarily concerned in the integration of the regions or parts of an organism in organismic reaction is a relation of dominance and subordination" (p. 36). "... whether we are primarily concerned with the organism or with human society, we cannot help but see the fundamental similarities in the processes of integration in the two patterns ..." (p. 270).

Memory, Recall, Learning, and Intelligence

The two great principles of British psychology—*empiricism* in its subvariety *sensationalism*, and *associationism*—had their origin in Aristotle. As for sensationalism, consider the following passage:

> Since according to common agreement there is nothing outside and separate in existence from sensible spatial magnitudes, the objects of thought are in the sensible forms, viz. both the abstract objects and all the states and affections of sensible things. Hence (1) no one can learn or understand anything in the absence of sense, and (2) when the mind is actively aware of anything it is necessarily aware of it along with an image; for images are like sensuous contents except in that they contain no matter [*P* III, 8:432a].

As Randall (1960, p. 96) says, "It is surprising that, for a man so wedded to *logos*, to language, as Aristotle, he seems to have been, psychologically, as much of a visualist as the major British empiricists." "For thought images serve as if they were contents of perception (and when it asserts or denies them to be good or bad it pursues or avoids them). That is why there is no thinking without an image" (*P* III, 7:431a).

The theory of the "association of ideas" is the oldest theory of psychological organization in terms of learning. The older history of association psychology has been reviewed by Warren (1921), and its modern status has been discussed by Robinson (1932). Guthrie (1935) remarked that "Associative learning has been recognized in some form or other by every writer on psychology since Aristotle" (p. vii), and he made the Aristotelian principle of association by contiguity the basis of his influential doctrine of learning (on which see the judicious critique of Mueller and Schoenfeld, 1954).

The concept of the association of ideas appears first in Plato, who exemplifies the principles of contiguity and similarity in a passage of the *Phaedo* (73-76), where, having said that "The knowledge of a lyre is not the same as the knowledge of a man," he continues,

> And yet what is the feeling of lovers when they recognize a lyre, or a garment, or anything else which the beloved has been in the habit of using? Do not they, from knowing the lyre, form in the mind's eye an image of the youth to whom the lyre belongs? And this is recollection. In like manner any one who sees Simmias may remember Cebes; and there are endless examples of the same thing. . . . And recollection is most commonly a process of recovering that which has already been forgotten through time and inattention. . . . So much is clear—that when we perceive something, either by the help of sight, or hearing, or some other sense, from that perception we are able to obtain a notion of some other thing like or unlike which is associated with it but has been forgotten [transl. Jowett].

This passage in Plato seems to have been long forgotten, and in modern times the history of associationism has usually been begun with Aristotle, although Aristotle and his successors—including Hobbes—were also forgotten or unknown by John Locke, who in 1695 thought that the principle of the "connection of ideas" had not been "hitherto considered"; one is tempted to take this as an early example of that neglect of history in which psychology seems to lead the other sciences.

Aristotle emphasized the principles of contiguity and frequency, and of attention or set of the individual. He also mentioned the factors of intensity and of organization of the material. It is not difficult to see in his analysis foreshadowings of the "laws" of association which Thomas Brown formulated more than two thousand years later. The following quotations will suggest how much of modern associationism was anticipated by Aristotle (the explanatory phrases in square brackets are in Beare's translation):

> The process of movement [sensory stimulation] involved in the act of perception stamps in, as it were, a sort of impression of the percept, just as persons do who make an impression with a seal [*M* I:450a30].
>
> Acts of recollection, as they occur in experience, are due to the fact that one movement has by nature another that succeeds it in regular order. If this order be necessary, whenever a subject experiences the former of two movements thus connected, it will [invariably] experience the latter; if, however, the order be not necessary, but customary, only in the majority of cases will the subject experience the latter of the two movements. But it is a fact that there are some movements, by a single experience of which persons take the impress of custom more deeply than they do by experiencing others many times; hence upon seeing some things but once we remember them better than others which we may have seen frequently [*M* II:451b10].
>
> For, in order of succession, the mnemonic movements are to one another as the objective facts [from which they are derived]. Accordingly, things arranged in a fixed order, like the successive demonstrations in geometry, are easy to remember [or recollect], while badly arranged subjects are remembered with difficulty [*M* II:452a1].
>
> For as regular sequence of events is in accordance with nature, so, too, regular sequence is observed in the actualization of movements [in consciousness], and here frequency tends to produce [the regularity of] nature. And since in the realm of nature occurrences take place which are even contrary to nature, or fortuitous, the same happens *a fortiori* in the sphere swayed by custom, since in this sphere natural law is not similarly established. Hence it is that [from the same starting-point] the mind receives an impulse sometimes in the required direction, and at other times otherwise, [doing the latter] particularly when something else somehow deflects the mind from the right direction and attracts it to itself [*M* II:452a28].

Compare with the above statement about the regularity of nature the following statement of Hull (1930, p. 523):

> Sequences in the outer world evoke parallel reaction sequences in sensitive organisms. By the principle of redintegration the organismic sequences acquire a tendency to run off by themselves, independently of the original world sequences. The organism has thus acquired an intimate functional copy of the world sequence, which is a kind of knowledge.

We have here, perhaps, an illustration of the fact that the novelty of much modern psychological "theory," compared with that of centuries or even millennia ago, is the verbal novelty of such terms as "redintegration"; in a similar way, a student knows that a horse has four legs before we teach him that the horse is a quadruped.

We find in Aristotle the first recorded example of a chain association: "milk, white, mist, moist, Autumn" (*M* II:452a15).

Beginning with Hobbes in the seventeenth century, a series of British philosophers adopted the concept of the association of ideas as a means of explaining the empirical origins of human knowledge —and of error, as well as of organization in general—in opposition to the doctrine, of which Descartes was usually taken to be the chief exponent, of innate ideas. "Associationism" thus came to be the name for a body of doctrine developed by the British empiricist philosophers of the seventeenth, eighteenth, and nineteenth centuries—Hobbes, Locke, Hume, Hartley, Brown, James and John Stuart Mill, Bain. The doctrine varied with its various exponents, but might be summarized as follows. All mental life arises from sensations, the elementary experiences resulting from stimulation of the sense organs. Experiences similar to the sensations may subsequently occur in the absence of the corresponding sense organ stimulations; these derivative experiences are "ideas." Complex mental states or processes arise by the process of association. That is, a sensation or idea will arouse other ideas—simultaneously, as in perception, or successively, as in trains of thought—which had on previous occasions occurred in temporal contiguity with the instigating sensation or idea. Some writers made similarity, contrast, causality, etc., coordinate with contiguity; others reduced all of these to contiguity. It is obvious that the fundamentals of this scheme—the empiricism and the principle of associative connection—were anticipated by Aristotle. This becomes still more obvious when we read the statements of the founders of British associationism: Hobbes and Locke. Hobbes states that

> The cause of the *coherence* or consequence of one conception to another, is their *coherence* or consequence at that time when they are produced by sense: as for example, from St. Andrew the mind runneth to St. Peter, because their names are read together; from St. Peter to a *stone*, for the same cause; from *stone* to *foundation*, because we see them together; and for the same cause, from foundation to *church*, and from church to *people*, and from people to *tumult*: and according to this example, the mind may run almost from anything to anything [Hobbes, 1650, Chap. 4].

> But because in sense, to one and the same thing perceived some-
> times one thing sometimes another succeedeth, it comes to pass in
> time that in the imagining of any thing there is no certainty what we
> shall imagine next; only this is certain: it shall be something that
> succeeded the same before at one time or another [Hobbes, 1651,
> Chap. 3].

Trains of thought may be—apparently—unguided, or they may be
"regulated by some desire and design." Locke, like Aristotle, distinguished between "natural" connections among ideas—those in
accordance with the laws of logic or nature—and those dependent
upon chance or custom:

> *Custom* settles habits of thinking in the understanding, as well as
> of determining in the will, and of motions in the body: all of which
> seems to be but trains of motions in the animal spirits, which, once
> set a going, continue in the same steps they have been used to; which,
> by often treading, are worn into a smooth path, and the motion in it
> becomes easy, and as it were natural [Locke, 1700, Book 2, Chap. 33].

Anyone who has read William James's *Principles*, particularly the
chapters on "Habit," "The Stream of Thought," and "Memory," will
have a feeling of familiarity on reading many passages in Aristotle.
Thus James's distinction between primary and secondary memory
strongly suggests Aristotle's between memory and recollection, and
James's famous passage on trying to recall a forgotten name is
paralleled by Aristotle's description of the "feeling of discomfort"
(M II:453a15) which is excited in the effort to recollect. Indeed,
one is tempted to describe James as Aristotle amplified; with, to be
sure, brain substituted for heart, but with hardly more explanatory
power, particularly as to learning and thinking, and with equal
uncertainty as to the physiological status of "consciousness"—Aristotle's "mind."

In the founding of experimental psychology, associationism was
one of the great strands which united in the nineteenth century
with Darwinism and with those other strands which could also be
traced back to Aristotle: German functionalism and act psychology,
from Leibnitz to Brentano; and German biology, which appeared
in a philosophical form in Lotze and Beneke, and became experimental with Johannes Müller, Ludwig, Helmholtz, and Ludwig's
Russian pupil, Sechenov. These men, or their teachers, were steeped
in Aristotle.

E. R. Guthrie, the most Aristotelian of American psychologists,
was, like Aristotle, interested in formulating psychological principles which could serve as guides in human life. His basic principle

was that "we learn only what we do" (1942, p. 24). He defined "personality" as consisting "of those modes of [a man's] behavior which we judge will show comparatively strong resistance to change" (1938, p. 136), and emphasized that these "conservative" modes of behavior are most thoroughly established in childhood. With these views compare the following passage in Aristotle:

> . . . by doing the acts that we do in our transactions with other men we become just or unjust, and by doing the acts that we do in the presence of danger, and being habituated to feel fear or confidence, we become brave or cowardly. The same is true of appetites and feelings of anger; some men become temperate and good-tempered, others self-indulgent and irascible, by behaving in one way or the other in the appropriate circumstances. Thus, in one word, states of character arise out of like activities. . . . It makes no small difference, then, whether we form habits of one kind or of another from our very youth; it makes a very great difference, or rather *all* the difference [*N* II, 1:1103b].

Guthrie's *The Psychology of Human Conflict* might well be regarded as a 1938 revision of Aristotle's psychological and ethical works; it begins with chapters on "The Nature of Living Organisms" and "The Nature of Mind." The spirit is the same: critical, empirical, practical, functional. One might think that Guthrie's denial of the heuristic value of neurological explanations of learning distinguishes him from Aristotle the biologist, but this is not really true: Aristotle was completely ignorant of the nervous system, and Guthrie utilized whatever seemed helpful to him in the modern literature of physiology, but was critical of the imaginary neurology of psychologists. There may well however have been a more subtle difference: the difference between Aristotle as a biologist who had had a life-long habit of working directly and personally with animal tissues, and Guthrie as a philosopher-psychologist whose activities had been mostly verbal, though based on sharp observation of human affairs. But then we have such a philosopher-psychologist in the Aristotle of the *Ethics* and *Politics*. There is another possible parallel between Aristotle and Guthrie which might be suggested, though not too seriously: the parallel between Aristotle versus Empedocles and Guthrie versus Tolman. Aristotle reproached Empedocles for identifying thinking and perceiving, and thereby failing to account for error (*P* III, 3:427a20). Guthrie declined to accept Tolman's identification of learning with the acquisition of "sign-gestalt-expectations," arguing that this explanation does not account for "wrong acts," but only for "the behavior of very nice and very wise people" (Guthrie, 1937, p. 528). The need to account for error is much emphasized in Aristotle (e.g., *P* III, 3-6), as in Guthrie.

Motivation and habit formation are the two basic principles of Aristotle's explanation of socialized behavior. There are certain universal needs and appetites—especially those of hunger and sex —which account for classes of recurrent behavior, but contingencies of environment—especially of social environment—account for individualized motives and habits; if these are to be socialized, teachers and law enforcement are necessary. Where Guthrie (1935, p. 1) in his first paragraph contrasts an animal with a brick, Aristotle contrasts him with a stone: "For instance the stone which by nature moves downward cannot be habituated to move upwards, not even if one tries to train it by throwing it up ten thousand times" (*N* II, 1:1103a21). What is innate in man is not socialized habits but the capacity to acquire them; it is as in the arts: "It is from playing the lyre that both good and bad lyre-players are produced."

A survey of recent discussions of "the processes by which a child acquires the values of his culture," such as that of Hill (1960), may leave a reader puzzled as to how the explanatory power of theory has advanced beyond the statements of Aristotle and of Guthrie. Verbal complexity—particularly the Freudian and Hullian—has certainly increased; as Hill remarks, "This area of research has become a battleground for conflicting terminologies, with one term often having a multiplicity of half-distinct meanings, and with what appears to be the same meaning often bearing different labels" (p. 317).

Like modern authors, Aristotle emphasizes as factors in human intelligence the structure and function of the hand and of the speech organs. His account of speech anticipates some of the essential features to be found in modern accounts. He points out that the respiratory and oral mechanisms have been utilized, "in accordance with [nature's] not uncommon practice," for different functions: not only respiration and nutrition but also the production of voice. "Voice is a sound *with a meaning*," "a luxury subserving its possessor's well-being," i.e., a by-product, having adaptive value, of the physiologically more fundamental visceral functions (*PA* II, 16:659b30; *P* II, 8:420b). Hearing contributes more than does vision to the development of intelligence: "For rational discourse is a cause of instruction in virtue of its being audible, which it is, not directly, but indirectly; since it is composed of words, and each word is a thought-symbol. Accordingly, of persons destitute from birth of either sense, the blind are more intelligent than the deaf and dumb" (*S* I:437a). Moreover, language makes possible human social organization; man is more of a political animal than are other gregarious animals, and this is because speech enables him to "set forth the expedient and inexpedient" (*Pol* I, 2:1253a).

In view not only of this passage but also of Aristotle's great interest in linguistic analysis, several writers (e.g., Shute, 1941, p. 110) have expressed regret that he did not follow out what would seem a natural development of his thought and interpret "mind" (*nous*) in terms of language (*logos*—a word which meant both 'language' or 'discourse' and 'reason'). Instead, as Randall (1960, pp. 98-106) says, Aristotle "turns Platonist" and describes an "active intellect" which is "deathless and eternal," rising above "the limits and conditions of its bodily instrument," and thinking the "intelligible system or order" of the universe (*P* III, 5-8:430a ff.). Randall points out that the prominence in subsequent philosophical literature of this notion of an immortal, separable, active intellect, requiring no bodily organ, is actually the product of religious preoccupations in Hellenistic and medieval times, and that Aristotle himself perhaps introduced a Platonic metaphor into an otherwise naturalistic context. Randall (1960, p. 102) then goes on to say,

> Of course, what Aristotle *ought* to have meant by "the *nous* that makes all things," the active intellect, in terms of his own thought, is clear enough. To his question, What makes us know? What actualizes universals? the answer is, it is *logos*, discourse, language and communication. The "active intellect" is actually *logos*. Moderns like Mead and Dewey seem not only to be right—they are also thoroughly Aristotelian. But it is striking that, important as Aristotle makes *logos*, what things can be said to be, he never treats *logos* itself in biological and functional terms, as an activity of organisms with the power of *nous*: he never treats *logos* as a "part" of the *psyche*, as one of the functions making up "life." Such a treatment is not in the *De Anima* at all, but it ought to be.

Visceral Processes

Aristotle appears to have dissected some hundred species of animals, including echinoderms, arthropods, mollusks, fishes (elasmobranchs and pisces), amphibians, reptiles, birds, and, among mammals, dolphin, hare, deer, horse, ox, and pig. It is improbable that he ever dissected a human body, though he may have inspected the human embryo or fetus. Descriptions of the movements of the heart of chameleon and tortoise, including descriptions of movements after removal of the heart from the body, indicate vivisection.

But in spite of his numerous dissections and many careful observations and descriptions, and in spite also of his theoretical emphasis on function, Aristotle's notions of the physiology of the internal organs were mostly erroneous (see especially *R, passim; H* I, 17). He described the heart as the origin of the blood vessels, giving as one of the main reasons for this origin—rather than an origin in the head as previously supposed—the requirement that the origin should be in a hot part of the body. "Innate heat" is an important concept in Aristotle's physiology; it is produced from the food and is the agent of digestion—the old notion of digestion as a "cooking." The innate heat, which is different from ordinary heat, is identified with the vital principle—a notion which goes back to the observation of the difference between a living body and a corpse. Death is always the result of loss of heat; in old age the feeble flame is easily extinguished. The animal heat must be regulated within narrow limits so as not to be destructive; this regulation is provided in air-breathing vertebrates by the lungs, whose tubes, running alongside the blood vessels, constitute a cooling system; Aristotle pointed out that the inspired air is cool while the expired air is hot. The brain is an accessory cooling organ, not a sensory or cognitive organ. There is a common wall between the parallel respiratory tubes and blood vessels through which breath can pass to the heart. The heart is a reservoir from which the blood passes to the vessels but to which it does not return; in the smallest blood vessels the blood is transformed into epidermal structures, flesh, or sweat and vapor. Aristotle, and his successors until Harvey, did not know that the heart is muscular; they attributed its beating to a swelling caused by fluid expanding under the influence of heat. The demonstration of the impossibility of this notion and the discovery of the true mechanism of the circulation of the blood had to await the seventeenth century and William Harvey. Without thermometers, Aristotle could not of course investigate body temperatures; it was not until the mid-nineteenth century that Helmholtz demonstrated the heat production of muscle and attributed this to combustion; his researches convinced him that animal heat was to be explained in terms of physics and chemistry and that the notion of a "vital force" was incompatible with progress in physiological knowledge (cf. Fulton, 1926, p. 42 ff.). It must be said, however, that Aristotle's approach also was "physicochemical"; in saying that innate heat is "produced from the food," he went about as far toward a physical explanation in terms of combustion as was possible in his time, and the same is true of what we might call his "homeostatic" explanation of respiration as a heat-regulating mechanism. His explanations were based on observations and dissections; it was his interpretations that were wrong, but these interpretations were not mystical, a priori, nor even "vitalistic."

Since in the above discussion "innate heat" is the main functional concept—the physiological agent of nutrition, sensation, and motion (*PA* II, 7:652b)—whereas in our discussion of motor processes we found the innate "pneuma" described as the physiological agent, it should be mentioned that, as Ross (1955, pp. 40-43) points out, some commentators have treated the two principles as the same; what distinction Aristotle may have intended between these two speculative notions need not detain us. We recall that both body heat and breath were primevally regarded as the signs of life, and their departure as death, and they were so regarded by Aristotle (cf. *LD* I).

The systemic functions of the gonads were observed by Aristotle in terms of the changes which occur in eunuchs: "The reason of this is that some of the parts are principles, and when a principle is moved or affected needs must many of the parts that go along with it change with it" (*G* 766a).

Sleep, Dreams, and "Parapsychological" Phenomena

Aristotle defines sleep as an inhibition of sensory function, and waking as a release from this inhibition. Since sensory processes are correlated with appetitive and aversive processes, the latter too enter into the definition of waking (*SW* I:454b25). Sleep is a functional state, controlled by a primary organ of sense (the heart), and alternates by physiological necessity with waking; it differs from abnormal states of loss of consciousness as in syncope or circulatory obstruction (*SW* II:455b).

Dreams are likened both to after-sensations and to illusions. (It is here that "Aristotle's experiment" is mentioned: an object placed between the crossed middle fingers feels like two objects.) The effects of previous sensory excitations persist. Sensory excitations may be aroused by causes within the body, as in emotional states or in delirium. In sleep, as in illusions, the excitations are not adequately controlled by sensory—exteroceptive—input (*D* II-III).

As for the significance of dreams, the author of the Hippocratic treatise *On Diet* had, in Book IV, distinguished two kinds of dreams: those of divine origin, presaging good or bad luck, whose interpretation is the business of diviners, and those of physiological origin, which must be interpreted by physicians; he took a view opposite to that of Aristotle by describing mental processes in sleep as more reliable than those in waking life because the mind is not distracted by the external world. Plato (*Republic* 571cd, 572b) speaks in Freudian terms of "a lawless wild-beast nature, which peers out in sleep." Aristotle (*PS* I) is sceptical concerning the prophetic significance of dreams; there may be something in it, since it is almost universally accepted. "Yet the fact of our seeing no probable cause to account for such divination tends to inspire us with distrust"—a remark which seems applicable to the interpretations of contemporary "parapsychologists." In some cases there may be a causal naturalistic relation between dream and event: just as, after we have been planning or performing some action in waking life, we may then dream about it, so a vivid dream may pave the way for an action in waking life. But most cases of apparent prophecy are to be regarded as coincidences.

> As, then, one's mentioning a particular person is neither token nor cause of this person's presenting himself, so, in the parallel instance, the dream is, to him who has seen it, neither token nor cause of its [so-called] fulfilment, but a mere coincidence. Hence the fact that many dreams have no "fulfilment," for coincidences do not occur according to any universal or general law. [Of course, if someone has enough "previsions" he may make a hit now and then.] For the principle which is expressed in the gambler's maxim: "If you make many throws your luck must change," holds good in [this] case also [*PS* II].

Aristotle was a naturalist rather than a "parapsychologist"; he assumed that the world is orderly and that our knowledge of it comes through our senses. His statistical attitude toward the notion of prophetic dreams is suggestive of the similar attitude of Galton toward the efficacy of prayer.

8

Aristotle:

Man in Society

ELEATIC STRANGER: Why, obviously we can make two divisions of
the art of measurement. . . . One of its branches will consist of all
the arts in which number, lengths, depths, breadths, velocities are
measured . . . ; the other of those which employ the standard of
due measure, decorum, seasonableness, obligatoriness, or any other
which is safely located in *a mean* between extremes.—Plato, *The
Statesman,* 284e. Taylor's transl.

Murphy (1949) begins his chapter on "Social Psychology" with
the statement that "From the time of Aristotle until late in the nineteenth century, psychology was a study of individual minds. The
problem of group interaction or interpersonal relations was a problem for the historian, the moralist, or the jurist, and—especially
during the eighteenth and nineteenth centuries—for the political
economist." The meaningfulness of this statement turns upon the
use of the term "psychology," a term which was, it is true, first used
in the sixteenth century, and which was then used for some three
hundred years as the name for "the study of individual minds," as
Murphy says. The purpose of the present chapter is to show that as
a matter of fact Aristotle created, in addition to the biological psychology which we considered in the preceding chapter, a social
psychology in his *Ethics, Politics, Rhetoric,* and *Poetics.* The titles
of these works are perhaps, for the modern student, unfortunate.
Had Aristotle organized all of the material in them into a single

systematic work, which a modern translator might have entitled *Social Psychology*, it would have been a more instructive textbook than was the one most used by psychologists in the first two decades of our century, that of McDougall.

Peters (1953, p. 709) presents Aristotle as the first in the long history of the nativistic approach to social phenomena which culminated in McDougall and Freud; and similarly LaPiere and Farnsworth, in their scholarly *Social Psychology* (1942, pp. 7-8), write:

> Aristotle . . . found the cause of society in the "nature" of the individual. He believed that society is but a consequence of the instinctive and therefore unchangeable character of the individual. Thus, since it is impossible to change men's nature, it is impossible to modify society. . . . Such a conclusion reduced men to the status of biological slaves, removed in degree but not in kind from social insects.

Plato, on the other hand, is described as an environmentalist, who

> . . . proposed the setting up of a new social system and in so doing advanced a concept of the origins of human behavior that is now, some twenty centuries later, not entirely incompatible with sociopsychological findings. He insisted that people behave as they do because they have been taught so to behave. . . . Plato anticipated the idea of innate differential capacity to learn and yet did not, as has since been done, assume a direct relationship between the social position of parents and the biological capacity of their offspring.

Plato's model, as we have seen, was Sparta, and the modern Platonic state is Soviet Russia, where the principles of environmentalism have been improved by Pavlov and Michurin; the "Soviet Man" is man-made-to-order. I hope to show that Aristotle, on the other hand, rejected "total unity" and favored the maximum of individual freedom and democracy compatible with the viability of the state, and that he held that the behavior and capacity for thought of an individual are the resultants of heredity, early habit formation, and education. As for "the relationship between the social position of parents and the biological capacity of their offspring," we may recast Aristotle's views in modern terms by saying that what happens to an individual in a certain cultural environment in early life is just as "biological" as the processes determined by his genes; as Aristotle says, the childhood habit patterns—the individual's character—are for practical purposes nearly as irreversible as are the gene-determined traits, and are just as much a limitation on the "biological capacity" of individuals and also of populations of individuals as they exist at any given time. We have been in the throes of discovering this fact in our attempts to spread democracy and industrialism throughout the world. It was Aristotle, and not, as LaPiere and Farnsworth suggest, Machiavelli, who wrote the first "manual of political craftsmanship," based upon "realistic" assumptions concerning the "natural character of man," and Aristotle's account would be quite relevant to an analysis of present-day social and political behavior.

Aristotle distinguishes between "theoretical" and "practical" science. The motivation of theoretical science is pure intellectual curiosity. Theoretical intelligence deals with universals and with ultimate and invariable principles, from which phenomena can be deductively "demonstrated." It is not concerned with human purposes nor does it instigate to action (*P* III, 9:423b25). The thinking of practical science is goal-directed and prescriptive of action; it deals with particular and hence variable, contingent, and relative environmental objects and with "things that are good or bad for man." Practical intelligence depends upon established habits of intelligent foresight. "It is not science, because matters of conduct are relative." "It is also clear that theoretical wisdom cannot be the same thing as political intelligence; for if we are to call knowledge of our own interests wisdom, there will be a number of different kinds of wisdom, one for each species" (*N* VI, 5&7:1140b&1141a).

Aristotle classes physics as a theoretical science, and defines it as the science concerned with the study of objects which are both material and capable of motion. Biology is a subdivision of physics which deals with the special kinds of change and motion peculiar to living organisms, including those forms of change and motion which constitute the objects of study of psychology. The practical sciences, on the other hand, are exemplified by medicine and the social sciences: ethics, economics, politics; they are really *arts*: bodies of rules of conduct which do not have the general validity of scientific laws but which hold good in the main. "It is the mark of an educated man to look for precision in each class of things just so far as the nature of the subject admits" (*N* I, 3:1094b24). In medicine a drug may have a certain "average" effect in most patients but widely deviating effects in some; treatment in general must be adjusted to the individual patient. The effects of social measures are relative to cultures, and the utility of moral maxims is dependent upon the indoctrination, acquired insights, and situations of the individuals concerned. These arts can therefore aim only at practical rules of conduct, the means of attaining certain personal or social ends, based on observed statistical probabilities.

There was here a relativism reminiscent of Protagoras and fore-shadowing the cultural and moral relativism of modern times as well as the "treat the patient, not the disease" movement which has been recurrent in the history of medicine. Aristotle points out something that has been much emphasized recently: that in a sense politics is the "master art," since it ordains which of the sciences shall be studied, uses the sciences and arts and legislates with a view to the welfare not merely of individuals but of the state (*N* I, 1-3).

Aristotle's method in the social sciences—especially in his *Politics*—is to investigate the laws, mores, and institutions of the societies known to him and to formulate on the basis of this investigation rules of law and conduct by which the personal and social goals important in these various cultures might be attained. In this process he utilizes both his own observations and the opinions of others: not only the opinions of philosophers but also the commonly accepted opinions of people in general. Here, as in his biology, he faced the difficulties—the deficiencies of fact and language—of a pioneer in a vast area. The boredom which often overtakes one in reading Aristotle—a boredom however no greater than that experienced in reading many modern textbooks of social psychology—results from the necessity he felt of detailed analysis and definition of traditional verbal usage. Moreover, Aristotle had a pragmatic aim, and he did not wish to depart too far from received opinion and usage but rather to systematize them and give them greater accuracy. Randall (1960, Chap. XII) emphasizes the distinction between Aristotle's *method* and his *conclusions*: the method—that of empirical investigation—could be applied to any culture; the conclusions and recommendations are relevant chiefly to the culture and values of the leisure class in the Greek city-states. However, a review of Aristotle's "social psychology" may persuade us that not only with respect to his general empiricism, relativism, and pragmatism, but also in more specific ways, his analyses have a wider application, and in particular, a disquieting relevancy to the social phenomena of our own times.

Principles of Individual Behavior

Let us first review the principles of individual behavior which we have hitherto examined and which Aristotle utilized in his social works.

1. Man is a biological organism characterized by the functions or activities of nutrition, reproduction, perception, movement, and thought.

2. Sensory processes leave traces which can be reactivated and which can then function in a manner similar to that of the original sensory processes.

3. Such mnemic processes become chained together under conditions of contiguity, frequency, and intensity of the original sensory processes. These sequences are however subject to environmental distraction and to the set of the individual at a given moment.

4. Behavior is causally related to environment, but action ensues only when sensory, mnemic, or thought processes are associated with motivational processes. Effective stimuli elicit either appetitive or aversive movements.

5. Action is always directed toward an end appropriate to existing motivation, and achievement of this end is accompanied by a state of pleasure which acts as a reinforcement of the action, whereas interference with such achievement, or unmotivated action, is accompanied by a state of displeasure which is expressed as aversive behavior (*N* VII, 13; X, 5).

6. There may be conflict between simultaneously aroused motivations, especially when these are related, respectively, to more immediate satisfactions and to more remote, socialized, and rational goals.

7. The most basic motivational processes are hunger, thirst, sex, anger, fear, and desire for bodily comfort (e.g., in relation to body temperature). These are "instincts" in the sense of "drives" which man shares with other animals; they are inborn tendencies. Emotions are treated as motivating forces. Many other "desires" are mentioned as explanations of behavior: the familiar behavior tendencies called, e.g., envy, affection, shame, curiosity, hate, emulation, rivalry, pity, joy, etc. These have been conveniently catalogued, with citations, by Griffin (1931, Chap. III). Interesting in view of a modern usage of "appetite" is Aristotle's mention of "a separate kind of desire answering to each kind of nourishment" (*Rh* I, 11:1370a20). Some "needs" or "drives" are described as "natural" or "necessary," others as resulting from acquired habits, and still others as sequelae of organic injury, disease, or insanity.

8. Reactions to stimuli depend on the state of the body at the time, and bodily states may eventuate in profound emotional reac-

tions in the absence of relevant external situations. Moreover, emotional outbursts, e.g., in rage or sexual excitement, may alter the bodily condition in a manner similar to that of madness or drunkenness.

9. Basic differences between individuals are determined by heredity, but the habit patterns established in early life are almost equally unmodifiable. Wickedness which is an expression of character is like an incurable disease, whereas incontinent behavior under the influence of a powerful appetite, accompanied by conflict and followed by repentance, is like an intermittent disease such as epilepsy (*N* VII, 8). The behavior of adults is the expression of their characters, and their characters are sets of habits which were established in childhood. Genetic explanation is the preferred method.

10. Variety in behavior, and hence in individual character formation, is insured by (a) variety of external stimulation, (b) variable operation of motivations, according to life circumstances and training, (c) different *combinations* of motives on various occasions, (d) type and details of supervision and training in youth and of social compulsion in adulthood, and (e) satiation and exhaustion resulting from long continuance of any activity.

11. Some thought processes—"practical thought"—eventuate in movements, but others—"theoretical thought"—end in verbally expressible logical conclusions. Motivated behavior may be delayed by processes of "practical thought" or "deliberation" in which alternative actions are weighed and a choice arrived at. There may be conflict between a more rational or ethical action represented by thought and an action motivated by a more primitive instinct or emotion. Relatively few men achieve a consistently rational control of their behavior; most men act in accordance with the variable kinds and degrees of childhood training and the socially enforced laws and mores, and for the rest behave in accordance with the capricious fluctuations of individualistic motivations: hunger, thirst, sex, anger, fear, envy, greed, etc.

In passing now from these principles of individual or physiological psychology to those of social psychology, we shall naturally find an overlapping of the two sets, since human beings are biological organisms modified by and interacting with social environments. Nevertheless, the question we shall have to consider in the end is whether Aristotle's thesis—that there is a basic difference in method, in probability-status of generalizations and in aims between natural science and social science—is justified.

The Psychological Bases of Society

Aristotle postulates a gregarious instinct which man shares with other animals. But "man is more of a political animal than bees or any other gregarious animals" because he has the gift of speech and can thereby formulate pragmatic and ethical rules of conduct. The capacity of men to regulate their behavior by such rules makes possible the family and the state. The isolated individual is not self-sufficing; man is normally a part of a whole which is the state. Socialized man "is the best of all animals, but, when separated from law and justice, he is the worst of all . . . the most unholy and the most savage of animals, and the most full of lust and gluttony" (*Pol* I, 2:1253a).

The sexual instinct is basic in the relationship of husband to wife and hence in the formation of the family. Also important in establishing family relationships are the desire for reproduction and the paternal, maternal, and filial motivations which arise during the prolonged human infancy; these last three kinds of motivation are proportionate in intensity to the amount of activity expended, so that the maternal motivation is greater than the paternal and the paternal than the filial (*G* III, 2:753a7; *N* IX, 7). In the family, justice requires that the father rule his children as a king his kingdom, in the interest of his subjects, and rule his wife "constitutionally" in accordance with his superior role; "democracy is found chiefly in masterless dwellings . . . and in those in which the ruler is weak and every one has license to do as he pleases"—as we would say, in "permissive" households, where frustrations are minimized and asocial behavior maximized.

The above motivations enter into the disposition of *friendship*, which is described as essential in holding states together. The conditions favoring friendship are kinship, similarity in race, character, interests, occupation, etc., and the sharing of the same friends and enemies. The long list of qualities desirable in friends (*Rh* II, 4:1381ab) is worth reading as a compendium of "social adjustment": desirable friends are those "with whom it is pleasant to live and spend our days . . . who are not too ready to show us our mistakes . . . who have the tact to make and take a joke . . . who praise such good qualities as we possess, and especially if they praise the good qualities that we are not too sure we *do* possess . . . who have some serious feeling about us, or belief in our goodness, or pleasure

in our company . . . those whom we help to secure good for themselves, provided we are not likely to suffer heavily by it ourselves."
This passage may serve as an example of Aristotle's very shrewd
and realistic observation. He remarks elsewhere that "Most people
seem . . . to wish to be loved rather than to love; which is why most
men love flattery; for the flatterer is a friend in an inferior position,
or pretends to be such . . . and being loved seems to be akin to
being honoured, and this is what most people aim at" (*N* VIII,
8:1159a13). We are reminded of the Freudian concept of "sublimation" when we read that the reproductive instinct expresses
itself not only in the desire for and love of children but also in
charitable actions and in the production of works of art: "Every
man loves his own handiwork . . . and this happens perhaps most of
all with poets; for they have an excessive love for their own poems,
doting on them as if they were their children. This is what the position of benefactors is like; for that which they have treated well is
their handiwork" (*N* IX, 7:1167b35).

The tendencies to imitate and to take pleasure in the acquisition
of knowledge are fundamental in education, science, and art.

> Imitation is natural to man from childhood, one of his advantages
> over the lower animals being this, that he is the most imitative crea-
> ture in the world, and learns at first by imitation. And it is also
> natural for all to delight in works of imitation. . . . The explanation
> is to be found in a further fact: to be learning something is the
> greatest of pleasures not only to the philosopher but also to the rest
> of mankind, however small their capacity for it [*Poet* 4:1448b5].

From the most fundamental motivational tendencies, which are
innate, are derived more specialized ones which operate in socialized life. Thus the gregarious, sexual, and reproductive instincts
enter into the development of social and political motivations.

Griffin (1931, p. 114) summarizes the factors in socialization
mentioned by Aristotle:

> The influences which lead to obedience to the laws of society are
> much the same as in the case of the family: (1) the force of circum-
> stances, e.g., earning one's living, (2) the impulse to imitate, (3) the
> desire to please one's fellows due to an affection which is usually
> weaker than in the family, (4) fear of the punishment dealt out by
> society . . . (5) the desire, arising from shame, to avoid loss of repu-
> tation, and (6) the desire to achieve honour, position, wealth, etc.

Law is likely to be a more effective instrument of socialization than
the commands of parents or of most rulers because it is more com-

pulsive, more likely to be based on "practical wisdom," and more impersonal: "people hate *men* who oppose their impulses." The majority of people are incapable of achieving an individual standard of conduct superior to the requirements enforced by law.

> For these do not by nature obey the sense of shame, but only fear, and do not abstain from bad acts because of their baseness but through fear of punishment. . . . What argument would remould such people? It is hard, if not impossible, to remove by argument the traits that have long since been incorporated in the character; and perhaps we must be content if, when all the influences by which we are thought to become good are present, we get some tincture of virtue [*N* X, 9:1179b11].

For only the few, gifted at birth and properly trained, is a high individual standard of conduct attainable; "the mass of mankind are evidently quite slavish in their tastes, preferring a life suitable to beasts" (*N* I, 5:1095b19).

The Psychology of Politics

From the above we see that Aristotle, like Horst (1951), arrived at the conclusion that "most men are created unequal," and like Horst regarded this conclusion as having political implications. Horst recommends selection of both electorate and political candidates by means of "qualifying tests"; Aristotle favors a "rule by the best," but in the absence of a testing technique his preferred form of government is actually an aristocracy in which the ruling class is a "natural" class selected by birth, wealth, and education. The men of this class, presumed to be characterized by intelligence and courage, are to be warriors in youth, councillors in later manhood, and priests in old age; they are citizens, among whom there is to be democratic and economic equality. The majority of the population —the mechanics, tradesmen, farmers, and slaves—are excluded from citizenship; for the proper performance of political duties, and the development of superior character and intelligence, requires leisure, which such "ignoble" occupations do not afford. The citizenship should be kept small enough to permit election of officers on the basis of personal acquaintance, a method of probably higher validity than that of paper-and-pencil tests. Experience shows, says Aristotle, that a very populous city can rarely, if ever, be well governed; there is a limit to the size of states as of everything else in nature. Modern experience seems to confirm this conclusion.

Aristotle's doctrine of "natural" classes—a dominant minority of the wealthy, privileged, and leisured versus a majority of the poor and powerless who provide the economic support and services required by the leisure class—and his assumption of a species-difference between freemen and slaves, may seem reprehensible to us, but it was founded on observation which could be replicated today; there were and are such classes—determined in varying degrees by education, wealth, and economic and political skills, and we have found that capacity for education and rationality are limited not only by heredity but also by the cultural level of childhood and racial environment. When Aristotle says that "some men are by nature free and others slaves, and for these latter slavery is both expedient and right," we properly deprecate his confounding of heredity and environment, but we must concede that in our own society there is a large class of individuals deficient in mental and moral qualities; we recognize that these deficiencies may be attributable either to heredity or to environmental deprivation, but the presence of such a class is a fact and has political importance.

While we might see some advantage in information tests as prerequisites for political candidacy, it is doubtful whether we could recommend "personality tests" as a practical means of assessing moral character, which was for Aristotle at least as important as intelligence; or rather, the two were inseparable. At any rate, modern governments are as likely as were the ancient ones to lead to general ruin because of incompetence, irrationality, demagoguery, and corruption of their members. Or rather, they are more likely to do so; for while those of our "philosophers" who are concerned with "virtue" and "happiness"—which were the chief ends of social life for Aristotle—are now as in ancient times objects of suspicion to the warriors, tradesmen, and politicians, those "philosophers" who concern themselves with physics provide the rulers with the means of ever more complete destruction and human misery.

The difference between Plato and Aristotle was that Plato was a mystic and fanatic, whereas Aristotle was an objective observer with—for his times—a rational and humane attitude not unlike that of Bertrand Russell. Aristotle did not, like Plato, devote his entire effort to the theoretical construction of an "ideal," that is, a totalitarian state, but surveyed all the kinds of government known to him, analyzed their organization, and suggested techniques whereby they might be made more tolerable and viable. As a Greek, Aristotle regarded order, justice, and moderation as desirable both in individual lives and in states, so that he gave especial attention to techniques for avoiding injustice, disaffection, and, in particular, revolution. He recognized—what perhaps has not been sufficiently recognized in recent times—that different populations and different situations may require, for viability, different forms of government, and that any viable form and practice of government represents a dynamic equilibrium and a set of compromises. He therefore suggested techniques of practical adaptation of institutions and laws to the prevailing situations in given communities.

How does Aristotle's political advice compare with that obtainable from modern "behavioral science"? There are three forms of government which constitute our great contemporary problems: democracy in the United States, with an admixture of oligarchy; oligarchies in South America, with variable admixtures of democracy; and tyranny in Russia and China—similar to that of the defunct Nazi state—with an admixture of oligarchy. Let us see what Aristotle's prescriptions are for each of these. But first let us examine certain general ethical and political principles underlying these prescriptions.

Ethical and Political Principles

1. The aim of human life and of political science is *happiness.* The happiness of an individual is defined as lifelong activities in accordance with virtue. Happiness is virtuous activity, which may be thought-activity and need not be pursued for the sake of practical results in order to have practical significance (*Pol* VII, 3). There are certain prerequisites for complete happiness, such as adequate wealth, good birth, physical endowment, and virtuous friends (*N* I, 7-8). "Those who say that the victim on the rack or the man who falls into great misfortunes is happy if he is good, are, whether they mean to or not, talking nonsense." "Happiness is prosperity combined with virtue" (*Rh* I, 4). It requires early training in habits of moral character on the basis of which intellectual education, imparted by teachers, becomes possible. Since the capacity which distinguishes man from the other animals is that of rational thought, the greatest human happiness attaches to the life of reason of the self-sufficient philosopher—endowed of course with the

amenities of leisured life—who contemplates truth without ulterior motives (*N* X, 7). (There would probably be general assent to this proposition on the part of university professors whose "necessaries of life" do not depend upon applied research.) As for political happiness, a happy city is so in regard to all of its citizens, not merely a portion of them.

2. *Virtues* are states of character, i.e., dispositions. They consist of ingrained habits of right action—action in accordance with justice, wisdom, and temperance—whose expression is guided by intellectual insight. "Virtue makes us aim at the right mark, and practical wisdom makes us take the right means." Pleasure and displeasure are essential factors in motivation, and moral excellence depends upon these having become attached to the appropriate forms of behavior (*N* II, 1-5). The highest kinds of virtue are those which are most useful to others (*Rh* I, 9).

3. The various traits of character can exist in either an excessive or a deficient degree; virtue consists in "the mean"; that is, in moderation and justice in accordance with the ancient maxim "Nothing to excess." Examples of socially undesirable extremes are vanity and humility, prodigality and stinginess, buffoonery and boorishness. This is the same principle as that of Greek medicine; virtue like health consists in a proper balance between opposites.

4. Just actions are learned by doing, not by talking. "But most people do not do these, but take refuge in theory and think they are being philosophers and will become good in this way, behaving somewhat like patients who listen attentively to their doctors, but do none of the things they are ordered to do" (*N* II, 4:1105b12). (This is a principle commonly ignored by modern religious and legislative bodies.) "Even medical men do not seem to be made by a study of textbooks" (*N* X, 9:1181b). In statesmanship as in medicine, experience is required; indeed, politicians seem to be made almost wholly by experience.

5. "Among statements about conduct those which are general apply more widely, but those which are particular are more genuine, since conduct has to do with individual cases, and our statements must harmonize with the facts in these cases" (*N* II, 7:1107a26). Thus since all laws are universal, they must be corrected in individual cases for the sake of equity, and equity must take account of a man's character, his intention, "the whole story." The proper means for the various character traits vary with individuals and situations (*N* V, 10; *Rh* I, 13).

6. The well-adjusted man is he whose level of aspiration is appropriate to his ability and achievement (*N* IV, 3).

7. "In one sense we call those acts just that tend to produce and preserve happiness and its components for the political society . . . what, as a relation to one's neighbor, is justice is, as a certain kind of state without qualification, virtue" (*N* V, 1:1129b15). "That form of government is best in which every man, whoever he is, can act best and live happily" (*Pol* VII, 2).

8. Awards should be according to merit. For example, in the simple case of two individuals, the ratio of their rewards should be the same as that of their merits. Since goods and services differ in kind, and "the number of shoes exchanged for a house must correspond to the ratio of builder to shoemaker," it has been necessary to introduce money as a means of common quantification; money measures in units of demand (*N* V, 5).

This problem of the quantification of the social values of disparate human activities was taken up in the nineteenth century by Galton, and has recently received much attention. Thus Thorndike (1940) estimated the values of individuals and of cities in terms of the money spent for various purposes, and Horst (1951) suggests that "if adequate psychophysical means were devised for evaluating a person's contributions to, and requisitions from, society and the one plotted against the other, the points should define a curve whose derivative was at every point greater than zero." Moreover, Horst specifies that rewards must be "in kind"; in goods and services, i.e., in money, not in "spiritual" values. The same problem has arisen in the effort to quantify and compare the academic performance of students by averaging standard scores in, e.g., folk dancing and chemistry.

Aristotle mentions a problem of exchange valuation which must still be solved *ad hoc* in law courts rather than by statistical calculations:

> In the friendship of lovers sometimes the lover complains that his excess of love is not met by love in return (though perhaps there is nothing lovable about him), while often the beloved complains that the lover who formerly promised everything now performs nothing. Such incidents happen when the lover loves the beloved for the sake of pleasure while the beloved loves the lover for the sake of utility, and they do not both possess the qualities expected of them (*N* IX, 1:1164a).

9. "Justice exists only between men whose mutual relations are governed by law." Since men tend to act in their own interests and

in positions of power to become tyrants, political rule should be not by men but by rational principles embodied in laws (*N* V, 6:1134a).

10. Unanimity of action is possible only among public-spirited men:

> Bad men cannot be unanimous . . . since they aim at getting more than their share of advantages, while in labour and public service they fall short of their share; and each man wishing for advantage to himself criticizes his neighbor and stands in his way; for if people do not watch it carefully the common weal is soon destroyed (*N* IX, 6:1167b).

11. Excessive unity destroys a state; for "the nature of a state is to be a plurality"; it "is not made up only of so many men, but of different kinds of men." Such schemes of unity as that proposed by Plato, involving common property and common wives and children, would lead only to lack of personal interest and responsibility, and to quarreling and disunity; unity does not result from uniformity. "Such legislation may have a specious appearance of benevolence; men readily listen to it, and are easily induced to believe that in some wonderful manner everybody will become everybody's friend," whereas the evils whose abolition is promised are in fact the products of human nature, which cannot be abolished. In Plato's state—as in modern totalitarian states—the "guardians" become "a mere occupying garrison" (*Pol* II, 1-5).

12. It is more important to limit population than to limit property. Neglect of this principle causes poverty, and poverty causes crime and revolution (*Pol* II, 6).

13. It is not the possessions but the desires of mankind which need to be equalized, by training the educable and restraining the rest. Poverty is not the sole cause of crime; human desires, including those for superfluities, also beget crime, and desires are insatiable; they grow with their satisfaction (*Pol* II, 6-7).

14. Different kinds of government are adapted to different states. The best is often unattainable; hence the statesman should consider not only what is best in the abstract but what it best relative to circumstances; political writers are often unpractical (*Pol* IV, 1). In writing constitutions it is unwise to assume an extraordinary standard of virtue or education; there should be adjustment "to the life in which the majority are able to share." The safest state is that with a large middle class; for the wealthy from childhood learn to be despotic rather than obedient, and the poor are degraded and

envious. The more perfect the mixture of the political elements the more lasting will be the constitution (*Pol* IV, 11-12). The legislator "must not think the truly democratical or oligarchical measure to be that which will give the greatest amount of democracy or oligarchy, but that which will make them last the longest" (*Pol* VI, 5). Military states are safe only while they are at war, for their people have never learned how to live the life of peace. "Governments which have a regard to the common interest . . . are true forms; but those which regard only the interest of the rulers are all defective and perverted forms" (*Pol* III, 6:1279a).

15. Oligarchy is "the rule of the few" because it is the rule of the rich, who are always few; and democracy is "the rule of the many" because it is the rule of the poor, who are many (*Pol* III, 8). "Democracy arises out of the notion that those who are equal in any respect are equal in all respects. . . . Oligarchy is based on the notion that those who are unequal in one respect are in all respects unequal. . . . Here then are opened the very springs and fountains of revolution." "Still democracy appears to be safer and less liable to revolution than oligarchy" (*Pol* V, 1). But any form of government pushed to an extreme ends in ruin, and those who think that their own party privileges alone constitute virtue push matters to extremes. "The aim of democracy is freedom; of oligarchy, wealth; of aristocracy, the promotion of education and cultural institutions; of tyranny, the protection of the tyrant. . . . We shall learn the qualities of governments in the same way as we learn the qualities of individuals, since they are revealed in their deliberate acts of choice; and these are determined by the end that inspires them" (*Rh* I, 8).

16. Man is easily spoilt; hence under no form of government is it safe to permit any citizen to gain excessive power or wealth. Opposing elements in a state should be balanced against one another. There should be such legal provisions that magistrates cannot possibly make money out of their offices; only then will public office attract men of merit rather than the avaricious; moreover, the people will not be irritated by the spectacle of graft.

17. The most important factor contributing to political stability is education adapted to the form of government. This education should be the same for all citizens and should be public, not private. There should be a balance between education in practical arts useful in business, and education in liberal arts and intellectual activities to be **practiced in leisure** and without ulterior purposes. The

proper end of work is leisure spent in intellectual enjoyment. Vocational training which contributes nothing to the formation of taste and character is fit only for slaves. Balance is important in education; e.g., "parents who devote their children to athletics, while they neglect their necessary education, in reality vulgarize them."

Let us summarize now the principles which Aristotle suggests for the regulation of the three kinds of governments which were mentioned above as being of prime importance to us in our present precarious world situation.

Principles of Democratic Government

The principle that the multitude ought to be supreme is justified in so far as group judgments may be superior to individual judgments. But this principle cannot be universally applied, "for the argument would equally hold of brutes; and wherein, it will be asked, do some men differ from brutes?" But assuming that the principle is applicable to some populations, corruption and disaster will result if those without personal merit are permitted to hold the great offices of state; on the other hand, political danger will be incurred if a large number of poor freemen are excluded from political participation. The practical solution is to give them the power of electing and of calling to account the magistrates, in the hope that their collective judgment will be sound—although it may well be argued that just as the physician should be judged by physicians, so a right election can only be made by those who have relevant knowledge (*Pol* III, 11). However, again, there is the hope that there will be among the many a majority of responsible citizens who collectively will be less corruptible and will perhaps not be swayed in unison by the same passion. In political administration, the analogy with medicine is not exact; while it is true that an intelligent man does not wish to be doctored out of a book, but calls in a physician who can unemotionally judge his particular condition, this action implies reliance on the professional integrity of physicians; whereas magistrates, who also have the task of adjusting textbook rules to individual cases, "do many things from spite and partiality"; for magistrates, therefore, law is a necessary control (*Pol* III, 16). Where the laws are not supreme, demagogues spring up, and the government becomes equivalent to a tyranny.

The principles of democracy are freedom and equality of individuals and the equating of justice with majority vote. Accordingly, there must be popular elections, rotation of offices among all the citizens, no—or very small—property qualifications for office, brief tenure of offices, and payment for services in office. The great offices should be filled by election from persons having relevant qualifications. Democracies are debased both by poverty and by demagogic distribution of money; the poor should be assisted to buy farms or enter trades.

In democracies as in other kinds of states the problem may arise of dealing with persons who come to predominate too much because of wealth or political influence. Democracies, whose aim is equality above all things, have practiced ostracism, but have unfortunately extended this practice to those whose pre-eminence is in moral and intellectual virtue (*Pol* III, 13). [This difficulty may be illustrated by a quotation attributed to Heraclitus: "The Ephesians would do well to hang themselves, every grown man of them, and leave the city to beardless lads; for they have cast out Hermodorus, the best man among them, saying, 'We will have none that is best among us; if there be any such, let him be so elsewhere and among others.'" This Ephesian sentiment has often been echoed in the United States Senate.]

In an effective democracy a board of magistrates, who have the necessary knowledge, prepare measures for the people's approval. But in the extreme form of democracy the people, receiving abundant pay and having nothing else to do, are always holding assemblies and deciding everything for themselves. In this situation, the excesses of demagogues—who are likely to be either generals or spellbinders—lead to revolutions by those against whom they have directed persecution.

Principles of Oligarchic Government

It is unwise for oligarchs to oppress the people, for then someone is very likely to inspire a revolution among the disaffected. Experience has shown that such leaders may be members of the oligarchy itself, or wealthy persons excluded from the government, or generals. Trouble often arises when the oligarchs engage in extravagant living and support this by raids on the rich or on the treasury.

Generals are a great hazard and often become dictators; for, in the mutual distrust between rulers and people, the generals and the army have to be entrusted with the defense of the country in war and of the government in peace. Personal quarrels among the oligarchs often cause revolutions, as do also inequities in honor, property, and power among citizens of a superior and high-spirited class. In general, the greater the distribution of power and property the greater is the degree of political stability. Power in the hands of the rich tends to make them insolent and avaricious, and their violations of the constitution and of justice may result in revolution (*Pol* V, 7). Clever political tricks, such as manipulations of registration and property qualifications for the ulterior purposes of class control, are likely in the long run to prove useless. The stability of oligarchies can be increased by attention to good relations with the unenfranchised, by introduction of leading spirits of the latter into the government, by limited tenures of office, and by attaching to high political offices the requirement of large personal expenditures for public purposes. Great care should be taken of the poor.

Principles of Tyrannical Government

A tyrant should purge out any who rise too high or are too independent; prohibit unsupervised organizations, assemblies, meetings, and education; keep surveillance over all residents and keep them in a state of subservience. He should employ spies and informers, including members of families; promote quarrels and mistrust among his subjects; impoverish his people so that, being kept busy scraping a living, they will have no time or strength to conspire; another way to keep them busy is to make war. Not as a prescription specifically for tyrannies but in a more general context occurs the ethnocentric argument, which was put into practice by Nazi Germany: plants exist for the sake of animals, and animals for the sake of man, "and so, in one point of view, the art of war is a natural art of acquisition, for the art of acquisition includes hunting, an art which we ought to practice against wild beasts, and against men who, though intended by nature to be governed, will not submit; for war of such a kind is naturally just" (*Pol* I, 8).

Alternatively, a tyrant may adopt a program based upon an almost opposite principle of action. He may strive to become a "father figure." In that case he will show himself very careful about public revenues and give an accounting of them, thus avoiding popular discontent; he will be seen to collect taxes only for public purposes; avoid any offensive personal behavior; adorn and improve his city; practice religion and align himself with the gods; honor men of merit personally but distribute punishments by deputy; present himself as the protector of the rich against the poor and of the poor against the rich; maintain the character of a great soldier.

The Art of Persuasion

That branch of social psychology which nowadays is called propaganda—defined as "the planned use of any form of public . . . communication designed to affect the minds and emotions of a given group for a specific purpose" (Linebarger, 1948)—was not neglected by Aristotle. In his *Rhetoric* he says that there are three modes of persuasion: the first depends on the speaker presenting himself in an attractive and friendly character—as having "good sense, good moral character, and goodwill"; the second, on putting the audience in a receptive and placable state of mind; the third, on presenting plausible—not necessarily valid or honest—arguments. Aristotle has of course a good deal to say about virtue, justice, etc., but his book deals in very practical terms with methods of getting results; of utilizing "in any given case the available means of persuasion." Whether one is on this side or on that of any given case, Aristotle suggests a plausible argument and rebuttal. "The duty of rhetoric is to deal with such matters as we deliberate on without arts or systems to guide us, in the hearing of persons who cannot take in at a glance a complicated argument or follow a long chain of reasoning." The rhetorician must not only be skilled in dialectic but he must understand human character and know how to manipulate emotions; how, e.g., to arouse hostility against a man by utilizing feelings of vengefulness, frustration, insecurity, or dissonance with an established set. The *Rhetoric,* in short, is a catalog of motives, dispositions, and practical situations, and of the methods of gaining advantage from them. Its detailed thoroughness as an applied psychology of attitude manipulation can only be appreciated by reading the whole. On the techniques of "mass communication," it is difficult to see what, in principle, could be added by modern textbooks in the way of practical advice. Consider a few examples: "One great advantage of maxims to a speaker is due to the want of intelligence in his hearers, who love to hear him succeed in expressing as a universal truth the opinions which they hold themselves about particular cases." Maxims also "invest a speech with moral character." Since any given thing usually has both good and bad consequences, the speaker can use whichever suits his purpose: "e.g., education leads both to unpopularity, which is bad, and to wisdom, which is good. Hence you either argue, 'It is therefore not well to be educated, since it is not well to be unpopular'; or you answer, 'No, it is well to be educated, since it is well to be wise.'" It is very effective to take advantage of the fact that "The things people approve of openly are not those which they approve of secretly." There are very few modern political speeches for which the principles could not be found in Aristotle's *Rhetoric*. As for forensic oratory, "you have a basis in the law, and once you have a starting-point, you can prove anything."

Very useful to rascals of all sorts, but especially to those who practice scapegoating, libel, blackmail, or fraud is the very complete list of descriptions of the kinds of persons who can be attacked with impunity: e.g., "those whose character has been attacked in the past, or is exposed to attack in the future . . . those who are hated or unpopular."

9

Psychology as Philosophy

Anyone who has at some time or another been influenced by Kant,—
anyone who has adopted an idealistic standpoint, and has been
unable to get rid of the last traces of the notion of the 'thing in
itself,' retains a certain inclination towards solipsism, which may
appear more or less clearly. . . . But when a man of science tells
me that solipsism is the only consistent standpoint, he excites my
astonishment. I will not emphasize the fact that this standpoint is
better suited to a fakir who dreams his life away in contemplation,
than to a serious, thoughtful and active man. But what I do believe
is that the man of science who inclines this way is making a confusion between philosophical and scientific methods.—Ernst Mach,
The Analysis of Sensations, p. 357 f.

I have been told that, in philosophy, errors never die; and it may
be that they die hard, in psychology, because that earlier habit of
immortality is still strong upon them.—Edward Bradford Titchener,
Lectures on the Elementary Psychology of Feeling and Attention,
p. 86.

We have reviewed three centuries of intellectual activity in
ancient Greece and its continued echoes in modern science. The
Greek developments relevant to the theory and program of psychology reached their ultimate expression in the work of Aristotle,
which we considered under the heads of "The Linguistics of Science," "Man as a Biological Organism," and "Man in Society." In
the remaining three chapters I shall discuss, under similar heads,
some modern writings, especially of the nineteenth and early twentieth centuries, with a view both to suggesting their continuity with
the older history and to assessing their significance for the present
state and future program of psychology.

Scientific method, as we saw it in Aristotle, consists of two kinds of technique: that of linguistics—including logic and mathematics —and that of observation. The two techniques are interrelated: observations lead to generalizations, and generalizations must agree with observed facts. With Archimedes of Syracuse (287-212 B.C.) the main principles of scientific method, as they are usually expounded in modern philosophies of science, had become clear: the formulation of definite and limited problems; the mathematical formulation of hypotheses; the experimental testing of deductions from the hypotheses. Moreover, Archimedes' treatise on *Method* (Heath, 1912) discusses the actual process of scientific research, which is usually concealed in the subsequent formal presentation, and which, as we saw, had already been described by Aristotle: first "intuitions" resulting from empirical observations; then testing of the intuitive principles—either "mentally" or by manipulations; and finally the construction of logical proofs or demonstrations. Archimedes was a physicist who worked particularly in that division of mechanics known as statics, the doctrine of equilibrium; much of his research had to do with the principles of the lever. This is a field in which the relation between logical deductions from hypotheses and experimental tests is relatively obvious. In theology and metaphysics, hypotheses may be immortal, and in biology and psychology their lives may be almost as long. It is not surprising, therefore, that in the effort of psychology to attain the status of a science, as well as in that of philosophy to rationalize the methodology of science, the model of mathematical physics should have been attractive. The suitability of this model for psychology, however, seems highly questionable.

Psychology and Philosophy

Linguistic techniques are regarded by philosophers as their peculiar domain. The difficulty is that most of the matters which philosophers have to verbalize about are products of scientific research, and any science is an on-going enterprise in which verbal formulations have reference to past and projected techniques of manipulation, observation, and recording. The linguistics of a science is its *organon*; it is an instrument or tool, having the same pragmatic status as its laboratory techniques. Both verbalizations and techniques are provisional, and depend for their significance upon their mutual interrelations. Science, in other words, is not an autonomous linguistic process, nor can its rules be legislated by logicians. Many have been misled by the vision of Einstein penetrating the secrets of the universe by means of a page of equations, as though no physical research had preceded and as though the devastating physical confirmations which followed were entirely the products of purely linguistic processes. The reading of most of the writers of "philosophies of science" has been concentrated on the literature of mathematical physics rather than that of biology or experimental psychology. Nevertheless, in their chapters or pages referring to these latter sciences, they do not hesitate to summon them before the bar of metaphysics—disguised as "philosophy of science" or "logic"—and to reproach them with declining to continue such ancient dialogues as that of the "mind-body problem" (cf., e.g., Feigl, 1958; Hook, 1960). The choice of his linguistic instruments—of his vocabulary, semantics, and syntax—is no less the responsibility of the scientist than is the choice of his laboratory instruments; the layman can judge the validity of both only in terms of some outcome communicated and intelligible to nonspecialists. In biological research, e.g., in such areas as cytology, genetics, or neurophysiology, the validity of results and conclusions depends upon a complex series of steps in the preparation of the material and on sophisticated controls of conditions; only the research scientist can evaluate the results in terms of the preparation and the experimental conditions, and the language in which he reports his research refers technically to preparation, conditions, and methods of recording and measurement.

As for psychology, the vagaries which can arise when linguistic processes are associated not with objective observation but with private meditation can be illustrated from the history of "logical positivism." Philosophers of this school found "behaviorism" to be an expression of the tendency—which at least in one of their phases they approved—toward "physicalism." But behaviorism and objective psychology were the creation not of philosophers but of biologists and biologically trained psychologists who had found their linguistic tools inadequate to their laboratory researches. When therefore, with an abatement of physicalistic zeal, some positivist philosophers assert the "necessity" of reintroducing the term and concept of "introspection," it seems reasonable to reply that this is a matter to be decided on pragmatic grounds by the scientists concerned. Hanson (1962) concludes a discussion of the relative roles of logicians and scientists by stressing

. . . the fact that mastery of the techniques of science and the techniques of logic requires experience and study and that logicians of science have perceived the need for both techniques, whereas practicing scientists, although they very often undertake both, are usually trained in only one [p. 1314].

However, the "conceptual analyses" and "argument structures" which serve him as illustrations are as usual those of Newton, Schrödinger, Heisenberg, Dirac, and Einstein. It is difficult to see how specialists in "argument structures" can usefully operate on an amorphous conglomeration of physiology, sociology, "mental" and "personality" testing, psychoanalysis, parapsychology, techniques of propaganda, advertising, salesmanship, and machine operation, and paramedical therapy. Perhaps the linguistic specialists can be more helpful when psychologists have reached some agreement as to what the subject matter of psychology is; the logicians who will then be useful will be those who will have diligently studied biology, and who, as a result of their professional training, will not confuse logic with metaphysics or experiment with meditation.

With the rapid development of science in the nineteenth century —the century which saw the rise of experimental psychology— there was increasing recognition of the necessity of correlating linguistic with laboratory methodology. The traditional metaphysical view was that science was a—perhaps minor—department of philosophy, and that it was the business of philosophers to formulate accounts of the universe in general. The semantics and syntax of these accounts were determined by philosophical tradition and by the personalities and conditions of life of the individual philosophers. Typically, the philosopher began by "intuitively" formulating certain a priori principles, and his subsequent account of the world consisted in "rationalistic" deductions from these principles. In science, on the other hand, it became evident that verbal statements must be correlated with experimental operations and observations. The notion, which had been adumbrated by Aristotle, that in science all linguistic formulations should be controlled, if not step by step then at least at certain points, by technically controlled observations, became widely current. Besides the technical (experimental, statistical, etc.) control there was required social control of the sort emphasized by Protagoras; that is, science as an institutionalized activity came to require independent confirmation of observations, and social agreement as to definitions of terms and as to procedures for testing hypotheses.

The verbal patterns of philosophers had been subject to no such close controls; on the other hand, they had been subject to extrascientific motivations which resulted from the fact that the professional responsibilities and interests of philosophers included religion, ethics, esthetics, and, paradoxically, the ineffable world of each philosopher's private "experience." Initial assumptions and subsequent attitudes toward hypotheses tended in varying degrees to be determined by such traditional and extrascientific preoccupations. Again, philosophers were individualists; since there was no institutionalized technique of checking philosophical verbalizations against technically and socially controlled observations, and since many—or most—philosophical verbalizations were incapable of such check, there was no prospect of progressive convergence of statement such as was to be expected in science. Such assimilation of philosophies to scientific discoveries and hypotheses as did occur was not usually attributable to habits of systematic, continual, and specific check, but rather to the influence on philosophers of the general atmospheric effect of some of the more publicized conceptions of science. Thus, for example, the theory of evolution and the post-Newtonian changes in physical theory came to influence philosophy, but by way largely of seeming to offer encouragement to ancient philosophical dogmas, an encouragement to which some eminent physicists and biologists gladly contributed.

A number of the "problems" which continue to be discussed in contemporary literature have histories which began several thousand years ago. When we call certain questions *problems,* we imply that we may possibly find *solutions* for them. Now a solution may be either—as in philosophy—a terminal verbalization which satisfies its maker, or—as in science—an experimental operation which confirms one of the alternatives contained in the question. Some questions can be answered in the scientific manner, others only in the philosophical manner. The sorting out of these two kinds is essential to efficient work in science.

Anyone who enters upon intellectual work must be prepared for the existence of different systems of discourse, each with its own vocabulary and rules of semantics and syntax, and must learn that it is just as injudicious to mix such systems as it is to mix the rules of different games or the conventions of different social groups. In scientific discourse, questions which are said to be insoluble are treated as questions which—so far as science is concerned—are improperly stated. If questions which first arose several thousand years ago, out of a background of magic and religion, have still not attained generally acceptable answers in science or philosophy, we are justified in suspecting that they do not conform to the rules of scientific discourse. There is a great advantage, I think, in treating such questions as historical and linguistic problems rather than as problems of "reality." For example, the "mind-body problem" is advantageously treated, not as the question of whether we must assume that human beings consist of both a body and a mind, but as the question of how this way of talking arose and whether it has any heuristic value in modern experimental science. It is a question of *pragmatics*: "that portion of semiotic which deals with the origin, uses, and effects of signs within the behavior in which they occur" (Morris, 1946, p. 219). This treatment of such questions is advantageous, I say, if at a given time we are agreed that we are practicing science and hence are using the scientific system of discourse. The fact that terms have long been used imposes on us no obligation to continue to use them. Of course it may happen that as we study the history of some of these ancient verbalizations, we may find ways in which they can be translated into language having operational significance in current science. So, for example, the old distinctions between perception and thinking, sensations and ideas, or inner and outer sense may perhaps be translated into the distinction between afferent and intrinsic (autonomous) functional activity of the cortex. That is, the rules of scientific discourse change with the available instrumental techniques; in the 1920's, when little was known about cerebral physiology, it was a rule—at least among behaviorists—that behavior must be explained in terms of peripheral correlations, and explanations in terms of central processes were considered by many psychologists to be "unscientific." Thus one task of history is to record the continual amendments to the linguistic rules of science, and another is to inquire whether any old and perhaps neglected questions can be translated into language which makes them amenable to new experimental techniques.

The Paradox of Positivism

The belief in the social mission of science found expression in the nineteenth century in the movement known as *positivism*. As Frankel (1950) says, positivism "stands for a certain temper of mind as well as a particular system of philosophy." It is the temper

of mind which has come to seem most natural to modern scientifically educated men and which is characterized by such propositions
as the following: that it is idle to speculate about the "ultimate
nature" of the world and of man; that science is a set of techniques
for solving particular problems; and that the methods of science
constitute the only intelligent approach to the problems not only
of the physical world but also of human affairs. A familiar expression of this attitude is the statement that the difficulties which have
arisen from the rapid advance of the physical sciences can be rectified by a comparable application of scientific methodology in the
social sciences. Positivism thus presents a paradox: on the one
hand, positivists recommend an objective, matter-of-fact method
which seeks to determine how things *are* rather than how they
should or *must* be; on the other hand, it seems typical for positiv-
istically oriented scientists to be concerned about moral and social
problems. The intellectuals of the eighteenth and nineteenth centuries who experienced in their own lives the rapid rise of science
were greatly troubled by the conflict of the scientific attitude with
the traditional metaphysical and theological beliefs which had been
accepted as the supports of moral and social behavior and institutions. Increasingly in the twentieth century our discomfort has
resulted from the impact on human affairs of the technological
applications of science. We can thus appreciate the force of the
following statement by Frankel (1950, p. 330):

> In short, most of modern philosophy has been wrestling with the
> positivistic temper of mind, as though it could neither live with it nor
> without it. The question of the interpretation to be placed on science,
> and the question of its bearing on human values, have been the most
> vexed issues of modern thought, and have given rise to a bewildering
> variety of philosophic schools of both a positivist and an anti-positivist
> persuasion.

The history of positivism might be said to extend from ancient
times to the present. In ancient Greece it was represented by such
thinkers as Epicurus, who sought to free men from theology by
offering them an explanation of the universe in terms of natural
law, and the Sophists, who wished to bring positive knowledge to
bear on human affairs. The cumulative successes of the scientific
method in the seventeenth and eighteenth centuries increasingly
favored the acceptance of the positivistic attitude among intellectuals. In England, the empirical philosophy, beginning with
Francis Bacon and culminating in Hume and John Stuart Mill,

became an essential part of the positivist tradition. The contributions of the philosophers of the French and German Enlightenment were also important: Descartes' attempt at a mathematical method, his criterion of truth—the clearness and distinctness of ideas, and his mechanistic model for the universe and for animal behavior; Leibnitz's plan for a universal science to be formulated in terms of a universal scientific language; Kant's limitation of theoretical knowledge to the realm of experience; the opposition to theology and other authoritarianism and the scientific and humanitarian orientation of such French writers as Voltaire, Diderot, Helvetius, Holbach, and LaMettrie. It must be remembered that the seventeenth and eighteenth centuries—the era of the "Enlightenment" —were highly dynamic: moral corruption and misrule of governing classes, starvation and misery of the masses, chaos of religious and political wars and revolutions resulted in widespread disillusionment with both temporal and spiritual authority, and with philosophical dogmas as well. Age-old authoritarian secular and religious doctrines were challenged by doctrines of "natural rights," and philosophical dogmas by the programs of those who, encouraged by the great discoveries of science, were confident that human reason could conquer everything. It is against this background that we must seek to understand the French philosopher *Auguste Comte* (1798-1857) who gave positivism its name and expounded its doctrines in his *Cours de Philosophie Positive.*

Comte's main purpose was social reform, and his interest in science resulted from his belief that it could serve as an instrument of social reorganization. He wrote, "I have a supreme aversion to scientific labors whose utility, direct or remote, I do not see." He wished to substitute science for theology as the moral foundation for social institutions. He defined science as the study of the laws of phenomena, of the constant relations of coexistence and succession observed to hold among the elements of experience. His slogan was "Savoir pour prévoir"—"Know in order to predict"; knowledge of the regular sequences of phenomena permits the prediction and control of events—the slogan which John B. Watson transmitted to American psychology. Comte arranged the sciences in a hierarchical order: mathematics, astronomy, physics, chemistry, biology, and sociology. Each of these presupposed the preceding ones, but the phenomena of a "higher" science could not be "reduced" to those of a "lower"; however, since psychology was classed under biology, the difficulty of its "reduction" to biology would presumably not arise. (But G. W. Allport, 1954, has pointed out that "What most students do not know is that toward the end of his life Comte was wrestling with a 'true final science' which, if fully worked out, could only have been what today we call psychology, even though Comte preferred to label it the science of "la morale positive" [p. 7]. This science was to be dependent upon *both* biology and sociology.)

The other great positivist, *Ernst Mach* (1838-1916), held that all scientific statements could be "reduced" to statements of sensations, a view which made possible the development of the concept of the "unity of science" by his successors. But more important in the present connection is Mach's statement that "my ideal of psychology is that it should be purely physiological" (Mach, 1959, p. 340, *note*); though he added that "I should nevertheless think it a great mistake to reject so-called 'introspective' psychology entirely," he "repeatedly emphasized the unity of the physical and the psychical" (p. 339), and actually identified psychology with neurophysiology:

> Thus the great gulf between physical and psychological research persists only when we acquiesce in our habitual stereotyped conceptions. A color is a physical object as soon as we consider its dependence, for instance, upon its luminous source, upon other colors, upon temperatures, upon spaces, and so forth. When we consider, however, its dependence upon the retina . . . , it is a psychological object, a sensation. Not the subject-matter, but the direction of our investigation, is different in the two domains [Mach, 1959, p. 17 f.].

Here again, a psychology which is "purely physiological" would not need to be "reduced" to biology, since it would *be* biology.

Mach's doctrine, which was "phenomenalistic" in that the universal "elements" which were to assure the unity of science were said to be "sensations," became "physicalistic" in the course of its development by the "Vienna Circle," a group which evolved in 1923 from a seminar at the University of Vienna led by Moritz Schlick, and which included among its members and affiliates a number of men whose names are now familiar in American science: Feigl, Neurath, Frank, Bergmann, Hempel, Reichenbach. Their program came to be called "logical positivism" or "logical empiricism." An interesting illustration of the intent of this program is given in a quotation from Neurath by Joergensen (1951, p. 76):

> The universal language of science becomes a self-evident demand, if it is asked, how can certain singular predictions be derived; e.g., "the forest fire will soon subside." In order to do this we need meteor-

ological and botanical sentences and in addition sentences which contain the terms "man" and "human behavior." We must speak of how people react to fire, which social institutions will come into play. Thus, we need sentences from psychology and sociology. They must be able to be placed together with the others in a deduction at whose end is the sentence: "Therefore, the forest fire will soon subside."

Carnap and Neurath agreed that the most expedient universal and intersubjective language in which such sentences could be expressed would be that of physics, or, as it was presently called, a "thing-language." Carnap (1959) presented the thesis that *"every sentence of psychology may be formulated in physical language"* (p. 165), and further, that "a sentence about other minds states that the body of the person in question is in a physical state of a certain sort" (p. 175). Carnap offered rebuttals to the usual objections to this thesis; in particular, he answered the objection that physiology is at an insufficient stage of development by stating that "Our ignorance of physiology can therefore affect only the mode of our characterization of the physical state of affairs in question. It in no way touches upon the principal point: that sentence P_1 ["Mr. A. is now excited"] refers to a physical state of affairs" (p. 175 f.). As for "intuitive psychology," Carnap observed, "Science is not a system of experiences, but of sentences" (p. 185), a statement which recalls Urban's (1939, p. 14) remark that "All knowledge, including what we know as science, is in the last analysis, discourse." Like the physician, the "intuitive" psychologist establishes by his diagnostic reaction "nothing but the existence of some specific physical condition of the experimental subject," and like the physiologist, he must "find a way of physicalizing the indirect characterization" (Carnap, 1959, p. 185). After distinguishing between an "actual property"—"a property which is defined by characteristics that can be directly observed"—and a "disposition" —"a property which is defined by means of an implication (a conditional relationship, an if-then sentence)"—Carnap points out that "more accurate insight into the micro-structure of the human body should enable us to replace dispositional concepts by actual properties (p. 186 f.). These remarks of Carnap's, made in 1932, about the progress possible in this direction are far better supported today. In a later paper, Carnap (1956) suggested that

Both these approaches [the introspective and the behavioristic] in psychology will probably later converge toward theories of the central nervous system formulated in physiological terms. In this physiological phase of psychology, which has already begun, a more and more prominent role will be given to quantitative concepts and laws referring to micro-states described in terms of cells, molecules, atoms, fields, etc. And finally micro-physiology may be based on micro-physics. This possibility of constructing finally all of science, including psychology, on the basis of physics, so that all theoretical terms are definable by those of physics and all laws derivable from those of physics, is asserted by the thesis of physicalism (in its strong sense) [p. 74 f.].

There have been many shifts in point of view and changes in formulation of logical positivist doctrine, so that a psychologist who wished to be guided by it would, like a lawyer, have to consult the successive revisions of the code and the varying judicial interpretations or "argument structures." Moreover, the psychologist might be disconcerted by the observation that the formulation of the code seems to be based, at least in part, on pragmatic judgments by individual philosophers on such matters as the "mind-body problem," "telepathy," "psychokinesis," the causal efficacy of "mental states," "free will," and the nature of language (cf. Feigl, 1958). Or, more formally expressed, there seems to be an insistence by the philosopher on the retention of traditional psychological terms and sentences, regardless of their utility in experimental research or their acceptability to experimental psychologists. Characteristically, philosophers, in writing on psychological topics, do not refer to specific experimental research, but "illustrate" their views by examples beginning with such phrases as "Suppose that . . ." Feigl's ultimate arguments against "hard-boiled behaviorists" and "crass materialists" (an interesting historical study would be that of the development by philosophers of a "technical" vocabulary of vituperation) seem to be "such persuasive or *ad hominem* questions as, "Don't you want anesthesia if the surgeon is to operate on you? And if so, what you want prevented is the occurrence of the (very!) raw feels of pain, is it not?" (p. 390). I would have thought that for the purposes of psychological *science* this argument had been met by Carnap (1959), who pointed out that unless a sentence about "minds," whether "other minds" or "one's own mind," is taken to refer to physical processes in the body of the person in question, the sentence becomes "untestable and thus meaningless" (p. 191). "Meaningless," that is, in the special language of scientific psychology; not "meaningless" in the language of everyday life and of philosophy in its hermeneutic and supportive role. But it is *science* which is under discussion, and it seems unreasonable for a philosopher to disregard, interdict, prescribe, or redefine the terms which are a part of the technical apparatus of a science.

As Aristotle recognized, logical analysis presupposes a previous analysis of natural language. This latter is the responsibility, not of philosophers, but of linguists. Linguistic science has undergone a highly accelerated development in the past three decades. It is absurd for a philosopher to ignore this development and to offer an individualistic redefinition of language as Feigl (1958, p. 402) does in the following passage:

> For the present I submit that by a "language" one is not compelled to mean an instrument of interpersonal communication. The idea of the soliloquy (*intra*-personal communication) may be restricted and modified in such a manner that it refers to unexpressed and inexpressible thoughts.

I am reminded of a sentence attributed to Goethe: "Jeder Mensch, weil er spricht, glaubt über die Sprache sprechen zu können." Similarly, we might say, "Jeder Mensch, weil er denkt, glaubt Psychologie betreiben zu können." Or, as Wundt said, "Alle Vulgärpsychologie besteht also kurz gesagt in der Hinübertragung einer subjektiven Reflexion über die Dinge an die Dinge selbst" (1911, p. 28). The psychologist might well conclude that contemporary "positivists" cannot be regarded as neutral technical consultants on the logical syntax of language; they are rather amateur psychologists—psychologists without laboratories, but with philosophical prepossessions. The Vienna Circle has thus completed a full revolution: from the metaphysics from which Mach—who, unlike many of his followers, was himself a scientist, both in physics and in psychology—sought to free science; through antimetaphysical phenomenology and physicalism; and back to the ancient "problems" of philosophy; we might well ask with Mach, "Are we here being led round in a circle by some evil spirit?"

We are touching here on a problem which has until recently been neglected: that of the influence on philosophical and scientific discourse of the philosophical and religious tradition, social and political environment, and consequent internal organization of the philosopher and scientist. As Weiss (1929b) pointed out, the developments in subatomic physics had a traumatic effect on physicists, some of whom in reaction turned psychologists. But, "The physicists who are now writing on the philosophical or psychological aspects of modern physics are using a psychology which they acquired during their undergraduate years." And, "Modern psy-

chology is a closed field for the physicist as such. He may indulge
in certain literary speculations and poetic flights, just as any one
else may do, but he is no more an authority in the field of human
behavior or social organization than any popular writer." The
physicist, said Weiss, translated experimental limitations into properties of the universe; as a matter of fact, "The physical properties
which are assigned to an electron depend on the physical (anatomical and physiological) properties of the physicist." And finally, in
commenting on the following peroration of an essay by Bridgman
(1929),

> And in the end, when man has fully partaken of the fruit of the
> tree of knowledge, there will be this difference between the first Eden
> and the last, that man will not become as a god, but will remain for-
> ever humble.

Weiss remarks,

> Bridgman is humble now, and there are a number of other physi-
> cists who feel the same way, but this is because they are baffled by
> the complexity of the physical situation which must be fitted into a
> social system. Humility is the attitude of the conquered. Man tri-
> umphant has never been humble.

The philosophers have of course been affected by this mood of the
physicists, whose theoretical constructions and extrascientific lucu-
brations they tend to take as models and from whose methodological bafflement they draw both cosmic and moral inferences. But
they have been affected also by the general pessimism appropriate
to our times—to the world since 1914. Like the Cynics and Cyre-
naics in the troubled times of the fourth century B.C., they tend to
turn inward; they feel impelled to return once again to the subjective world of Plato, Descartes, Husserl, and Heidegger; they find,
e.g., the Freudian "analysis" more congenial than the objective
experimental research in psychological and physiological laboratories. It was otherwise when Viennese positivism was founded;
then everything was possible, and there were endless vistas of
scientific discovery and of human progress. This brief period—from
1870 to 1914—was a time also of relative political and economic
stability, a golden age in which "pure science," undeflected by commercial, political, or religious demands, could be practiced by men
of lofty and independent character—such men as Helmholtz, Ludwig, and Mach—who had no hesitation in rejecting the ancient
philosophical verbalisms which were of no utility in experimental

research. That in our own time there has been a "loss of nerve" is quite understandable, but it is also a most depressing feature of our situation.

Subjectivistic Incursions into Psychology

In Chapter 2 I called attention to Marett's distinction, in the life of primitive peoples, between routine, commonsensical, or proto-scientific behavior in "normal" or favorable environments, and magical or religious behavior in catastrophic situations. In the history of philosophy and science of civilized peoples there have occurred, with changes from the one to the other of these two kinds of environmental situations, alternating cycles of optimism, rational analysis, and objectivism, and of pessimism, subjectivism, and anti-intellectualism. We first encountered these cycles in ancient Greece, where the objective, free-ranging thought of the Milesians in a time of prosperity and expansion was followed by Platonic and post-Platonic subjectivism and hostility to science in times of increasing social chaos and individual insecurity. We have now to consider some subjectivistic phases of such cycles in modern times which have influenced that congeries of activities whose relatedness consists in their being called "psychology."

The tradition of "romanticism," subjectivism, and irrationality which began in the latter part of the eighteenth century and which has entered at various points into modern psychology may be said to have had three main sources. First, there were the reactions against general social, political, and economic conditions, as in the period leading up to the French Revolution of the late eighteenth and the German Revolution of the mid-nineteenth century, and in the ensuing period of the growth and conflict of nationalities down to 1870; since 1914 chaos and insecurity have reached new heights, and have given rise to that revival of subjectivism known as "existentialism." Secondly, there was the conflict, very severe for some individuals, between the old and the new in theology and philosophy: the authoritarian versus the individualistic, the rationalistic versus the empiristic, the subjectivistic versus the objectivistic, the religious or metaphysical versus the scientific, the holistic versus the analytic. And thirdly, there was the occurrence, in times of social conflict, of neurotic and psychotic individuals.

Romanticism is not of course the only possible reaction in difficult times. The same age which produced Rousseau (1712-1778) also produced that representative of mechanistic materialism, LaMettrie (1709-1751); in von Haller (1707-1777), the founder of modern experimental physiology, the scientific and the romantic strains were united in one man, whose creativity was consequently marred by religious melancholy. In different individuals, the grounds for reaction-style may be predominantly constitutional-physiological, or biographical, or socio-historical. But individuals of different constitutions react differently to similar biographical and social conditions, and individuals whose behavior might otherwise be "normal" may become neurotic, melancholy, and pessimistic under sufficiently severe conditions. Such severe conditions are permanent possibilities of all human life; death or incurable disease of an individual or of his loved ones are irreversible catastrophes. In recent times large populations of individuals have suddenly found themselves impoverished, driven from their homes, tortured, their status as human beings abolished. For individuals caught in such ultimate realities, science and rationality are irrelevant; for the extreme conditions, *nothing* is relevant; for less extreme conditions, the ancient religious formulae may assist in some sort of survival. "Psychologically regarded," says Marett, "the function of religion is to restore man's confidence when it is shaken by crisis."

But religion, Marett goes on to say, is a traditional social institution which involves conventional doctrine. When, in the period beginning about 1750, new theological, social, and scientific doctrines came into conflict with traditional doctrines, constitutionally predisposed persons reacted with over-compensatory romanticism, anti-intellectualism, antisocial rebellion, or "nihilism." Psychologists, reading the writings and the biographies of these persons, would, I think, class most of them as neurotics, and neither humanitarians nor scientists would be likely to select from among their number a model of the humane intellectual.

The Philosophers of Rationalism

The rationalistic and analytic *thesis* to which the romantic and holistic movement was the *antithesis* and reaction was represented by Descartes, Leibnitz, Kant, and the British empiricists Locke,

Berkeley, and Hume; the antithesis was represented by Rousseau, Schopenhauer, Kierkegaard, Nietzsche, and, in recent times, Heidegger and Sartre. Not that the dialectical contrast was "pure"; both traditions were strongly subjectivistic; within the rationalistic tradition this tendency was at war with the scientific trend of the age. In both traditions there were religious and mystical preoccupations and motivations. Both traditions were combined in Hegel.

Descartes (1596-1650) reflected the contrary influences of his time by developing *both* a mechanistic theory and *also* a psychophysical interactionism. (On the one hand, Galileo and Harvey were driving animism out of physics and physiology; on the other, the reactionary movement in theology induced self-preservatory caution in philosophers. Descartes, like modern professors, loved peace and quiet; he had no desire to follow Bruno to the stake, nor even to risk the less painful death which at Paris in 1624 had been threatened a scholar who wished to discuss the atomic theory in public.) In Descartes' mechanistic physiology, animals are machines whose processes are to be explained in terms of the arrangement and motions of their material parts. The nervous system operates as a *reflex* mechanism: the nerves open from the ventricles of the brain by valves; these nerves not only serve as hollow pipes, which upon the opening of the valves convey the "animal spirits"—a subtle fluid described as being "like a wind or very fine flame"— from the brain ventricles to the muscles, but also contain "little threads" which can be mechanically "pulled" by motion induced at a sensory surface under stimulation. Reflex action thus results when stimulated sensory threads pull—"just as by pulling at one end of a rope one causes to strike at the same instant a bell which hangs on the other end"—at the valves in the brain and thereby permit the animal spirits to flow through the nerves to the muscles, which they inflate "just as the air in a balloon hardens it." (This entire scheme has been excellently described by Fearing [1930, pp. 15-28], whose translations of the *Traité de l'Homme* I have used.) Like Aristotle, Descartes had an automaton model: the hydraulically operated figures in the royal gardens which could leap, gesture, make sounds, and play instruments. I really do not see that this scheme of Descartes' was a notable advance over that of Aristotle; Descartes did have some additional biological knowledge, but not nearly as much as he might have had in his time had he been more of a biologist and less of a philosopher-theologian. Descartes furnishes the classical example of the neglect of a principle stated by Fulton (1926, p. 11) when he said that "a knowledge of structure must precede a study of function"; the neglect of this principle has been characteristic of philosopher-psychologists down to recent times; the "brain-fields" and "electrical tensions" and "closures" of the gestalt psychologists were no more correlated with cellular structures than were the threads and valves of Descartes, nor were they put forward by men who, any more than Descartes, had talent and interest for physiological research; the gestalt analogies were taken from more modern physics than the hydraulics of Descartes, but they were still analogies, with no foundation in neuroanatomy.

It is true that Descartes studied some medicine and made some dissections at the abattoirs, but he made no discoveries, and failed in important respects to understand those which had been made, or to anticipate those which were about to be made. Thus, while he generalized to the neuromuscular system Harvey's demonstration of the mechanistic principle of the circulatory system, he substituted for Harvey's proof of the pumping action of the heart the old notion of the heart expanding under heat; the ancient "animal spirits" and muscle inflation doctrines which he espoused were experimentally disproved within two decades of his death. But though he was a philosopher rather than a biologist, he was enormously influential in expressing the scientific tendency of his age, and it was he who most effectively introduced the mechanistic mode of thought into modern biology; in reaction, there soon arose the vitalistic movement, initiated by Stahl, which ever since has made capital of the unfinished business of biology. (Since the terms "mechanism" and "vitalism" have often a strongly affective value, it is worth-while to recall their cognitive reference: mechanism asserts that living phenomena.*can* be explained—not that they have at a given time *been* explained—in physicochemical terms; vitalism insists that their explanation is now known to require the postulation of a "vital" or "spiritual" force. Here two misconceptions have caused confusion: the notion that correlation, coordination, and mnemic processes—"integration"—in brain centers must consist of "something more" than physicochemical events in anatomical structures, and the notion that the mathematical quandaries of the atomic physicists have spiritualistic implications for biology—a new form of the old Pythagorean grasping for the "secret of the universe." Since Descartes' day, physics has added new concepts and laws—notably those of electricity—to those of mechanics, and the term "mechanism"—as the opposite of "vitalism"—has tended to extend its meaning so as to become synonymous with "physical-ism," which is a variety of both naturalism and positivism.)

But besides introducing mechanism into biology, Descartes intro-duced subjectivism and mind-body dualism into philosophy and psychology. His philosophy, says Russell (1945, p. 567), "brought to completion, or very nearly to completion, the dualism of mind and matter which began with Plato and was developed, largely for religious reasons, by Christian philosophy." The famous "Method" of "Cartesian doubt" arrived at the conclusion that the only cer-tainty from which philosophy can begin is that "I think" (*cogito*). It is only through the "mind," not through the untrustworthy senses, that knowledge of the external world is possible, and then only because Descartes has "proved" the existence of God. "Rea-son," it will be recalled, had been said by Plato to be the only source of true knowledge, and the "true-born" knowledge appre-hended directly by the soul had been contrasted by Democritus with the "bastard" knowledge received by the senses. In psychol-ogy, Descartes' dualism took the form of assuming that in man, while there is, as in animals, a body consisting of matter defined as "extended substance" and deterministically governed by the laws of physics, there is also a spirit or soul defined as "inextended think-ing substance." The question then arose of how an immaterial soul could interact with a material body. Descartes "solved" this prob-lem by assuming that the soul and body interact through the pineal body; the "animal spirits" by impinging on the pineal body bring sensory impressions to the soul, and the soul, also by very slightly inclining the pineal body, directs the animal spirits toward particu-lar motor nerve openings; the difficulty of this interaction was attenuated by describing the required pineal movements as "very slight," on the same principle as the excuse of the girl for her illegit-imate baby: that it was, after all, "a very little one."

Thus Descartes introduced into modern biology and psychology both a mechanistic and hence an objectivistic tradition, and also a dualistic and subjectivistic one. The mechanistic tradition found expression in the physiological researches of such men as Helm-holtz and Sechenov. The interactionistic dualism appeared in Wil-liam James and William McDougall; the dualism palliated as "psychophysical parallelism" filled the fat journal volumes of introspective psychology—of what might paradoxically be called "conventionalized idiosyncrasy" or "verbalized ineffability"—of Wundt, Bain, and Titchener; the subjectivism was the root from which grew the "psychological" movements of phenomenology and existentialism.

In *Leibnitz* (1646-1716) we have the classic example of what happens to "psychology" at the hands of a philosopher whose main interests and intellectual apparatus are theology, mathematics, and logic, and who uses the concepts of physical and biological science in the service of metaphysical speculation; we have in Leibnitz a seventeenth-century Parmenides. As Höffding (1924, I, p. 353) observes: "It is decidedly prejudicial to the clearness and significance of the Leibnitzian philosophy that, from beginning to end, theological points of view play so large a part in it. It by no means furthers the solution of problems to clothe them in theological form." As for the Leibnitzian logic, it is, says Russell (1945, p. 595) a clear-cut example of "drawing inferences from syntax to the real world." Leibnitz's problem was that of the intellectuals of his age: how to reconcile the new scientific discoveries, which as intellectuals they could not but accept, with the old theology, which they regarded as the foundation of individual and social morals and order. Leibnitz effected this reconciliation by means of the assumption that the aims of God find their satisfaction in the operation of the laws of natural science. A consequence of this assumption was that the actual world is the best possible world, and that experienced evil is a small but necessary aspect of a universe in which there is so much light and perfection that even if the majority of men were subjected to eternal torment their pain would be as nothing compared with the infinite sum of happiness. It is easy to see why men of more sombre temperament and experience, notably the followers of Schopenhauer, Kierkegaard, and Nietzsche, revolted against such philosophical optimism, combined as it was with the presupposition of the complete rationality of existence, which was equally unacceptable to them.

Leibnitz's "psychology" is a mixture of physics, biology, introspection, and metaphysical speculation. In physics, his starting point was the atomic theory; introspectively, he started from his observation of his own inner experience. This self-observation revealed not only sensations, feelings, and thoughts, but a fundamental characteristic of all mental states; namely, effort or striving; *activity* is a basic concept of Leibnitz's system, which is therefore a forerunner of the various "act psychologies." By the "law of analogy," all other existence was considered as differing only in degree from our own. Here there occurred an admixture of biology; by means of the microscope, which had then just been invented, Leibnitz was able to see that ". . . life exists everywhere, even where the eye cannot see it; it was thus but a short step to the conclusion that the smallest particles of matter are life-principles—not dead atoms, but living 'monads'" (Nordenskiöld, 1928, p. 128). The universe consists of an infinite number of "monads," indivisible real beings, each different from every other and each containing from the first the potentiality of its whole subsequent history; each develops according to its own indwelling laws by its own force ("force" being defined as the present state of things that brings about a change in the future). The various monads composing the universe enjoy differing degrees of consciousness, of darkness or clearness; the soul of man has the highest degree, while the souls of animals have a kind of consciousness comparable to our duller half-waking states; the monads of inert matter are of a still lower order. The human being is an aggregation of monads of different psychical levels, the soul being the highest monad of the system. There is no causal interaction among the monads; none of them have holes, windows, or doors through which anything from outside can enter in. Nothing in the body can penetrate the soul; hence no impressions enter the soul through the senses, but all our ideas are innate; an individual's ideas however become "clearer" as he "unfolds" according to his own nature. Body and soul *seem* to act on each other, but this appearance of causal interaction is actually attributable to the harmony of their natures pre-established by God at the moment of their creation, just as an infinitely skillful watchmaker might make and set two watches so perfectly that they would forever after show the same time. The mental states of an individual exist in all degrees between darkness and clear consciousness. Below the threshold of consciousness are the *petites perceptions,* illustrated by the sounds of the individual water drops in the roar of the sea; the sum of such small sensations may give rise to *perceptions* of varying degrees of clearness; the highest degree is *apperception,* the stage of voluntary attention. That which presents itself clearly to consciousness is always a combination of more obscure elements. The obscure states of which an individual is not conscious form the connecting links between the conscious states, which would otherwise often appear contradictory. The life of the soul is thus continuous through states of consciousness and unconsciousness, sleep and waking. The obscure organic sensations of which we become aware only when we attend to them exemplify the mental activity which determines us unknown to ourselves; there is more in us than we know, e.g., we use principles of which we can only later become aware.

It will be evident that Leibnitz supplied much of the stock in trade of subsequent psychology and pseudopsychology. In the first place, there is the doctrine of psychophysical parallelism, which, following Spinoza, Leibnitz developed as an alternative to the interactionism of Descartes. At this distance in time we can only marvel that this doctrine, grounded in theology, should have become the foundation of the experimental psychology which according to the conventional account was founded by Wilhelm Wundt. That Wundt, trained as a physiologist, should have projected a science of man in which men were to be regarded not as biological organisms but as congeries of private sensations and feelings is testimony to the power which the German idealistic metaphysics exercised over most—but not all—German psychologists and their British allies, such as Bain, Ward, and Stout. Secondly, the notion of a hierarchy of levels of consciousness provided the program of "animal psychology," which consisted of inferring the "consciousness" of animals from their behavior, in accordance with Leibnitz's "law of analogy." I once witnessed a dramatic demonstration given by Madison Bentley, before a large audience, of the consciousness of an earthworm; Bentley progressively feigned blindness, deafness, abolishment of limbs, etc., until he had arrived at the requisite stage of sensory deprivation. Boring (1950, p. 623) says that "the rule is: if you want to appreciate the animal consciousness, put yourself in the same situation and see what it is like." He asserts that this technique has contributed greatly to the understanding of the performance of the rat in the maze, but concedes that "it is much harder for man successfully to play the role of the free-swimming protozoan." This approach to the study of animal behavior was embodied in Washburn's *The Animal Mind* (1908; fourth edition, 1936), which was for several decades the reigning textbook of "animal psychology."

Thirdly, the doctrine of innate ideas began the tradition of nativism in German psychology which eventuated in gestalt psychology, whereas the doctrine of the combination of sensations and of apperception was a part of the background of Wundt's atomistic associationism. Fourthly, the doctrine of activity appeared both in Wundt's fundamental principle of psychic causality and in his concept of apperception as "active association," and also in Freud's notion of "libido." Fifthly, the doctrine of degrees of consciousness, threshold of consciousness, and the unconscious gave rise to Fechnerian psychophysics and "mental mensuration," to Herbartian "psychical mechanics"—which also involved the notion of "activity," and to the "theoretical" elaborations of Freud, who like Leibnitz needed no experimental techniques nor controls but was able to intuit the laws of life, though he substituted the language of Greek mythology for that of Christian theology.

It is interesting to observe how William James (1890, I), who has exerted so great an influence on American psychology, wrestled with the Leibnitzian conceptions in his chapters on "The Mind-Stuff Theory" and "The Stream of Thought." He begins by saying that

> . . . one easily makes the obscurest assumptions in this science [of psychology] without realizing, until challenged, what internal difficulties they involve. When these assumptions have once established themselves (as they have a way of doing in our very descriptions of the phenomenal facts) it is almost impossible to get rid of them afterwards or to make any one see that they are not essential features of the subject. . . . One of the obscurest of the assumptions of which I speak is *the assumption that our mental states are composite in structure, made up of smaller states conjoined* [I, p. 145].

Of Leibnitz's notion of perceptions as summations of *petites perceptions* James says,

> This is an excellent example of the so-called 'fallacy of division,' or predicating what is true only of a collection, of each member of the collection distributively. It no more follows that if a thousand things together cause sensation, one thing alone must cause it, than it follows that if one pound weight moves a balance, then one ounce weight must move it too, in less degree. . . . And so each infrasensible stimulus to a nerve no doubt affects the nerve and helps the birth of sensation when the other stimuli come. But this affection is a nerve-affection, and there is not the slightest ground for supposing it to be a 'perception' unconscious of itself ⌊p. 164].

Of the argument that "in addition to the fully conscious way in which an idea may exist in the mind, there is also an unconscious way," as seems to be the case when "we deliberately analyze our motives, and find that at bottom they contain jealousies and cupidities which we little suspected to be there," James says that "It would be difficult to believe that intelligent men could be guilty of so patent a fallacy, were not the history of psychology there to give the proof" (p. 172). Of the notion that "Every brain-cell has its

own individual consciousness which no other cell knows anything
about. . . . There is, however, among the cells one central or pontifi-
cal one to which *our* consciousness is attached" (I, p. 179), James
says,

> We are back at Leibnitzian monadism, and therewith leave physiol-
> ogy behind us and dive into regions inaccessible to experience
> and verification; and our doctrine, although not self-contradictory,
> becomes so remote and unreal as to be almost as bad as if it were
> [I, p. 180].

And yet, in attempting to account for the continuity of the "stream
of thought," James describes "transitive states" of consciousness in
a way reminiscent of Leibnitz's "obscure states" which form the
links between conscious states.

It is, I think, obvious that Leibnitz foisted upon psychology a
vast tangle of linguistic blind alleys which occupied its attention
and its books and journals down until the 1920's, and which still
determine much of its non-experimental, intuitive literature.

The empiricism and associationism introduced by the British
philosophers Hobbes and Locke were discussed in Chapter 7. The
"ideas" of which they spoke were of course subjective phenomena,
but *David Hartley* (1705-1757), who was a physician, extended
the principle of association to include muscular movements, and
suggested a neurophysiological hypothesis to account for mnemic
and associative processes; under the influence of Newton's writings,
he substituted for the traditional "animal spirits" hypothetical
"longitudinal vibrations" in the nerves and brain; the physiological
correlates of the ideas of memory are "diminutive vibrations" to
which the medullary substance of the brain becomes disposed by
repetitions of sensory vibrations. *Thomas Brown* (1778-1820)
made an analysis of the variations in stimulating conditions and
in the history and state of the individual which would influence the
process of association. *Alexander Bain* (1818-1903), in his analysis
of "will," started from an assumed tendency of the organism to
"spontaneous movements," and hypothesized that acts which bring
pleasant results are retained while those which bring unpleasant
results are eliminated; in this, Bain anticipated by some forty years
the Thorndikian theory of trial and error learning. The influence of
the British philosophers was great and various; their subjectivistic
empiricism affected German idealistic philosophy through Kant,
and this feature, combined with their associationism and psychophysical parallelism, determined the nature of the pioneer German

"experimental" psychology; most importantly, the seminal work of Ebbinghaus. Through their influence on Beneke they were part of the tradition which led to Sechenov and the Russian objective physiologists. The introduction into the associationistic scheme of muscular movements and trial and error learning by Hartley and Bain prepared the way for the experimental study of learning by Lloyd Morgan and Thorndike. Bain's two works—*The Senses and the Intellect* (1855) and *The Emotions and the Will* (1859)— together constituted the standard British psychological textbook for almost half a century. His parallelism gave to his textbook the pattern of a "physiological psychology" which was followed by subsequent British and American psychologists; characteristics shared with a long line of later textbooks included the attempt to describe both the physical and the mental "aspects" of every topic, a long introductory chapter on the nervous system which was but indifferently correlated with the matter of the subsequent chapters, detailed analysis of the senses, and emphasis on movement as a physiological category. Bain's classification of mental phenomena into cognition, feeling, and volition is still characteristic of British psychology.

If the reader will recall the discussions of Chapter 7, he will be reminded of how much of all this—the sensationalistic empiricism, the associationism, the attempt at physiological correlation—was a recapitulation of Aristotle's analysis which was necessitated by the intervening centuries of theological preoccupations.

Immanuel Kant (1724-1804) had an overpowering influence on German philosophy and psychology. Ernst Mach, in his *Analysis of Sensations* (1959, p. 30) wrote: "I have always felt it as a stroke of special good fortune, that early in life, at about the age of fifteen, I lighted, in the library of my father, on a copy of Kant's *Prolegomena to any Future Metaphysics*. The book made at the time a powerful and ineffaceable impression upon me, the like of which I never afterwards experienced in any of my philosophical reading." If Mach then goes on to describe his long struggle to free himself from the Kantian idealistic metaphysics, he thereby emphasizes how pervasive this metaphysics was and how responsive it was to the contrary influences of the German Enlightenment and the Romantic movement.

The intellectual environment in which Kant grew up included Prussian Pietism—the formalized dogmatic theology of the Lutheran church, Swedenborgian mysticism, and Wolffian metaphysical dogmatism. *Emanuel Swedenborg* (1688-1772) illustrated in his life the conflicting tendencies in the northern Europe of his time; until middle age he was a scientist and man of affairs who made many contributions to pure and applied science, some of which were remarkable anticipations of much later research. But then he began to have visions of heaven and hell and to receive revelations from God; it then became his mission to teach the doctrines thus received: that the essence of God is infinite love; that the two worlds of nature and spirit are distinct but intimately related by analogous substances, laws, and forces, etc. *Christian Wolff* (1679-1754) might be called the first German "professor" of psychology; Pillsbury (1929, p. 107) has remarked: "German universities were no more backward than those elsewhere, but psychology elsewhere was written by independent scholars, and in Germany, when written at all, was the work of the university men." (It is interesting to reflect that all psychologists today are institutionalized.) Wolff was the popularizer of the "great systems," the rationalistic, subjectivistic, dogmatic philosophies of Descartes, Spinoza, and, most particularly, Leibnitz; like Leibnitz, he illustrated the tendency "to unite physical science with theology, by conceiving the world as a huge mechanism, designed to serve the divine ends, and brought into agreement with conscious life by means of a pre-established harmony" (Höffding, 1924, I, p. 370). Wolff also has traditionally been regarded as the typical exponent of German "faculty psychology." Like the Scottish psychology represented by Thomas Reid, Wolffianism described the soul as unitary but as having the capacity or "faculty" of entering into various activities. This was the ancestor of the doctrine of instincts, according to which, e.g., animals fight "because of" an instinct of fear.

At the university, Kant was particularly attracted to physics and mathematics; the strong influences during this period were Newton and Wolff, though in his early writings Kant was critical of both. The most notable of these early writings suggests by its title his orientation toward physical science: *General Natural History and Theory of the Heavens, or an Attempt to Explain the Composition and Mechanical Origin of the Universe on Newtonian Principles*. After about 1760 Kant turned to his main life work, which might be described as the seeking of solutions to two ancient philosophical problems: that of the relations among sense data, thought processes, and external objects, and that of the nature and sanctions of ethical principles.

The first of these problems had been made critical by Berkeley and Hume. Berkeley's position opened the way for solipsism, according to which the universe consists solely of the individual in question and his own experiences, so that the position of science as an objective social activity becomes precarious. In Hume, subjectivistic scepticism reached its climax; all that is available to a human being is his succession of mental states; there can be no rational justification for the concept of causation, the principle of induction, or the belief in the existence of external objects. Theoretically, these conclusions would entail the impossibility both of practical life and of science; Hume however in the end adopted the same adjustment to solipsistic scepticism as did those scientists who saw it as a problem: "If we believe that fire warms, or water refreshes, 'tis only because it costs us too much pains to think otherwise." Knowledge of the external world, said Hume, actually rests on *belief*, which in turn is based upon customary conjunctions and sequences of mental states. Russell (1945, p. 669) remarks that

> So far as the physical sciences are concerned, Hume is *wholly* in the right: such propositions as "A causes B" are never to be accepted, and our inclination to accept them is to be explained by the laws of habit and association. These laws themselves, in their accurate form, will be elaborate statements as to nervous tissue—primarily its physiology, then its chemistry, and ultimately its physics.

With Russell's statement compare that of the behavioristic psychologist A. P. Weiss (1929a, p. 61):

> The solipsism of the behaviorist follows from the assumption that the *individual* is regarded as a locus in the movement continuum. Human behavior is, of course, restricted to bodily movements and no event of an external world can be discriminated until it acts on the sensori-motor mechanism of the individual himself. Solipsism is merely a recognition of the fact that all discrimination is sensori-motor discrimination; there is no other form of movement.

That is, any scientist who finds his highly motivated enterprise threatened by solipsistic paralysis can escape to continued productivity by adopting certain *postulates*: that there is an external world to which the scientist is functionally related, and that induction can validly yield probability estimates.

Kant found himself confronted with the conflict between the dogmatic metaphysics of Leibnitz and Wolff and the subjectivistic scepticism of Hume. His solution was to assume (1) that the "things-in-themselves" of the outer world are not directly accessible to human knowledge, (2) that sensory data are the raw material of cognitions, (3) but that this raw material is given form, organized into concepts, by the activity of thought or "understanding." If we were to put this in modern terms, we would say that the brain *integrates* sensory data—which are "coded messages" and not external objects—and imposes upon them certain organized patterns which are determined by the properties—mostly mnemic and contextual—of the nervous system. This would then be a truism of neurophysiology. However, Kant asserted that certain of the "forms" which the "understanding" imposes on experience are innate: e.g., space, time, causality, The importance of the Kantian analysis for the history of psychology is that it influenced many German psychologists; thus it was largely responsible for the nativism of Hering, Stumpf, and the gestalt psychologists, and for the subjectivism of Herbart, Fechner, Wundt, Avenarius, Mach, Titchener, and the "phenomenologists." This history is a depressing illustration of how philosophical introspection and speculation uncontrolled by biological research can lead to an enormous amount of largely fruitless activity on the part of psychologists. The requisite techniques of biological control were of course not available to these men; in this situation, psychologists under the influence of subjectivistic philosophy seek short cuts: introspection, phenomenology, "depth psychology," "verstehende Psychologie," etc. There seems to be a perennial delusion that a wise man can gaze comprehensively at a total situation, or penetratingly into his own "mind," or empathically at a fellow man, and seize the essence or grasp the categories of these; into this intuitive world the serpents of reliability estimation and physiological validation do not intrude.

Kant's ethics was a product of his Pietistic upbringing and his reading of Rousseau. His models of Pietism were his parents, particularly his mother; they represented for him the patterns of uprightness and moral virtue. Rousseau, on the other hand, who, as Russell (1945, p. 685) says, "was destitute of all the ordinary virtues," and who rejected science, learning, reason, and social decorum, found the rules of conduct "in his own heart"; that is, in the undisciplined impulses of the individual. The ideal good man was for him a fictitious "savage," uncorrupted by human culture. It is paradoxical that Rousseau, the prototype of the "beatnik," should have been an inspiration of Kant's rigorous ethics. The idea of lasting influence which Kant derived from Rousseau—again paradoxically—was that of the dignity of man as a personal being. But though he began by deriving ethical judgments from "feelings," in accordance with Rousseau, he finally rejected emotional motivations, religious sanctions, practical consequences, and personal happiness as proper sources or criteria of right conduct. He also denied that the universally valid moral law is derived from experience; it is a priori "in the reason," and autonomous; it is spoken by the "inner voice" of conscience. The highest ethical precept is *Do your duty,* regardless of personal inclinations or consequences. There is a "categorical imperative": "Act only according to those maxims which thou canst at the same time wish to be general laws." From this Kant thought that he could deduce a second ethical formula: "So act as to treat humanity, whether in thine own person or in that of any other, in every case as an end withal, never as a means only." In the vast literature of ethics there are of course many valid criticisms of Kant's principles, and to us as psychologists it seems obvious that there is no such thing as an absolute moral sense, universally valid, and that moral principles are products of social evolution and of individual learning. And yet we have perhaps fallen into errors far more serious, both for science and for the welfare of mankind, than are the errors which we recognize in Kant; the modern successors to Plato and Hobbes have succeeded on a large scale in making applications of scientific research or pseudoresearch in ways which contravene Kant's ethical formulae. Perhaps Kant's principles, regarded not as a priori but as expressing the "wisdom of the race," would be safer guides to moral conduct—and to the viability and happiness of the human race—than the relativism which we have learned from anthropology or the "adjustment" recommended by psychology or the spiritualistic metaphysics and "free will" which some physicists have professedly deduced from their calculations; perhaps relativism and tentativeness are useful in science, but some fundamental absolutes are desirable in ethics. The itch for consistency and Hegelian wholeness is perhaps our undoing: the demand that all be science or all be religion, for example, or that these be "reconciled," or that scientists throw themselves into the public arena and direct practical affairs, or that philosophers and theologians make value judgments of scientific research and hypotheses. It might be well to recognize that human beings play different games according to different rules, and that even in Aristotle's day, and far more today, competence in one area is but indifferently correlated with competence in others. There have been many objections lately to the view that scientists as such do not make value judgments; they do indeed make such judgments—of objectivity, replicability, nature of relevant variables, statistical reliability. They may act as consultants concerning the means to social ends or concerning the probable effects of certain programs; in judging and applying this advice, however, the guardians of the public weal had better hold fast to the Kantian absolutes.

The philosophy of *Georg Wilhelm Friedrich Hegel* (1770-1831) was the culminating expression of the German idealistic philosophy which stemmed from Kant. In Hegel's formative years the influence of Kant was modified by his interest in classical antiquity—particularly in "the Hellenic idea of a man who is calmly tranquil in the consciousness of his unity with God" (Muirhead, 1910), in medieval Christian mysticism, and in Rousseauism. The philosophy which he evolved was a strange mixture of rationalism and mysticism; it was both an expression of German Romanticism and also the model of intellectualistic philosophizing against which Romantics and existentialists revolted.

Parmenides, we recall, had identified thought with reality, and described reality as a spherical whole, indivisible and homogeneous. Hegel also identified the rational with the real—"Being is thought"—and asserted that the only ultimate reality is the "whole," which he called "the Absolute," and described as "spiritual." He did not maintain that reality was homogeneous, but he did describe the apparent separateness of things as an illusion; their reality, he said, consists in their being parts of the whole.

> The view of Hegel, and of many other philosophers, is that the character of any portion of the universe is so profoundly affected by its relations to the other parts and to the whole, that no true statement can be made about any part except to assign its place in the whole. Thus there can be only one true statement; there is no truth except the whole truth [Russell, 1945, p. 743].

This is of course the metaphysics which has been made familiar to us by gestalt psychology; as Russell says (p. 744), the question at issue "is the question that divides the friends of analysis from its enemies." It is odd that the quarrel between two offshoots of German idealistic philosophy—the post-Hegelian "wholeness" represented by the Berlin gestalt psychologists and the peculiar subjectivistic "analysis" represented by the Leipzig psychologists—should have become so great a preoccupation of American psychology. There were also Hegelian echoes in that branch of American *behaviorism* which mysteriously stemmed from Berlin; thus we find Weiss, Max Meyer's pupil, describing the universe as a dynamic whole of interacting electrons and protons in which individuals and objects are merely temporary loci; of social organization he said, "The organization as a whole exhibits such a complexity and variety of movements that it approaches more closely than does any individual in it, a hypothetical limit which may be characterized as omnipotent, omnipresent, and omniscient" (Weiss, 1929a, p. 432)—a statement, innocently "theoretical" in the 1920's, which has since then acquired ominous implications. Weiss's ideal of social organization was, however, the Kantian ideal of a league of nations for perpetual peace, rather than the Hegelian ideal of the Prussian state organized for war. (Hegel asserted that war "preserves the moral health of peoples.") The cultural center of the area in which Max Meyer spent most of his professional life and in which Weiss was educated was St. Louis; this was the headquarters of a remarkable group that studied Kant and Hegel and published works by and on Hegel; it was a unique center of German idealistic philosophy in America.

Hegel's notion that the social "whole" is a super-person led him to the view—contra Kant—that the individual is a means to an end, that citizens exist for the sake of the State. LaPiere and Farnsworth (1942, pp. 51-52, 394-395) have discussed this "fallacy of personification" and the illegitimate extension of the "organic analogy" in sociology and social psychology; as they indicate, these fallacies have served as rationalizations for totalitarian governments. In psychology, McDougall's is a curious case; by a sort of Hegelian dialectic—*thesis*: acceptance; *antithesis*: rejection; *synthesis*: "germ of truth"—applied to Hegel's political philosophy, McDougall (1920) arrived at his concept of the "group mind," whose prototype is found in the "patriot army." McDougall quoted with approval a writer who declared that the school which derived its inspiration from Kant and Hegel "could satisfy the new needs of social progress, because it refused to worship a supposed individual liberty"; this seeming "revolution of ideas" was however only a "restoration of the *Republic* of Plato" (McDougall, 1920, p. 23 f.).

Gustav Theodor Fechner (1801-1887) was the agent of the most notable incursion of the Hegelian *Naturphilosophie* into experimental psychology: that of "psychophysics." Like Swedenborg he began his career as a physical scientist and ended as a mystic; on the way he invented psychophysics as a means of attaining, as Brett

(1953, p. 555) says, "a unified world of thought, spirit, and matter linked together by the mystery of numbers." Matter was to become one with spirit by means of an equation. Thus through Fechner and Hegel our current experimental psychology is linked with the number-mysticism of Pythagoras. From Hegel too Fechner received that vision of "the wisdom of the East," that "dream of Absolute Spirit," which found expression in Fechner's *Zend-Avesta*. Pillsbury has suggested, half-seriously, that Fechner's "nervous breakdown" and subsequent abandonment of physics for philosophy and psychology might be treated "as a neurosis developed as a defence mechanism."

> It appears that he was either unwilling or unable to learn the mathematics required if he was to do much in physics. One might suggest that he developed an inferiority complex on this account, or in terms of another system, that he took flight from reality, and found an excuse for himself in blindness and accompanying symptoms [Pillsbury, 1929, p. 174].

The Philosophers of Irrationalism

The philosophers whom we have just been considering assumed that the world is operated in accordance with universal laws which human reason can discover, and that the discovery of these laws is the business of philosophy. Hegel described the contingencies and particulars of nature as illusions; nature, he said, "is full of freaks," but the richness and variety of its structure "gratifies none of the higher interests of reason." For the "irrationalists," on the other hand, contingencies and particulars—"concrete existence"—were all-important. The quarrel is the ancient one, which we noted in our discussion of Aristotle, between "essence"—the qualities of things which can be expressed in the genera and differentiae of definitions and which can serve as terms in generalized formulae— and "existence"—the unique, "the state of being actual," "that which is experienced," "the presence of a given datum in the physical universe at some date and place" (Runes, 1942, *s.v.*). The concept of "existence" has entered recent experimental psychology as the methodological principles of "concreteness" and "contemporaneity" of Lewin, in whose doctrine it is combined with Hegelian "wholeness." But existentialism was introduced into modern philosophy by three men—Schopenhauer, Kierkegaard, and Nietzsche—

in whom personal, social, and theological conflicts led to intensely pessimistic views of human life as a struggle with evil, or with "nothingness," or with man's tendency toward optimism and happiness.

Arthur Schopenhauer (1788-1860), like Hegel, began his intellectual life under the influence of Kant, Plato, and Indian metaphysics. Kant had declared the "will," man's "practical nature," to be the innermost essence of man, from which proceeds the fundamental moral law. While the principle of the phenomenal world is determinism, that of the moral world is freedom and responsibility; the will of the individual is an autonomous, self-active principle which transcends experience and authority and comes most clearly to expression when duty conflicts with strong egoistic motivations; duties easy to perform are suspect. Whereas the rationalists had identified reality, "the Absolute," with thought, Schopenhauer, following Kant, identified it with "will," and identified individual will with the "cosmic" will. This universal drive to activity leads only to futility and suffering, for which the only palliation is surrender of the will and attainment of nirvana or non-existence. It will no doubt seem incredible that this philosophical tour de force should have influenced modern philosophy, and through it psychology; the facts however seem to be as stated by Russell (1945, p. 759):

> In one form or another, the doctrine that will is paramount has been held by many modern philosophers, notably Nietzsche, Bergson, James, and Dewey. It has, moreover, acquired a vogue outside the circles of professional philosophers. And in proportion as will has gone up in the scale, knowledge has gone down. This is, I think, the most notable change that has come over the temper of philosophy in our age.

Sören Kierkegaard (1813-1855) was a very melancholy Dane whose writings have been very influential in the existentialist reaction to the tragical events in Europe since 1914. His philosophy was the expression of intensely personal factors: "As a boy he was delicate, precocious and morbid in temperament." He "lived in studious retirement, subject to physical suffering and mental depression" (*Encyclopaedia Britannica*, 1911). Ostensibly because of his mission—the Socratic one of bringing people to a realization of the tragic meaning of life—he renounced his betrothed, and thus illustrated his central theme: that the only important problem of life is the choice which the *individual* must make—"either-or"—between pleasure and suffering. In this choice there can be no objective

criteria, but only subjective belief. Barrett (1958), in his sympathetic chapter on Kierkegaard, says that

> Kierkegaard advances two general principles that are in advance
> of nearly all current psychologies: (1) Despair is never ultimately
> over the external object but always over ourselves. . . . what we can-
> not bear is that in being stripped of an external object we stand
> denuded and see the intolerable abyss of the self yawn at our feet.
> (2) The condition we call a sickness in certain people is, at its center,
> a form of sinfulness [p. 151].

Friedrich Nietzsche (1844-1900) was in his youth a brilliant
student of classical philology who was cursed with ill health, weak
eyesight, and a "nervous stomach." His sufferings became progressively greater, so that at the age of thirty-two he had to give up his
professorship and at the age of forty-four became hopelessly
insane. It seems plausible therefore to describe his philosophy as
the overcompensatory expression of a revolt against everything:
science, culture, philosophy, religion, morality, democracy, and the
state. His central idea, understandably, was that of the "will to
power," a universal dynamic principle of both inorganic and
organic life reminiscent of the "force" of the Leibnitzian monads;
the social consequence of this principle was his ideal of a ruthless
elite, free of compassion, to whom the mediocre majority were to
be subjected, like animals or like the slaves of the silver mines in
Plato's Athens, with whatever suffering might be requisite to the
purposes of their masters; the "superman" is beyond good and
evil." Barrett (1958) has pointed out that our contemporary civilization can with some justification be described as "post-Nie-
tzschean": "the psychoanalyst sometimes finds it necessary to tell a
patient that he *ought* to be more aggressive and selfish"; Adler
declared "that the Will to Power was basic"; the modern world is
characterized by "an energetic and dynamic will to conquer nature
and transform the conditions of life"; this is the meaning and
appeal of Communism, and it is also the drive whose slackening
would spell economic catastrophe in America. Neither intellectual
analysis nor Christian ethics seems able to mitigate this drive which
is headed by way of interstellar space toward Nothingness (Barrett, 1958, pp. 158-183). That Nietzsche would not have liked the
petty bourgeois "blond beasts" who carried out his program was of
little moment to mankind; as Kahler (1961, p. 584) says, "Down to
the last details, the Nazis have made his prophecy come true. But
airy thoughts are very different from their concrete realization."

Even thoughts, one might add, which have arisen in clinic or laboratory. Our judgment of Nietzsche's influence on psychology as a science will depend on our estimation of the contributions to science of Freud and Adler and upon our definition of "science."

In the period since 1914 two representatives of "phenomenological existentialism," Heidegger and Sartre, have been particularly influential. *Martin Heidegger* (1889-   ) combined and modified the ideas of Kierkegaard and Husserl. *Edmund Husserl* (1859-1938) in his turn had modified Kant's ideas under the influence of *Franz Brentano* (1838-1907). Where Kant had held that the "phenomenon"—the datum of human conscious experience—is the mere appearance of the true object-in-itself which cannot itself be known, Husserl asserted that philosophy and science must begin with a description of what is presented to us in experience without obscuring preconceptions. From Brentano he borrowed the idea that the "immanent components" of the stream of consciousness "intend"—point to—real or possible "worldly objects." Perhaps this will be enough to suggest that Husserl carried logical and mental "analysis" to an ultimate degree of verbal abstraction; the version of Husserl's philosophy which entered psychology through Stumpf, Külpe, Bühler, and the gestalt psychologists is perhaps sufficiently characterized by Boring's (1950, p. 367) statement that phenomenology is "a discipline that claims to deal with pure consciousness by a method of immanent inspection." Katz (1950, p. 18) tells us that ". . . the critique which Gestalt psychology directs against the older psychology, and its positive contributions as well, stand or fall on the merits of the phenomenological method." Its critique and contributions stand or fall therefore on the merits of subjectivistic description in psychology.

Existential philosophy, says Barrett (1958, p. 30) is "a product of bourgeois society in a state of dissolution." It is a rejection of the Western philosophical tradition, which began in ancient Greece, of intellectual analysis and scientific systematization. In the face of the terrible experiences of recent decades, it returns to Kierkegaard's preoccupation with the predicament of individual man in the basic attitude of "dread," anxiety, and "concern" with such ultimates as death and "nothingness." The sort of human situation out of which recent existentialism arose and which accounts for the existentialist emphasis on conscience and choice is described by Sartre:

> Exile, captivity, and especially death (which we usually shrink from facing at all in happier days) became for us the habitual objects

of our concern. We learned that they were neither inevitable accidents, nor even constant and inevitable dangers, but they must be considered as our lot itself, our destiny, the profound source of our reality as men. At every instant we lived up to the full sense of this commonplace little phrase: "Man is mortal!" And the choice that each of us made of his life was an authentic choice because it was made face to face with death, because it could always have been expressed in these terms: "Rather death than . . ." [Sartre, *The Republic of Silence*, quoted by Barrett, 1958, p. 213 f.].

And here, in a final quotation from Barrett's eloquent book, are the arguments, succinctly expressed by a philosopher, which have induced some psychiatrists and clinical psychologists to adopt the existential philosophy as a rationale for their practice:

There seem to me two objections—one practical, one in principle— to the attempt to interpret man in his totality from the point of view of the behavioral sciences. First, these sciences are as yet very youthful, and very poorly provided with reliable general conclusions. If, honoring the requirements of the severely scientific conscience, we restrict ourselves to the *reliable* results now afforded by these sciences, we shall have a picture of only a tiny fragment of man. . . .

The second objection—one of principle—to the view of the behavioral sciences is that they must be perpetually incomplete. From what has been established in our time about the incompleteness of mathematics, the most rigorous of all the sciences, we know that such vague and complex amalgams (not yet systems) as the behavioral sciences can never even pretend to completeness; consequently man as a totality will always elude their grasp. Any attempt to interpret man *completely* from the view of these sciences is bound to be reductive in nature [p. 259 f.].

May (1961, pp. 11-51), after mentioning his own encounter, as a patient in a tuberculosis sanitorium, with personal "non-being" and with Kierkegaard, describes the dilemma of the clinician facing a patient who has come into his office for the first time: between "technical and diagnostic concerns" based on systematic theory, on the one hand; and on the other, intuitive "understanding" of the individual patient, by avenues which include "subliminal, empathetic, 'telepathic' communication." The "fundamental unit of study" is "*two-persons-existing-in-a-world, the world at the moment being represented by the consulting room of the therapist*" (p. 40). But the same situation is faced by the practitioner of internal medicine, who must also, as Hippocrates emphasized, deal with the total patient as an individual in an environment. The difference is that the physician, in a wide area of his practice, has available the knowledge and techniques derived from the basic medical sciences:

anatomy, physiology, biochemistry, etc. When a patient reports, e.g., gastrointestinal or cardiac distress, the physician can apply objective diagnostic techniques; were he to stop with intuitive "understanding" based on "experience," his patient might very well die of his complaint, and this not infrequently happens. But when thorough physical diagnosis reveals no pathology and hence suggests no medical therapy—when the patient's trouble is Kierkegaardian "anguish"—there is no basic medical science to serve as a guide; there is only a research field occupied jointly by persons called psychologists, physiologists, biochemists, etc. This research field is however rapidly maturing; the methods and knowledge particularly of electrophysiology and brain chemistry are bringing within the range of science the last great unknown organ system; it might be said that in the twentieth century we have been crossing a frontier with respect to the nervous system comparable to that across which Harvey in the seventeenth century showed the way for the circulatory system.

Throughout the philosophical history which we have been rehearsing, not only were the descriptions of "mental" processes based wholly on introspection and meditation, uncontrolled by physiological observations, but the methods required for the relevant observations were not available. Even such contacts as certain philosophers—e.g., Descartes, Leibnitz, Hartley—had with the biology of their times were superficial. And yet, in the eighteenth century, while the British and German philosopher-psychologists were preoccupied with private analyses of sensations, "pure reason," "will," etc., French philosophers were emphasizing, in Aristotelian fashion, the conception of function as the activity of a biological organism. Thus Cabanis described the brain as "a special organ whose particular function it is to produce thought just as the stomach and intestines have the special function of carrying on the work of digestion, the liver that of filtering the bile, etc." (Fearing, 1930, p. 89). Today we are still likely to find both philosophers and psychologists referring to LaMettrie and Cabanis as representatives of a "crude materialism" which we have fortunately outgrown. Boring (1950, p. 214) speaks of LaMettrie as "enslaving the soul to mechanical law," but he has just previously said that "Science of necessity tends toward mechanism and so away from animism. . . . Science is thus naturally monistic, not dualistic, and its logic and techniques are adapted to defining mechanisms for the body but not animisms for the soul" (p. 212). This is, I think, the crux of the matter; in so far as psychology is a biological *science*, its business is to investigate recordable processes in identifiable structures. The world of private experience and of empathic "understanding" may serve the individual scientist as a source of ideas for experimental research, but they do not themselves constitute scientific knowledge. Every experimentalist is likely to have had the experience, in the course of an experiment, of "seeing" certain relationships which subsequent statistical analysis showed to be illusory. Here again I would emphasize the desirability, both for science and for other human interests, of recognizing that science is not all of human life: it is not religion, nor ethics, nor esthetics, nor a means of expressing or escaping from personal anguish. Science consists of a very special set of interrelated objectives, attitudes, concepts, and techniques. The dilemma of the psychiatrist is of course very real; as a physician he must try to palliate his patient's distress, but he has available only very imperfect knowledge and techniques for dealing with the relevant organ-system. He is somewhat in the position of the Hippocratic physician who had to do something for his patient's abdominal distress in almost complete ignorance of visceral physiology. Even more precarious is the position of the "clinical psychologist," who has entered upon the cure of souls without a basic medical education.

There have been from time to time discussions of the reasons for the laggard development of psychology as a science. The most important reason, I have just suggested, is the unavailability of relevant biological knowledge and techniques. This fact becomes most obvious where ignorance has the most obvious human consequences; namely, in psychiatry or "medical psychology." Here the place of knowledge has been taken either by imaginary physiology or by what might properly be called "poetry." Imaginary physiology began with the ancient Greeks; e.g., Alcmaeon and Empedocles; in modern psychiatry it has appeared as the irrational fads of phrenology, psychosurgery, shock therapy, and ataractic drug therapy. Poetry or mythology as pseudomedical doctrine and therapy also began in Greece, notably with Parmenides and Pythagoras; its modern manifestations, derived largely from the German philosophers of the period from 1700 to 1850, have been the equally irrational psychoanalytic "movement," or "depth psychology," and existentialism. The unhappy history of these shots in the dark and wrestlings with the ineffable has been reviewed by Altschule (1957) and, with an extensive bibliography, by Bailey (1956); the latter calls attention to the panegyrics which have attended the introduction of each of these "physiological" techniques and poetical constructions—panegyrics very like the clinical success stories with which drug manufacturers introduce their "wonder drugs." When we read the accounts which pharmacologists (e.g., Irwin, 1962; Modell, 1963) give of the technical and practical difficulties of statistically reliable evaluations of drugs, we realize, a fortiori, how unreliable are the "data" on which "psychotherapies" have been based; and indeed, the enthusiasms for "new" psychiatric concepts and techniques, like those for new drugs, sooner or later fade away. Bailey quotes from F. A. Weiss a list of Freudian "ideas which must be given up":

> The priority of sexual events in childhood, the castration complex, penis envy, the Oedipus complex and cure by *Abreaction* of old trauma. How could it be otherwise when we remember how Freud built up his theories? Just before his seventieth birthday he remarked that he had spent his life guessing how the mental apparatus is constructed. He sat in his study, pondered on these matters and scribbled his ruminations. Unfortunately that is all he did. Thrice in his early life he essayed the experimental method and thrice he failed. . . . I know that there are attempts to prove that psychoanalysis is a science. They do not convince me and have convinced very few objective observers [Bailey, 1956, p. 394 f.].

Disquiet has been increasingly expressed in America over the fact that basic and seminal scientific theory has originated mostly in Europe. But the European, particularly the German, heritage of *psychology* has been in large part a hindrance to its development, at least in so far as the German psychologists were by tradition and education philosophers. The two notable exceptions, Helmholtz and Ebbinghaus, were most nearly independent of the tradition. And yet, in our most scholarly history of psychology, that of Boring (1950), Wundt, who for a time fastened upon a large segment of American psychology his sterile "existential" dualism and introspective methodology, is celebrated as the great founder of experimental psychology; whereas Ebbinghaus, who single-handedly invented the experimental psychology of learning, is spoken of in a rather patronizing tone as one who "left no deep imprint on the psychological world after his death." But Boring goes on to say, very truly, that "Ebbinghaus was especially important to experimental psychology because he helped to make articulate and effective the spirit of the times that called for an emancipation of psychology from philosophy" (p. 392). This spirit is beautifully expressed in the first two chapters of Ebbinghaus's *Memory* (1913). The world in which Helmholtz and Ebbinghaus lived and worked was a far different world from that of the seers of "wholeness," "orality-anality-genitality," "the ineffable sense of I am I," and the "dynamic unconscious which is beyond causal and scientific explanation" whose reports we still find in the clinical sections of the *Psychological Abstracts*.

10

Psychology as Social Science

It would be fruitless to attempt to differentiate among social psychologists, group dynamicists, and sociologists on the basis of the specific research they do or the nature of the data and generalizations they use in their thinking. They, together with economists, political scientists, and anthropologists, are all *social scientists.*— Krech and Crutchfield (1948), p. 25.

Aristotle, as we saw, distinguished *theoretical* sciences, which included physics, biology, and psychology, from *practical* sciences, which were *arts* dealing with variable and contingent human affairs: ethical, political, and esthetic valuations, actions, and productions; and, in general, with "socially significant behavior." In practical science, Aristotle, as an "objective relativist," assumed that for each particular human situation the proper adjustment could be objectively determined. The task of practical science was thus diagnosis and prescription according to the presented case, as in medicine. There was however a normative political theory, stated as follows by Randall (1960, p. 255):

The best *polis* is the one that best fosters all human excellences, all conduct in accord with moral excellence and intelligence. . . . Aristotle thus stands for the omnicompetence of the state. There is nothing that political government must refrain from doing, if it makes for human welfare. Aristotle thus quite literally is stating the theory of the "welfare state."

As Randall points out, Hobbes, who assumed, contrary to Aristotle, that men are by nature asocial and that the purpose of the state is to prevent them from destroying one another, rationalized by these assumptions a view of social organization which resembled that of Plato in having totalitarian implications. In troubled times, such as those of the Stoics, Descartes, Rousseau, and ourselves, programs and attitudes of social disengagement, individualism, liberalism, and "existentialism" have been rationalized by other assumptions, such as those of "natural rights" and of the dependence of all knowledge or of all values on individual conciousness. Some early twentieth-century psychologists—e.g., A. P. Weiss (1929a)—under the influence of nineteenth-century optimistic scientism, positivism, progressivism, and social Darwinism, and of the Wilsonian vision of a League of Nations, projected a civilization in which all aspects of human life would be brought under the control of social science; Weiss rationalized this program as the inevitable goal of a world-process which began with electron-proton aggregates; the principle of entropy found no place in this scheme, nor did the concept of cycles of creation and dissolution of the Greek philosophers. In contemporary America, in a period of unprecedented general prosperity combined with social disintegration, we have the doctrine of "permissiveness," rationalized by theories of conflict and frustration. In Russia there is in official operation a program, scientifically authenticated in terms of conditioning theory, of political control of men by systematic application of the Pavlovian principle of the "second signaling system"; uniform verbal conditioning of all individuals is designed to substitute an authorized and unifying verbal environment for individualizing "real" environments, so that the mass of socialized men may become an efficient instrument in achieving the goals set by their leaders. "For the Bolshevik, [man] is a robot who can be trained to act independently within specified limits" (Bauer, 1952, p. 178). In America, the generalizing of conditioning techniques from laboratory rats and pigeons to human social control has been advocated by Skinner (1948b, 1953, 1955). While Skinner, like Plato, Aristotle, Hobbes, Comte, Weiss, and many another philosopher-psychologist, undoubtedly had the praiseworthy aim of increasing human welfare by rationalizing society, his program, as dramatized in his novel, *Walden Two*, aroused, as mentioned in our discussion of Plato's "ideal state," great misgivings among some of his colleagues. This disquiet might well be reinforced by what we have learned from the tragic role of the physicists; namely, that it is not the research scientist who will control the applications of his discoveries and that the scientist whose advice will most influence the rulers will not necessarily be a man who is much concerned about the fate of mankind. There is by no means general agreement among psychologists that the applications of psychological theories and techniques to education, "psychotherapy," business, and politics have made for a net improvement in human welfare; the judgment of thoughtful laymen is expressed in such "dystopias" (Walsh, 1962) as Aldous Huxley's *Brave New World* and George Orwell's *1984.*

We cannot, it seems, escape a value judgment concerning the relation of science to human affairs. In modern times the role and value of science in practical life and its relation to such other interests as religion, morals, and esthetics have been much discussed; such questions have become more serious with the recent accelerated influences of applied science on the patterns of living of large populations and on the capacity of the human race to destroy itself. There could hardly be a worse epoch in human history in which to undertake the justification of science. We have least difficulty when we consider the biological sciences and experimental medicine. We might perhaps expect little serious disagreement with the proposition that these sciences are socially valuable and justifiable; the sort of progressive control of nature which they provide is intimately related to basic human urgencies; in the words of Castiglioni (1947, p. 10), "the identity of human suffering under all skies must create a solidarity both of science and of scientists." However, it is true that at the point of contact between biological science and the general population there is an area—that of medical practice and the dispensing of drugs—in which there is an attenuation of scientific and humanitarian and an accession of extrascientific—commercial and political—factors. Moreover, the increased preservation of life which science has made possible has resulted in population pressures which may have disastrous consequences. And finally, we see looming ominously in the background, and seldom mentioned, that most obscene prostitution of biological science, "biological warfare," which may constitute the final cancelling out of the humanitarian contribution of biology. Still more dubious is the net contribution of the physical and chemical sciences to human welfare; here the commercial, political and military interests enormously outweigh the humanitarian. As for psychological science, many psychologists would probably wish to have the judgment suspended.

When Nagel (1962, pp. 636-639) cites as an expression of a "malicious philosophy of science," easily refuted, the assertion that "Science deals with instrumentalities and is incapable of determining values," he seems to me to be blind to our contemporary predicament. It is not necessary to indict "scientific intelligence as solely responsible for our present difficulties," nor to deny that "some philosophic and theologic ideas" have perpetuated "economic inequality and human slavery." It is enough to point out that scientific "solutions" at any given time are contingent, incomplete, and of less than perfect reliability; that they may presently be found to be erroneous; that all this is particularly true of practical applications; and that the "methods of controlled inquiry," which, if not prevented by "vested interests and the cake of custom," would solve human problems, are practiced by *scientists* with vested interests in their programs and theories. If we attach any importance to the ancient moral maxims, such as those concerning the dignity of the individual and the rights to "life, liberty, and the pursuit of happiness," our experience with the scientists who have been solving problems in atomic and bacteriological warfare, pharmacology, eugenic programs, applications of "psychology" to public education—from Rousseau through Dewey and Thorndike to Skinner, social applications of "personality tests," and techniques of social control can hardly encourage us to substitute scientists for theologians, philosophers, and statesmen as arbiters of our fate. For while it is true that science is not *solely* responsible for our present difficulties, it does not seem to follow that scientists can be relied upon to preserve us from such difficulties. That the scientists who determine policies affecting the fate of mankind may be moral imbeciles has been documented, e.g., by Feuer (1963, pp. 393-402).

Social Psychology Before 1920

Nagel (1961, pp. 447-546) has made an extensive analysis of the methodological problems and theoretical structure of the social sciences. He points out that until quite recent times the literature dealing with social behavior must be classed as social and moral philosophy rather than science, and that its "data" have been mostly anecdotal and tendentious. The purpose of the authors of most of this literature has been, not objective inquiry, but defense or confutation of social systems or beliefs. This was certainly true of Plato's writings; Aristotle, on the other hand, strove to derive principles from objective and comparative surveys, and this method, as Randall (1960, pp. 241 ff.) remarks, has baffled many modern readers. Until recent decades the European writers on social behavior have been philosophers or propagandists rather than scientists: the Stoics and Epicureans, Machiavelli, Hobbes, Montesquieu, Hume, Rousseau, Bentham, Hegel, Comte, Gobineau, Spencer, Wundt, LeBon, Tarde, Marx; the speculations of many such writers have been discussed in previous chapters. Though, as Nagel says, some of these writings might be described as containing "penetrating insights into the functions of various social institutions," to none of them could the canons of scientific method be meaningfully applied. This earlier history has been admirably reviewed by G. W. Allport (1954), who has described the various "simple and sovereign theories"—the unitary explanations by which the older writers sought to systematize and simplify the variable phenomena of social behavior. Prominent among these simplistic explanations were the pleasure-pain theories, transmogrified or transmuted nowadays as the Freudian "pleasure principle," or as "reinforcement," or as "tension reduction"; the "will to power" of Hobbes, Nietzsche, and Adler; and the various doctrines which placed chief emphasis on either rationalism—"reason" or "cognition," or irrationalism—"emotion" or "will." Very prominent have been the "three fundamental concepts" of sympathy, imitation, and suggestion, around which has accumulated a vast literature of more literary than scientific interest. The argument as to whether "aggression" or "cooperation" is the more basic feature of "animal nature" is still going on. The British empirical philosophers sought a unifying principle in the association of "ideas"; in recent times, when "ideas" have been replaced by "reflexes" or "responses," Russian and American psychologists have applied the principle of conditioning or redintegration to social behavior. As we shall presently see, some of the principles appealed to in recent social psychology, though having a conceptual continuity with the older philosophical literature, have gained some operational definition in experimental research; the dubiousness of their generalized application to social and moral problems however remains.

Rather than repeat the history which Allport has so adequately reviewed, I shall discuss at some length the contributions to "social psychology" of McDougall and Weiss: the former, because in my opinion his contribution—like that of Freud—has been vastly over-rated (Allport speaks of "the gigantic impact of Darwin, McDougall, and Freud"); the latter, because he has been ignored.

The Social Psychology of William McDougall: Psychical Causation and Instinct

In the second and third decades of the present century, social psychology was introduced as a university course and rapidly gained popularity. There were two textbooks available: that of William McDougall (1908; last ed., 1931) and that of E. A. Ross (1908; last ed., 1925). There were two social psychologies: that taught by psychologists, who used McDougall, and that taught by sociologists, who used Ross. McDougall sought to erect a social psychology on the basis of hereditary "instincts"; Ross described human nature as a set of habits socially acquired, largely through "suggestibility" and "imitation." As M. B. Smith (1953) remarks, in a review of some modern textbooks of social psychology,

> The dialectic interplay between the psychological and sociological approaches that runs as a persistent theme through the subsequent development of the discipline is still with us, as the current crop of texts attests. . . . It is doubtless a sign of persisting immaturity that the basic textbook with its necessarily limited scope still recommends itself to competent social psychologists as a vehicle for their major theoretical contributions.

Dominated as we are by the concept of historical progress, and by the belief, common among scientists, that older writings have perhaps a "cultural" but actually a scientifically irrelevant anti-quarian interest, we are apt to assume that anything written by a scientist in the twentieth century must represent a vast advance over anything written in the fourth century B.C. It is therefore instructive to compare McDougall's social psychology with that of Aristotle.

There was, in the first place, very little that was "social" in McDougall's *Social Psychology*; it was used as a textbook for no better reason than that it had that title and was written by a "psychologist." It proposed to "explain" human behavior in terms of a limited number of "instincts" and some "general innate tendencies." McDougall's list of instincts and tendencies was taken, not from a literature of controlled research, which was nonexistent, but selectively from the traditional literature of "naturalistic" observation; as Boring (1950, p. 718) says, psychologists presently "discovered that anyone can make up his own list of instincts and that there is no way to prove that one list is more certainly correct than another." In McDougall's (1918) account, "Every instance of instinctive behavior involves a knowing of some thing or object, a feeling in regard to it, and a striving towards or away from that object" (p. 27). The function of cognition is to initiate and guide action; action implies the evoking of a striving; pleasure and pain are conditioned by the success or failure of the striving. Instinctive dispositions may acquire "new perceptual inlets in accordance with the principle of association in virtue of temporal contiguity" (p. 39). A further complication results from the fact that sense-presentations may be reproduced in ideas. Instincts are innate dispositions correlated with biological structures and functions and are shared by man with other biological organisms. The postulated instincts include fear, rage, curiosity, sex, hunger, and gregariousness. The "general innate tendencies" include sympathy, imitation, and play. A "law of habit" is stated as "the tendency for every process to be repeated more readily in virtue of its previous occurrence" (p. 119). "Will" is said to be definable as "that which proceeds from character," and character "is something built up in the course of life" (p. 264); any action is to be explained "as the expression of some single conative disposition, or of a conflict of, or of some conjunction of, such tendencies, according to the plan of organization of the character" (p. 392).

As far as I can see, there is nothing in all of this that we did not find in Aristotle, though McDougall himself considered his book "novel" and "revolutionary" (1920, p. ix). Even the concept of "sentiment" as "an organized system of emotional tendencies centred about some object," a concept which McDougall described as "a very important discovery" astonishingly "reserved for a contemporary writer [Shand] to make," and which McDougall makes the main principle of personality organization, was adumbrated in Aristotle's discussion of the factors making for variety in behavior and in character formation, among which factors he included different combinations of motives on various occasions. The reader of the *Social Psychology* will look in vain for citations of experimentally or statistically controlled research; what he will find is dogmatic assertions and quotations from philosophers.

In a sympathetic review of McDougall's social psychology by

Heidbreder (1939, p. 158), there is a paragraph which concisely summarizes his "hormic psychology":

> He made use of [the word "hormic"] not only to emphasize the conative aspects of mental life, but also to distinguish his own view of motivation from that of the hedonists. For McDougall, purposive striving was literally goal seeking—not toward pleasure and away from pain in themselves. Pleasure and pain might be important in influencing the means toward an end, but they were not in themselves the ends sought or avoided. This part of his theory has received less attention than it deserves. . . . It is interesting, however, that an essential part of his teaching was the conception of psychological processes as directed toward objects—a conception prominent in various enterprises today, in social psychology and in psychology generally.

This paragraph could, I think, serve very well as a summary of Aristotle's views. It is commonly stated that McDougall and Freud revolutionized psychology by introducing the factor of motivation into modern psychology, which had previously been preponderantly concerned with cognitive factors. This statement should, in the first place, be qualified by a recognition of the fact that the principle of "active striving," of "conation," generalized to the universe, and the attempt to temper the mechanistic trend of natural science with teleology, had been introduced into German philosophy by Leibnitz, who strongly influenced the founders of modern psychology. But the principle of motivation had been stated by Aristotle two millennia before Leibnitz in an objective biological context which seems more akin to modern research than does the animism of McDougall or the mythology of Freud.

It seems doubtful, not only whether McDougall's psychology achieved any important advance beyond that of Aristotle, but also whether it was not in its most emphasized features a retrogression. Aristotle began as a Platonist and metaphysician but became a biologist, and as a biologist he approached the problems of human social life in an objective and realistic spirit. McDougall, like Freud, began as a biologist but became increasingly dedicated to the promulgation of theses not amenable to biological research, and his forays into research were attempts to find evidence *for* his emotionally based beliefs. These beliefs, of which the *Social Psychology* is also an expression, are presented in a number of other works (e.g., 1923, 1930a, 1930b). In these, his animus against American psychology, "academic psychologists," and "crude behaviorists" might perhaps be thought to be matched by Aristotle's critiques of other philosophers, although Aristotle is more judicious and less arrogant. But in his insistent arguments for "animism" and "psychical causation," in his hostility to "mechanistic" (which I would translate "natural science") explanations, in his belief that the phenomena of "psychical research" provide reliable evidence against "the mechanistic dogma"—in all of these respects McDougall seems to me to illustrate an attitude, an invasion of the scientific enterprise by extra-scientific interests, which compares very unfavorably with the objective biological attitude of Aristotle. Though he claims that his "hormic psychology" is "the truly physiological psychology," he says that its essence may be conveyed by the following: "To the question—Why does a certain animal or man seek this or that goal?—it replies: Because it is his nature to do so" (1930a, p. 13). This hardly seems an advance over Aristotle, nor does it suggest a twentieth-century program of natural science research. For Aristotle an "end" was the last stage in a regular sequence; he referred thus to the observed "uniformities of nature." In biology, he had in mind either the model of embryonic development or that of human planning and production; only the latter did he regard as "purposive." As Randall (1960, p. 128) points out, we need, in Aristotle's view, to know outcomes in order to understand processes, but ends are never efficient causes; "they never 'do' anything. . . . Only motion can 'do' anything, or 'make' anything take place." For McDougall, on the other hand, all biological processes—from metabolism to complex behavior—are manifestations of "purposive striving," and every attempt to explain such processes in terms of natural science—"mechanistically"—is foredoomed to failure. His point of view comes out very clearly in the following:

> Of the two types of process, we certainly understand the appetitive more intimately than the mechanical; for we directly experience appetition, we have an inside acquaintance with it, as well as acquaintance of the purely external kind which is the only kind of acquaintance that we have with mechanical process. And when metaphysicians attempt to go behind the distinction of mechanical and appetitive processes (which for science is fundamental) and attempt to show that processes of the two types are really of like nature, the most plausible view seems to be that which regards mechanical process as reducible to the appetitive type or regards it as, perhaps, representing a degradation of process of the appetitive type [1918, p. 370].

Presumably introspection would thus become a universal scientific method. At any rate, the method is not that of natural science: in the preface to his *Group Mind* (1920, p. ix f.) McDougall says,

All this part of psychology labours under the great difficulty that the worker in it cannot, like other men of science, publish his conclusions as discoveries which will necessarily be accepted by any persons competent to judge. He can only state his conclusions and his reasoning and hope that they may gradually gain the general approval of his colleagues. For to the obscure questions of fact with which he deals, it is in the nature of things impossible to return answers supported by indisputable experimental proofs. . . . The only test and verification to which any scheme of human nature can be submitted is the application of it to practice in the elucidation of the concrete phenomena of human life, and in the control and direction of human conduct, especially in the two great fields of medicine and education.

The distinction here is obviously that which Aristotle made between "theoretical" and "practical" science: the former seeks universal laws, the latter must be content with rules about matters which "may be otherwise." The distinction is however somewhat obscured by McDougall's dogmatism; moreover, it might have been expected that a psychologist writing in 1920 would have emphasized that where experimental proofs are impossible, intuitive satisfaction is not an adequate substitute for estimates of statistical probability. As for medicine, that branch of it which is in question has owed its unhappy history to the verification of schemes by "application to practice," without benefit of experimental proofs, and something of the sort has happened not infrequently in education.

As for the attempt which McDougall made, in his *Group Mind*, to write the social psychology at which he had not arrived in his *Social Psychology*, such leading concepts as that of the "group mind," the "idea of a nation," and the "extension of the self-regarding sentiment" seem more remote from social realities than the analyses of Aristotle's *Politics*, unless one identifies them with the unhappy German mythology which was adopted by the Nazi state, an identification which McDougall indignantly but not quite intelligibly rejected. The concept of "group soul" like that of individual soul has been the rationalization of great mischiefs in human history. Ellwood (1921) stated as his fundamental criticism of the book that McDougall "takes the crowd as the starting point for the interpretation of group spirit," whereas Cooley (1902) "would take the primary groups of men, especially the family and the neighborhood groups, as the starting point for understanding the whole process of interaction between individuals and, hence, collective behavior" (p. 222). In this, Aristotle anticipated Cooley. Ellwood calls attention to the indeterminate boundary between psychology and sociology, and to the fact that McDougall makes no clear distinction between group psychology and sociology. Ellwood remarks:

> To the careful student of society it would seem, indeed, that the psychology of group behavior in any given situation is inextricably bound up with historical, biological, geographical, economic and many other conditions. The careful consideration of all of these influences, if possible with some quantitative analysis of them, is indeed just what is necessary to make any science of collective behavior truly scientific. This is the program of the sociologist, but as yet many group psychologists do not seem to sense the difficulties of the task which they are undertaking" [p. 221].

Ellwood mentions the contrast between Giddings, who held that sociology is "the psychology of society," and the earlier psychologists, such as Baldwin, who held that psychology concerned itself with the individual, while sociology concerned itself with the group. There is here an unresolved problem. It was not unreasonable for Aristotle to be the head of a school and a professor of philosophy, biology, psychology, and social science, but in our times we have the anomaly of two social psychologies, or rather of a "lack of consensus on the boundaries and organizing conceptions of social psychology" (M. B. Smith, 1953, p. 151), and we award doctorates to "psychologists" who may be physiologists, sociologists, or paramedical psychiatrists.

The "Biosocial" Psychology of A. P. Weiss

So much for McDougall. Let us examine, by way of contrast, another twentieth-century neo-Aristotelian psychology which seems in spirit quite the opposite of McDougall's. Albert Paul Weiss, like McDougall, had a training in biology, and his first research was, like McDougall's, in sensory function. Still, again like McDougall, he had a strong interest in social behavior. But whereas McDougall (1930b) "rebelled" (as he says he did against any theory "widely accepted in the scientific world") against German physiology and psychology (which he encountered at Göttingen as a student of G. E. Müller, and at Cambridge through Rivers, an exponent of Kraepelin and Hering), Weiss, as a pupil of Max Meyer, was a product of the German tradition of anti-vitalistic physiology (Ludwig, Bois-Reymond, Brücke, Helmholtz), "objective psychology" (Loeb, Beer, Bethe, Uexküll), and positivism (Mach and Avenarius). There was certainly a contrast in backgrounds here, between the schools of Wundt and Müller on the one hand (plus the French clinical psychologists) and that of the men of the Ludwig-Helmholtz tradition on the other. But while Müller was a philosopher turned psychologist, Wundt, like McDougall and William James, had been trained as a physician and physiologist; there are many examples of the fact that it takes more than a training in biology to insure a life-long biological attitude; the—apparently—same general cultural background which produces natural scientists can produce mentalists, vitalists, and those mystics among physicists who leap from mathematics to spiritualism, bearing with them the more impressionable among psychologists. In the psychologies of McDougall and of Weiss we have excellent illustrations of the existence of blank pages in our philosophies of science: those which should deal with the psychology of scientists. Lashley (1923, pp. 344–346) remarks, "Adherence to mechanism or finalism seems to be wholly a matter of temperament; the choice is made upon an emotional and not a rational basis," and he gives a humorous psychoanalytic account of the two temperaments, whose complete lack of communication in controversy does indeed suggest extra-scientific motivations.

It should be noted that a very important and pervasive part of the German academic tradition was Aristotle. Müller had been grounded in Aristotle by Trendelenburg; and Stumpf, Max Meyer's teacher, by Brentano. Brentano, the founder of Austrian "act psychology," strongly influenced James Ward, whose subject-object conative psychology and categorization of human activity into cognition, feeling, and conation transmitted Aristotle's concepts to British psychology and in particular, through Stout, to McDougall.

Weiss's interest in social psychology was, I think, of early origin. He had entered academic life somewhat late, after some practical experience of the world in the engraving and photographic trades, and had taken an active interest in political socialism. His lifelong interest in social applications of science, in "biosocial behavior," "behavioristic ethics," and "social status" perhaps owed more to his early experience than to Meyer, although the latter too had some decided opinions about the social mission of psychology. At any rate, Weiss's whole program is expressed in the following quotations from Meyer (1921):

> We psychologists must often hear the (unjustified) reproach that our psychology is nothing but physiology or neurology or some simi-

lar "unpsychological," materialistic science, against which you would better protect the unsuspecting, pure soul of the college freshman. But we psychologists have no difficulty in distinguishing our interests from those of other biological departments. We study the organism as an organism, it is true, but only in so far as its functions have distinctly social significance. We do not study the stomach, because its function is an individualistic affair with which society is not directly concerned. It is the physiologist's business. . . . But we are concerned with the possibilities of developing habits and with the limitations, if there are any, which Nature may have placed upon the development of habits. We are convinced that habits are the mysterious entities so much and so vaguely talked about under the name of social forces.

A hundred years ago Johannes Mueller, the father of modern physiology, made the famous remark: "Nemo psychologus nisi physiologus." That was a valuable statement at his time when psychology was still mixed up with speculative philosophy and very little psychology in the modern sense existed. Today a still more valuable statement would be this: "Nemo psychologus nisi sociologus" [p. 405].

In religion and in politics the worst intolerance, the most inhuman atrocity is found correlated with the most one-sided preference of spiritual, subjective, idealistic terminology. Can you blame the psychologist when he, who regards the study of human life as his particular sphere of interest, confesses to you that he prefers to think of a human being as a bodily organism rather than as a soul, of a nation as a society of such organisms rather than a collective soul? [p. 415].

In the cultural background of both Meyer and Weiss was the German tradition which began in the eighteenth-century Enlightenment as an attempt to reconcile natural science with religion and which became increasingly concerned with the application of natural science to humanitarian purposes. This tradition was transmitted to Meyer and Weiss particularly by Ebbinghaus, whose *Abriss der Psychologie* Meyer (1908) translated (see particularly the *Introduction* and Chapter IV), and by Friedrich Lange (1925). We gain insight into Lange's motivation from his biography: in Höffding (1920, II, p. 542 f.) we read:

After spending some years as *docent* and teacher in a *Gymnasium* Lange became an editor and social agitator. He took part in the movement against Bismarck's domestic policy; also in the struggles of the Working Men's Association for a fixed organization. His work entitled *Die Arbeiterfrage* dates from this time. Like Mill's *Political Economy* this is one of the first books in which the social question is treated impartially and from a general point of view. Lange's view of the matter is that there must be a struggle with the struggle for existence, and that to carry on this first struggle is the peculiar duty of man. . . . He considered the political significance of the labour ques-

tion to lie in the fact that it exercises a continual pressure on conservative institutions, the banks of which will give way if canals are not
soon dug. Free-thinking men of the upper classes now have to choose
whether they will strengthen banks or assist in digging canals.

Lange's student days fell in the stormy revolutionary period around
1848, and we, shaken by more universal convulsions, can sympa-
thize with what he wrote in a letter of 1849: "Should it not be clear
to every reasonable man that civilised Europe must enter into one
great political community?"

Lange's purpose, like that of Fechner, was to come to terms with
natural science in order to reserve a place for idealism as the necessary validation of ethical religion and moral law, of "spiritual
values." But in doing this he presented with uncompromising
cogency the arguments for materialism, and in particular the evidence and implications of neurology. It was in Lange's time that
the researches of Flourens, Pflüger, Meynert, Hitzig, Nothnagel,
and Ferrier became available, and the problems of brain localization, reflex action, and the nature of the nerve impulse were under
active discussion. Considering the fact that at this time Gerlach's
theory that the processes of neurons in gray matter constitute a
nerve-net was widely accepted, and that Waldeyer did not formulate his neuron theory until 1891, it is startling to read in Lange
(III, pp. 144-145) the statements:

> There is not a special nervous process of sensation and another of
> motion, but the physical process is in all cases of the excitation of a
> nerve essentially the same, and differs only in strength or weakness,
> quickness or slowness, &c. [And in a footnote:] Here then exists the
> very important principle that a weak state of irritation already exist-
> ing in a nerve at the same time increases the irritability of the nerve
> by a fresh stimulus.

Lange insists that the functions of the nervous system must be
explained in terms of general physical and chemical laws and in
accordance with the principles of the conservation of matter and
of energy. The physiological sequence from stimulation through
afferent, central, and efferent processes to contraction is an unbro-
ken causal chain of which consciousness is not a member. Idealism
must not be permitted to intrude into theoretical science, where
strict mechanical explanations are required; on the other hand
materialism has a limit beyond which it must not trespass on the
subjective world of ideals and values. The objective nervous processes and the subjective conscious processes are in a Spinozistic

double-aspect relation. In Lange, then, we see clearly the currents which entered into the controversies in American psychology of the 1920's, as they were recorded, notably, in the *Psychological Review.* The partisans of those controversies might be said to have expounded different aspects of Lange's doctrine: the behaviorists the objective aspect, with consciousness excluded; the mentalists the subjective, introspective aspect; the compromisers, the double-aspect view; and the burgeoning social psychologists, whether behaviorists or functionalists, the moral and social values. As to the latter, Lange's chapters, in the third volume, on "Scientific Psychology" and on "Political Economy and Egoism" will repay reading: we find there many things reminiscent of Aristotle and many which anticipate such psychologists as Weiss. Lange says,

> To what extent now scientific method can be applied to psychology must be shown by the result. We will premise that it is not merely the borderlands of nervous physiology which admit an exact treatment. However undefined we may leave the boundaries of psychology, at all events we must for the present include in it not only the facts of sentient life, but also the investigation of human action and speech, and generally of all manifestations of life, so far as an inference is possible from them to the nature and character of man [III, p. 177 f.].

He then goes on to discuss as fields for investigation animal psychology; the study of newborn infants ("It is astonishing with what phlegm our good philosophers can conduct an argument on the origin of consciousness, without ever feeling it necessary to go into the nursery and see exactly what takes place there in connexion with this problem"); ethnopsychology; the study of the laws of the succession of ideas (or as we would say, of learning); and "anthropological statistics" (i.e., the application of the mathematics of probability to social phenomena). This last had been suggested in the years following 1835 by the pioneering, though as Lange points out, uncritical work of Quetelet, who paid insufficient attention to the nature of his populations and in particular to their dispersions.

If this seeming digression on Lange seems overlong, I must assure the reader that I leave Lange only because I must, and that anyone familiar with twentieth-century American psychology who reads through the third volume of Lange's *History* will experience many a familiar passage—expressed, it is true, in a language of humane scholarship to which we have grown unaccustomed.

Weiss, like Aristotle and Aristotle's predecessors, felt it necessary to begin with "primary" physical elements and motion. Aristotle, in accordance with the thought of his time, postulated earth, water, air, and fire as the elements, in whose transformations there was a quantitative equivalence suggestive of the nineteenth-century "conservation of energy"; moreover, the compounds of these elements "may be different from their constituent elements"; thus novel properties are generated. The dynamic principle underlying all creation and dissolution is that of *motion*:

> In our own physics, motion is understood in terms of the "laws of motion," Newtonian or Einsteinian. Aristotle's answer, the Unmoved Mover, is just such an answer to just such a question: it is the Aristotelian counterpart of Newton's *principia mathematica* of motion, the laws of motion of the science of dynamics [Randall, 1960, p. 134].

All of this will be found in the first chapter of Weiss's *Theoretical Basis* (1929); he of course substituted electrons and protons as his ultimate elements, with the proviso that the impending regressions in physical analysis would be accepted and "need not disturb the psychologist":

> If the mathematicians can construct the universe as we now have it, out of merely an assortment of whirling spaces, well and good,—if it runs itself. But to introduce into such a system some mystical, non-material force or psychic ultimate, as some eminent physicists persist in doing, simply shows a lack of knowledge of the most recent advances in the study of human behavior. A physicist turned poet should not expect the type of recognition for his poetry that is accorded him for his physics [Weiss, 1929, p. 16, note].

For Weiss as for Aristotle, biology is a branch of physics and psychology is a branch of biology. The human individual is "a locus in the [cosmic] movement continuum, and a function (in the mathematical sense) of the changes that are occurring in all other electron-proton aggregates" (p. 57). Weiss's hierarchy of increasing complexity of organization—atoms, molecules, cells, tissues, organs, organisms, families, tribes, nations—is practically identical with that of Aristotle except for the insertion of cells and the addition of electrons and protons at one end and the League of Nations at the other.

With this basis and this beginning, one might expect that psychology would be built up as a biological science, with close attention to structural-functional relationships. But not at all! Two emotionally-reinforced motivations had entered American psychology to determine much of its subsequent development. First, there was the rejection of the central nervous system, partly because of impatience with the speculative nature of neural theory resulting from the limitations of neurophysiological methods of the time, but also because of the odium of "guilt by association"; the brain had been the "seat of the soul," of the "consciousness" reported by introspection, so that it became the part of objectivistic virtue to refuse to deal with this *baquet magnétique*. Jacques Loeb brought this attitude to America from the anti-metaphysical and anti-vitalistic wars of German science. The "ganglion-cells" of the central nervous system had been supposed to be the residences of "ideas" and memories, and the control centers of coordination. These notions Loeb rejected, saying, e.g., that the movements of orientation toward light "are governed by exactly the same external conditions and depend in the same way upon the external form of the body" in animals with nerves as in plants without nerves. "These heliotropic phenomena, consequently, cannot depend upon *specific* qualities of the central nervous system" (1900, p. 4). The nervous system is essentially a multiplicity of protoplasmic bridges between the sensory organs and the muscles. As for "the mechanisms which give rise to the phenomena called psychic or conscious," Loeb declared,

> Consciousness is only a metaphysical term for phenomena which are determined by associative memory. By associative memory I mean that mechanism by which a stimulus brings about not only the effects which its nature and the specific structure of the irritable organ call for, but by which it brings about also the effects of other stimuli which formerly acted upon the organism almost or quite simultaneously with the stimulus in question [p. 12].

This is the concept of "double stimulation" (equivalent to but anticipating Pavlov's principle of the conditional reflex), which Max Meyer and Weiss adopted as their "physiological" explanation of habit-formation or learning. Meyer's development of the notion from Loeb was independent of Pavlov, and was supplemented by the concept of "deflection ["drainage"] of nervous currents" which was based on the hydraulic analogy whose history we traced in Chapter 5. "Deflection" was made the physiological mechanism of learning and attention, and of the phenomena which Pavlov subsumed under the term "inhibition." From Ebbinghaus, Meyer adopted the concept of a "hierarchy of nervous levels." The total neurophysiological model of Meyer and Weiss was then as follows: a nested system of "reflex arcs" in which at successive higher levels more and more of the "arcs" at lower levels are interconnected, until at the highest (presumably cortical) levels, "all sensory points are interconnected with all motor points." Through this system flow "currents" originating at sense organs and varying in intensity with the stimulus intensities and with the "resistances" of the various possible pathways. The effect of a "current" flowing through a pathway is to "reduce its resistance," and in the case of "double stimulation" a "weaker current" is "deflected" by a "stronger," and the result is the establishment of a new sensory inlet for a response or a new motor outlet for a sensory process.

Now what was the purpose of this neurophysiological model? The purpose was pedagogical and disciplinary; it was a rite of exorcism by which soul, mind, and consciousness were to be driven out of psychology, which, having been thus purged, could become a domain of natural science. Rites, however, to be effective must be presented in the guise of authenticity, and the neural model was presented as neural fact, and the pedagogy reinforced by exercises in the calculation of distributions of "neural flux" according to Ohm's law. The model was not a scientific hypothesis, for it was unrelated to any program of research.

The other emotionally-reinforced motivational current which led psychology away from biology was the interest in the "social significance" of behavior, and in social reform and "progress." This interest was derived from the humanistic side of the mechanistic-humanitarian dilemma of nineteenth-century European intellectuals, and was reinforced by the positivistic sociology of Comte. Comte's credo, as succinctly stated by Boring, is the credo of Meyer's *Psychology of the Other-one,* and of Weiss: "Comte believed that the basic data are social, that introspection of the single private consciousness is impossible, that there can be no individual psychology but only social science, that we can investigate not the *me* but the *us,* since man can be understood only in his relation to his fellows" (Boring, 1950, p. 633).

Weiss's program for psychology is most concisely expressed in his discussion of "The Measurement of Human Behavior and of Human Achievement" (1929a, pp. 433-439). Here, after presenting an equation which defines "social status" as a summation of "attainments in education, vocation, administration, recreation, and special personal accomplishments," and two other equations which define a "specific response" and the "historico-social environment," he says,

> These equations differentiate psychology from physiology and neurology in that psychology studies those sensori-motor and social processes as factors which establish the individual's *social status* and not

as anatomical or physiological conditions in themselves. Further these equations represent the fundamental postulates upon which the social sciences may be based [p. 438].

Basic to this view of psychology is the distinction between "bio-physical" and "biosocial" equivalence. Two responses are biophysically equivalent to the extent that they consist of the same physiological processes in the same structures; they are biosocially equivalent to the extent that, as stimuli, they evoke the same response in other individuals. Weiss says, "I do not believe that any neurological insight alone will enable us to determine what the *stimulating effects* of a given neuromuscular configuration will be *upon other individuals*" (p. 88). This statement is undoubtedly true, the more so that those effects will vary with the cultures, individual life histories, and momentary states of those other individuals. And yet, many psychologists would, I think, be reluctant to agree that the sole or main measuring instruments of psychology are the response mechanisms of "other individuals." Here it almost seems that behaviorism doubled back on its historical trail and proposed to use human neuromuscular systems not as objects of research but as laboratory instruments, as introspective psychology had done. I have wondered whether there was some relevance in the fact that in the laboratory in which Weiss trained apprentice psychologists (in my time, at least) most of the exercises were taken from Titchener's *Manual,* and the reports which were to be entered in the tables were in terms of the attributes of sensation.

The issues raised by Weiss's presentation came to amusing expression in an interchange between Weiss and Howard C. Warren in the *Psychological Review.* This was in the time of the great war between the psychology of consciousness and behaviorism, and Warren, who was distinguished among psychologists as a scholar and a gentleman, thought he saw a way to be a peace-maker. He assumed that behaviorists meant what they said when they declared the data of psychology to be *responses,* defined as "a class of phenomena indicative of neural activity." The "states of consciousness" of traditional psychology "are not merely subjective occurrences" but are "somehow conditioned on the operations of the nervous system." Warren's proposal was that

A balanced view of the field of psychology, then, would seem to make its central feature the *specific activity of the nervous system.* Behavior may be regarded as the end-result of neural activity, and the conscious experiences which the introspectionists investigate are in some way 'bound up' with this same neural activity. . . . The two [schools of psychology] have at least this in common, that they . . . agree that the main function of the nervous system is the integration of incoming impulses and the coordination of outgoing impulses— both of which occur at the centers. . . . psychology is the branch which deals with stimulation of organisms by their environment, central nervous activity resulting therefrom, and responsive activity of whatever sort consequent on this central activity [Warren, 1921b, pp. 250-251].

Warren argues that "the essential adjustment operations are central." As against the "peripheral" theory of thinking, which involves proprioceptive feedback from serial responses, he suggests that the central process may be "the significant feature of neural activity." In sum, his suggestion is that "All three methods throw light on these central operations. Neurology, behavior, and self-observation are all needed for a broad, systematic development of the science" (p. 269). As for behavior equivalence, such as that between the "same" word spoken or written, or spoken in different languages, Warren places this equivalence in the central nervous system of the individual. Warren called his view "the double-aspect hypothesis," and its logical form was therefore nominally in the tradition of Spinoza and of Fechner and Lange. Fechner interpreted soul as appearance to oneself and matter as appearance to others, both representing the same reality differentiated only in point of view; Lange thought it justifiable to assume that behind the subjective state of consciousness and the objective nervous process there is an unknown third thing; Warren postulated "but one set of primary occurrences . . . which may be observed either *objectively*, by means of apparatus registering the nerve impulses, or *subjectively*, by living these events." But if, as Warren asserted, "the fundamental concern of psychology is with the operations of the central nervous system," then his program for psychology might have been stated as the investigation of those operations by correlated neurophysiological and behavioral techniques, the latter including the recording and analysis of both verbal—including "introspective"— and non-verbal—including visceral—behavior. The nervous system would then become the *tertium quid* which manifests itself both in neurograms and in behavioral records; this *quid* would have the advantage of being a *hoc* which has a determinable structure.

The reader will not be surprised to hear that Weiss would have none of Warren's kindly meant mediation. He declared that the basis of response "equivalence" is "not in the nervous system of the reactor but in the nervous systems of *other* individuals of the same social status" (Weiss, 1922, p. 340). It might be that introspective reactions could be used as "precision instruments for the indirect measurement of [certain] neural conditions," but "this type of problem is not of any particular interest to the behaviorist unless it is brought into relationship with those overt reactions which have social significance" (p. 341). "Whether the neural processes go over one neuron or another, or through one center rather than another, is quite irrelevant except in so far as the nature of the neural mechanism limits those overt reactions which, when expressed in abstract form, represent the civilization or culture of some social unit, whether this be a nation or a colony of ants" (p. 343). Between behaviorist and introspectionist there can be no compromise: "As time goes on the gap between them will grow wider." Warren (1922) in his reply comments on the two main points of disagreement between himself and Weiss: the latter "rejects or minimizes the occurrences within the central nervous system as unimportant for psychology, while [Warren regards] them as among its most significant data" (p. 481). And, "The investigation of the social and general environmental conditions of organic reaction is surely an important task; but it is not the whole program, nor even the chief problem of psychology" (p. 488).

What was there in Weiss that was not in Aristotle? In Aristotle we have the linguistics, the physics and metaphysics, the biology, and the "social science," including ethics, politics, "communication," and esthetics. In Weiss we have an emphasis on language as a system of substitute stimuli-and-responses which makes possible the "compound multicellular"—i.e., social—organization whereby "the sense organs and the muscles of all individuals are placed at the disposal of all other individuals," and past environments and cumulative behavior organization are made available to successive generations; moreover, the adaptive significance of discrimination, generalization, and abstraction is expounded. Weiss had these ideas from Meyer (cf. Meyer, 1911, 16th Lecture), and Meyer had them from Lazarus Geiger (1878), a philosopher-philologist who was well grounded in the history of his subject. The germs of the "biosocial" interpretation of language we have noticed in Aristotle, and we noted how he stopped just short of identifying, as Geiger in effect did, and as did the behaviorists of the 1920's with great sounding of trumpets and many a counterblast, *thinking* with *language*. The important thing about Weiss's version was that he communicated

it to Leonard Bloomfield, who, abandoning the sterile Wundtian-
ism of his first edition, adopted in his *Language* (1933) the functional behavioral point of view as the psychological foundation of
an analysis which ushered in a new era in the science of linguistics,
or at least in that aspect which has come to be known as "psycholinguistics," and which has become so active a field in recent
psychology.

Fries (1961) has felt it necessary to depreciate the influence of
Weiss on Bloomfield. He writes: "But in general, the evidence seems
to show, *not* that, through the influence of Weiss from 1922, Bloomfield became a 'behaviorist' and then shifted his fundamental
approach to that of a 'mechanist,' but rather that Weiss, through
Bloomfield, gained new insights into the significance of language
which harmonized with and filled out his own understanding of
'some of the possibilities of human achievement when scientific
mechanism is taken as a fundamental postulate in human behavior'" (p. 204). This judgment, this assertion of a one-way influence,
is not, I think, one which Bloomfield himself would have made. In
an obituary notice, Bloomfield (1931, pp. 219-221) wrote:

> Weiss was not a student of language, but he was probably the first
> man to see its significance. He saw that language supplied the key to
> those phenomena of human conduct and achievement which hitherto
> had been attributed to non-physical forces. There had always been
> students who refused to believe in the spectres of our tribal animism
> (*mind, consciousness, will,* and the like) but these students had never
> given a clear-cut and satisfactory explanation for the super-biological
> actions of man—the actions which transcend the possibilities of the
> animal world. In our time these students are the behaviorists,—an
> ugly name, said Weiss, but accepted it for want of better. Weiss was
> a devoted pupil of Max Meyer; the latter's system, most thorough in
> eliminating animism and finalism, formed the basis of Weiss's work.
> The pupil's enormous advance was due to his evaluation of language.

Fries is concerned to give "maximum emphasis" to Bloomfield's
doctrine that "we can pursue the study of language without reference to any one psychological doctrine." To this two rejoinders
might be made. First, Bloomfield was speaking against the background of the history of both "philology" and *Voelkerpsychologie*.
Every philologist had been his own psychologist; I remember hearing an eminent linguist give a public lecture in this tradition at a
Linguistic Institute in which he spun a wonderful "psychological"
theory of sound change. Bloomfield (1933, p. 17) mentions the
classical example of Hermann Paul's "insistence upon 'psychologi-

cal' interpretation." "He accompanies his statements about language with a paraphrase in terms of mental processes which the speakers are supposed to have undergone." And Wundt—whose two thick volumes on *Die Sprache* it was once necessary for the student of language to struggle through—insisted "upon the importance of psychological interpretation in terms of his system, while Delbrück says that it does not matter what particular system of psychology a linguist may choose" (Bloomfield, p. 18). My second rejoinder to Fries is suggested by Bloomfield's (1933) preface, which Fries also quotes:

> The deep-rooted things about language, which mean most to all of us, are usually ignored in all but very advanced studies; this book tries to tell about them in simple terms and to show their bearing on human affairs. In 1914 I based this phase of the exposition on the psychologic system of Wilhelm Wundt, which was then widely accepted. Since that time there has been much upheaval in psychology; we have learned . . . that we can pursue the study of language without reference to any one psychological doctrine, and that to do so safeguards our results and makes them more significant to workers in related fields. In the present book I have tried to avoid such dependence. . . . The mentalists would supplement the facts of language by a version in terms of mind,—a version which will differ in the various schools of mentalistic psychology. The mechanists demand that the facts be presented without any assumption of such auxiliary factors. I have tried to meet this demand not merely because I believe that mechanism is the necessary form of scientific discourse, but also because an exposition which stands on its own feet is more solid and more easily surveyed than one which is propped at various points by another changeable doctrine.

It will be noted that what Bloomfield rejected was "versions in terms of mind" put forward by "mentalists," and that what he proposed to do was to "meet the demand of the mechanists." In other words, he proposed to study language objectively, as Weiss proposed to study *all* behavior.

Is "psycholinguistics" a part of linguistics as well as of psychology? Bloomfield must have thought so, or he would not have devoted twenty pages of his book to the subject. Those linguists must have thought so who have participated with psychologists in seminars and conferences during the past two decades. Did Weiss influence Bloomfield in the direction of "behaviorism"? Here I must observe that Weiss was one of those men, like Lotze and Brentano, whose personal influence was greater than that of his writings: the sense of this is eloquently conveyed by Bloomfield's obituary: "In word and deed, as in his writings, Weiss was completely the man of science . . . in everyday converse he spoke accurately and without prejudgment, so that his hearers sometimes found depth or wit in what for him was only straightforward speech . . . in daily life his helpful competence, his utter divorcement from the simian and the rapacious traits of our species, led one to see a high grace or a saintly unselfishness in what for him must have been merely plain, sensible conduct." Weiss and Bloomfield lived for several years in the closest intimacy; such of their protracted conversations as I overheard would not lead me to agree with Fries's thesis of a one-way influence. Some linguists, particularly students of Sapir, have been very hostile to Bloomfield's "behaviorism"; e.g., Swadesh (1948) speaks of "mechanical materialism," "mechanistic fetishism," and "the fetish that anything related to the mind must be ruled out of science." Fries declares that "the 'image' of Bloomfield as a thoroughgoing 'behaviorist' now dominated in his approach to language by the crassest type of behavioristic psychology as popularly understood, is wholly without foundation in fact" (1961, p. 205); psychologists will recognize the adjective "crass" as a vituperative trade term of idealistic philosophy and Bergsonism. The tradition of "every philologist his own psychologist" is still alive in linguistics. On the interrelationships of psychology and linguistics, Carroll's (1953, pp. 71-82) discussion will be found of interest.

As for Weiss's physics, metaphysics, and biology, we can no doubt agree that electrons and protons are an improvement over earth, water, air, and fire, and reflex arcs over the push and pull of the *pneuma* in blood vessels, but we may doubt whether it was an unalloyed improvement over Aristotle's notion of the heart as an integrating center for sensory, emotional and motor processes to assume that "there are *no* central *control* or cerebral *integrating* mechanisms," and that the central nervous system is a system of conductors differing from the metallic conductors of an electric wire network only in the property of change of resistance with function (Weiss, 1929a, p. 202). In actuality, Weiss's physics and physiology were largely irrelevant to his main interest in behavior as socially significant; they were weapons for combating (one thinks of Lucretius) mysticism, psychical causation, and mentalistic entities; they were unrelated to any program of either physiological or psychological research, except in the very general sense of ruling out introspective techniques and mentalistic categories.

How shall we compare Weiss's *social* psychology with that of

Aristotle? For Weiss as for Aristotle the key concept is "happiness." Aristotle defined it as intellectual and moral activity; Weiss as an optimal compromise or ratio between individual variability and socially required conformity. Perhaps the two definitions might be thought to be united in the definition by a contemporary historian of the "progress" which has occurred in recent decades: the change from a belief in impersonal "laws of nature" governing man's social life to the concept of "the application of reason to human affairs." After speaking of "the diversification of individual skills and occupations and opportunities which is the concomitant of an advancing civilization," Carr (1962, p. 190) continues, "Perhaps the most far-reaching social consequence of the industrial revolution has been the progressive increase in the numbers of those who learn to think, to use their reason." The difference would be that whereas Aristotle would probably have considered this hypothesized development to be time-limited or cyclical, Weiss would have thought it a segment of a cosmical asymptotic curve. Weiss, making the leap from biological to social evolution that was natural for the heirs of the optimistic late-nineteenth century, envisaged a "cosmical evolution'" towards a universal "biosocial destiny" in which all men would attain their individual "optimal ratios." Aristotle, perhaps, from our more pessimistic point of view, more realistically surveys the means, in individual and in social and political life, which will, for a time at least, insure as much individual freedom as is compatible with the viability of the state.

There would be no great gain, I think, in carrying the comparison further. Suffice it to say that when one reads in parallel Weiss's sections on desire, purpose, volition, motivation, emotion, esthetics, and ethics, and Aristotle's works on ethics, politics, and rhetoric, one is likely to get the impression that Aristotle stays closer to the realities of social behavior and that his discourse would be more helpful to a "social engineer" than the rather doctrinaire writing of Weiss. But this comparison is not entirely fair; it neglects the long history of mystification and philosophical obfuscation, the esoteric verbiage of German and British closet-psychology, which had intervened between Aristotle and modern psychology; it was largely on the negative task of demolishing these barriers that Weiss expended his energies; one needs to read the journals of those days to realize the sterility of mentalistic psychology. The important point for our present purpose is that Weiss illustrates that peculiar tendency in modern psychology which claims to study behavior in stimulus-response terms but, neglecting or rejecting neurophysiology, concentrates its interest on goals, purposes, social significance, practical prediction, or the promotion of individual "adjustment" or social reforms.

Social Psychology Since 1920

There has been a good deal of disagreement as to the definition of "social psychology" and as to its relation to psychology on the one hand and to sociology on the other. When in 1924 Floyd Allport published his *Social Psychology*, he introduced a new spirit into what had been largely a "theoretical"—i.e., speculative, mentalistic, and verbose—subject. In his preface he said that "there are two main lines of scientific achievement which I have tried to bring within the scope of this volume. These are the *behavior viewpoint* and the *experimental method*." He defined social psychology as "the study of the social behavior and the social consciousness of the individual" (p. 12), and declared,

> There is no psychology of groups which is not essentially and entirely a psychology of individuals. Social psychology must not be placed in contradistinction to the psychology of the individual; *it is a part of the psychology of the individual*, whose behavior it studies in relation to the sector of his environment comprised by his fellows. His biological needs are the ends toward which his social behavior is a developed means. Within his organism are provided all the mechanisms by which social behavior is explained [p. 4].

As for the relation to sociology, Allport held that "While the social psychologist studies the individual in the group, the sociologist deals with the group as a whole" (p. 10), and that "the two sciences must remain separate branches of inquiry" (p. 11).

In Floyd Allport's social psychology, the individual is regarded as a biological organism "within [which] are provided all the mechanisms by which social behavior is explained," and Allport devotes three chapters to the physiological basis of behavior; instinct, maturation, and learning; and the physiology and conditioning of emotional responses. In this scheme therefore the correlation between biological structures and behavioral functions is maintained, and there would be no great difficulty in regarding this extension of general psychology, which investigates the influence of social stimuli upon a biological organism, as a biological science.

In the pioneer text of "social psychology" by a sociologist, however, E. A. Ross (1908) had described social psychology as a branch of sociology, which differs from sociology proper in that it deals with cooperative and conflictive behavior whereas sociology proper deals with groups and structures. "Social psychology deals only with uniformities due to *social* causes," and excludes all other causal factors, notably heredity and physical environment. The point of view was expressed in the following passage:

> Looking at their heredity, we should expect people to be far more dissimilar and individual than we actually find them to be. The aligning power of association triumphs over diversity of temperament and experience. There ought to be as many religious creeds as there are human beings; but we find people ranged under a few great religions. It is the same in respect to dress, diet, pastimes, or moral ideas. The individuality each has received from the hand of nature is largely effaced, and we find people gathered into great planes of uniformity [p. 1].

Ross's chapter headings were in accordance with this point of view: e.g., Suggestibility, The Crowd, Mob Mind, Fashion, Imitation. The individual organism is "largely effaced," and we have the movements of "groups and structures."

The contrast between the social psychology of psychologists and that of sociologists has persisted. G. W. Allport (1954, p. 50) remarks that "A final and chief cause of the great diversity in textbooks lies in the sociological-psychological bifurcation that marks the entire history of social psychology." It might be said that two different morphological references are involved; on the one hand, a reference of behavioral functions of the individual to the structure of the nervous system, and on the other, a reference of social functions to the structure of social groups. This difference in reference can be seen in the history of research techniques. The first controlled researches which subsequently became influential in social psychology were those on "set," "determining tendency," etc., in which it was shown that the nature of instructions—self or experimental—influenced a subject's reaction time and the nature and course of his thought and behavior. This was the origin of the explanatory concept of "attitude," which historically we associate with the Würzburg school (cf. Boring, 1950, pp. 401 ff.), and which has become so prominent in contemporary social psychology that G. W. Allport speaks of it as "probably the most distinctive and indispensable concept in contemporary American social psychology" (1954, p. 43); the "measurement" of attitudes has become a chief research preoccupation of social psychologists. The laboratory study of the influence on individual performance of the presence of other people began with the studies of Triplett (1897), A. Mayer (1903), and Moede (1913), and made its definitive entry into American laboratories through the work of F. H. Allport (1920) and Whittemore (1924). In all such studies the experimenter was still working with the individual subject, and whatever behavior he recorded, even though he might in a given experiment be chiefly interested in the influence of social—e.g., linguistic—stimuli, he could still, in so far as his competence and available techniques permitted, correlate this behavior with biological processes and structures. But in 1891 G. Stanley Hall introduced the questionnaire into American psychology, and Thorndike (1904), Thurstone (1924), and Kelley (1923) introduced the statistical methods of dealing with "mental test" data which had been developed in England by Galton, Pearson, Spearman, and Yule. With these developments the individual disappeared into the group, as he was destined also to do, of course, in sociological surveys and opinion polling and in the "attitude measurement" of psychologists. Though the "attitude unit," "the primary building stone in the edifice of social psychology," is said to connote "*a neuropsychic state of readiness for mental and physical activity*" (G. W. Allport, 1954, p. 43), this "state" as it appears in the statistical products of attitude research is no longer a functional state related to the neural structures of—necessarily—an individual, but a disembodied statistical abstraction characterizing a group.

The Topsy-like growth of "psychology" since the 1920's has been in large part a response to extra-scientific "valences." The founding of psychology as an experimental science in the last decades of the nineteenth century was the work of men trained in physiology—Weber, Helmholtz, Johannes Müller, Wundt—and scientific psychology was called "physiological psychology." The peculiar subject matter of psychology was said to be "consciousness," as nowadays it is said to be "behavior," but it was assumed that the correlation of consciousness with nervous function and structure was an essential part of the psychologist's task. Thus Wundt, in his basic textbook (1904, p. 2) wrote:

Practically everything that the physiologists tell us, by way of fact or of hypothesis, concerning the processes in the organs of sense and in the brain, is based upon determinate mental symptoms: so that psychology has long been recognized, explicity or implicitly, as an indispensable auxiliary of physiological investigation. Psychologists, it is true, have been apt to take a different attitude towards physiology. They have tended to regard as superfluous any reference to the physical organism; they have supposed that nothing more is required for a science of mind than the direct apprehension of conscious processes themselves. It is in token of dissent from any such standpoint that the present work is entitled a "physiological psychology."

There are many psychologists today who "regard as superfluous any reference to the physical organism." Some of these are stimulus-response experimentalists whose historical roots are traceable to the anti-brain-localization movement represented by Jacques Loeb (1900), whose influence we have noted in Max Meyer and Weiss. According to Loeb, the prime functions of the nervous system are irritability and conductivity, the providing of "protoplasmic bridges" between peripheral sensory and motor organs; the reactions of an animal "depend in reality upon the peripheral structures, and not on the structures of the ganglia" [i.e., nuclei of the central nervous system] (Loeb, 1900, p.147). Skinner (1956), describing his graduate studies at Harvard, says:

> I soon came into contact with W. J. Crozier, who had studied under Loeb. It had been said of Loeb, and might have been said of Crozier, that he "resented the nervous system." Whether this was true or not, the fact was that both these men talked about animal behavior without mentioning the nervous system and with surprising success. So far as I was concerned, they cancelled out the physiological theorizing of Pavlov and Sherrington and thus clarified what remained of the work of these men as the beginnings of an independent science of behavior.

Thus in the work of Skinner and of his many followers the total biological activity of an animal appears only symbolically in the movements of a lever, summated by a polygraph. Innumerable experimentalists have followed in the tradition of Ebbinghaus, who, inspired by Fechner, thought that in averaged curves of learning and retention he had discovered a method of measuring levels above and below the threshold of "consciousness"; his followers have not only continued to accept his view that the relation between the arbitrary units—in any given experiment—of correct items or errors and number of trials represented some unitary function of the learner, but have gone further and thought to achieve a more reliable estimate of the "true function" by averaging the scores of many individuals, thus dissolving the individual organism in the group as effectually as did the social psychologists.

But the farthest remove from the *biological* individual—as contrasted with the individual as a congeries of hypothetical constructs —was achieved by those psychologists who participated in "the flight from the laboratory" (Skinner, 1961). Speaking of "the intellectual climate of 1947"—which he did not find greatly changed in 1959—Skinner said, "Experimental psychology was then at the nadir of its popularity. Graduate students were turning to social, personal, clinical, and applied psychology in ever increasing numbers, and defections from the ranks among older men were common" (p. 50). In this trend, psychologists were responding to "contingencies of reinforcement"; e.g., classes in social and abnormal psychology were more popular than those in experimental and physiological, and textbooks enlivened with case histories sold better than those which had the look of scientific textbooks. Every psychologist who has had experience in curriculum advising knows the stock answer of students who are asked why they wish to major in psychology: "I have always been interested in people"; it will seldom be found that students who give this answer have also been interested in the study of physics, chemistry, and biology. There are also the factors of differential monetary rewards—including "grants"—for work having "social significance," and of the substitution of automation—computer programming—for laboratory drudgery. For many students, moreover, the prospective delights of manipulating or "working with" other people are highly attractive.

The Hobbesian trichotomy of *corpus-homo-civis*—"physical bodies-human being-social man"—has been reduced again to the Aristotelian dichotomy of theoretical and applied science; the break in objectives and in methodology occurs between *homo* and *civis;* as for a general theory generated by the former that might be applied to the latter, recent writers tend to regard this as a hope for the future. Skinner (1961, p. 51) remarks that "A general theory of human behavior was needed, and only an experimental science could supply it. Separate technologies of behavior could temporize with particular theories, but the special control of variables attainable only in laboratory experimentation would ultimately supply the account which, being in closest accord with the actual properties of the human organism, would be most useful in every field of human affairs." And again (p. 52), "We do not really explain 'disturbed behavior' by attributing it to 'anxiety' until we have also explained the anxiety. The extra step required is in the spirit of an experimental science: it is a search for a manipulable variable rather than a verbal explanation."

The enormous multiplication of social psychologists and of their publications, and the lack of general agreement concerning both theoretical foundation and methodology have been commented upon by a number of writers who have reviewed the post-1920 history of social psychology. Thus Faris (1945), a sociologist, speaks of the "great outburst of energy resulting in thousands of research projects" which has been accompanied by a "loss of interest in the analysis of human nature into elements." "The diligent work of the physiological psychologists, the speculations of the instinct school, and the similar attempts of the depth psychologists, together with other less plausible formulations have lost their interest." The indispensable application of quantitative methods has brought with it "offenses against sound method, as when arbitrary values are assigned to arbitrary terms and correlations worked out to the third decimal under the illusion that exactness means accuracy" (Faris, 1945, p. 428). G. W. Allport (1954) describes the sudden burgeoning of social psychology as a response to the catastrophic events which began in 1914 and remarks that "Practical and humanitarian motives have always played an important part in the development of social psychology, not only in America but in other lands as well" (p. 4). Although he states that "No sharp boundaries demarcate social psychology from other social sciences," he nevertheless defines a difference in spheres of interest: whereas the other social sciences "wish to know the course of society with the individual extracted," social psychology "wishes to know how any given member of a society is affected by all the social stimuli that surround him. . . . Social psychology is above all else a branch of general psychology. Its center of emphasis is the same: human nature as localized in the person" (p. 5). But he points out that "The theories of social psychology are rarely, if ever, chaste scientific productions. They usually gear into the prevailing political and social atmosphere" (p. 11). He surveys the numerous varieties of "theoretical concepts" which have been utilized by writers on social behavior: rationalistic, irrationalistic, phenomenological, instinctive, cognitive, behavioristic, "group mind," etc. Of particular interest are his comments on the influential French sociologist, Emil Durkheim (1858-1917), who denied the relevance both of physiology to the explanation of mental processes and of individual psychology to

the explanation of social facts. "Cultural determinists" have "quoted
with favor" Durkheim's adage: "Every time a social phenomenon
is directly explained by a psychological phenomenon, we may be
sure that the explanation is false" (p. 37 f.). As Allport points out,
the lack of consensus in "social psychology" is reflected in the textbooks, which vary between the extremes represented by Durkheim
and F. H. Allport, and also between emphasis on experimental
research and emphasis on speculation. Cartwright (1961), reviewing the history of social psychology in the period 1945-1957, speaks
of "the tremendous increase in the total number of people calling
themselves social psychologists"; most of these people are new-
comers to the field who show little awareness of the history of the
subject. The "excitement and optimism" of social psychologists at
the end of the war has died down, but publications, doctoral
programs, and research organizations requiring administrative functions," "program planning," "team work," "electronic data reduction," and, of course, large financing, including generous provision
for "overhead," have shown phenomenal growth. Cartwright finds
little consensus as to theory: the question "whether social psychology is really a distinct field of knowledge," and if so, how it is to be
defined "has never been satisfactorily settled" (p. 16). Cartwright
lists "four fundamental orientations currently . . . contending for
acceptance": that which regards social psychology as a subarea of
general psychology, that which regards it as a branch of sociology,
that which regards it as a separate field whose distinctive subject
matter is "social interaction," and that which "looks toward the
development of a general theory of behavior" encompassing all of
the "social sciences": psychology, sociology, anthropology, political
science, economics, linguistics, etc. This last orientation is obviously
that of university, government, and foundation administrators and
of the organizers of "interdisciplinary symposia" who class psychology as a "social science" and speak generally of the "behavioral
sciences." This lumping together of interests and activities does not
seem to be justified by a survey of research methods: it is a far cry
from the techniques of analyzing the physiological correlates of
behavior to the techniques of "interviewing, sampling, content
analysis, scaling, and of experimentation on small groups" (Cartwright, p. 21), and a still farther cry to opinion polling, analysis of
economic trends, and structural linguistics.

Nagel (1961, pp. 447-546) has given a careful analysis of the
methodological problems and the status of explanations in the

"social sciences." He states that "In short, the social sciences today possess no wide-ranging systems of explanations judged as adequate by a majority of professionally competent students, and they are characterized by serious disagreements on methodological as well as substantive questions" (p. 449). He seeks to show, however, that there are no insuperable difficulties *in principle* in either research methodology or theory construction which would prevent the "social sciences" from becoming "real sciences." He gives the arguments against the "reductive thesis" of "methodological individualism", e.g., "no set of premises about the conduct of *individual* human beings might suffice for deducing some given statement about the actions of a *group* of men."

But the question which I wish to raise is not whether social psychology or "social science" generally can be scientific or experimental, or whether its statements can be "reduced" to statements about the biological individual; it is the question rather whether in the present state of affairs it is advantageous—to the advancement of science—to group a biologically oriented study of the individual with social psychology and the other "social sciences." I would suggest that here, as in the linguistics of science, the question is a pragmatic one; it is not a question to be settled by logical argument, traditional usage, nor administrative convenience, but by the nature of the objectives, language, methodology, and training of the respective practitioners.

As to objectives and training, there can be little doubt that there is a sharp dichotomy as between physiological and social psychologists, and a consequent dichotomy in language and methodology; they constitute different "populations," both initially and finally. Probably the most important selective factor is that described by Cartwright (1961, p. 23):

> The very nature of social psychology means that social psychologists must get involved, in one way or another, with society and its problems. This involvement takes three primary forms: (1) social psychology depends upon society for its financial support, (2) it obtains its data from society, and (3) its findings may be used to influence the course of events in society.

Powerful motivations, which determine both curricular programs and life careers, are consequently involved: humanitarian dedication, monetary rewards, social recognition, incessant attendance on conferences, the prestige of consultantships in socially important matters—somewhat the same motivations which induce men to desert the laboratory for the administrative suite.

Because of their inevitable reference to practical problems, there are historical relationships and contemporary parallelisms between social and clinical psychology. G. W. Allport (1954, p. 26) speaks of "the marriage between abnormal and social psychology" which resulted from the application, beginning about 1890, of Charcot's concept of dissociation to social behavior, and which was betokened in 1922 by the change in the title of the *Journal of Abnormal Psychology* to *Journal of Abnormal and Social Psychology*. As for the parallelisms, Kelly (1961), in reviewing the decade following 1947, reports that "Even among clinical psychologists, there is relatively little agreement as to just what should be included or excluded by the term clinical psychology" (p. 31). He points out that "clinical psychology has become a professional specialty attracting nearly half of all graduate students in psychology and is the name of the largest division of the American Psychological Association"; this hypertrophy was produced, beginning in 1946, by the creation by the federal government of a large number of jobs "at attractive salaries" and of Ph.D. training programs with equally attractive subventions. "Motivated in part by a desire to be of service and in part by the wish to be in position to utilize federal funds in developing their graduate programs, departments of psychology, in spite of limited staff and facilities, undertook to develop Ph.D. training programs with specialization in clinical psychology" (p. 35). The difficulty of rationally planning such programs is suggested by Kelly's (p. 44) statement that "In fact, the variation with respect to theoretical orientation and techniques of practice is so great that it is extremely difficult to identify any real entity of clinical psychology as a substantive discipline." And he further summarizes the situation as follows:

> In a word, the *practice* of clinical psychology is of necessity still largely an art because the *science* of psychology has not yet provided the basic knowledge and techniques which permit clinical psychology (or psychiatry) to be practiced as an applied science. This unfortunate state of affairs leads different psychologists to very different conclusions. The tough-minded say in effect: "Since we don't know what we are doing, let's not waste any time in doing it—time that might be better spent in developing our science to the point that it can sometime be useful." The more tender-minded say: "While it's true that we are woefully ignorant, we know enough to be helpful in our artistic endeavors—and besides, only clinical activity permits certain essential kinds of observations, and tends to stimulate those hypotheses which are most likely to contribute to the development of our science" [p. 45].

The question is whether the work of those who are to advance the science of psychology is facilitated or hindered in an atmosphere which nurtures tender-minded artists or socially-minded pollsters. The term "psychology" has undergone so great an extension of meaning as to have lost its usefulness in science. It is inevitable that its use will be continued by those practitioners who deal with laymen, but its use as an administrative category in university teaching and research, or as a category for the organization of scientific societies and the publication of journals does not seem justified by any community of theory, methodology, terminology, training, interests, or attitudes; a glance through any recent number of the *Psychological Abstracts* will illustrate this statement—but any reader who has been a member of a large university department of psychology and has participated in curriculum planning and Ph.D. examining can furnish his own illustrations. It is somewhat the situation in which departments of physiology would find themselves if through similar accidents of historical development they included subgroups of practitioners of psychiatry, clinical medicine, public health medicine, etc., etc.

An interesting overview of the situation of social psychology in 1950 was provided by a conference of psychologists and social scientists (Rohrer and Sherif, 1951). There seemed to be general agreement on the desirability or even necessity of a marriage between psychology and sociology (e.g., Newcomb, pp. 31-49); the reader, however, may be moved to forbid the banns on the ground of the immaturity of the groom—psychology—and the cultural disparity of the parties. In psychology we have various learning theories, cognition theories, and theories of motivation; as in the nineteenth century every psychiatrist had to have his own nosology, so in recent times every psychologist has felt the need of a distinctive theory, and all these theories exist in a state of intramural rivalry. (The political epithet "imperialism" has been borrowed by some writers.) The two articles by MacLeod (pp. 215-241) and Postman (pp. 242-272) illustrate Sherif's (p. 15) statement that "At present, at least, the majority of social psychologists seem to be proceeding along the perceptual (cognitive) approach," rather than in terms of learning theory. Both articles might be said to be in the Würzburg tradition: MacLeod advocates a Husserlian phenomenology and Postman presents a modernized—and lucid—version of Achian "determining tendency" and in particular of the interaction between set and environmental cues. But while these refurbished versions of traditional psychological concepts necessarily refer to research on individuals and hence retain their implications of biological function, the articles which deal with *social* "social psychology" operate —with a redundancy and tendency to platitude which psychologists used to associate with sociological literature—with such concepts as "group interaction," "group norms," "group conflict" or "cohesion," "roles," and "attitudes" (this last defined in terms of test scores). The working relation between psychology and sociology, I would suggest, had better be correspondence rather than cohabitation; they are divided on the one hand by a difference of morphological reference—to biological structures and to group structures, respectively, and on the other, by differences in training, attitudes, interests, and language—and often in extrascientific involvement. Bloomfield's recommendation to linguists that they "pursue the study of language without reference to any one psychological doctrine" and his judgment "that to do so safeguards our results and makes them more significant to workers in related fields" might be applicable to other fields of social study. I doubt, e.g., whether anything of permanent value has accrued to social science through the wide-spread "theorizing" in terms of Freudian concepts or whether the analysis of group structures and interactions would be improved by a phenomenological approach.

11

Psychology as a Biological Science

In the nervous system we see two basically different constituents, ganglia and nerve fibers, that is, centers of stimulation and lines of transmission; although each of these two elements offers an array of varied phenomena, which we admittedly are not able to refer back to specific mechanical particulars, we see nevertheless a complicated web of arousal and transmission, of interlinkage and isolation, of inhibition and reinforcement, which complicates investigation to such a degree that a really unparalleled impertinence is committed when people who have themselves never lifted a little finger in the investigation of these difficult matters place before those tireless investigators who devote their lives to research the naive question: "How then can the soul be explained from movements of constituents of the brain?" Can these gentry themselves explain how their personal psyche, their precious ego, manages to embody itself in matter?—Rudolf Virchow: *Scientific Method and Therapeutic Standpoints* (1849).

We have seen that there are four ways of defining "psychology": it can be defined as a branch of philosophy, or of social science, or of biology, or as a relatively self-sufficient science of "mind," "consciousness," or "behavior." The ancient Greek naturalists regarded man as a "locus in the movement continuum," composed of the same elements and subject to the same laws as the rest of the universe. Aristotle defined psychology as a division of biology; so too did Comte—at least until his last days. For Aristotle—as a biologist —animal functions were functions of animal structures, and the structures of a given species were to be understood in terms of their survival value for that species. But for the next two thousand years, discourse about man was dominated by the Platonic-Christian concept of man as a soul or mind or consciousness, unfortunately or at least irrelevantly conjoined with anatomical structures. This tradition has persisted into our own times as the notion of a science whose business it is to correlate "behavior" or "traits" or "attitudes" or "constructs" with "stimuli" or with sequences or combinations of external conditions or events, or merely with time; the behavior is often "measured" in arbitrary units of apparatus operation, designated as "errors" or "correct moves" or "operant responses" or "goal attainment."

In the University of Washington laboratory some thirty years ago there was a model which illustrated the principle of "conditioning." A doll which "reached" when a rabbit was presented and "shivered" when a clapper was sounded, would, after a joint presentation of rabbit and clapper, shiver on presentation of the rabbit. Stevenson Smith observed that most students were content with the front view of the apparatus, but that a few stepped to the rear to examine the mechanism responsible for this phenomenon; he suggested that this differential reaction might serve as an aptitude test for psychologists. But most psychologists, we might say, have been content with the front view. We have now to consider the historical reasons for this lack of curiosity, the dissatisfactions which it has engendered, and the accelerating technical developments of the past century which have been decreasing its justification.

Before entering upon these discussions let me anticipate the conclusion to which they seem to me to lead. If there is to be a *basic* science of man, it seems to me inescapable that this science should correlate functions—including "behavior"—with structures; it would in fact be the science of *physiology*—"the branch of biology dealing with the processes, activities, and phenomena incidental to and characteristic of life or of living organisms"; when Webster's adds that "the phenomena of mental life are usually regarded as outside the ordinary scope of physiology," it expresses a dualism which seems no longer useful. We are habituated in clichés which have become inconsistent with our practice and our capability; we say that physiology studies the processes in organs while psychology studies "the whole organism"; or that physiology but not psychology studies the actions of visceral organs; or that psychology studies only those bodily movements which have "social significance." Hebb, who has so forcibly called attention to the necessity of relating behavior to neural mechanisms, nevertheless asserts that "Psychology cannot become a branch of physiology. We cannot escape the need of large-scale units of analysis, nor the need of the special methods of behavioral study on which such analysis is based" (1958b, p. 264). "To discuss what goes on inside a rat's head as he runs the maze, for example, we use such terms as 'hunger drive,' 'expectancy of food,' 'stimulus trace' and 'the stimuli of the choice point.' Such constructs have little direct reference to neural function. They were invented and subsequently refined in the context of studying behavior, and their use does not require any detailed knowledge of what is happening in the CNS" (p. 262 f.). But it seems an odd situation that one discipline should make constructs about what goes on in the head while another discipline investigates the actual processes which go on there; moreover, if the constructs have little direct reference to neural function, the problem might seem to be to gradually make the reference *more* direct; the reference need not be limited to *neural* function, but may be more generally to *physiological* function, as would be true of the "constructs" which Hebb mentions. The dichotomy between construct-makers and process-investigators may be regarded as the result of the dualistic origins of American experimental psychology and of what became the traditional training of psychologists. In the early years of the century, psychologists tended to "minor" in philosophy; as the century wore on, they became more and more preoccupied with "mental tests," "social psychology," and the behavior-observation methods introduced by Lloyd Morgan, Hobhouse, and Thorndike on the one hand and Ebbinghaus, G. E. Müller, and later Pavlov, on the other. As for the physiologists of the nineteenth century, they were the first experimental psychologists, and Johannes Müller's *Handbuch der Physiologie des Menschen* (1833-1840) contained in its books iii-vi the first textbook of experimental psychology; from the ranks of Müller's pupils —especially Helmholtz, du Bois-Reymond, and Ludwig—and of *their* pupils came the first "objective psychologists," who were of course also physiologists.

But the tradition taken over by the founders of the American laboratories of psychology was that established by German professors of philosophy, especially Wundt and G. E. Müller, who were much concerned to demonstrate that psychology was an independent science. Techniques taken over from physiology, especially those of sensory physiology, "psychophysics," and reaction-time, plus the memorizing technique of Ebbinghaus and the word-association technique of Galton, when combined with "introspection" were thought to constitute a peculiar methodology which distinguished psychology—as the study of the "mind"—from physiology. Meanwhile in physiology there was occurring a slowly accelerating technical development which presently gave access to the processes in peripheral nerves, and in reflex mechanisms as peripherally recorded; only in the last few years have techniques become available for studying processes in the central nervous system. With the most recent developments, the barriers which had been created between physiology and psychology have been breaking down; one finds "psychologists" in physiology departments and "physiologists" in psychology departments—that is, persons with degrees in the respective departments—working on the same sort of problems with the same techniques and apparatus, although, of course, because of the intervening historical developments, the workers in psychology departments inhabit a small enclave within an enormous multiracial empire. But throughout this history the absence of available knowledge and techniques, and the absence of intent to test physiological theory by physiological research, has not prevented psychologists from giving their "constructs" the form of hypothesized anatomico-physiological mechanisms. Classical examples were the explanations of learning as a "reduction of resistance at synapses," and of inhibition, attention, or absent-mindedness as "neural drainage." More recent examples are the "quasi-neurological principles" of Hull, who, though he claimed to be a "peripheralist" and to talk in the language of behavior, nevertheless introduced "intervening variables" which were at the same time "hypothetical constructs" for which physiological reality was implied; and again, there are Köhler's theory of "electrical fields," Lashley's theory of "interference patterns," and Hebb's conceptions of "cell-assemblies" and "phase sequences."

Hebb (1958a), in presenting his views concerning the relation of psychology to the biological sciences, begins with the statement that "I suppose it is because of its history, the course of its earlier development and its origins, that psychology is not yet fully integrated with the realm of biology though, inescapably and permanently, it is now in that realm," and he ends with the statement that "Our strategy calls for maximal utilization of data and ideas from both sides of this fence; and in fact we must get rid of the fence as far as possible." With these statements I thoroughly agree, but I am dubious about what might be stated as three theses of the intervening paragraphs: (1) that the basic science of psychology—"physiological psychology"—differs from physiology in that it operates on a "molar" level; (2) that it must nevertheless "devise physiological hypotheses about the nature of some of psychology's 'intervening variables'"; (3) that the barrier between psychology and physiology is one of communication, and that this barrier can be removed by a sort of "adult education" whereby the psychologist and biologist do homework on each other's subjects. But since there are, on the one hand, "psychologists" who perform surgical operations, implant electrodes, and record visceral processes, and on the other, physiologists who work with the techniques devised for the study of discrimination, learning, motivation, emotion, etc., the adequacy of the first thesis as a basis for professional or educational differentiation is questionable. As for the second thesis, was Hebb, in developing the concepts in his *Organization of Behavior* (1949)—or Johannes Müller in his *Handbuch*, or Ladd in his *Physiological Psychology* (Ladd and Woodworth, 1911)—a psychologist or a physiologist? If we try to define the concept of "psychologist," how much do we have left when we have eliminated the criteria of peripheralism, mathematical models, factor analysis, experimental design, Freudianism, hedonism, and group interaction? On the other hand, when a man "gets up" neurology to the extent which was necessary for the working out of Hebb's theories, is he not at least an honorary physiologist? And physiologists ignorant of behavioral research, like those ignorant of statistical controls, are members of a passing generation. And so to the third thesis: "communication" suggests symposia, conferences, and "teams," or at least taking in each other's washing. There seems however to be good reason for asserting that, however stimulating such communication may be, information which is to be creatively integrated must be fed into an individual brain. Since there exist brains in which this has occurred, there seems to be no necessity for maintaining institutional or curricular barriers. As Livingston (1962, p. 52) says, "A real union will be established between psychology and neurophysiology when a large number of scientists are well grounded in both disciplines."

The Antecedents of Neurophysiology

Of the sixteen centuries from the second century A.D. to the beginning of the nineteenth century—from Galen to von Haller,

Whytt, Galvani, and Bell—the first three-fourths were blank for physiological science. The Greeks had had certain great intuitions, notably those of the atomic structure of the universe, of metabolic equilibration, of disease as a disequilibrium, of biological evolution, of muscular movement as a reflex response to sensory stimulation, and of a peripheral transmission system communicating through central integrating organs. But the fleshing out of these intuitions was prevented by the lack of technical development. In neurophysiology, there were the primitive beginnings of dissection and vivisection, from Alcmaeon through Aristotle, Herophilus, and Erasistratus to Galen. The Hippocratics had arrived at the conception of the brain as serving the functions of perception, motor control, memory, thought, and emotion, and of abnormal states of the brain as the causes of temporary or persistent behavioral aberrations. Erasistratus in the third century B.C. distinguished the peripheral nerves from the arteries and veins. Galen distinguished between sensory and motor nerves and gave the first anatomical description of the autonomic nervous system; by sectioning the spinal cord he demonstrated the connection of different levels to the various parts of the body. The gross anatomy of the brain— the main subdivisions and the ventricles, membranes, sinuses, and convolutions—were known. At this point further progress would in any case have had to await technical inventions, but progress was conceptually interrupted by the Platonic soul-body dualism and mysticism and by the subsequent centuries of religious dogmatism.

The great scientific developments between 1500 and 1800 were, so to speak, propaedeutic to the rise of neurophysiology; they provided both the general scientific climate—the release from the bonds of dogma as well as the positive ideas of scientific method— and also more specifically the beginnings of the techniques and the models of biological explanation necessary for biological research. Science had lived on, with decreasing vitality, for some five hundred years after the death of Aristotle. Aristotle, it will be recalled, was the tutor of Alexander the Great, who in 332 B.C. founded Alexandria, which became the great center of Hellenistic and Jewish culture. Here in the period between 300 and 200 B.C. mathematics, astronomy, physics, anatomy, and physiology flourished. Euclid wrote his *Elements*; Aristarchus anticipated Copernicus' heliocentric theory of the planets; Herophilus and Erasistratus dissected the human body, distinguished the gross structures of the brain—which they recognized as the center of the nervous system and the seat of intelligence—and distinguished experimentally between the dorsal (sensory) and ventral (motor) nerve-roots of the spinal nerves. In this period also Archimedes of Syracuse founded the sciences of mechanics and of mathematical physics, and contributed to the understanding of the relationship between intuition, experiment, and formal proof in scientific discovery. Further developments in mathematics occurred in the last two centuries B.C., particularly at the hands of Apollonius. Singer (1959, p. 76) tells us that

> Archimedes and Apollonius between them originated two great problems which have ever since occupied geometers. The first is the quadrature of figures outlined by curves. This gave rise in due course to the infinitesimal calculus. The second is the theory of conic sections. This gave rise in due course to the theory of geometrical curves of all degrees so that, for example, a circle could be treated as a special case of the ellipse.

In the first two centuries A.D., when all the lands of the Mediterranean world had become provinces of the Roman Empire, the two great figures are those of Ptolemy and Galen. Ptolemy developed a mathematical astronomy which was not superseded until the seventeenth century. Galen (131-201 A.D.) was the last great biologist of antiquity; the enormous mass of his writings transmitted the medical knowledge of the ancient world across the barren intervening centuries to the men who revived medical research in the sixteenth century. Two erroneous doctrines of Galen persisted into modern times: one was the notion of "animal spirits" supposed to flow through the nerves so as to produce the phenomena of sensation and of movement, and the other was the assumption that wherever peripheral nerves join one another they communicate so that the animal spirits may flow freely from one part of the body to another and thus bring about "sympathy" between various parts of the body. Singer (1959, pp. 100-101) remarks that "the vast, windy, ill-arranged treatises of Galen" survived until the sixteenth century, while the biological works of Aristotle, Theophrastus, and the Ionian and Alexandrian biologists disappeared, because Galen's theologically expressed teleology, according to which human structure and function are to be understood in terms of a Creator's design, "fitted in with the prevailing theological attitude of the Middle Ages." "This attitude removes the foundation of scientific curiosity. After Galen there is a thousand years of darkness, and both medicine and biology almost cease to have a history."

Three "psychiatrists" of the first two centuries A.D. are worthy of mention. *Celsus* (ca. 25 A.D.) wrote a celebrated treatise on Roman medicine of which one chapter was devoted to mental diseases. He deserves credit, I think, for denying a notion common in his time that whereas the physician properly treats the ills of the body, the ills of the "mind" are the province of the philosopher (or as we would say, the psychologist). *Aretaeus of Cappadocia* (81-138? A.D.) wrote the first descriptions of "prepsychotic personalities," described mania and melancholia as expressions of one illness, and distinguished mania from both senile disorders and from states (schizophrenic?) in which patients appear "stupid, absent, and musing." *Soranus* (fl. 98-138 A.D.) was representative of those physicians who appeared from time to time in the history of psychiatry and recommended humane treatment of the mentally ill, attention to the needs of the individual, tranquil environment, etc. Such physicians alternated with those of the opposite persuasion, represented by Celsus and in the seventeenth century by Willis, who recommended "retraining" or "bringing the insane to their senses" by punishment, confinement, starvation, sudden fright, bloodletting, enemas, purges, emetics, etc. During the first three centuries A.D. medical science and science in general were more and more overwhelmed by waves of oriental mysticism, superstition, and anti-intellectualism. Intellectuals sought refuge in contemplative passivity, resignation, and mystical subjectivism, a posture which some intellectuals in our own time are recommending. Following the establishment of Christianity as the official religion of the western world in 313, demonology took over the field of mental disease and dominated it for twelve centuries. Persons suffering from mental diseases were regarded as being possessed by demons or the devil; in the earlier centuries the treatment consisted of conjurations, exorcisms, application of holy relics, etc. Mental diseases were sometimes also attributed to the influences of the stars and planets and treated by various magical concoctions and incantations. Increasingly, especially following the institution of the Inquisition (1233), the mentally diseased were treated as witches and heretics. The inquisitors checked whole populations for *stigmata diaboli*—"marks of the devil"—such as pigmented or anesthetic areas of skin. Hallucinations and delusions were attributed to demoniac possession, and self-accusations were taken at face value. Torture and burning at the stake were the legal procedures against "witches," and hundreds of thousands were burned.

In the twelfth and thirteenth centuries western Europe began to recover some of the science and philosophy of the ancient Greeks through Latin translations from the Arabic. But the chief "recovery" was the logical and cosmical works of Aristotle as adapted to ecclesiastical requirements by such theologians as Albertus Magnus and Thomas Aquinas; the result was scholasticism—authoritarian dogmatism and the mystical picture of the world as presented by Dante.

In the late fifteenth and early sixteenth centuries the rebirth of science was signalized by the appearance of Greek texts and translations of the biological works of Aristotle and of the medical works of Hippocrates and Galen. In the realm of physical science there occurred a series of great events which greatly accelerated the development of modern science in general. *Copernicus* in 1543 introduced the proposition that the earth revolves upon its own axis and around the sun. This was the beginning of that spectacular series of discoveries which eventually demolished the hold of dogmatic theology upon the intellectual world. Dingle (1959, p. 21) asks, "Why was it, then, that a century after his death his work became the centre of one of the most violent intellectual controversies that the world has known?" and he answers,

The reason was that, though apparently simple and harmless, it in fact gave the death-blow to the whole medieval system of thought, for it touched that system at its most vital spot. It is hard for us to realize today, when so many quite dissimilar departments of knowledge surround us on all sides, that medieval thought was essentially a unity. The subjects we know as astronomy, physics, chemistry, theology, psychology, physiology, and so on, were then all fused together in a single system. Above the outermost sphere of astronomy was the heaven of theology, pictured in the same diagram.

This passion for unity between the natural sciences and theology, metaphysics, and morals found unedifying expression in the nineteenth-century controversy about the theory of evolution, and it still manifests itself in some philosophers and elderly scientists. The lesson of history seems to be that theologians, metaphysicians, and humanitarians would do well not to attempt intervention in scientific theory and research and to concentrate instead on controlling the *applications* of science. *Galileo* (1564-1642), the creator of modern physics and astronomy, by his exact quantitative studies of motion made untenable in the realm of inorganic nature the notion of "animation," the conception of non-physical agents, such as "will," which could influence a sequence of physical events. He affirmed, says Höffding (1924, I, p. 181), that "it is only possible to understand the qualitative changes in nature when these can be traced back to quantitative changes, which means here to motions in space." His slogan was: "To measure what can be measured and to make measurable what cannot be measured."

Francis Bacon (1561-1626) sought to abolish slavish dependence on authority, especially that of the "Aristotle" of the theologians, and to demonstrate the futility of a priori reasoning. He urged the substitution of induction based on exhaustive observation and experiment. He declared that when we assume "final causes" and apply them to science, we are carrying into nature what exists only in our imagination. Instead of understanding *things,* we dispute about *words,* which each man interprets to suit himself. Also, we continually confuse the objects of science with those of religion. The control over the environment and human health which science has given us was totally lacking in Bacon's day, and there was no connection between science and the practical world; the learned men of Bacon's time were dominated by Thomistic Aristotelianism; that is, by the habit of syllogistic "reasoning" and the dogmas of the Aristotelian "science" of the Schoolmen. It was against this background that Bacon asserted that science should be brought to bear on the problems of human life (cf. Broad, 1959). But he did not urge a concentration on immediate practical problems; on the contrary, he emphasized that science could only give rise to useful applications by discovering the fundamental laws and structure of nature; it should seek to "explain" rather than to "anticipate." The proper method was induction from experiments and testing of the resulting generalizations by experiment. Bacon's philosophy of science has been much criticized on the ground of overemphasis on induction and underemphasis on insight, tentative hypotheses, mathematical deduction, and tests of deductions (cf., e.g., Dampier-Whetham, 1930, p. 138). However, such criticisms seem to neglect both Bacon's position in history and also what Bacon actually said. His approach was perhaps sounder than that in recent psychology in which we sounded the slogan of "prediction and control" and upon an inadequate theoretical foundation tried to erect a vast structure of applied psychologies. Like Hebb (1958a) and Skinner (1956), Bacon was distrustful of mathematical formalism in science. Bacon urged a "crash program" requiring a huge research organization and vast expenditures;

moreover, scientific method was to be so standardized that most of the work could be done by what we call "technicians" and Darwin called "fourth rate men"; this "faith in the common man" has touched the heart of Eiseley (1961, p. 1201), but in others it has aroused misgivings. Thus Dubos (1961, p. 1209) has called attention to the hostility toward science and scientists expressed by two widely read authors, Miguel Unamuno and Ortega y Gasset, who "have accepted Bacon's claim that the scientific method is so mechanical and foolproof as to be readily and effectively handled by small minds." Dubos (p. 1210) quotes Ortega: "Anyone who wishes can observe the stupidity of thought, judgment, and action shown today in politics, art, religion, and the general problems of life and the world by the 'men of science.'"

With *Isaac Newton* (1642-1727) the developments in physical science which we have been sketching reached their climax. His theory brought all the motions in earth and sky under one unifying system of law. His conception of a clockwork universe, set in motion by God but thereafter operating automatically, provided the reconciliation between science and religion which eased the conflicts of intellectuals in the eighteenth and nineteenth centuries; it provided also, however, the model of universal "mechanistic" explanation which so many in our times have been proclaiming to be obsolete, often seeming to mean by this that the world which science seeks to study is capricious—or, in more ancient language, animistic. That the world is capricious is a notion which we, like primitive men, are free to adopt, and it accords with much of our personal experience, but it is incompatible with science.

In biology, great events occurred in the sixteenth and seventeenth centuries. *Andreas Vesalius* (1514-1564) founded modern anatomy and physiology; he pioneered the modern techniques of dissection, inventing the necessary instruments, and published a great textbook of human anatomy. Before the sixteenth century, the relation between verbal and manual behavior, which is an essential part of our definition of science, was very slight, and in medical education it was very peculiar: a reader read passages from the works of Galen, the professor in his pulpit explicated the passages, and the demonstrator at the table pointed to the organs in the cadaver which the barber-surgeon carved up. With Vesalius began the advancement of anatomical knowledge by means of dissections carried out by medical scholars. (It is interesting to note that the education in anatomy of most psychologists is still carried

out—in so far as it occurs at all—by means of a modern equivalent
of the ancient demonstration method: textbook plus films.)
Vesalius gave physiological demonstrations of the dependence of
muscle contraction upon the motor nerves, and of the effect of
sectioning the spinal cord on sensation and movement of parts supplied by nerves leaving the cord below the level of section. The
spirit of Vesalius' research is conveyed by the following quotation
(transl. by Foster, 1901, p. 258):

> But how the brain performs its functions in imagination, in reason-
> ing, in thinking and memory . . . I can form no opinion whatever.
> Nor do I think that anything more will be found out by anatomy or
> by the methods of those theologians who deny to brute animals all
> power of reasoning, and indeed all the faculties belonging to what we
> call the chief soul. For as regards the structure of the brain, the
> monkey, dog, horse, cat, and all quadrupeds which I have hitherto
> examined, and indeed all birds, and many kinds of fish, resemble man
> in almost every particular.

William Harvey (1578-1657) in 1628 demonstrated the circulation of the blood, and thus demolished the whole Galenic doctrine
of "spirits." Since his explanation was in purely physical and
mechanical terms—the motion of the blood being ascribed to the
muscular contraction of the heart—the possibility of the physical
explanation of all bodily activities was greatly strengthened, and
the concept of mechanism was extended into the biological world.
It must be remembered that the doctrine of "spirits" had been
appealed to as offering a connecting link between body and soul.
Singer remarks that "The knowledge of the circulation of the blood
has been the basis of the whole of modern physiology and with it of
the whole of modern rational medicine" (Singer and Underwood,
1962, p. 121 f.).

The Beginnings of Modern Neurophysiology

In the eighteenth century began the development of modern
neurophysiology. *Albrecht von Haller* (1708-1777) began as an
infant prodigy and became one of those universal geniuses who, we
are told, are no longer possible—poet, novelist, botanist, anatomist,
physiologist, public official and diplomat. He wrote the first modern textbook of physiology, in eight volumes. In his neurophysiology he still held to the ancient ideas that the same nerves served
both sensation and motion, and that the nerves conveyed a "nervous liquor." But he demonstrated that muscles do not contract

because they are made to swell like balloons by inflowing fluid but that they possess a *vis insita,* an intrinsic capacity to contract, as shown by excised heart or intestine. A muscle, he showed, could be caused to contract either by direct stimulation or by stimulation of its nerve, whose *vis nervosa* he distinguished from the *vis insita* (contractility) of muscle. Haller distinguished also, in a rather vague sort of way, between reflex, involuntary, automatic reactions and voluntary actions "arising from the mind" (cf. Fearing, 1930, pp. 70-74).

Luigi Galvani (1737-1798) discovered "animal electricity" through a chance observation that frogs' legs developed spasms when hung by copper hooks from an iron balustrade, the spasms being induced whenever the muscle came into contact with the iron. The physicist *Volta* denied Galvani's statement that the contractions resulted from the conduction of "animal electricity" by the metal, and maintained that they were produced by electricity generated by contact of dissimilar metals. In this he was correct, and he went on to develop the "voltaic pile" or electric battery. Galvani however went on to demonstrate, by his experiments "without metals," that when the nerve of a nerve-muscle preparation is brought into contact with an injured point of the muscle, the nerve is stimulated and the muscle contracts. The existence of potential differences in physiological tissues was thus proved. The evolution of the electrophysiology of the nervous system between 1600 and 1800 has been usefully outlined by Brazier (1958). Static electricity, as revealed by the attraction of light bodies by a piece of amber which has been rubbed with a flannel cloth, had been known since about 600 B.C. About the year 1600 Gilbert discovered that a large number of substances possess the same property as amber, and he accordingly called them "electrics," from the Greek word for amber, *electron.* In 1729 it was discovered that Gilbert's "nonelectrics," which do not show electrification by friction, convey away the "electric virtue" as fast as it is excited; these therefore are *conductors,* and thus the concept of electricity as flowing like a fluid current was born. Beginning about 1660 frictional machines which produced electrostatic charges mechanically by the turning of a crank began to be invented. In 1745 the "Leyden jar," the first effective condenser, made it possible to store electric charge. These primitive electrostatic machines and condensers were available to Galvani for the stimulation of irritable tissues. The impact of these discoveries upon eighteenth century intellectuals and upon the public in general is conveyed by the following quotations:

Certainly this [electricity] was the most striking, the most original, and the most progressive branch of eighteenth-century physics. The spectacle of the erect hair, the nasal sparks, of an electrified youth hung in silk cords from the ceiling excited the rather coarse humor of the age; the mystery of lightning drawn off down an iron rod and confined, like a jinn, in a Leyden bottle, was witness to the strange power of nature and man's intellectual mastery of it; while, at a more serious and prosaic level, a new corpus of experimental and theoretical knowledge was taking shape, of incalculable importance for the future. No one could have foreseen, in Franklin's day, the extent to which physics was to become the science of electricity, yet already by 1800 almost every experimental physicist was to some degree an electrician [A. R. Hall, 1954, p. 347 f.].

The announcement of the discoveries of Galvani and Volta led to an intellectual outburst which can only be compared with the political upheaval of the time. One finds in the literature of the period from 1791 to 1798 no less than fifty separate titles of contributions to the subject of animal electricity. As du Bois-Reymond has remarked, wherever frogs were found and where dissimilar metals could be obtained, everybody attempted to see how the mangled limbs of the frogs could be once more brought to life. Visions were entertained of new vital forces and powers, and one can judge of the importance of the discoveries by the rich fruition of knowledge to which they eventually led [Fulton, 1926, p. 37].

As we have seen, the Galenic doctrine of nervous action as consisting in the flow of "animal spirits" in nerves regarded as hollow tubes was still dominant, and was defended by so eminent a physiologist as von Haller, who, like Robert Whytt, specifically rejected electricity as the agent in nerve action. It was Galvani's experiments which sounded the death knell of Galen's doctrine of fluid in pipes after a life of more than 1500 years in physiology; its ghost however took up residence in psychology, under the protection of Freud, McDougall, and Max Meyer.

At the close of the eighteenth century the great von Humboldt demonstrated the validity both of Volta's "bimetallic electricity" and of Galvani's intrinsic "animal electricity," and showed that these were not mutually exclusive. Controversy and puzzlement about the phenomena in nerve and muscle continued, however, for fifty years, and it was not until the middle of the nineteenth century that electrophysiology—which is almost synonymous with neurophysiology—was able to resume its advance with the demonstration of electric currents in nerve by du Bois-Reymond by means of the newly perfected needle galvanometer.

Robert Whytt (1714-1766) gave the first modern statement of the principle of the reflex control of movement. The historical background of this subject was the conflict between the Cartesian conception of the animal body as a reflex machine, applied unreservedly to man by LaMettrie (1748), and the animistic-vitalistic theory of *Georg Ernst Stahl* (1660-1734), according to which there was an unbridgeable gap between living and non-living things. Stahl held that the chemical processes in a living body are different from those of the laboratory, being characterized by complexity and easy decomposability of chemical associations, which are held together by the soul; if the soul relaxes its control of the body, decomposition ensues, and this is what occurs in sickness and death. Mental disease results when the life force is inhibited by a contrary mood or idea—which may suggest the notion of "conflict" or the Freudian "repression of instinctual drives." Stahl might be regarded as the ancestor of modern vitalistic, anti-mechanistic, organismic, and anti-organic tendencies; characteristically, he expressed great contempt for anatomical and microscopic investigation (cf. Nordenskiöld, 1928, pp. 178-183, and Zilboorg, 1941, pp. 277-280).

Whytt (who exemplifies the precocity which contrasts so painfully with the extended academic infancy of our own times—he received the M.A. degree at the age of sixteen) distinguished between voluntary motions—which "proceed from an immediate exertion of the active power of the will," involuntary, and "mixed" motions; it is the latter two which are of interest for subsequent history. The involuntary motions were those of the list which has become familiar to us: those of the alimentary canal, heart, bladder, pupil, salivary glands, respiratory organs, etc. These he showed to be controlled through the spinal cord; his demonstration was that of the "basic experiment" (cf. Fearing, 1930, pp. 74-83) of the decapitated frog. He thus provided the experimental basis for the conception of reflex action and invalidated the notion of "sympathy" between body parts by means of anastomosing peripheral nerves; he wrote,

> There is no sympathy between the different muscles or other parts of the body as was observed while the spinal marrow was entire; from whence it seems to follow that the nerves distributed to the several parts of the body have no communication but at their termination in the brain or spinal marrow, and that to this, perhaps, alone is owing the consent or sympathy between them.

Whytt noted the phenomenon of muscle tonus: a constant state of tension in muscles that have antagonists which is produced by the continuous influence of the nerves. His "mixed motions" are those which can occur above or below the level of consciousness; here he includes automatized habits; his discussion is very like that of William James. His reference to the fact that "the sight, or even the recalled *idea* of grateful food, causes an uncommon flow of spittle into the mouth of a hungry person" is cited by Fearing as a "remarkable anticipation of an observation which physiologists of 150 years later were to recognize under the term 'conditioned reflex.'" A discussion of Whytt's contributions has been provided by Carmichael (1927).

The contrast between Whytt and his contemporary, David Hartley, is interesting; Whytt was a physiologist who performed actual physiological experiments; Hartley, though trained as a physician, takes his place in the ranks of the philosophers of association theory as a specialist in wholly hypothetical neural "constructs." The one was an important link in the progress of science, the other is a paragraph in histories of philosophy and psychology. To credit Hartley with having been the originator of physiological psychology, as Brett (1953, p. 422) does, would be to give a philosophical, non-biological meaning to the word "physiological." It is also to be noted that Hartley took his notion of "vibrations" in the nerves and brain, not from contemporary physiological researches, but from the physical doctrine of Newton's *Principia*. In this analogical borrowing from physical theory he was to be followed by many a later psychologist.

Sir Charles Bell (1774-1842) is known chiefly as the formulator of "Bell's Law," which states that the ventral roots of the spinal nerves contain only motor fibers and that the dorsal roots contain only sensory fibers. On the basis of this discovery (which according to Singer [1959, p. 68] had been anticipated by Erasistratus c. 280 B.C.), Bell suggested that separate regions of the brain and spinal cord might serve the sensory and motor functions; he thus initiated the analysis of the nervous system into functional components, an analysis upon which modern neurology is based. (It must be remembered that von Haller and other eighteenth-century physiologists had continued to believe that the same nerves transmitted both sensory and motor impulses.) Another great contribution made by Bell was the postulation of a muscle sense and the demonstration of the regulatory role of proprioceptive feedback. Fearing (1930, p. 120) quotes him:

Between the brain and the muscles there is a circle of nerves; one nerve conveys the influence from the brain to the muscle, another gives the sense of the condition of the muscle to the brain. If the circle be broken by the division of the motor nerve, motion ceases; if it be broken by the division of the other nerve, there is no longer a sense of the condition of the muscle, and therefore no regulation of its activity.

Carmichael (1926), in the course of an excellent account of Bell's contributions, remarks,

For certain psychologists any knowledge of the nervous system is considered as merely preparatory physiology; for others it is truly a part of psychology. All, however, save a few belated 'mentalists,' admit the importance of a knowledge of the nervous system for one who would understand 'mind.' From the early experiments of Wundt's institute down to the work of the present day there are few laboratory problems which do not make use, in the course of their development, of certain generalizations which are based upon Bell's Law [p. 197].

And in a footnote Carmichael observes, "It is interesting to note that the so-called 'introspective psychologists,' who study experience as dependent upon the experiencing individual, and the 'behaviorists,' who study the activity of the organism as a whole, agree at least on the one point of considering physiology as extra-psychological. . . . Other students admit the study of the nervous system as an integral part of "psychology." Developments since Carmichael's writing have made of "psychology" a merely administrative and bureaucratic catchall whose relation to physiology can hardly be discussed, although the problems of a basic science of human life—in health and disease—remain.

Johannes Müller (1801-1858) was renowned as a teacher—his pupils included Helmholtz, du Bois-Reymond, Ludwig, and Virchow; as a systematizer—his *Handbook of Human Physiology* was a monumental survey of contemporary knowledge in the fields of physiology and psychology; and as the formulator of the theory of the "specific energies of nerves." According to this theory (whose history has been reviewed by Boring, 1950, pp. 80-95), which in its essentials had already been stated by Bell, each sensory nerve, however stimulated, gives rise to its own specific kind of sensory process; the same stimulus affecting different nerves gives rise to the different experienced qualities appropriate to the particular nerves; conversely, different stimuli affecting the same nerve always give rise to the particular quality of that nerve. Fundamental to this doctrine was the principle that the "sensorium"—the sensory part of the brain—receives, not "copies" of external objects, but changes in the states of the nerves induced by external energy sources. We are directly "aware," not of objects, but of neural activity, since the functional activity of the nerves intervenes between the outer world and "us." This is the problem of sensory "coding," which still awaits clarification (cf., e.g., Ruch, 1961, p. 302, and Rosenblith and Vidale, 1962). To what relative degrees is the "specificity" to be attributed to sense organ, nerve processes, and central connections? Müller spoke of the "specific irritability" of the sense organs, a property to which Sherrington in 1906 referred by the term "adequate stimulation"; light is the "adequate" stimulus for the eye, which is however also, though less, sensitive to other—"inadequate"—stimuli, such as mechanical pressure. Ruch compares the sense organs to the color filters of photography and suggests that they "translate the complex impression into an intricate pattern of action currents which are recombined in the cerebral cortex . . . to give a picture of the external world" (p. 302). But he expresses doubt as to whether the differential sensitivity necessarily depends on morphologic differentiation of the end-organ, and remarks that "Could coding of nerve impulses be established, the concept of end-organ specificity could be abandoned." Müller was uncertain whether the specificity was in the nerves or in the areas of the brain in which they terminated, although he inclined to the latter alternative; on this question we find Ruch (p. 303) saying, "Dramatic evidence of this is the production of visual sensation by stimulation of the cortical visual area in conscious human patients and of somatic sensation by stimulation of the cortical somatosensory area." Evidently Bell and Müller raised questions concerning fundamental principles of operation of the nervous system which when definitively answered will be part of the final unravelling of the problems of perception, action, and thought.

Neurophysiology in the Nineteenth Century

Progress in neurophysiology was greatly accelerated in the nineteenth century by the invention of two instruments: the needle galvanometer, about 1825, and the compound microscope, about

1827. The galvanometer made possible the work of *Emil du Bois-Reymond* (1818-1896), the founder of modern electrophysiology. In 1838 it had been established that a difference of potential exists between a damaged and a normal area of nerve or muscle surface, so that when such areas are connected to a galvanometer, a current, called the "current of injury," flows in a direction indicating that the damaged area is electrically negative to the rest of the surface. Du Bois-Reymond demonstrated that when a muscle or nerve is stimulated, a transient diminution of the current of injury occurs, indicating that the difference of potential between injured and undamaged regions is momentarily decreased. Hence the electrical sign of nerve and muscle activity was at first called a "negative variation of the current of injury." The work of a number of investigators in the latter part of the nineteenth century led to the view that the electrical phenomena of nerve and muscle result from the presence of surface membranes, having selective ion permeability, interposed between solutions of different electrolytes. This view was formulated as the "membrane theory" in 1902 by *Julius Bernstein* (1839-1917), who ascribed the electromotive force revealed by the locally injured muscle fiber to selective permeability to potassium ions, present inside the fiber in greater concentration than outside. The action potential wave following stimulation he described as a self-propagating depolarization by breakdown of this selective permeability. This explanation in terms of the movement of ions in progressive local electrolytic circuits—rather than in terms of the flow of electrons as in metallic conductors—was consonant with Helmholtz's demonstration in 1850 that the velocity of impulses in human nerves was 100 meters per second or less, whereas Müller and others had inclined to the view that it was of the order of the velocity of light. In his excellent chapter on "Psychophysiology in the First Half of the Nineteenth Century," Boring (1950, pp. 27-49) comments,

> The importance for scientific psychology of the discovery that the transmission of the nervous impulse is not practically instantaneous, but relatively slow, is not to be underestimated. In the period under consideration, the mind had come to be largely identified with the brain, but the personality seemed rather to be a matter of the entire organism. Every one thought, as the average man thinks now, of his hand as of a piece with himself. To move his finger voluntarily was an act of mind in itself, not a later event caused by a previous act of mind. To separate the movement in time from the event of will that caused it was in a sense to separate the body from the mind, and

almost from the personality or self. At any rate, Helmholtz's discovery
was a step in the analysis of bodily motion that changed it from an
instantaneous occurrence to a temporal series of events, and it thus
contributed to the materialistic view of the psychophysical organism
that was the essence of nineteenth century science [p. 42].

The invention of the capillary electrometer in 1872 and of the
string galvanometer in 1901 made possible further progress in
electrophysiology. *Francis Gotch* (1853-1913) demonstrated the
refractory period in nerve. *Keith Lucas* (1879-1916) showed that
the contraction of muscle fibers is in accordance with an "all-or-
none" principle, and that the nerve impulse leaves behind it a
phase of diminished excitability.

Adrian (1932) remarked that "The history of electrophysiology
has been decided by the history of electric recording instruments,"
and, as of his time of writing, he said that "The advent of triode
valve, or vacuum tube amplification has so altered the whole position that we can compare ourselves to a microscope worker who
has been given a new objective with a resolving power a thousand
times greater than anything he has had before" (pp. 2, 5). The
most important result of the introduction of this new instrument
was that it became possible to record the activity of single nerve
cells, as Adrian was the first to do. Gasser and Erlanger were able
to show that the congeries of fibers in mixed nerve trunks, differing
in caliber and in thickness of myelin sheath, exhibit correlated differences in functional properties, such as stimulus threshold, conduction velocity, and action potential voltage. Previous to these
developments the activity of the nervous system could be studied
only in peripheral *nerves*; that is, what was recorded was the summated action potentials of many nerve fibers, of varying properties,
within the nerve, just as electroencephalography records summated
potentials of the brain. It now became possible to record the activity of single neurons and to trace the progress of functional activity
from the periphery through the central nervous system; this
method, far more than any of its predecessors—incomparably more
than the method of ablation—offers hope that we may arrive at an
understanding of the modes of operation of the nervous system.

By about 1827 the compound microscope was sufficiently
improved to permit the observation of cell structure. The following series of developments occurred: the method of cutting thin
sections of the brain, chemically hardened (1824); discovery that
the gray matter of the brain is cellular, and description of the fibers

of the white matter (1833); discovery that a severed nerve trunk degenerates in its peripheral portion only (1839); method of cutting a continuous series of sections so that structures like nerve fibers can be traced through the series (1842); demonstration that every nerve fiber is connected to a nerve cell body, and that degeneration of a sectioned fiber occurs in the part distal to the section, facts which Waller utilized to develop a method of tracing nerve tracts (1852); discovery of a staining method, using carmine (1858); Golgi's method of staining with silver nitrate, which brings out the entire nerve cell with all its ramifications (1873); Cajal's description of the synapse (1889); Waldeyer's formulation of the neuron theory, according to which the nervous system is composed of individual cellular units, the neurons. Previous to this it was possible to think of the nervous system as a continuous network of fibers. An important result of these discoveries was that the revealed histological differentiation and complexity suggested a corresponding differentiation of functions, so that the case for a simple unitary function—e.g., of the cerebral hemispheres—became more doubtful.

The question of unitary versus differentiated functions has had a long and not very edifying history under the title of "localization of functions in the brain." The history began with *Franz Joseph Gall* (1758-1828), who, on the basis of statistically uncontrolled observations, asserted that each of some thirty-five mental traits or "faculties" has its seat in a definite region of the brain, and that the relative development of these traits in an individual is revealed by correspondingly localized protuberances of the skull. Gall's pupil Spurzheim elaborated and popularized this doctrine and gave it the name "phrenology." While phrenology was rejected by most scientists of the period, it did bring into prominence the problem of the correlation of brain function and structure. *Pierre Flourens* (1794-1867) developed the method of extirpation or ablation in a series of skilful experiments on the brains of pigeons. He found that extirpation of the cerebral hemispheres abolishes "voluntary" action and perception; animals remain as in a coma when undisturbed, although they can walk, stand, and right themselves; normal responses to visual or auditory stimuli are lost, although reflex responses—e.g., pupillary reflex—are still present. Flourens concluded that the cerebral hemispheres are the sole organs of a *unitary* faculty of volition and perception. "All perceptions and volitions have the same distribution in the hemispheres; the facul-

ties of perceiving, understanding, and willing constitute a single
function which is essentially unitary." Thus he denied that there
is any localization of function in the hemispheres; intelligent behavior is an indivisible function of the activity of the entire hemispheres. *Paul Broca* (1824-1880) found in several patients a coin-
cidence of motor aphasia with a lesion in the inferior frontal gyrus
of the left cerebral hemisphere, and concluded that this cortical
area was a "speech center." This observation suggested to him the
possibility that every convolution of the hemispheres had its own
particular functions and that Flourens' doctrine of unity of function was untenable. *Gustav Fritsch* and *Eduard Hitzig* in 1870
found that electrical stimulation of the frontal cortex of various
mammals caused movements of the extremities of the opposite side
of the body, and that with strong stimuli the movements were
convulsive and general but that with weak stimuli there appeared
to be different cortical foci for different groups of muscles.

The great clinical neurologist *John Hughlings Jackson* (1835-
1911) had a few years earlier arrived at similar conclusions from
the observation of the origin and spread of epileptic convulsions.
Hitzig however "made the precarious step from the localization of
movements to that of psychic functions" (Riese, 1959, p. 108). He
declared that "abstract thinking demands a special organ and this
I seek provisionally in the frontal lobes." *Paul Emil Flechsig* (1847-
1929), having in 1827 noted the white streaks formed by early mye-
linating tracts in brain sections from the human newborn, recognized
myelogenesis as a method of functional analysis, and in the years following 1893 developed, on the basis of this method, his theory of
projection and association centers, dividing the cortex into primary
and secondary projection areas and association or cognition areas;
he considered the parietotemporal-occipital "association zones"—
not the frontal—as most important for mental life. (Flechsig was
"quite a character"; see Haymaker's, 1953, pp. 31-35, account.)
Flechsig's distinction between projection and association areas reinforced the notion that certain parts of the brain are particularly
concerned with intellectual activities. However, *Hermann Munk*,
having in 1880, on the basis of extirpation and clinical data, localized the visual sensory area in the occipital lobe, and having thereupon divided the cerebrum into visual, auditory, tactual, etc.
"sensory spheres," in each of which he assumed that the images and
ideas associated with a single sensory mode are stored and elaborated, concluded that the interconnections between the sensory

spheres were adequate for the most complex integrations, so that there was no need to postulate specialized association areas devoted to the higher intellectual processes. "I considered the whole cerebral cortex," he said, "the aggregate of all the sensory spheres, to be the seat of the intelligence, which I defined as the combination and product of all the ideas arising from the sense-perceptions." Conclusions somewhat similar in effect were reached by *Friedrich Leopold Goltz* (1834-1902), who may be regarded as the classical "ablationist." Removing at first small portions of the cerebral cortex of dogs, he eventually succeeded in producing decerebrate animals, "Hunde ohne Grosshirn." "He observed that a direct relation existed between the amount of cerebral cortex removed and the degree of resulting dementia, and thus he anticipated the holistic concepts formulated by S. I. Franz and K. S. Lashley, namely, that except for the visual area there are no well defined functional centers" (Haymaker, 1953, p. 133). He anticipated Lashley also in stating that dementia is of essentially the same type after lesions of any area and in reporting "vicarious functioning" of remaining parts of the cortex for parts extirpated or involved in pathological processes. He was also the first to report the "sham rage" of animals with frontal decortications and to draw the conclusion that there are subcortical mechanisms for integrating emotional reactions, being thus a forerunner of Cannon and Bard. It is interesting to note that among Goltz's pupils were Sherrington and Loeb.

The history of brain "localization," is, as I said, not very edifying; it is the prime example of fruitless theorizing based on inadequate knowledge of structure and inadequate physiological methodology. It began with the nonsensical notion that arbitrary "traits" could be correlated with gross areas of the brain; when the cellular structure of the nervous system was discovered, the notion arose of "a cell for every idea," which fitted in well with associationistic psychology, since the cells, like the "ideas," were interconnected. When "habits" and "conditioned reflexes" replaced "ideas," "reflex arcs" became the localized structural units. Lashley began with such a concept. He stated that "The original program of research looked toward the tracing of conditioned-reflex arcs through the cortex, as the spinal paths of simple reflexes seemed to have been traced through the cord" (Lashley, 1929, p. 14). But, "The experimental findings have never fitted into such a scheme. Rather, they have emphasized the unitary character of every habit. . . ." From these results he drew the inference that

> The learning process and the retention of habits are not dependent
> upon any finely localized structural changes within the cerebral
> cortex. The results are incompatible with theories of learning by
> changes in synaptic structure, or with any theories which assume that
> particular neural integrations are dependent upon definite anatomi-
> cal paths specialized for them. Integration cannot be expressed in
> terms of connections between specific neurons [p. 176].

This inference was obviously a *non sequitur,* since Lashley's methodology provided no information concerning "finely localized" functional activity or structural changes within the cerebral cortex,
which would necessarily be cellular, involving cell processes,
somata, and synaptic junctions. The antistructural implications of
Lashley's inferences have, I think, strongly encouraged the peripheralistic, "stimulus-response" tendency of American psychology,
and in this respect his work, reinforcing as it did the influence of
gestalt psychology, was of doubtful service to physiological psychology. The "bowlful of porridge" notion of the brain was the
most egregious expression of the age of physiological innocence
among psychologists.

The only possible principle of research on brain function had
been stated in 1868 by *Theodor Meynert* (1833-1892): "If we look
upon the cortex as an organ functioning as a whole then the information that it subserves the processes of the mind is all that can be
said. . . . To think further about the cortex is impossible and unnecessary. . . . But our hope to understand eventually the function of
the hemispheres is raised again by the opposite assumption which
leads us straight to an organology of the central surface" (quoted
in Haymaker, 1953, p. 64). The extraordinary histological complexity and regional differentiation of the cerebral cortex were
brought to light by the researches of *Santiago Ramón y Cajal*
(1852-1934), *Gustav Magnus Retzius* (1842-1919), and *Rudolf
Albert von Kölliker* (1817-1905); the brief biographies of these
men in Haymaker's *Founders of Neurology* (1953) are well worth
reading; thus it is interesting, especially for scientists who sit on
"selection" committees, to read that the future Nobel Prize winner
Cajal was considered by his teachers to be a dolt (cf. the description of David Hume by his mother as "a fine, good-natured crater
but uncommon weak-minded"). The cellular structure and interconnections of the cerebral cortex have been described by Lorente de
Nó in the third edition of Fulton's *Physiology of the Nervous System* (1949). Of particular interest is the following passage:

Cajal assumed that the large number of cells with short axons was the anatomical expression of the delicacy of function of the brain of man. At present that assumption is almost a statement of fact, for it is known that synaptic transmission demands the summation of impulses under strict conditions, and it is evident that the more heterogeneous is the origin of the synapses on the cells with descending axons, the more rigid become the conditions for threshold stimulation, and the more accurate the selection of the paths through which the impulses may be conducted [p. 308; italics in original].

Some Recent Developments in Neurophysiology

Ruch (1961, pp. 249-276), in surveying recent research on the cortex, points out that "Electrophysiologists, by using microelectrodes which can record from single cells throughout the depth of the cortex, are developing a physiology of the cortex comparable to the histologic studies of the cortex made with silver stains" (p. 252), and, so far as the motor cortex is concerned, he remarks that "the controversy over cortical localization can be traced to neurophysiologists' thinking in terms of a morphologically complex structure . . . rather than in terms of its various cellular components —single units or classes of like neurons" (p. 266). Pribram (1958) has provided a discussion of the present state of knowledge of "neocortical function in behavior," indicating revisions which seem to be required in our traditional picture of the brain. Most interesting is his suggestion for a reconciliation between the "localizationistic" and the holistic views of cortical function; for the traditional "transcortical reflex model," according to which input from sense organs is organized in "sensory" areas, elaborated in "association" areas, and relayed to "motor" areas, he suggests that the so-called "projection" and "association" areas *both* discharge to subcortical nuclei. "According to this conception, the 'associative' functions of the central nervous system are to be sought at convergence points throughout the central nervous system, especially in the brain stem and spinal axis, and not solely in the intrinsic ["associative"] cerebral sectors" (p. 167). This suggestion seems to be consonant with the general plan of organization of the nervous system as it has been revealed in recent decades: its hierarchical organization and the incredibly complex system of interconnections—successively superimposed in the course of evolution—between nuclei, as in the reciprocal connections between thalamus and cortex, and between these and the basal nuclei and cerebellum.

Brooks (1958) concludes his review of the history and present status of the problems of integrative function with the statements that ". . . I believe it is reasonable to say that most of the basic concepts of function pertinent to brain and nervous system physiology were derived during the previous century and first quarter of this," and "It seems to me they [the neuro-biochemists] are assembling at the mark or perhaps approaching the first hurdles—we wish them speed and we hope that they in their coming day will bring us closer to an understanding of the great mysteries: learning, memory, thought and consciousness which seem to have some relationship to the brain" (pp. 249-250). We psychologists may wish them speed too, for thus our literature may win its freedom from its great burden of hypothetical constructs and theories of learning, perception, motivation, personality, and pathology. Brooks remarks that "Anatomical knowledge and knowledge of function have usually developed in parallel," and he proceeds to show how "the development of a few anatomical concepts and a similarly small number of ideas concerning function have made possible the modern procedure for analysing the brain's functional activity and the physico-chemical processes involved" (p. 236).

The paradigm, so to speak, of the basic concepts of neural integration and plasticity is afforded by the soma—the cell body and adjacent dendritic surfaces—of a neuron of the central nervous system, together with the clusters of synaptic knobs of the axons of other neurons which are scattered over the surface of this soma. On this surface is produced, by various combinations of action at the various knobs, that "algebraic summation" of excitatory and inhibitory effects which is the basic mechanism of integration. The concept of this mechanism was the creation of Sir Charles Sherrington, beginning with his famous *The Integrative Action of the Nervous System* (1906), which was a milestone in the history both of neurophysiology and of psychology. The history and present status of ideas on the synapse have been reviewed by Eccles (1959). We have seen the dependence of the previous development of neurophysiology on the invention of instruments and techniques; Eccles shows how, since 1951, intracellular recording and the use of the electron microscope have made possible a "very satisfactory synthesis of the structural and functional observations on the synapse"

(p. 57); the prospects seem good that this structure is in process of yielding the ultimate secrets of neural action.

However, the operations of the central nervous system involve hundreds of synaptic endings on each of some ten billion neurons, and these billions of neurons are organized in complexly interconnected subsystems. The remarkable advances in neurophysiology since ca. 1950, helpfully reviewed, e.g., by Livingston (1962), have revealed functional relationships which give physiologically operational meaning to such ancient psychological concepts as attention, emotion, mood, purpose, and memory. The methodology of earlier neurological research had restricted knowledge chiefly to the conspicuous tracts of nerve fibers and the definite gray masses —"nuclei"—with which they were connected. This system, whose cell bodies were large and whose axons were long myelinated fibers, was, according to the scheme of Hughlings Jackson, arranged in hierarchical levels, the successively higher horizontal levels of the central nervous system exercising progressively "higher" and more dominant control over lower levels. It was known that throughout the brain stem there was a dense feltwork of small cells and short branching fibers, the "neuropil." New methods of research in the past two decades have made it possible to investigate this "longitudinally organized," phylogenetically older, nervous system, which receives inputs not only from sense organs but also from brain stem and forebrain nuclei and contributes its influence, by a diffuse projection system, to the forebrain; its relations are particularly close with the older parts of the forebrain— limbic lobe, hypothalamus, etc. The significance of these discoveries has been thus described by Livingston (1962, p. 68):

This increasing emphasis upon the organization of vertical systems running lengthwise through the neuraxis puts a new light upon ablation experiments which traditionally cut across the neuraxis. By means of stereotactic instruments, it is now possible to destroy relatively discrete pathways in the neuraxis and to show that consciousness, emotional experience, and motivation are not exclusively dependent upon classical sensory and motor projection systems, nor upon the neocortical mantle itself. Instead they seem to be more dependent upon projection systems belonging to the phylogenetically older, transactional parts of the brain stem and limbic systems. Stimulation and ablation of neocortex, and disruption of the classical sensory and motor projections seem to interfere with subjective experiences in rather objective, depersonalized, detached ways. Similar interventions into the reticular formation and limbic system, and other phylogenetically older parts seem to affect the individual's internal state more intimately by interfering with his attention, by awakening him from sleep or obtunding his consciousness, and by inducing pervasive motivational and affective reactions.

Two other ancient concerns of psychology have been illuminated by recent physiological research: it has been shown that the fate and effect of incoming sensory signals depend upon the total ongoing activity in the central nervous system, and that the central nervous system is in continuous "spontaneous" activity to which afferent influx can merely contribute in greater or lesser degree. Thus the "stimulus-response," peripheralistic, "empty organism" point of view which has dominated so much of "behavioral" psychology has become absurd. Organization, distortion, and "meaning" in perception and the "autonomy" of thought processes receive physiological interpretations.

The German "Objective" Biologists of the "Mechanistic" Nineties

The mechanistic view of the animal organism which had been introduced by Descartes in the seventeenth century was espoused and developed in the second half of the nineteenth century by a number of eminent German biologists, and vigorously opposed by other biologists and by ecclesiastical and political authorities. This was the "mechanism versus vitalism" controversy which has persisted into our own times.

In 1845 four pupils of Johannes Müller, who was himself a vitalist, entered into an agreement to combat vitalism. These men, then all in their twenties, were destined to become famous leaders of biology: Karl Ludwig, Emil du Bois-Reymond, Ernst Brücke, and Hermann von Helmholtz. These men pledged themselves to establish the principle that "No other forces than common physical-chemical ones are active within the organism."

In 1847 Helmholtz, in a paper on the conservation of energy, presented evidence that this principle is applicable to the living organism. He had been anticipated in this by Julius Robert Mayer, who in 1845, on the basis of his studies of the heat-work ratio, the relation between muscular action and the digestion in the body's exertion of energy, and the dependency of terrestrial life on assimilation of plants and thus ultimately on solar energy, concluded that it is unnecessary to assume a special life-force as a source of the metabolism in the living body. It was Helmholtz however who gave the definitive empirically based and mathematical formulation to the principle of the conservation of energy. This formulation gave a great impetus to physiological research, since it seemed to bring all the phenomena of biology within range of the explanatory principles of physics and chemistry.

An event which worked to the same effect was the synthesis, by Friedrich Wöhler in 1828, of urea from ammonium cyanate, which was the first synthesis of an organic compound from components which could be produced from inorganic elements. Thus what had been taken to be an unbridgeable gulf between organic and inorganic was closed, and biology became continuous with chemistry.

The publication of Darwin's *Origin of Species* in 1859 enormously reinforced the natural-science view of animal and human life. The impact of the Darwinian theory, like that of the other developments to which I have referred, was not due merely to its technical importance for biological science; the enthusiastic reception and bitter opposition aroused by these developments were the results of their application to radical movements and conservative reactions in the realms of philosophy, religion, and politics. In politics, the revolution of 1848 and the harsh counter-measures of the government resulted in even such scientific issues being transformed into liberal-conservative controversies. Thus, for example, Rudolph Wagner, a "Christian conservative" biologist at Göttingen, friend of those in political authority, in 1854 violently attacked materialistic soul-theories, and was answered in kind by Karl Vogt, who had been dismissed from his professorship at Giessen for revolutionary activity; Vogt asserted that the soul is a product of the brain, which "produces ideas as the liver produces bile and the kidneys urine." The polemics between these two men were famous and scurrilous, and were regarded as expressions of the hostility between the government and the liberal opposition. As is usual, the radical liberals were influenced by humanitarian motives and saw scientific materialism as a means of combating entrenched superstition and injustice; this motivation recurs throughout the history of Western thought, as far back at least as Epicurus and Lucretius. In the period which we have been discussing, a prime example is Friedrich Büchner, whose book *Energy and Matter* was one of the most widely read popular scientific works of the time. "He was," says Nordenskiöld (1928, p. 452), "of noble character and a keen upholder of liberty and justice, and from his early youth he enthusiastically adopted materialistic ideas, in which he saw a means of bringing humanity out of darkness and superstition."

In philosophy, the anti-empirical romantic philosophy of Schelling and Hegel was losing ground both because of internal decay and also because of the great successes of natural science. In religion, the church authorities were naturally on the side of philosophical idealism and vitalism, whereas the intellectual radicals, who saw a glorious future for natural science—having no premonitions of its modern applications—were attracted by the mechanistic view.

Mention must be made of *Ernst Haeckel* (1834-1919), for many years professor of zoology at Jena. He was the great proponent in Germany of Darwinism, and it was upon this theory that he based his belief in the possibility of a mechanical explanation of all nature. In this matter he became an enthusiast, not to say a fanatic; biology, he claimed, could unite "natural science research with the psychical sciences and thus [form] the basis for a uniform view of life, which would gradually reconstruct the whole of human existence on general humanitarian lines, and which would therefore constitute the foundations of all education" (Nordenskiöld, p. 521). Such statements led to the banning in Prussian schools not only of Darwinism but also of biology. Haeckel naturally became very popular among the political and religious "free-thinkers," while to the conservatives he was a promoter of "socialism," a word with the emotional value which "communism" has today. Goldschmidt (1956), in his fascinating book of reminiscences of German biologists of the period around 1900, says that "The present generation cannot imagine the role [Haeckel] played in his time, far beyond his actual scientific performance," although that performance included a two-volume work which "established the basis of evolutionary thinking in morphology." Goldschmidt relates the results of being sent by his parents to get books from the stacks of a lending library:

Of course, once in the stacks, I began to browse and to look for books which might satisfy my interests, and thus I struck the revolutionary books by Karl Vogt and the wild *Energy and Matter* of Büchner, a kind of atheistic Bible. As I could not dare to bring home such books openly, I hid them under my coat, read them secretly, and returned them to the shelves the same way, some weeks later. In this way I found Haeckel's history of creation one day and read it with burning eyes and soul. It seemed that all problems of heaven

and earth were solved simply and convincingly; there was an answer
to every question which troubled the young mind. . . . There was no
creation, no God, no heaven and hell, only evolution and the wonderful law of recapitulation which demonstrated the fact of evolution to
the most stubborn believer in creation [p. 35].

Haeckel's materialistic monism may be regarded as an ancestor of
the theoretical approach adopted in the 1920's in the psychology of
Max Meyer and Albert P. Weiss.

Against the historical background sketched above, we can understand the "objectivistic" movement among German biologists of
the turn of the century. It should be emphasized, however, that
while the greatest among these biologists shared the historical background of the mechanist-vitalist controversy, their motivation in
urging an objectivistic approach was professional; they advocated
a strictly natural science approach and a vocabulary operationally
defined in terms of physical, chemical, and biological observations,
and they did this on pragmatic and heuristic grounds; they thought
that such a program would be conducive to scientific progress in
biology. The considerations which were influential with them
appear in numerous articles in the *Biologisches Centralblatt* of the
years 1898-1902, of which I have translated or abstracted illustrative
passages in what follows.

Albrecht Bethe (1898) remarked:

Except for the theologians—who have an interest in preserving a
mediaeval standpoint in these matters—and some philosophers, we
hardly find anywhere a denial any longer of the fact that the phenomena which we call psychical are linked in the closest way with material processes and states in our nervous system. The numerous
experiences in medical practice, the numerous experiments of our
great investigators of the nervous system, the knowledge that everywhere else in nature everything seems to be subject to the law of
causality . . . all this justifies us in assuming that events here are not
qualitatively different from those in the rest of the world. [It does
not matter, Bethe says, whether we regard the subjective aspect of
physiological processes as being itself identical with or an accompani-
ment of material processes, for] whatever the position we take toward
this question, the actually psychical aspect of these processes, the
"subjective," remains unknowable, and all that we can hope to discern
of the phenomena in question is the chemical and physical processes
which occur with them—concerning this philosophers and scientists are
pretty well agreed. . . . These chemicophysical processes and their
effects, i.e., the "objective" aspect of the psychical phenomena, can
be the object of natural-science research—but only these. [Moreover,
all "mental" activity is dependent upon external stimulation, without
which we sleep. Bethe cites a pathological case described by Strüm-

pell in 1878:] He observed a 15-year-old quite talented cobbler-
apprentice who gradually lost the sensibility of his entire body surface and body orifices, lost smell and taste, became blind in one eye
and deaf in one ear. With the seeing eye he could still write and
perform many manipulations (so far as his partly paralyzed limbs
permitted); when however his good eye was blindfolded, he was
completely helpless. If his good ear was stopped up and his good eye
covered, he invariably fell into deep sleep within two or three
minutes. . . . If no gateways are open by which differentiated external
stimuli can reach a human being, he remains, in spite of his beautiful
central nervous system, on the lowest level. [There is here an anticipation of quite recent work on "sensory deprivation" and in particular
of the evidence which suggests the dependence of normal functioning
of the brain on a continuing arousal reaction generated in the reticular formation, which in turn depends on sensory bombardment; this is
however an area awaiting reconciliation of inconsistent results, e.g.,
in regard to "autonomous" activity of the brain.]

In 1899 Bethe joined with Th. Beer and J. V. Uexküll in an article entitled "Proposals for an Objectivistic Nomenclature in the
Physiology of the Nervous System." Here it is said that

Each person knows sensations and everything that is built up of them
—the subjective, psychical—only in himself; external to himself he
observes only the phenomena of movement, and arrives only by the
help of analogical inferences . . . at the assumption of psychical
characteristics for other humans and the higher animals; to ascribe
sensations to the lower animals and to the lower centers of human
beings there is lacking even this unscientific method. [Since psychology deals only with the subjective, it can keep the traditional subjective terminology, but in comparative physiology such terminology
leads to misunderstandings. A new objective terminology is therefore
proposed which] presupposes the existence of a nervous system and
therefore aims only at an agreement for the physiology of the Meta-
zoa [Beer, Bethe, and Uexküll, 1899].

Ludwig Arnhart (1899) in an article entitled "Objective Psychology" tells how he had arrived at this notion by way of the
Kantian theory of knowledge:

It is clear that we can experience one another only through our outer
senses, and can observe nothing of another's soul, or as Bethe would
say, of his "subjective." What I can observe in him are only movements. If I can explain these movements of my fellow man in relation
to the stimuli acting upon him without the help of the inner experience of my fellow man, which experience indeed can never be given
to me, then I have done everything that it is possible for me to do. . . .
The study of the movements of my fellow man without regard to his
inner experience, in relation only to the presuppositions required by

my external experience, I call *objective psychology*. . . . Hitherto we have been accustomed, upon observing in our fellow men movements similar to our own, to assume by analogy the same inner experience in them and to attribute to them as to ourselves an inner being, the soul. One can now, if one can explain all movements of one's fellow man without a soul, invert the analogical inference and say: in my fellow man I need no soul in order to explain his movements; his movements are similar to mine and hence I need no soul in myself in order to explain all my movements. Just as I before reasoned from the known psychical in myself to the unknown psychical in my fellow men, so I reason now from the known physiological of my fellow man to the unknown physiological in myself, which I, because I cannot look into my own brain, cannot observe. It is to this that S. Exner refers when he remarks: "the psychical phenomena are still regarded today as several thousand years ago the stars were regarded, before for the first time the thought was expressed that 'this movement could be an apparent one, conditioned by the movement of the earth.'"

Arnhart concludes with the statement: "If both biologists and psychologists pay attention to our standpoint, much controversy will be avoided. Biology will truly lead, at the expense of psychology, to a new understanding of the world."

In an article by Ziegler (1900) we read:

. . . all scientists who concern themselves with the comparative physiology of the nervous system must endeavor to use only such concepts as are independent of the philosophical tradition and which are based upon objectively observable characteristics and take into account the established knowledge of the structure of the nervous apparatus. . . . For nothing whatever can be accomplished in comparative physiology and animal psychology by the differentiation between conscious and unconscious processes, since in animals it is impossible to determine this by observation. . . . It is not necessary to attach much significance to the demarcation of psychology from physiology, since the psyche is nothing other than the physiological function of certain organs. . . . It is not advisable to use the word *psychical* in natural science as a technical term. The philosophers usually designate as psychic only that which comes into consciousness. The scientist can place no great value on the differentiation of conscious and unconscious, since [these] continually interact, since moreover many different degrees of consciousness occur, and since finally the conscious is only the subjective copy of physiological processes. For natural science it would be practical to regard the word *psychic* only as a general popular designation [Vulgärbezeichnung] for the relatively higher functions of the nervous system, and then to differentiate between the *objective-psychical,* that which one can observe in other humans and in animals, and the *subjective-psychical,* the field of inner experience, which in a strict sense one can observe only in himself.

A vigorous polemicist against the views illustrated above was the Jesuit biologist Erich Wasmann, an authority on the "psychology" of ants. Uexküll (1900) quotes from Wasmann (1900):

> The principle that a scientist cannot know whether an ant or a horse behaves with selfconsciousness or not would logically have to be extended to include all the other psychical qualities of animals which we can no more see directly than we can selfconsciousness. From this would follow that it would not be permissible for the scientist to ascribe to animals perception and sensation. From that principle therefore flows the inescapable conclusion *that for the scientist there can be no animal psychology.*

Uexküll replies:

> But this conclusion we too have drawn, exactly as Wasmann expresses it, that one should no longer speak of animal psychology but only of neural physiology. Why do we renounce the drawing of inferences from visible behavior of animals to the processes in their psyche, since elsewhere we are accustomed to infer cause from effect? . . . When an animal performs a movement, this movement was produced by muscle contractions. The muscle contractions were caused by the arrival of the electrical wave in the nerve endings. The wave did not arise spontaneously in the motor nerve but was produecd in it by similar physical phenomena in certain centers of the central nervous system. But these had themselves received more or less direct impulses which came from certain centripetal nerves. The waves which passed over the centripetal nerves arose from the sense organ of the nerve, after the latter had been stimulated by a movement-process of the environment. We have now done what Wasmann desired. We have successively inferred the cause from the effect and in this way have again emerged from the animal, without meeting anywhere a psychical element. . . . When a conscientious researcher presents the results of his experiments in subjective terms, he does not by a hairsbreadth say any more than could be expressed in objective form. Instead of saying: the memory of the odor of the nest came on this occasion again into consciousness, one can, e.g., say: the stimulation by the nest material, having remained in residual form in the central organ, on this occasion again becomes effective. The subjective mode of expression gives the reader the illusion that the researcher actually knows something about the memory images in the soul of the ant, and in addition it misleads the researcher himself into believing that we may without difficulty assume the existence of an animal soul.

There are many other articles on the mechanism-versus-vitalism question in these volumes of the *Biologisches Centralblatt*, notably the long and thoughtful articles by Albrecht (1901) in which he discusses most perspicaciously what later became the wearisome questions of "emergence" and "whole-versus-part." Friedenthal (1901) expressed a hope shared by other biologists (cf. Nordenskiöld, 1928, p. 272) that psychology might play the role for physiology of the Gadarene swine, by bearing away with it the devils of neovitalism, psychical entities, and scientific pessimism, leaving physiology free to concentrate on scientific problems, which more and more required the education of researchers in physical chemistry, higher mathematics, and general physics and chemistry.

Jacques Loeb (1859-1924) brought the German mechanistic tradition of biology to America, but in an unfortunate form for psychology. His teaching at American universities (Universities of Chicago and California and the Rockefeller Institute) and his books (1900, 1912) were very influential among animal psychologists. Loeb's model was the tropisms of plants: e.g., "We have seen that, in the case of animals which possess nerves, the movements of orientation toward light are governed by exactly the same external conditions, and depend in the same way upon the external form of the body, as in the case of plants which possess no nerves. These heliotropic phenomena, consequently, cannot depend upon *specific* qualities of the central nervous system" (1900, p. 4). The only function of the central nervous system is to provide "protoplasmic bridges" between the sensory organs of the surface of the body and the muscles. This was the historical source of the Skinnerian "empty organism" concept; it was a prime source also of the imaginary neurology of Max Meyer, A. P. Weiss, and many another American teacher of psychology who "explained" behavior by diagramming "reflex arcs." There was a good deal of justification for Oscar Hertwig's famous lecture in 1900 on the history of biology in the nineteenth century in which he attacked the "empty mechanism," divorced from morphology, into which many physiologists had fallen; none exemplified this more egregiously than Loeb, who "explained" everything, from the segmentation of eggs to the movements of animals, by an "oxidizing" process. "Indeed," says Nordenskiöld (1928, p. 606), "in the opinion of Loeb, there exist no structural conditions whatever; there is hardly any question of the organism's possessing a chemical composition of its own; all that takes place in the organism is the result of outside impulses." This is the assumption, explicit or implicit, of American stimulus-response psychology. It is a very peculiar form of "mechanistic" physiology, for which the admissible alternative, however, as Hertwig emphasized, is not vitalism. The events within the organism, even "spontaneous" or "autonomous" processes, are just as "mechanistic" and "physicochemical" as the peripheral ones, although the physiologist must of course take account of the functional organization of tissues, organs, and systems, and these structures and functions cannot be taken into account by those whose education and "experimental design" preclude their doing so.

The Russian Reflexologists

The most remarkable—for the history of physiological psychology—of the mechanistic biologists was a Russian, *Ivan Michailovich Sechenov* (1829-1905), the founder both of modern physiology and of modern psychology in Russia. His psychological essays were not translated from the Russian until 1935, although his basic *The Reflexes of the Brain* was published in 1863 and the other essays within the next two decades; hence his name does not appear in our histories of psychology until Boring's (1950) second edition, except for a description of his pioneer work on central inhibition, which had been published in German in 1863, in Fearing's (1930) history of the study of reflex action. Sechenov was the link between the mechanistic—i.e., anti-vitalistic—movement which arose among German biologists of the second half of the nineteenth century and the reflexology of Bechterev and Pavlov. Thus he is important as a source both of the German and of the Russian backgrounds of American behaviorism. As a participant in the German tradition he studied with Ludwig and worked in the laboratories of Helmholtz and other German physiologists; he revisited the German laboratories from time to time to do research or demonstrate his discoveries; and his lifelong correspondence with Ludwig shows how close were his ties with German physiology and how highly his work was regarded by the great German physiologist. His influence on Russian science and upon the intellectual circles of Russia in general was immense.

In his days as a medical student in Russia Sechenov spent much time on the works of the German philosopher *Friedrich Eduard Beneke* (1798-1854), who played an important role in introducing British empiricism and associationism into German psychology, standing thus in explicit opposition to the prevailing idealistic transcendentalism of German philosophy. Beneke's most important work, *Psychologische Skizzen* ("Psychological Sketches"), was published in 1825-1827, and the more usually cited shortened version of this, significantly titled *Lehrbuch der Psychologie als Natur-wissenschaft* ("Textbook of Psychology as a Natural Science"), in 1833. Beneke was regarded by the Hegelians at Berlin as so much of a radical in philosophy that he was for a time forbidden to teach at the University; he was told by the authorities that a philosophy which did not deduce everything from the Absolute was not worthy to be called philosophy. His death by drowning, after a life of poverty and illness, was presumed to have been a suicide. In the tributes of his friends and pupils he appears as a man of noble and lovable character. (On his life and philosophy, see Brandt, 1895.) In histories of psychology Beneke is usually bracketed with Herbart, largely because he was accused of plagiarism by the Herbartians and wrote an extensive refutation of the charge. While Herbart's basis was metaphysical and his method mathematical, Beneke intended his basis to be empirical and his method genetic. "Empirical" is here, of course, used in its historical philosophical sense; in the sense that the philosopher, instead of starting from an alleged intuitive knowledge of ultimate reality, begins with an introspective examination of his own conscious experience, the nature of which obviously depends upon his linguistic, literary, and general social background and upon the detailed contingencies of his individual life. Such examination can yield hypotheses, but it cannot yield scientific data, i.e., data which are subject to experimental, statistical, and replicative control. It may appear that Beneke's hypotheses were just as a priori as Herbart's; the difference is that Beneke intended them as hypotheses of a natural science, while Herbart regarded psychology as being metaphysical and non-experimental, and as differing in this respect from natural science. Boring (1950, p. 252), who makes no mention of Beneke, says that Herbart regarded metaphysics "as being quite as basic to psychology as are experience and mathematics. It was much later that psychologists began to write 'antimetaphysical' chapters—as Mach did in 1886. What Herbart gave to psychology was status. He took it out of both philosophy and physiology and sent it forth with a mission of its own." It would have been appropriate for Boring to have mentioned that, long before Mach, Beneke rejected metaphysics and philosophy in general as the basis for psychology, and instead made psychology the basis for philosophy. As for giving psychology status and sending it forth on a mission, one hesitates

to believe that Boring regards the mathematical elaboration of fictitious data as being the mission of psychology. It is not Herbart's
metaphysical-mathematical scheme that appears to anticipate modern biologically oriented psychology; it is rather the genetic
approach of Beneke.

Beneke assumed that the mind of an individual develops through
the interaction of his native disposition with his cumulative sensory
experience. Confusion has resulted from Beneke's use of the term
Vermögen. This term may be translated "faculties," but Beneke
rejected the concept traditionally associated with it in "faculty
psychology"; he described its rejection by Herbart as one of the
two great stages in the development of psychology; the other was
the rejection of innate ideas by Locke. By *Vermögen* Beneke meant
the capacities or tendencies of an individual. The mind is the totality of such capacities, which are defined by the activities which
are their expressions. The *Urvermögen* ("prime faculties") are the
capacities for sensation and movement with which an individual is
born. These are *active* tendencies; they seek external stimuli, and
undergo progressive development and differentiation as a result of
their interaction with them. Thus continually new and more complex capacities—such as perception, judgment, reasoning, and will
—develop by a progressive integration of simpler capacities. Mental
elements combined in groups and series come by repetition to fuse
into percepts and concepts, which are refined and differentiated by
partial variation of the elements whereby inessential features are
eliminated. A mental activity aroused by a stimulus leaves behind
itself a *trace* which may again be aroused by a subsequent stimulus
or by a new activity. The accumulation of such traces interacts with
the external stimuli in the development of new activities, there
being thus continual reciprocal action between the conscious and
the unconscious. But Beneke hypothesized another process, a sort
of tendency toward equilibrium. Mental activities may be "moveable," i.e., one may "flow over" into another so as to reinforce it;
thus joy may heighten a perception, and the threshold for a sound
may be lowered if it is expected. This notion was offered as an
explanation of the varying strengths of elements at different times,
and as a necessary supplement to the principle of reproduction by
association, explaining why *A* at one time arouses *B* and at another
time *C*, when both *B* and *C* are similar to *A*. It is also a theory of
attention and interest. Thus in Beneke British associationism is
modified by the Leibnitzian notion of "activity" or "striving." In

this respect Beneke might be thought to have anticipated the notion of "drive" or "motivation"; blind strivings, he said, become strivings after something by being associated with definite satisfactions. Upon these empirical and genetic principles Beneke developed his treatments of aesthetics, religion, ethics, education, and everyday life. His educational writings gained him his widest audience.

Psychology, in Beneke's view, must not look to physiology for assistance but must develop hypotheses from an examination of the phenomena of conscious experience, a view which—if we substitute "behavior" for "experience"—is still represented by some psychologists of the mid-twentieth century. While Beneke used or suggested biological terms and concepts, he did so metaphorically or analogically. But such language probably made him more attractive to such a physiologist as Sechenov, who in large part adopted Beneke's genetic scheme of psychological analysis but declared that the problems of psychology must be investigated by physiologists. At the conclusion of his *Reflexes of the Brain*, Sechenov (1935, p. 335) says,

> Finally, I must confess that I have built up all these hypotheses without being well acquainted with psychological literature. I have only studied the Beneke system, and that in my school years. The works of the same author have given me a general knowledge of the theories of the French school of sensualism. Professional psychologists will probably point out the resulting defects of my work. But my task was to show the psychologists that it is possible to apply physiological knowledge to the phenomena of psychical life, and I believe that my aim has been partly attained. I think this justifies my attempt to write about psychological phenomena without knowing beforehand all that has been written on this subject, and knowing only the physiological laws of nervous activity.

When Sechenov had received his medical degree he was able to use a small inheritance to study physiology in Berlin. He attended the lectures of the aged and almost retired Johannes Müller and the course on animal electricity of du Bois-Reymond. After further preparation in chemistry, he began studies of the physiological effects of alcoholic intoxication. He continued this work at Leipzig, Jena, and Vienna. At Jena and Vienna he became the pupil and life-long friend of the great physiologist, Karl Ludwig. He worked also at Heidelberg in the laboratories of Helmholtz and Bunsen. Thus, early in his professional life, Sechenov came under the influence of three leaders—Ludwig, du Bois-Reymond, and Helmholtz—of the anti-vitalistic movement in German biology which provided the intellectual climate from which "objective psychology" emerged. His indoctrination is manifested in some statements in his doctoral dissertation of 1860; e.g., "Even if there exist forces peculiar only to animal and plant organisms and absent in the inorganic world, these forces must be subordinated to laws which are as inevitable as the laws governing the inorganic world." And, "The only correct approach to pathology in our time is the molecular [i.e., physicochemical] principle."

In 1860 Sechenov returned to Russia and was appointed assistant professor of physiology in the Military Medico-Surgical Academy in St. Petersburg. He began a course of lectures on bioelectric phenomena, with demonstrations of the apparatus and techniques of this new field of physiology. His lectures, says Shaternikov (1935) "produced an immense impression, not only on the academic world, but also on intellectual society in general." At this time, in spite of political repression and cultural isolation, there was a public in Russia ready to welcome new lines of thought, particularly if these seemed to be based on the inductive methods of science. This is evidenced by the reception of Buckle's *History of Civilization in England* (1857). D. M. Wallace (1877, I, p. 167) wrote:

> At the commencement of the present reign [that of Alexander II, 1855-81] there was a curious intellectual movement . . . among the Russian educated classes. The movement assumed various forms, of which two of the most prominent were a desire for encyclopaedic knowledge, and an attempt to reduce all knowledge to a scientific form. For men in this state of mind, Buckle's great work had naturally a powerful fascination. It seemed at first sight to reduce the multifarious, conflicting facts of human history to a few simple principles, and to evolve order out of chaos.

"The predisposition of the Russian intelligentsia to seek extremes," says Tompkins (1957, p. 246), "led its members to endow scientific hypotheses and philosophical theories with the character of dogmas." Thus they found Buckle irresistible when he declaimed,

> . . . the dominion of superstition, already decaying, shall break away, and crumble into dust; and new life being breathed into the confused and chaotic mass, it shall be clearly seen that, from the beginning, there has been no discrepancy, no incongruity, no disorder, no interruption, no interference; but that all the events which surround us, even to the furthest limits of the material creation, are but different parts of a single scheme, which is permeated by one glorious principle of universal and undeviating regularity [quoted by St. Aubyn, 1958, p. 114 f.].

What an eloquent expression of the positivistic and optimistic spirit of the nineteenth century! And how poignant, when we read that science and human progress are to bring an end of wars and persecutions! But these views were subversive of existing institutions, and it is not surprising that the Russian translation of Buckle's second volume was, like Sechenov's *Reflexes of the Brain,* forbidden publication by the Russian government.

In 1862 Sechenov went to Paris and in the laboratory of Claude Bernard carried out investigations of the cerebral mechanisms of inhibition of the reflex activity of the spinal cord in the frog. The hypothesis that the brain exercised an inhibitory influence had been proposed as an explanation of the increase in reflex movements which had been observed following decapitation, and this hypothesis was thought to be supported by Weber's celebrated discovery of the inhibitory influence of the vagus on the heart (Fulton, 1926, p. 526; Fearing, 1930, pp. 187-217). Sechenov observed the effects on the reflex activity of the spinal cord of sectioning the brain at various levels, of stimulating the brain cross-sections at these levels, and of cutaneous pain stimulation. He interpreted his results as indicating that the inhibitory mechanisms are located in the brain stem, from thalamic to upper bulbar levels; that they are nerve centers—i.e., central neurons; and that their functional activity is aroused by discharge into them of sensory fibers. He suggested that in the intact animal the inhibitory mechanism is continuously in a state of tonic excitation; when the animal is decapitated, this inhibitory influence is removed and the spinal reflexes are consequently augmented.

Later Sechenov, with a considerable number of pupils, investigated the effects of electrical and chemical stimulation of the sensory fibers of the sciatic nerve of spinal frogs and of frogs with cerebral hemispheres removed. In the free-sitting frog with hemispheres removed, he found that (a) a weak tetanization of the nerve released an immediate jump; (b) during strong tetanization the frog remained quiet and the sensitivity of the front paws to pinching disappeared; (c) interruption of the strong stimulus resulted in a jump and a return of skin sensitivity. The response to stimulus interruption, Sechenov thought, showed that the suppression of response during stimulation could not be attributed to "fatigue"; it appeared that inhibition resulted from excitation in the same nerve whose stimulation could also produce movement. These and other phenomena observed in a series of ingenious experiments seemed to Sechenov to be best explained by assuming two antagonistic central mechanisms, an excitatory and an inhibitory. With weaker stimulus intensities the excitatory factor predominates, but with increasing stimulus strength the inhibitory factor increases at a rate relatively greater than that of the excitatory factor. To the periodic interaction of these antagonistic mechanisms could also be attributed such periodic activities as those of locomotion and respiration. Inhibitory mechanisms are present in the spinal cord, but the action of the brain-stem locomotor center, as well as that of the spinal levels in the intact animal, is probably under the influence of the brain-stem inhibitory center previously postulated. Experiments with chemical stimuli suggested that the sensory fibers whose central discharge caused inhibition were different from those producing excitomotor effects.

Sechenov perhaps came as near to writing a complete "psychology" on a biological basis as was possible for his time. His development of this field is recorded in four treatises, the English translations of which take up some 224 pages of the *Selected Works* (1935). As an experimental researcher Sechenov was a physiologist, and his approach to a psychological analysis of man was ostensibly by way of his experimental results with frog brains. His views on human psychology seem however to have been largely predetermined by his early study of Beneke, and by the German mechanistic biologists, particularly Helmholtz. Psychology is said by Sechenov to study psychical activity, but this psychical activity manifests itself by muscular movements, which are the final expression of the activity of the brain. The task of psychology is that of "determining the way in which muscular movements in general issue from the brain." This task, Sechenov declared, must be carried out by physiologists. By the discovery of the laws governing muscular movements, "billions of diverse phenomena, having seemingly no relationship to each other, can be reduced to the activity of several dozen muscles." Speech constitutes one class of manifestations of brain activity; by speech "is understood a certain combination of sounds produced in the larynx and the cavity of the mouth, again by means of muscular movements" (1935, pp. 263-265). The most hopeful approaches to a scientific psychology are by way of the simpler phenomena of comparative psychology and of neural physiology; for the discovery of laws involves the reduction of complex relationships to simpler ones. The introspective observations of traditional psychology may provide a useful starting point, but its theories must be rejected; in particular, its treatment of mental categories as forces. Thus the doctrine of volition, according to which man has power over his body, thoughts, and desires, is nothing but a figure of speech. "The possibility of speculative blunders of this sort is due to the fact that since words are symbols of objects or of relations between objects, man can mentally perform the same operations upon words as he does upon actual objects of the external world, and apply the results of such mental operations to the sphere of reality" (p. 355).

Moreover, traditional psychology has regarded *psychical* as synonymous with *conscious*. But the chain of successive conscious processes of an individual's daily experience is largely without obvious relations to external factors or to bodily movements. These conscious processes correspond to the "middle phases" (i.e., central nervous processes) of complete reflex acts; but physiology must study not only the "middle phases" of reflexes but also their "end phases" (i.e., their sensory beginnings and their motor outcomes, including speech). "Shall we isolate the middle of an integral whole, calling it psychical, and opposing it to the rest of this whole, calling it material?" (p. 347-349). The question of whether it is useful to assume an impassable gulf between animals and man or between psychic and somatic processes is illuminated in the history of physiology by the mechanist-vitalist controversy: the opinions of the mechanists, however ridiculous in their details, gave rise to modern physicochemical physiology, whereas vitalism, "by regarding the nature of the human body as something entirely apart from more simple phenomena, could lead to nothing but a feeling of amazement before the facts observed, and could not further the analysis of the elements of these facts." There is no sharp distinction between definitely somatic nervous acts and definitely psychical phenomena; even the simplest reflexes involve sensation as their "middle phase." Psychology as studied by physiologists must use the *method of analogy*, which is the method to which "we owe the brilliant theories of physics which have identified heat with light, and both heat and light with the purely mechanical movement of particles." In psychology the method consists in identifying psychical with nervous processes; this is the only possible means of treating psychical facts analytically, and this is why psychology must be studied by physiologists (pp. 340, 347-349). It might be objected that we know nothing about the nature of the processes which go on in nerves, and that the concepts, e.g., of nerve center function and memory trace are hypothetical or based on generalizations from the frog. Sechenov replies that the lawfulness observed in pure reflexes justifies us in looking for a relationship between any mental phenomenon and reflex action. "And every time we find such a relationship (I am convinced it can be found in every case; but naturally my conviction is not an absolute truth for every one), we can say that the nature of the given conscious act of man is the same as that of reflexes" (p. 334). Sechenov offers his hypotheses in full recognition of "the insignificance of what I have done in comparison to what will be done in future." And in fact, the spinal reflex model for the activity of the brain and the notion that all brain processes are specifically initiated by sensory impulses and issue in motor responses have had to be abandoned by the discovery in recent decades of the integrative and the "autonomous" or "spontaneous" functions of the brain.

It might be said that the Russian Sechenov was by training and intellectual tradition a German mechanistic biologist who shared the German assimilation of British empiricism and associationism, including the geneticism of Herbert Spencer. With the help of his own experimentally derived concept of interacting excitatory and inhibitory mechanisms he wrote the first "objective psychology" and became the first "behaviorist" of modern times. To justify calling him a behaviorist we can point out that the main features which characterized American behaviorism of the first two decades of the twentieth century also characterized Sechenov's writings: anti-vitalism, an insistence on movements as the objects of psychological study, a rejection of introspection as a methodology, an emphasis on physiological analysis and interpretation of behavior, and the utilization of comparative and genetic methods. Perhaps all of this might be expressed as a *doctrine of continuity*: continuity of the sciences, from physics to psychology; of phylogeny, from the lowest to the highest living forms; and of ontogeny, from infant to adult. The spirit of objective psychology and behaviorism is derived from nineteenth-century positivism, and it has shown a close affinity for the other derivatives of positivism: logical positivism, physicalism, the unity of science movement, and operationalism (cf. Frank, 1949, pp. 165-171). In historical contrast to behavioristic psychology would be vitalistic and animistic psychology, psychology of consciousness, the non-genetic psychology of "gestalt" and of the "life-space," and the various semi-mystical, non-experimental, and non-physiological psychologies of psychoanalysis, "depth" psychology, existentialist psychology, etc. There is another resemblance between the *psychological* writings of Sechenov and those of the early American behaviorists; namely, that they are philosophical essays rather than analyses related to past and projected experimental research on the behavior of human beings—of which, of course, there was little or none to the purpose. Sechenov's hypotheses of neurophysiology were to be sure based on his own experimental research—with frogs—and were thus on a firmer footing than the imaginary and almost Cartesian neurophysiology of the Americans, but the sort of information on which the latter based their analyses of the human "higher processes" was no different from that relied upon, e.g., by David Hartley, who also is commonly said to have written a "complete psychology"; information, that is, consisting of the sum total of philosophical tradition and of the individual philosopher's uncontrolled observations and accumulated "common sense." The difference between them and Hartley was that nineteenth and early twentieth century objective psychology received a special coloring from the rise of positivism, mechanistic biology, and a general optimistic spirit of evolutionary progressivism; but Hartley too was biologically oriented and made ingenious analyses of behavior—e.g., of speech development—which anticipated later research. In the years between 1860 and 1920 many researches important for the future development of psychology were done; notably, the reflexological investigations of Bechterev and Pavlov, the laying of the foundations of endocrinology, and the beginnings of the laboratory study of animals and of human infants. But if we compare the books, e.g., of Max Meyer and A. P. Weiss, with the essays of Sechenov, we may find some difficulty in pointing out advances based on experimental citations. Watson's *Psychology from the Standpoint of a Behaviorist* (1919, 1924) gives much more the impression of experimental progress—progress due largely to the influence of Russian physiology. But Sechenov, who recognized clearly that almost all psychological research remained to be done, was more modest and less dogmatic than the early American behaviorists, for he shared the ideals and the spirit of the great German biological laboratories in which great discoveries had been made and in which he himself had done important work.

Ivan Petrovich Pavlov (1849-1936)—whose biography has been written by Babkin (1949)—like Sechenov studied in Germany after having finished medical school in Russia. He too worked in the laboratory of Ludwig in Leipzig, and also with Heidenhain in Bres-

lau; in the latter laboratory he learned the technique of preparing
a pancreatic fistula and a stomach pouch, and thus of studying
secretory functions in chronic preparations. Upon his return to
Russia, he worked in the laboratory of Botkin, the founder of
research-based clinical medicine in Russia. Here he began with the
study of the neural control of the cardiovascular system and of the
digestive glands, under the influence of Botkin's concept of "nerv-
ism," which emphasized the regulation of all bodily processes by
the central nervous system. (Botkin was a pupil of Virchow, the
founder of cellular pathology and the definitive promulgator of the
doctrine that "All cells arise from previously existing cells." While
they were both at Vienna, Sechenov and Botkin had a dispute, the
latter defending Virchow's concept of a "special life force" and the
former arguing in the physicochemical terms of Ludwig.) With
reference to Pavlov's work on the circulatory and digestive mechanisms—in particular, on the salivary glands—it should be mentioned
that Ludwig was a pioneer in these areas. While Pavlov was not a
pupil of Sechenov, he was immensely influenced by him; Pavlov
repeatedly acknowledged the influence of Sechenov's *Reflexes of
the Brain* on the development of his notions about the nervous
system.

For the work of the first half of his career—on the digestive
glands—Pavlov received the Nobel prize in 1904. In the course of
this work he improved on the gastric pouch technique of Heidenhain—the fashioning, by an abdominal operation, of a portion of
the stomach of a dog into a tubular pouch opening to the external
skin surface; Pavlov's improvement consisted in the preservation of
the vagal innervation of this miniature stomach. By means of the
externally opening fistula, Pavlov could observe the amount and
quality of the gastric juice. As a result of the preservation of the
vagal innervation he was able to observe, beginning about 1900,
not only the increased secretion when food was placed in the
mouth, which was a "native" reflex of the type studied by Sherrington and which Pavlov called "unconditioned," but also that
which resulted when the dog was merely allowed to *see* the food,
an acquired response which Pavlov at first called a "psychic secretion" and later a "conditioned reflex." During the next thirty years
Pavlov and an increasing staff of associates and students devoted
themselves to the study of conditioned reflexes, the main features
of which—the phenomena of simultaneous, delayed, and trace
reflexes, summation, inhibition, extinction and spontaneous recov-

ery, differential conditioning, etc.—are well known to all students of psychology. (A good brief review will be found, e.g., in Wolman, 1960, pp. 42-64.) I shall therefore not rehearse these matters but instead discuss some questions arising from Pavlov's general approach and from the theoretical superstructure which he erected on his empirical observations. The Pavlovian technique of the conditioned reflex arrived in America at the time of the rise of behaviorism, and was warmly welcomed by those intent on substituting objective recording for introspection; the sense of a new and productive methodology is communicated by the section on "The Conditioned Reflex Methods" in Watson's famous textbook (1924, pp. 28-38). But the load of "physiological" theory and terminology which Pavlov placed on this methodology, at a time long before true physiological methods were available for the study of the activity of central nervous structures, and the pattern which he set of creating "hypothetical constructs" in lieu of physiological knowledge, have been a heavy burden to psychology.

A characteristic of the Pavlovian methodology which is of theoretical interest was discussed at the First Conference on the Central Nervous System and Behavior (Brazier, 1959, pp. 166-169); namely, that in addition to the use of chronic animals—that is, of unanesthetized, healthy, "whole" animals, normal except for, e.g., the previously made and fully healed gastric or salivary fistula—and the holding of the animals in a natural position, extreme care was taken of the health and comfort of the animals and for their isolation from disturbing conditions during experiments. The result was an impression of the reproducibility of experimental results and hence a neglect of statistical controls which has received unfavorable comment from American researchers. As Leake said (Brazier, p. 167), "The Russians are thoroughly familiar with the theory of probability and they apply it, of course, in their physics, but it does not appear in their biological literature." (This was also true until recent times of some American physiological literature, in which a "true" relationship was often illustrated by a "good" kymograph record, selected from others in which there had been "disturbing conditions.") On the other hand, some critics of American methodology have accused it of the opposite extreme: the neglect of experimental and reliance on statistical controls. Presumably it was the Russian failing which was revealed by Loucks (1933) in an analysis which he summarized as follows:

It is pointed out that Pavlov's principle of cortical irradiation is the focal point of his entire systematization of behavior. Six studies from his own laboratory are analysed and found to oppose the fundamental assumption of this theory of cortical irradiation. Accordingly, it is concluded that Pavlov's explanatory formulation of sleep, learning, neuroses—his entire system of behavior—lacks experimental verification.

Gantt (Brazier, p. 169) emphasizes how contrary to the course of physiology in his time, as represented, e.g., by Sherrington, was Pavlov's concentration on the "irregularities in gastric and salivary secretion; his observation, for example, that the secretion began not only when the dog saw the man who fed him but also when he heard this man's footsteps. This therefore was one of those true scientific discoveries which involve attention to previously neglected "discrepancies." He seems however to have been anticipated by Claude Bernard (Brazier, p. 170), and he himself refers to Thorndike's *Animal Intelligence* (1898) as the starting point of systematic investigations of "the highest nervous activities of animals" (Pavlov, 1927, p. 6), seeming thus to make no particular distinction between "Pavlovian" and instrumental conditioning. Moreover, the concept of the attaching of an old response to a new stimulus was new only in the context of the physiological laboratory; it was as old as Aristotle in the context of philosophical psychology; Pavlov himself identified conditioning with "association by simultaneity" (e.g., Pavlov, 1957, p. 410). The interpretation of the associative process in terms of an imaginary neurology was, we recall, pioneered by Hartley in 1746.

The concept of the *reflex* was basic in Pavlov's thought. This concept, he wrote (1927, p. 4), was evolved by Descartes:

Starting from the assumption that animals behaved simply as machines, [Descartes] regarded every activity of the organism as a *necessary* reaction to some external stimulus, the connection between the stimulus and the response being made through a definite nervous path: and this connection, he stated, was the fundamental purpose of the nervous structures in the animal body. This was the basis on which the study of the nervous system was firmly established. In the eighteenth, nineteenth, and twentieth centuries the conception of the reflex was used to the full by physiologists. Working at first only on the lower parts of the central nervous system, they came gradually to study more highly developed parts, until quite recently Magnus, continuing the classical investigations of Sherrington upon the spinal reflexes, has succeeded in demonstrating the reflex nature of all the elementary motor activities of the animal organism. Descartes' conception of the reflex was constantly and fruitfully applied in these studies, but its application has stopped short of the cerebral cortex.

Sechenov, says Pavlov, made "a bold attempt" to represent the activities of the cerebral hemispheres as reflex—"that is to say, as *determined*." "Thoughts he regarded as reflexes in which the effector path was inhibited, while great outbursts of passion he regarded as exaggerated reflexes with a wide irradiation of excitation." "All this, however, was mere conjecture. The time was ripe for a transition to the experimental analysis of the subject—an analysis which must be as objective as the analysis in any other branch of natural science" (p. 5). Pavlov enumerates the influences favoring this transition: the theory of evolution, the resulting development of comparative physiology and rejection of anthropomorphic preconceptions, Loeb's doctrine of animal tropisms, the introduction by Beer, Bethe, and Uexküll of an objective terminology, and the study of the reactions of the lower animals to external stimuli. This complex of influences, "which appealed to the practical bent of the American mind," led to the work of "the American School of Psychologists" on "the highest nervous activities of animals"—notably the work of Thorndike. But whereas the Americans, "being psychologists," follow a mode of experimentation that "is mostly psychological"—"with the exception of a small group of 'behaviorists'"—Pavlov's group investigated and systematized "the whole subject by physiological methods alone," so that Pavlov considered himself to be in a position to present "a physiological interpretation of the activities of the cerebral hemispheres" (p. 7).

The contrast between American psychologists and Russian physiologists may be said to have been this: that while the Americans thought that they could arrive at an understanding—in terms of "prediction and control," which do not necessarily betoken *understanding*—of *behavior* by means of stimulus-response correlations, the Russians thought that they could arrive at an understanding of *brain functions* by means of such correlations. Both parties relied on *peripheral* observations; both made hypotheses about brain processes—the Russians giving their constructs the status of physiological reality, the Americans hypothesizing in varying degrees of implicitness, and some adopting the negative construct of Loeb by which the brain becomes negligible in stimulus-response correlations. But at the time when Pavlov (1932) was attacking American psychologists for their "psychological" approach, and Guthrie (1934) was replying, neither the Russians nor the Americans had available any techniques adequate for the physiological study of brain activity; neither Pavlov's extirpation of the cortex of dogs nor Lashley's extirpation of the cortex of rats advanced our knowledge of the functions of this organ beyond the point reached by Goltz, nor could the correlation of these gross surgical assaults with observations of salivation or maze running give *definitive* support either to Pavlov's concepts of "irradiation," "concentration," and "induction" or to Lashley's theories of "mass action," "equipotentiality," and "electrical field." Guthrie (1934, p. 205) was quite right when he wrote,

> It is evident that the differences between us do not concern Pavlov's laboratory findings. These have been of immense service to psychology. Our differences concern a strong tendency found throughout Pavlov's reports to interpret the facts in terms of supposititious events and states in the cortex. These events and states are not the characteristics of nerve conduction described by such men as Adrian and directly demonstrable in the laboratory. They are, on the contrary, quite unlike any of the properties of nervous tissue that have been so directly demonstrated, and they are of such a nature that they cannot be observed by any available technique.

Step by step in our review of the history of the study of the nervous system we have seen how each great advance had to await the invention of new instruments and techniques, and how great a spurt of research and knowledge followed each such invention. The futility of the sort of theorizing about brain function which we have just been discussing is more clearly seen now in the light of the developments of the past decade or so: the collision between the Pavlovian past and the electronic present is illustrated in the conversation of the participants in the "First Conference" (Brazier, 1959, pp. 178-182); e.g., Leake tells of Professor Sarkisov's work at the Brain Institute: "He had prepared a fixed gasket, so that he could insert special microelectrodes into the cortex of cats in order to take action currents from the six differentiated cortical layers" (p. 178). Teuber comments: "I have often wondered why the Pavlovian concepts, whose relation to actual events in the brain is so entirely hypothetical, have assumed this crucial role in theory construction in this country [e.g., in the theory of discrimination learning of Spence]. Perhaps the reason is that Pavlov's constructs had been enunciated in such a forceful way by a distinguished physiologist . . . as if they were physiological entities" (p. 181). The basic advances in the physical sciences have, as we know, originated in Europe, and American science has benefited from their importation. Importations of psychological theories—such as those of Freud, the gestaltists, and Pavlov—have had more the character of New York ticker-tape parades: sudden and widespread enthusiasms which caused the expenditure of vast amounts of energy and paper, of questionable long-term utility for science. Some of the dubious consequences of Pavlovian enthusiasm in America have been discussed by Loucks (1937).

There was, however, one principle enunciated by Pavlov which seems sound, even though he himself did not follow it: "the principle of structure" (1957, p. 421); i.e., the principle that the dynamic phenomena mediated by the nervous system "must be related to the most delicate details of its structure" (p. 423).

Platonism, Reductionism, and the Science of Man

In tracing the history of the science of man we have noted a cyclic tendency. But in discussing this history, we meet with a linguistic difficulty. I have called this book, *faute de mieux*, a "history of psychology," but the scope of reference of the word "psychology" has become as impossibly wide as has the membership of the American Psychological Association, extending as it does from neurophysiology to sociology and the arts of persuasion and pastoral counseling. We have lost the Aristotelian distinction between science and art, between the search for the basic principles of individual life and dealings with the contingencies of social life. We cannot use the etymologically appropriate terms for the basic science, "anthropology" or "physiology," for these have acquired special meanings. Perhaps this is the sort of situation in the history of languages in which semantic ambiguity leads presently to a semantic shift; possibly the invasion of physiological laboratories by "psychologists" will continue and result in a broadening of the reference of *physiology* and the abandonment of the absurd definition of physiology as the study of organs in isolation from each other, from the "whole organism," or from the environment. Certainly, it is difficult to say who are physiologists and who are psychologists when one reads the spate of recent reviews of work in what is variously called "neurophysiology," "neuropsychology," "biological psychology," and "physiological psychology." These compound words are makeshifts, marking a terminological vacuum which will surely be filled by a term without ambiguous and pretentious "multidisciplinary" implications. (There are other such awkward terms; e.g., "psycholinguistics": it is doubtful whether linguists and psychologists would agree that they are united in an "interdisciplinary" interest in the soul.) For the basic science of man various substitute terms have been suggested; e.g., Hunter (1930) suggested "anthroponomy." The terms "praxiology," "behavioristics," and "behavioral science" all emphasize the change from the introspective to the objective methodology, but in doing so emphasize also the peripheralist bias. The setting in of this tide is seen in the following paragraph by Dunlap (1930, p. 317):

> The course of development of modern psychology for some years has been towards the periphery as the place to search for the control of mental processes, and away from the brain as a *deus ex machina*. The brain is more and more conceived as having but one function, namely, integration expressed as transmission and habit formation. More and more we are convinced that all brain neurons have one and the same kind of function qualitatively. More and more we have become interested in muscle-patterns and glandular activity. The hypothesis I urge [i.e., the hypothesis which "assigns the source and basis of mental differences . . . to the periphery, instead of to the brain"] is but the logical conclusion of our progressive reconstructions.

As the study of man comes more and more to include techniques for and consequently increasing interest in the—objectively observed!—processes in the nervous system, glands, visceral organs, and in the underlying biochemistry and genetics, the peripheralist, "stimulus-response" bias becomes less and less appropriate. There has been a redress of balance: the abandonment of the inward look which behaviorism regarded as an essential feature of its program became for many an abandonment of internal processes, and this secondary prejudice against physiology was reinforced by impatience with the fruitless "theorizing" about the nervous system—in the absence of adequate research techniques—in the early decades of this century. The new "functional," "pragmatic," and "objective" motivations caused psychologists, like a colony of protozoans in a polarized field, to withdraw from their physiological boundary and congregate on the side of the social sciences—of "biosocial behavior," "socially significant behavior," etc. For many psychologists—working in cooperation with their physiologist colleagues—this phase has passed, and "internal" has come to mean "anatomicophysiological" rather than "psychical." (See the memorable paper of Loucks, 1941.) But "behavioral science" will continue to carry the complex of meanings imposed upon it by the vast "multidisciplinary" programs staffed by social psychologists, statisticians, psychometricians, clinical psychologists, sociologists, economists, and political scientists. We need not raise the question of the social value of these programs; it is commonly assumed that they are the last best hope for the human race, although dissenting voices are heard; e.g., Pfafflin (1963) suggests that ". . . a good many of psychology's current difficulties in its relation to society are due less to the fact that we can do so much than to the fact that we can do so little . . . there is a tendency on the part of psychologists to try to provide solutions, even in those cases where there is no adequate solution available." Forty years ago Dunlap (1926, p. 342) saw and commented on this tendency:

> The practical urge to lay hasty foundations and use them prematurely is not entirely the fault of the psychologist. Every psychologist knows how difficult it is to get appropriations and maintenance for purely scientific work, and how much more impressive to the powers that control money is something which is "practical," however flimsy and evanescent its "practicality." The amount of money wasted in practical work which might be saved if more were available for the fundamental scientific work on which eventual practical applications depend, is, of course, enormous. . . .

In 1963 we find Albee (p. 94) saying,

> We are torn between a humanitarian desire to do something to help present day neurotics and psychotics and the rational decision that only by research can we achieve our goal of reducing suffering. . . . Sensible or not, the growth in psychology continues to be in the direction of application rather than basic research.

Albee comments on the progressive watering down of the elementary textbooks which are the instruments of self-selection of the undergraduates who presently will enter graduate work. Nothing is more characteristic of these texts than the omission of the biological basis of behavior, or its relegation to an appendix where it can be ignored at the discretion of the instructor.

Having thus explained that I use the term "psychology" as an arbitrary counter with the meaning of "the basic science of man" (because I cannot hope to anticipate linguistic history by decreeing a more suitable term), I return to the sentence with which this section began, concerning the cyclic tendency in the history of psychology. The early Greek philosophers and the Hippocratics regarded man as a part of nature, as an object of natural science.

Plato introduced the language of psychophysical dualism. Aristotle, as a result of his biological researches, returned to the biological point of view. With the destruction of Greek culture and the rise of Christianity, the theologians adopted and fastened on the learned world the Platonic dualism. As a manifestation of the great renaissance of science in the seventeenth and eighteenth centuries, the view of man as a natural object, analyzable in terms of biological mechanisms, was powerfully reasserted by Descartes—however ambiguously—and LaMettrie. Then in the last half of the eighteenth and first half of the nineteenth centuries came the era of philosophical idealism, exemplified by the German romanticists from Kant to Hegel; this was the source of that "mentalism," subjectivism, and reliance on introspection which was communicated by the German philosopher-psychologists of the late nineteenth century to the early American psychologists. However, in this same late nineteenth century the great triumphs of biological science induced among biologists a positivistic temper which found expression in the "objectivist" movement in physiology and presently in psychology.

But in biology the dualistic or spiritualistic tradition has lingered on. This is most pronounced in those biologists who—despite their disclaimers—cling to a vitalistic conception. Thus Sinnott (1950, p. 106 f.), though he describes "the highest goal of biology" as attainable by "objective, experimental study of the regulation of form and function in plants and animals," goes on to say that

> When [this goal] is attained I believe we shall find that organization depends neither on the operation of only those physical laws which we now know nor on some superphysical or vitalistic agent about which nothing can be learned, but that a more perfect knowledge of nature and man wlil tell us how the physical and the spiritual are linked in that ascending, questing, creative system which is life. The answer may also be sought subjectively, I believe, in man's inmost experience and intuitive perceptions, at biological levels far different from those of science. "A poem," says Vannevar Bush in his recent book, "can touch truths that go beyond those that are examinable by test tube or the indication of needles on instruments." Life can be studied fruitfully in its highest as well as its lowest manifestations. The biochemist can tell us much about protoplasmic organization, but so can the artist. Life is the business of the poet as well as of the physiologist.

Characteristic of such contexts is Sinnott's statement that "An understanding of modern physics and of relativity has convinced

most thinkers that, as the old-fashioned, three-dimensional universe
with its solid atoms and its Newtonian laws is out of date, so, too, is
a philosophy which puts its trust in such a system" (p. 108). There
are very few biologists who "understand modern physics and relativity," and still fewer who realize that these modern mathematical
formulations of sub-atomic and cosmical physics have no discerni-
ble relevance or application to the work of the biologist or to such
ancient "problems" as those of "mind versus matter" or "free will
versus determinism." It would be a great gain to both biology and
psychology if those who wish to contribute to theoretical and
methodological discussions would refrain from using models or
arguments taken from modern mathematical physics. The foundation of biology lies at the molecular level of biochemistry.

Poetry is a noble art, but science too is a lofty expression of
human intelligence and dedication; of the laboratory we can say
what the poet James Kirkup (1955) said of the surgical theatre:
". . . this is imagination's other place." When we read the lives and
works of the greatest biologists, we do not find that they were deficient in their appreciation and knowledge of poetry, music, and
art in general, nor in their humanitarian interests. Their scientific
work, however, they thought worthy of complete dedication,
according to the strict rules of scientific method; they wrote their
scientific works with sobriety and precision, in the language of
science, and they did not commit the "Hamlet fallacy" of announc-
ing from time to time that their researches had revealed to them
the inadequacy (or adequacy!) of the scientific method to penetrate to the ultimate spiritual essence known to poets and mystics.
Poetry and mysticism, they might have said, can comfort and
inspire, but only science can hope to arrive, e.g., at a cure for can-
cer, and it will do so by such intellectual processes as exemplify
the highest achievements of mankind.

The confusion of tongues, the admixture in physiological contexts
of the ancient soul-body dualism, has reinfected physiological psychology through the agency of some of the neurologists to whom
psychologists have gone to school. Of these neurologists, the two
most influential have been Sherrington and Herrick; Sherrington's
Integrative Action of the Nervous System and Herrick's *Introduction to Neurology* and *Neurological Foundations of Animal Behavior* were the schoolbooks of physiologically inclined psychologists
during the first quarter of the present century. The genius of Sherrington and Herrick in neurological research and in its exposition in

the precise and sober language of science is unquestioned, but both of these men felt impelled to superadd to their scientific expositions philosophical statements which, though not definable in terms of their laboratory operations, tended by association to acquire—especially for psychologists—the authority of operationally validated observations. Thus we read in Sherrington (1953, p. 252),

> How can a reaction in the brain condition a reaction in the mind? Yet what have we sense-organs for, if not for that? This difficulty with sense is the same difficulty, from the converse side, as besets the problem of the mind as influencing our motor acts.
>
> I would submit that we have to accept the correlation, and to view it as interaction; body→mind. Macrocosm is a term with perhaps too medieval connotations for use here; replacing it by "surround," then we get surround⇌body⇌mind.

And in Herrick (1924, p. 304) we find such statements as:

> Consciousness, then, is a factor in behavior, a real cause of human conduct, and probably to some extent in that of other animals. We have endeavored to show that it belongs to the general class of individually modifiable action, whose manifestations in some form are coextensive with life itself. This series of activities as viewed objectively forms an unbroken graded series from the lowest to the highest animal species. And since in myself the awareness of the reaction is an integral part of it, I am justified in extending the belief in the participation of consciousness to other men and to brutes in so far as the similarities of their objective behavior justify the inference.

In the midst of our admiration for the brilliant advances in neurophysiological techniques and knowledge, as surveyed in the recent volumes edited by Delafresnaye (1961), Koch (1962), Brooks and Cranefield (1959), Poynter (1958), and Harlow and Woolsey (1958), we may be astonished by the reintroduction of the language of philosophical dualism. Thus Pribram (1962) begins and ends his chapter with quotations from Herrick, to the effect that the exclusion by biologists of everything "mentalistic" from their science is "a feckless subterfuge," because "the most significant things people do are consciously motivated and consciously directed," and that "our ultimate survival is endangered" by "the cleavage of the 'spiritual' from the 'natural.'" Pribram himself summarizes his approach as follows:

> All scientific inquiry begins with introspection. A first step toward precision is made when these introspections can be verbalized or in some other way communicated to others. . . . The job of psychologists

is to give precision to one aspect of the scientific universe of discourse. . . . Any concepts derived from behavioral data irrespective of their terminological cloak are considered to be psychological concepts. Such concepts are of two sorts: those derived from propositional statements about introspections, and those derived from instrumental behavior or from the nonpropositional aspects of verbal statements. . . . According to this view, the philosopher and the psychologist have the common task of relating observational and experimental data to phenomenological data [p. 149 f.].

This "psychological, subjective behaviorism," we are told, is neither a philosophical dualism nor an "extreme" monism. It involves "collating concepts derived from observed data with those introspectively derived" (p. 150). By following this program, "The horizons hitherto reserved for the poet and the humanist become the frontier of behavioral science" (p. 153). The series of experiments which Pribram offers as examples of "neurobehavioral analysis" involved the variables of differential brain extirpations and lever-pressing in monkeys, supported by interpretations based on the electrophysiological studies of others; the subjects, however, do not appear to have been trained to introspect. Certain interesting structural-functional relationships were observed and stated, but the problem was conceived and interpreted as an investigation of "the neurology of intention and will."

I know of no way out of this linguistic jungle other than the path of operationalism. The new techniques and the new knowledge of structural-functional correlations which the neurophysiologists have at their disposal are of such overwhelming interest that it is supererogatory of them to announce their discoveries as elucidations or confirmations of ancient philosophical concepts. This pouring of new wine into old bottles does an injustice to the new vintage. It is understandable that the neurosurgeon speaking to a patient, or perhaps the neurophysiologist speaking to a neurosurgeon, or a scientist speaking to the public may feel compelled, in the exigency of communication, to revert to the popular language derived from ancient philosophy and theology. But if there is such a thing as a basic science of man, this exigency should not exist there. The trouble arises, I think, from the concept of "interdisciplinary" relationships: the idea that there must be two "levels" of methodology and "constructs," that of physiology and that of "psychology." The methodology of physiology has become very sophisticated and requires not only intellectual acumen but also a high degree of instrumental and manipulative skill; it is not clear why men who have acquired these abilities should be precluded, by a frontier wall, from utilizing or understanding the modest armamentarium of experimental psychology—the problem boxes, mazes, discrimination apparatuses. The sensory, reaction-time, and conditioning techniques, of course, originated in physiology. As for constructs, those of physiology are both structurally and operationally defined; those of psychology are both hypothetical and ephemeral. Pribram is quite right when he says of "the translation of the phrases that refer to one system of hypotheses into the phraseology that refers to another such system (e.g., Hullian into Freudian)" that "Such translations, many times removed from data, provide a feeling of satisfaction much as does autistic thinking; unfortunately, little of enduring value is accomplished by either" (p. 142). The same is true, I think, of the attempt to report neurophysiological functions or correlations between behavioral and physiological observations in terms of the pseudophysiological constructs of psychologists whose training in physiology had been of the traditional superficial sort. The *basic* difficulty then is one of education: the problem of "levels" and of "reductionism" is a product of the history of psychology which made psychology first a "study of the mind," then a "science of (peripheral) behavior," and finally a heterogeneous mixture of physiology, social science, and paramedical practice. There are no reasons, other than bureaucratic ones, why there should not be a basic science of man. This science will however not be advanced by those who think that "the ivory tower concept is a nostalgic memory," or who accept "the rationale which both justifies and demands that psychologists address themselves to the broad matter of social control" (Ericksen, 1963). The relation between the "basic medical sciences" and medicine may serve us as a model; the physician faces daily immediate problems of life and death; in so far as he has means of dealing with these problems he has them from men who worked in "ivory tower" laboratories: men like Justus von Liebig, Claude Bernard, Karl Ludwig, Rudolf Virchow, Jakob Henle, Sir William Bayliss, and Robert Koch. In so far as psychology can be either a basic medical science or a basic science of man, it must follow the aphorism of Johannes Müller: *Nemo psychologus nisi physiologus*—"No one can be a psychologist without being a physiologist." This however, in terms of education and individual differences of abilities and interests, is incompatible with the slogan which Max Meyer (1921, p. 405) wished to substitute: *Nemo psychologus nisi sociologus*. The methodological and conceptual frontier is not between *corpus* and *homo* but between *homo* and *civis.*

I will end with a ghostly echo from the past. On the morning of August 5, 1896, at the second general session of the Third International Congress of Psychology, held at Munich, the most lively discussion of the Congress resulted from a paper by Paul Flechsig "On the Association Centers of the Human Brain." The discussion was touched off by some extemporary remarks made by Flechsig at the conclusion of his paper, to the effect that perhaps contemporary introspective psychology had less to contribute to problems raised by research on the brain than did concepts developed by persons who were not professional psychologists. Theodore Lipps said that to judge what brain processes mean psychologically one has to know what they *can* mean; neurologist and psychologist must each work in his own field, and each must learn from the other. To this August Forel replied:*

> To Professor Lipps I would reply "No" when he says that "Everyone should stay nicely at home in his own department." No and a thousand times no! It is only in appearance that there are two different departments, psychology and neural physiology, because our capacity for knowledge is inadequate. The things themselves, however, which are observed by both "departments" are absolutely the same. We shall never arrive at understanding, never will clarity in the advance of knowledge of these things be achieved, if we do not work together. Not only must the psychologist study brain physiology, but the brain physiologist must study psychology. The thing must be studied from both sides, and both sides must tally—so far naturally as our capacity for knowledge permits—if attainable truth is to be attained. But we must not stay at home, but explore also our neighbor's house!

Now arose Wladimir von Dechterew (*not* Bechterew), Director of the Central Insane Asylum of St. Petersburg, and delivered himself as follows:

> Gentlemen! Science has by decades of hard fighting achieved its advances and its present position. It had to break completely with the older scholastic and dogmatic conceptions. In the present discussion we still see the old quarrel between the old school of psychology and physiological psychology. I permit myself, because of the importance of the matter, to accentuate the antithesis somewhat more sharply!
> We are entering the twentieth century; I could hope that the future

---

* The quotations are my translations from the Minutes of the Congress, published at Munich by J. F. Lehmann, 1897.

Fourth Congress will be able to present itself as a purely physiological one. It is therefore all the more disagreeable to hear at the end of the nineteenth century that there are voices of the learned world which would drag psychology down again into the sphere of scholasticism and dogmatics. Our celebrated Russian physiologist Prof. Setschenoff, who was the first, in the sixties, to work on the inhibitory centers of the brain, answered the question, who should develop psychology? by saying, as the conclusion of a lengthy study, "the physiologist." In the last twenty years clinical psychiatry has assembled extensive material and cleared up many questions in conjunction with physiology. The same question must today be answered: the physiologists and the psychiatrists must elaborate psychology. Whoever has not completed serious professional studies in physiology and psychiatry will be looked upon and treated by serious persons in the coming century, if he calls himself a psychologist, like someone who calls himself an architect without having attended a technical school or academy of architecture. That is my firm conviction.

The chairman, Carl Stumpf, thereupon abruptly closed the discussion with the words: "In the face of such sharpening of the antithesis, further discussion seems to me fruitless." As a pupil of Lotze and Brentano, Stumpf no doubt thought to himself, *Da hörte eben einfach alles auf!*

Young Max Meyer, newly a doctor of philosophy, was there that morning, and fifty years later he remembered that Russian and told me about him.

LIST OF REFERENCES

Academy of Religion and Mental Health. *Religion, science, and mental health.* New York: New York University Press, 1959.

Adams, F. *The genuine works of Hippocrates.* New York: William Wood, n.d. (London, 1849).

Adrian, E. D. *The mechanism of nervous action.* Philadelphia: University of Pennsylvania Press, 1932.

Albee, G. W. American psychology in the sixties. *Amer. Psychologist,* 1963, 18, 90-95.

Albrecht, E. Die "Ueberwindung des Mechanismus" in der Biologie. *Biologisches Centralblatt,* 1901, 21, 97-106; 129-133.

Allport, F. H. The influence of the group upon association and thought. *J. exp. Psychol.,* 1920, 3, 159-182.

Allport, F. H. *Social psychology.* Boston: Houghton Mifflin, 1924.

Allport, F. H. *Theories of perception and the concept of structure.* New York: Wiley, 1955.

Allport, G. W. *Personality.* New York: Holt, 1937.

Allport, G. W. The historical background of modern social psychology. In G. Lindzey (Ed.), *Handbook of social psychology.* Cambridge, Mass.: Addison-Wesley, 1954. Vol. I, pp. 3-56.

Altschule, M. D. *Roots of modern psychiatry.* New York: Grune & Stratton, 1957.

Arnhart, L. Objektive Psychologie. *Biologisches Centralblatt,* 1899, 19, 521-526.

Babkin, B. P. *Pavlov: a biography.* Chicago: University of Chicago Press, 1949. (Reprint, 1960.)

Bailey, P. The great psychiatric revolution. *Amer. J. Psychiat.,* 1956, 113, 387-406.

Barrett, W. *Irrational man.* New York: Doubleday, 1958.

Barth, L. G. *Embryology.* New York: Dryden Press, 1953.

Barzun, J. *Teacher in America.* Boston: Little, Brown, 1945.

Bauer, R. A. *The new man in Soviet psychology.* Cambridge, Mass.: Harvard University Press, 1952.

Bayliss, W. M. *Principles of general physiology.* 4th ed. New York: Longmans, Green, 1931.

Beardslee, D. C., and O'Dowd, D. D. The college-student image of the scientist. *Science,* 1961, 133, 997-1001.

Beer, T., Bethe, A., and Uexküll, J. v. Vorschläge zu einer objektivierenden Nomenklatur in der Physiologie des Nervensystems. *Biologisches Central-blatt,* 1899, 19, 517-521.

Bergmann, G. Philosophy of science. Madison, Wis.: University of Wisconsin Press, 1957.

Bethe, A. Die anatomischen Elemente des Nervensystems und ihre physiologische Bedeutung. Biologisches Centralblatt, 1898, 18, 843-874.

Bitterman, M. E. Toward a comparative psychology of learning. Amer. Psychologist, 1960, 15, 704-712.

Bloomfield, L. Albert Paul Weiss. Language, 1931, 7, 219-221.

Bloomfield, L. Language. New York: Holt, 1933.

Bloomfield, L. Linguistic aspects of science. In International Encycl. of Unified Science. Vol. 1, No. 4. Chicago: University of Chicago Press, 1939.

Boring, E. G. The psychology of controversy. Psychol. Rev., 1929, 36, 97-121.

Boring, E. G. A history of experimental psychology. 2nd ed. New York: Appleton-Century-Crofts, 1950.

Boring, E. G. Science and the meaning of its history. The Key Reporter, 1959, 24 (No. 4), 2-3.

Boring, E. G. Introduction: Lashley and cortical integration. In F. A. Beach et al. (Eds.), The neuropsychology of Lashley. New York: McGraw-Hill, 1960. Pp. xi-xvi.

Bradbury, M. The taste for anarchy. Saturday Review, June 30, 1962.

Brandt, F. B. Friedrich Eduard Beneke: the man and his philosophy. New York: Macmillan, 1895.

Brazier, M. A. B. The evolution of concepts relating to the electrical activity of the nervous system 1600 to 1800. In F. L. N. Poynter (Ed.), The history and philosophy of knowledge of the brain and its functions. Oxford: Blackwell, 1958. Pp. 191-222.

Brazier, M. A. B. (Ed.) The central nervous system and behavior. Transactions of the first conference. New York: Josiah Macy, Jr., Foundation, 1959.

Brett, G. S. History of psychology. Edited and abridged by R. S. Peters. London: Allen and Unwin, 1953.

Bridgman, P. W. The logic of modern physics. New York: Macmillan, 1927.

Bridgman, P. W. The new vision of science. Harper's Magazine, 1929, 158, 443-451.

Bridgman, P. W. The nature of physical theory. Princeton: Princeton University Press, 1936.

Bridgman, P. W. Science: public or private? Phil. Sci., 1940, 7, 36-48.

Broad, C. D. Bacon and the experimental method. In Lindsay, J. (Ed.), A short history of science. New York: Doubleday (Anchor), 1959. Pp. 27-33.

Brooks, C. Mc. Current developments in thought and the past evolution of ideas concerning integrative function. In F. L. N. Poynter (Ed.), The history and philosophy of knowledge of the brain and its functions. Oxford: Blackwell, 1958. Pp. 235-252.

Brooks, C. Mc., and Cranefield, P. F. (Eds.). The historical development of physiological thought. New York: Hafner, 1959.

Brown, R. Words and things. Glencoe, Ill.: The Free Press, 1958.

Burnet, J. Greek philosophy. Part I: Thales to Plato. London: Macmillan, 1924.

Burnet, J. Early Greek philosophy. New York: Meridian Books, 1957.

Butterfield, H. The origins of modern science, 1300-1800. New York: Macmillan, 1951.

Carmichael, L. Sir Charles Bell: a contribution to the history of physiological psychology. Psychol. Rev., 1926, 33, 188-217.

Carmichael, L. Robert Whytt: a contribution to the history of physiological psychology. Psychol. Rev., 1927, 34, 287-304.

Carnap, R. The methodological character of theoretical concepts. In H. Feigl and M. Scriven (Eds.), *Minnesota Studies in the Philosophy of Science.* Vol. I. Minneapolis: University of Minnesota Press, 1956. Pp. 38-76.

Carnap, R. Psychology in physical language. In A. J. Ayer (Ed.), *Logical positivism.* Glencoe, Ill.: The Free Press, 1959. Pp. 165-198.

Carr, E. H. *What is history?* New York: Knopf, 1962.

Carroll, J. B. *The study of language.* Cambridge, Mass.: Harvard University Press, 1953.

Cartwright, D. A decade of social psychology. In *Current trends in psychological theory.* Pittsburgh: University of Pittsburgh Press, 1961. Pp. 9-30.

Castiglioni, A. *A history of medicine.* Transl. by E. B. Krumbhaar. 2nd ed. New York: Knopf, 1947.

Chapanis, A. Men, machines, and models. *Amer. Psychologist,* 1961, 16, 113-131.

Child, C. M. *Physiological foundations of behavior.* New York: Holt, 1924.

Clancy, F. J. *Doctor, come quickly.* Seattle: Superior Publishing Co., 1950.

Cleve, F. M. *The philosophy of Anaxagoras.* New York: Columbia University Press, 1949.

Commins, W. D. Some early holistic psychologists. *J. Phil.,* 1932, 29, 208-217.

Conant, J. B. History in the education of scientists. *Amer. Scientist,* 1960, 48, 528-543.

Cooley, C. H. *Human nature and the social order.* New York: Scribner, 1902-1922.

Copi, I. M. *Introduction to logic.* New York: Macmillan, 1953.

Cornford, F. M. *From religion to philosophy.* New York: Harper, 1957.

Creed, R. S., et al. Reflex activity of the spinal cord. Oxford: Clarendon Press, 1932.

Croce, B. *Theory and history of historiography.* London, 1921.

Dampier-Whetham, W. C. D. *A history of science and its relations with philosophy and religion.* New York: Macmillan, 1930.

Delafresnaye, J. F. (Ed.) *Brain mechanisms and learning.* Oxford: Blackwell, 1961.

Deutsch, J. A. *The structural basis of behavior.* Chicago: University of Chicago Press, 1960.

Dewey, J. Antinaturalism in extremis. In Y. H. Krikorian (Ed.), *Naturalism and the human spirit.* New York: Columbia University Press, 1944. Pp. 1-16.

Dickinson, G. L. *The Greek view of life.* 3d ed. London: Methuen, 1904.

Dingle, H. Copernicus and the planets. In *A short history of science.* New York: Doubleday Anchor Books, 1959. Pp. 18-26.

Dobzhansky, T. *Evolution, genetics, and man.* New York: Wiley, 1955.

Dodds, E. R. *The Greeks and the irrational.* Boston: Beacon Press, 1957.

Driesch, H. *Philosophie des Organischen.* 4th ed. Leipzig: Quelle and Meyer, 1928.

Driesch, H. *Biologische Probleme höherer Ordnung.* 2nd ed. Leipzig: Barth, 1944.

Dubos, R. Scientist and public. *Science,* 1961, 133, 1207-1211.

Dunham, B. *Man against myth.* Boston: Little, Brown, 1947.

Dunlap, K. The experimental methods of psychology. In C. Murchison (Ed.), *Psychologies of 1925.* Worcester, Mass.: Clark University Press, 1926. Pp. 331-351.

Dunlap, K. Response psychology. In C. Murchison (Ed.), *Psychologies of 1930.* Worcester, Mass.: Clark University Press, 1930. Pp. 309-323.

DuShane, G. Triage. *Science,* 1957, 125, 381.

Ebbinghaus, H. *Memory. A contribution to experimental psychology.* Transl. by H. A. Ruger and C. E. Bussenius. New York: Teachers College, Columbia University, 1913.

Eccles, J. C. The development of ideas on the synapse. In C. McC. Brooks and P. F. Cranefield (Eds.), *The historical development of physiological thought.* New York: Hafner, 1959. Pp. 39-66.

Eddington, A. S. *The nature of the physical world.* Cambridge: The University Press, 1929.

Eiseley, L. C. Francis Bacon as educator. *Science,* 1961, 133, 1197-1201.

Ellis, A., et al. Mowrer on "sin." *Amer. Psychol.,* 1960, 15, 713-716.

Ellwood, C. A. Review of McDougall's *Group Mind. Psychol. Bull.,* 1921, 18, 219-222.

Encyclopaedia Britannica, 1910-1911.

English, H. B., and English, A. C. *A comprehensive dictionary of psychological and psychoanalytical terms.* New York: Longmans, Green, 1958.

Ericksen, S. C. Legislation and the academic tradition in psychology. *Amer. Psychologist,* 1963, 18, 101-104.

Faris, E. The beginnings of social psychology. *Amer. J. Sociol.,* 1945, 50, 422-428.

Farquharson, A. S. L. De motu animalium. In Smith, J. A., and Ross, W. D. (Eds.), *The works of Aristotle.* Oxford: Clarendon Press, 1912. Vol. V.

Farrington, B. *Greek science. 1. Thales to Aristotle.* Harmondsworth, Middlesex, England: Penguin, 1944.

Farrington, B. *Greek science. 2. Theophrastus to Galen.* Harmondsworth, Middlesex, England: Penguin, 1949.

Fay, J. W. *American psychology before William James.* New Brunswick, N. J.: Rutgers University Press, 1939.

Fearing, F. *Reflex action. A study in the history of physiological psychology.* Baltimore: Williams & Wilkins, 1930.

Fechner, G. T. *Ueber die Seelenfrage.* Leipzig, 1861.

Feifel, H. et al. Symposium on relationships between religion and mental health. *Amer. Psychologist,* 1958, 13, 565-579.

Feigl, H. The "mental" and the "physical." In H. Feigl et al. (Eds.), *Minnesota Studies in the Philosophy of Science.* Vol. II. Minneapolis: University of Minnesota Press, 1958. Pp. 370-497.

Feigl, H., and Brodbeck, M. (Eds.) *Readings in the philosophy of science.* New York: Appleton-Century-Crofts, 1953.

Fell, H. B. Fashion in cell biology. *Science,* 1960, 132, 1625-1627.

Feuer, L. S. *The scientific intellectual.* New York: Basic Books, 1963.

Flourens, J. P. N. *Recherches expérimentales sur les propriétés et les fonctions du systeme nerveux dans les animaux vertébrés.* Paris, 1842.

Foster, M. *Lectures on the history of physiology during the 16th, 17th, and 18th centuries.* Cambridge: Cambridge University Press, 1901.

Frank, P. *Modern science and its philosophy.* Cambridge: Harvard University Press, 1950.

Frank, P. G. (Ed.) *The validation of scientific theories.* Boston: Beacon Press, 1956.

Frank, P. *Philosophy of science.* Englewood Cliffs, N. J.: Prentice-Hall, 1957.

Frankel, C. Positivism. In V. Ferm (Ed.), *A history of philosophical systems.* New York: Philosophical Library, 1950. Pp. 329-339.

Frazer, J. G. *The golden bough.* Abridged ed. New York: Macmillan, 1947.

Friedenthal, H. Ueber die Stellung der Physiologie innerhalb des Gesamtgebietes der Naturwissenschaften. *Biologisches Centralblatt,* 1901, 21, 497-503.

Fries, C. C. The Bloomfield 'school.' In C. Mohrmann et al. (Eds.), *Trends in European and American linguistics 1930-1960.* Utrecht: Spectrum Publishers, 1961, Pp. 196-224.

Frumkin, R. M. American arete and teacher education. *Ohio Parent-Teacher,* 1959, 37, 12-13.

Fulton, J. F. *Muscular contraction and the reflex control of movement.* Baltimore: Williams & Wilkins, 1926.

Fulton, J. F. *Physiology of the nervous system.* 3d ed. New York: Oxford University Press, 1949.

Garrison, F. H. *An introduction to the history of medicine.* 4th ed. Philadelphia: Saunders, 1929.

Geiger, L. *Der Ursprung der Spache.* 2nd ed. Stuttgart: Cotta, 1878. (1st ed., 1869.)

Goldschmidt, R. B. *Portraits from memory.* Seattle: University of Washington Press, 1956.

Goltz, F. Ueber die Verrichtungen des Grosshirns. *Arch. f. d. ges. Physiologie,* 1881, 26, 1-49.

Graubard, M. Review of *Integrated Basic Science,* by S. M. Brooks. *Science,* 1962, 137, 275-276.

Greenwood, M., and Smith, M. Some pioneers of medical psychology. *Brit. J. medical Psychol.,* 1934, 14, 1-30, 158-191.

Griffin, A. K. *Aristotle's psychology of conduct.* London: Williams & Norgate, 1931.

Guthrie, E. R. Pavlov's theory of conditioning. *Psychol. Rev.,* 1934, 41, 199-206.

Guthrie, E. R. *The psychology of learning.* New York: Harper, 1935. (Rev. ed., 1952.)

Guthrie, E. R. Tolman on associative learning. *Psychol. Rev.,* 1937, 44, 525-528.

Guthrie, E. R. *The psychology of human conflict.* New York: Harper, 1938.

Guthrie, E. R. Conditioning: a theory of learning in terms of stimulus, response, and association. In N. B. Henry (Ed.), *The forty-first yearbook of the National Society for the Study of Education.* Bloomington, Ill.: Public School Publishing Co., 1942. Part II, Chap. I.

Guthrie, E. R., and Horton, G. P. *Cats in a puzzle box.* New York: Rinehart, 1946.

Guthrie, W. K. C. *The Greek philosophers from Thales to Aristotle.* New York: Harper, 1960.

Hall, A. R. *The scientific revolution 1500-1800.* London: Longmans, Green, 1954.

Hall, G. S. The contents of children's minds on entering school. *Pedagog. Seminary,* 1891, 1, 139-173.

Hall, J. K., Zilboorg, G., and Bunker, H. A. (Eds.) *One hundred years of American psychiatry.* New York: Columbia University Press, 1944.

Hanson, N. R. Scientists and logicians: a confrontation. *Science*, 1962, 138, 1311-1314.

Harlow, H. F., and Woolsey, C. N. (Eds.) *Biological and biochemical bases of behavior*. Madison, Wis.: University of Wisconsin Press, 1958.

Harris, Z. S. *Methods in structural linguistics*. Chicago: University of Chicago Press, 1951.

Hartley, David. *Observations on man, his frame, his duty, and his expectations*. London, 1749.

Harvey, W. *De motu cordis et sanguinis*. 1628. Transl. by K. J. Franklin: *Movement of the heart and blood in animals*. Oxford: Blackwell, 1957.

Haymaker, W. (Ed.) *The founders of neurology*. Springfield, Ill.: Charles C Thomas, 1953.

Heath, T. L. *The method of Archimedes*. Cambridge: Cambridge University Press, 1912.

Hebb, D. O. *The organization of behavior*. New York: Wiley, 1949.

Hebb, D. O. Drives and the C.N.S. (conceptual nervous system). *Psychol. Rev.*, 1955, 62, 243-254.

Hebb, D. O. Alice in wonderland or psychology among the biological sciences. In H. F. Harlow and C. N. Woolsey (Eds.) *Biological and biochemical bases of behavior*. Madison, Wis.: University of Wisconsin Press, 1958. Pp. 451-467. (a)

Hebb, D. O. *A textbook of psychology*. Philadelphia: Saunders, 1958. (b)

Heidbreder, Edna. William McDougall and social psychology. *J. abnorm. soc. Psychol.*, 1939, 34, 150-160.

Herrick, C. J. *Neurological foundations of animal behavior*. New York: Holt, 1924.

Herrick, C. J. *An introduction to neurology*. 5th ed. Philadelphia: Saunders, 1934. (1st ed., 1915)

Hett, W. S. *Aristotle: Problems*. 2 vols.: Books I-XXI; XXII-XXXVIII. London: Heinemann, 1953; 1957.

Hilgard, E. R. *Introduction to psychology*. 2nd ed. New York: Harcourt, Brace, 1957.

Hill, W. F. Learning theory and the acquisition of values. *Psychol. Rev.*, 1960, 67, 317-331.

Hobbes, T. *Human nature*. London, 1650.

Hobbes, T. *Leviathan*. London, 1651.

Höffding, H. *A history of modern philosophy*. Transl. by B. E. Meyer. London: Macmillan. Vol. I, 1924; Vol. II, 1920.

Hook, S. (Ed.) *Dimensions of mind*. New York: New York University Press, 1960.

Horst, P. Most men are created unequal. *Sci. Monthly*, 1951, 72, 318-324.

Hull, C. L. Quantitative aspects of the evolution of concepts. *Psychol. Monogr.*, 1920, 28, No. 123.

Hull, C. L. Knowledge and purpose as habit mechanisms. *Psychol. Rev.*, 1930, 37, 511-525.

Hunter, W. S. A consideration of Lashley's theory of the equipotentiality of cerebral action. *J. gen. Psychol.*, 1930, 3, 455-468. (a)

Hunter, W. S. Anthroponomy and psychology. In C. Murchison (Ed.) *Psychologies of 1930*. Worcester, Mass.: Clark University Press, 1930. Pp. 281-300. (b)

Hunter, W. S. Lashley on "Cerebral control versus reflexology." *J. gen. Psychol.*, 1931, 5, 230-234.

Hyman, S. E. A critical look at psychology. *Amer. Scholar*, 1960, 29, 21-29.

Irvine, W. *Apes, angels, and Victorians.* New York: McGraw-Hill, 1955.
Irwin, S. Drug screening and evaluative procedures. *Science*, 1962, 136, 123-128.

Jaeger, W. *Aristotle. Fundamentals of the history of his development.* Oxford: Oxford University Press, 1962. (Reprint of 2nd., 1948, ed.)
James, W. *The principles of psychology.* 2 vols. New York: Holt, 1890.
Jeans, J. *The mysterious universe.* Cambridge: The University Press, 1930.
Jeans, J. *The new background of science.* Cambridge: The University Press, 1933.
Joergensen, J. The development of logical empiricism. *Internat. Encycl. of Unified Science.* Vol. II, No. 9. Chicago: University of Chicago Press, 1951.
Johnson, H. M. Are psychophysical problems genuine or spurious? *Amer. J. Psychol.*, 1945, 58, 189-211.
Jones, W. H. S. *Hippocrates.* Vols. I and II. New York: Putnam, 1923.
Jones, W. H. S. *Hippocrates.* Vol. IV. New York: Putnam, 1931.
Jones, W. H. S. Philosophy and medicine in ancient Greece. *Suppl. to the Bulletin of the History of Medicine*, 1946, No. 8.
Joos, M. Review of G. K. Zipf's *The psychobiology of language. Language*, 1936, 12, 196-210.
Joule, J. P. On matter, living force, and heat. *Manchester Courier*, May 5 and 12, 1847. (Reprinted in F. R. Moulton and J. J. Schifferes [Eds.] *The autobiography of science.* New York: Doubleday, 1945. Pp. 293-298.)
Jowett, B. *The Republic of Plato.* 3d ed. 2 vols. Oxford: Clarendon Press, 1908.

Kahler, E. *Man the measure.* New York: Braziller, 1961.
Kantor, J. R. *An objective psychology of grammar.* Bloomington: Indiana University Press, 1936.
Kantor, J. R. Preface to interbehavioral psychology. *Psychol. Record*, 1942, 5, 173-193.
Kantor, J. R. *Psychology and logic.* Bloomington, Indiana: Principia Press, 1945.
Kantor, J. R. *Problems of physiological psychology.* Bloomington, Indiana: Principia Press, 1947.
Kapp, E. *Greek foundations of traditional logic.* New York: Columbia University Press, 1942.
Katz, D. *Gestalt psychology.* New York: Ronald, 1950.
Kelley, T. L. *Statistical method.* New York: Macmillan, 1923.
Kelly, E. L. Clinical psychology: the postwar decade. In *Current trends in psychological theory.* Pittsburgh: University of Pittsburgh Press, 1961, Pp. 31-49.
Kirk, G. S., and Raven, J. E. *The presocratic philosophers.* Cambridge: Cambridge University Press, 1957.
Kirkup, J. A correct compassion. In Plotz, H. (Ed.) *Imagination's other place. Poems of science and mathematics.* New York: Crowell, 1955. Pp. 188-191.
Klemm, O. *A history of psychology.* Transl. by E. C. Wilm and R. Pintner. New York: Scribner's, 1914.
Kneale, W., and Kneale, M. *The development of logic.* Oxford: Clarendon Press, 1962.
Koch, S. (Ed.) *Biologically oriented fields: their place in psychology and in biological science.* (Vol. 4 of *Psychology: a study of a science.*) New York: McGraw-Hill, 1962.

Köhler, W. *Gestalt psychology.* New York: Liveright, 1947.

Korzybski, A. *Science and sanity; an introduction to non-Aristotelian systems and general semantics.* Lancaster: Science Press, 1933.

Kraft, V. *The Vienna Circle.* New York: Philosophical Library, 1953.

Kranz, W. *Empedokles.* Zürich: Artemis-Verlag, 1949.

Krech, D., and Crutchfield, R. S. *Theory and problems of social psychology.* New York: McGraw-Hill, 1948.

Kuhn, T. S. *The structure of scientific revolutions.* Chicago: University of Chicago Press, 1962.

Ladd, G. T., and Woodworth, R. S. *Elements of physiological psychology.* New York: Scribner's, 1911.

Lange, F. A. *The history of materialism.* Transl. by E. C. Thomas. 3rd ed. London: Kegan Paul, Trench, Trubner, 1925. (1st ed., 1865; 2nd and last by the author, 1873-1875.)

LaPiere, R. T., and Farnsworth, P. R. *Social psychology.* 2nd ed. New York: McGraw-Hill, 1942.

Lashley, K. S. The behavioristic interpretation of consciousness. *Psychol. Rev.,* 1923, 30, 237-272; 329-353.

Lashley, K. S. *Brain mechanisms and intelligence.* Chicago: University of Chicago Press, 1929.

Lashley, K. S. Cerebral control versus reflexology. A reply to Professor Hunter. *J. gen. Psychol.,* 1931, 5, 3-20.

Lashley, K. S. In search of the engram. In F. A. Beach et al. (Eds.), *The neurophysiology of Lashley.* New York: McGraw-Hill, 1960. Pp. 478-505.

Lashley, K. S., Chow, K. L., and Semmes, J. An examination of the electrical field theory of cerebral integration. *Psychol. Rev.,* 1951, 58, 123-136.

Ledley, R. S. Digital electronic computers in biomedical science. *Science,* 1959, 130, 1225-1234.

Lewin, K. The conflict between the Aristotelian and Galilean modes of thought. In K. Lewin, *A dynamic theory of personality.* New York: McGraw-Hill, 1935.

Line, W. Gestalt psychology in relation to other psychological systems. *Psychol. Rev.,* 1931, 38, 375-391.

Linebarger, P. M. A. *Psychological Warfare.* Washington: Infantry Journal Press, 1948.

Livingston, R. B. How man looks at his own brain: an adventure shared by psychology and neurophysiology. In S. Koch (Ed.), *Psychology: a study of a science.* Vol. 4. New York: McGraw-Hill, 1962. Pp. 51-99.

Locke, J. *An essay concerning human understanding.* 2 vols. New York: Dover, 1959.

Loeb, J. *Comparative physiology of the brain and comparative psychology.* New York: Putnam's, 1900.

Loeb, J. *The mechanistic conception of life.* Chicago: University of Chicago Press, 1912.

Loenen, D. *Protagoras and the Greek community.* Amsterdam: N. V. Noord-Hollandische Uitgevers Maatschappij, 1940.

London, P. The morals of psychotherapy. *Columbia University Forum,* 1961, 4, 38-43.

Lones, T. E. *Aristotle's researches in natural science.* London: West, Newman, 1912.

Loucks, R. B. An appraisal of Pavlov's systematization of behavior from the experimental standpoint. *J. comp. Psychol.,* 1933, 15, 1-47.

Loucks, R. B. Reflexology and the psychobiological approach. *Psychol. Rev.*, 1937, 44, 320-338.

Loucks, R. B. The contribution of physiological psychology. *Psychol. Rev.*, 1941, 48, 105-126.

Lucretius. *On the nature of the universe.* Transl. by R. Latham. Harmondsworth, Middlesex, England: Penguin, 1951.

Łukasiewicz, J. *Aristotle's syllogistic.* Oxford: Clarendon Press, 1951. (2nd ed., 1957.)

Lund, F. H. The phantom of the Gestalt. *J. gen. Psychol.*, 1929, 2, 307-323.

MacCorquodale, K., and Meehl, P. E. On a distinction between hypothetical constructs and intervening variables. *Psychol. Rev.*, 1948, 55, 95-107.

Mach, E. *The analysis of sensations.* New York: Dover, 1959. (Reprint of 1914 transl. of 5th German ed.; 1st ed., 1886.)

Mainx, F. Foundations of biology. *Internat. Encycl. of Unified Science*, 1955. Vol. 1, No. 9.

Malinowski, B. *Magic, science and religion.* New York: Doubleday, 1954.

Mandler, G., and Kessen, W. *The language of psychology.* New York: Wiley, 1959.

Marett, R. R. *Anthropology.* New York: Holt, 1912.

Marquis, D. G. The neurology of learning. In C. P. Stone (Ed.), *Comparative psychology.* New York: Prentice-Hall, 1951. Pp. 292-315.

Marx, M. H. (Ed.) *Psychological theory.* New York: Macmillan, 1951.

May, R. (Ed.) *Existential psychology.* New York: Random House, 1961.

Mayer, A. Ueber Einzel- und Gesamtleistung des Schulkindes. *Arch. ges. Psychol.*, 1903, 1, 276-416.

McDougall, W. The nature of the inhibitory processes within the nervous system. *Brain*, 1903, 26, 153-191.

McDougall, W. *An introduction to social psychology.* London: Methuen, 1908. (Subsequent editions to 1931; references are to 13th ed., 1918.)

McDougall, W. *The group mind.* New York: Putnam's, 1920. (2nd ed., 1927)

McDougall, W. *Body and mind.* 6th ed. London: Methuen, 1923.

McDougall, W. Hormic psychology. In C. Murchison (Ed.), *Psychologies of 1930.* Worcester, Mass.: Clark University Press, 1930. Pp. 3-36. (a)

McDougall, W. [Autobiography] In C. Murchison (Ed.), *A history of psychology in autobiography.* Vol. I. Worcester, Mass.: Clark University Press, 1930. Pp. 191-223. (b)

McKeon, R. (Ed.) *The basic works of Aristotle.* New York: Random House, 1941.

McVittie, G. C. Rationalism versus empiricism in cosmology. *Science*, 1961, 133, 1231-1236.

Meehl, P. E. The cognitive activity of the clinician. *Amer. Psychologist*, 1960, 15, 19-27.

Mettler, C. C. *History of medicine.* Philadelphia: Blakiston, 1947.

Meyer, M. (Transl. and ed.) *Psychology: an elementary textbook, by Hermann Ebbinghaus.* Boston: Heath, 1908.

Meyer, M. *The fundamental laws of human behavior.* Boston: Badger, 1911.

Meyer, M. *Psychology of the other-one.* Columbia, Missouri: Missouri Book Co., 1921.

Miller, G. A. *Language and communication.* New York: McGraw-Hill, 1951.

Miller, N. E. Learnable drives and rewards. In S. S. Stevens (Ed.), *Handbook of experimental psychology.* New York: Wiley, 1951. Pp. 435-472.

Modell, W. Hazards of new drugs. *Science*, 1963, 139, 1180-1185.

Moede, W. *Experimentelle Massenpsychologie*. Leipzig: Hirzel, 1920.

Morris, C. *Signs, language and behavior*. New York: Prentice-Hall, 1946.

Morris, W. W. Houston's superpatriots. *Harper's Magazine*, 1961, 223 (Oct.), 48-56.

Moulton, F. R., and Schifferes, J. J. (Eds.) *The autobiography of science*. New York: Doubleday, Doran, 1945.

Mowrer, O. H. "Sin," the lesser of two evils. *Amer. Psychologist*, 1960, 15, 301-309.

Mowrer, O. H. *The crisis in psychiatry and religion*. New York: Van Nostrand, 1961.

Mueller, C. G., and Schoenfeld, W. N. Edwin R. Guthrie. In Estes, W. K., et al., *Modern learning theory*. New York: Appleton-Century-Crofts, 1954. Pp. 345-379.

Muirhead, J. H. Hegel. In *Encycl. Brit.*, 11th ed., 1910, Vol. 13, *s.v.*

Multhauf, R. P. Review of L. Thorndike's *A history of magic and experimental science*. *Science*, 1959, 129, 90-91.

Murphy, G. *Historical introduction to modern psychology*. Rev. ed. New York: Harcourt, Brace, 1949.

Murray, G. *Five stages of Greek religion*. New York: Doubleday, 1955.

Nagel, E. *The structure of science*. New York: Harcourt, Brace & World, 1961.

Nagel, E. Malicious philosophies of science. In B. Barber and W. Hirsch (Eds.), *The sociology of science*. New York: Free Press, 1962. Pp. 623-639.

Nordenskiöld, E. *The history of biology*. New York: Tudor, 1928.

Ogden, C. K., and Richards, I. A. *The meaning of meaning*. New York: Harcourt, Brace, 1947.

Ogle, W. *Aristotle on the parts of animals*. London: Kegan, Paul, 1882.

Opler, M. E. Review of O. v. Mering's *A grammar of human values*. *Science*, 1961, 134, 186.

Panofsky, E. *Albrecht Dürer*. Vol. 1. 3rd ed. Princeton: Princeton University Press, 1948.

Patrick, G. T. W. *The fragments of the work of Heraclitus of Ephesus on nature*. Baltimore, 1889. (Citation from Jones, 1931, p. 456 f.)

Pauling, L. A molecular theory of general anesthesia. *Science*, 1961, 134, 15-21.

Pavlov, I. P. *Conditioned reflexes*. Transl. by G. V. Anrep. Oxford: Oxford University Press, 1927.

Pavlov, I. P. The reply of a physiologist to psychologists. *Psychol. Rev.*, 1932, 39, 91-127.

Pavlov, I. P. *Experimental psychology and other essays*. New York: Philosophical Library, 1957.

Pearson, K. *The grammar of science*. London: Dent, 1949.

Peck, A. L. *Aristotle. Generation of animals*. Cambridge, Mass.: Harvard University Press, 1943.

Penfield, W., and Roberts, L. *Speech and brain-mechanisms*. Princeton: Princeton University Press, 1959.

Peters, R. S. (Ed.) *Brett's history of psychology.* New York: Macmillan, 1953.

Pfafflin, S. M. Comment: "Rebuttals needed." *Amer. Psychologist,* 1963, 18, 319.

Pillsbury, W. B. *The history of psychology.* New York: Norton, 1929.

Plato. *Protagoras.* Ed. and transl. by W. R. M. Lamb. London: Heinemann, 1924.

Plato. *Theaetetus.* Ed. and transl. by H. N. Fowler. London: Heinemann, 1928.

Poincaré, H. *Science and method.* Transl. by F. Maitland. New York: Dover, 1952. (Orig. French ed., 1908.)

Popper, K. R. *The open society and its enemies.* 2 vols. London: Routledge, 1945.

Powers, D. Emotional implications of acne. *New York State J. Medicine,* 1957, 57 (No. 4), 751-753.

Poynter, F. N. L. (Ed.) *The brain and its functions.* Oxford: Blackwell, 1958.

Pratt, C. C. *The logic of modern psychology.* New York: Macmillan, 1939.

Pribram, K. H. Neocortical function in behavior. In H. F. Harlow and C. N. Woolsey (Eds.), *Biological and biochemical bases of behavior.* Madison, Wisc.: University of Wisconsin Press, 1958. Pp. 151-172.

Pribram, K. H. Interrelations of psychology and the neurological disciplines. In S. Koch (Ed.), *Psychology: a study of a science,* Vol. 4. New York: McGraw-Hill, 1962. Pp. 119-157.

Price, G. R. Science and the supernatural. *Science,* 1955, 122, 359-364.

Quine, W. V. O. *From a logical point of view.* Cambridge, Mass.: Harvard University Press, 1953.

Radin, P. *Primitive man as philosopher.* New York: Dover, 1957. (a)

Radin, P. *Primitive religion.* New York: Dover, 1957. (b)

Ramul, K. The problem of measurement in the psychology of the eighteenth century. *Amer. Psychologist,* 1960, 15, 256-265.

Randall, J. H. *Aristotle.* New York: Columbia University Press, 1960.

Rensi, G. *Introduzione alla scepsi etica.* Naples, 1921.

Rhine, J. B. Why national defense overlooks parapsychology. *J. Parapsychol.,* 1957, 21, 245-258.

Riese, W. *A history of neurology.* New York: MD Publications, 1959.

Rivers, W. H. R. *Medicine, magic, and religion.* London, 1924.

Roback, A. A. *History of American psychology.* New York: Library Publishers, 1952.

Robinson, E. S. *Association theory to-day.* New York: Century, 1932.

Robinson, V. *The story of medicine.* New York: New Home Library, 1943.

Rogers, C. R., and Skinner, B. F. Some issues concerning the control of human behavior: a symposium. *Science,* 1956, 124, 1057-1066.

Rogosin, H. An evaluation of extrasensory perception. *J. gen. Psychol.,* 1939, 21, 203-217.

Rohde, E. *Psyche. The cult of souls and belief in immortality among the Greeks.* Transl. by W. B. Hillis. London: Routledge & Kegan Paul, 1950.

Rohrer, J. H., and Sherif, M. (Eds.) *Social psychology at the crossroads.* New York: Harper, 1951.

Rosenblith, W. A., and Vidale, E. B. A quantitative view of neuroelectric events in relation to sensory communication. In S. Koch (Ed.), *Psychology: a study of a science.* Vol. 4. New York: McGraw-Hill, 1962. Pp. 334-379.

Ross, D. *Aristotle: Parva naturalia.* Oxford: Clarendon Press, 1955.

Ross, E. A. *Social psychology.* New York: Macmillan, 1908. (Subsequent editions to 1925.)

Ross, W. D. (Ed.) *The works of Aristotle.* 11 vols. Oxford: Clarendon Press, 1908-1931.

Ruch, T. C. Somatic sensation. In T. C. Ruch et al., *Neurophysiology.* Philadelphia: Saunders, 1961. Pp. 300-322.

Runes, D. D. (Ed.) *The dictionary of philosophy.* New York: Philosophical Library, 1942.

Russell, B. *The analysis of mind.* New York: Macmillan, 1921.

Russell, B. *An inquiry into meaning and truth.* New York: Norton, 1940.

Russell, B. *A history of Western philosophy.* New York: Simon & Schuster, 1945.

Russell, B. *Unpopular essays.* New York: Simon & Schuster, 1950.

Sarton, G. *A history of science. Hellenistic science and culture in the last three centuries B.C.* Cambridge, Mass.: Harvard University Press, 1959.

Sarton, G. *A history of science. Ancient science through the Golden Age of Greece.* Cambridge, Mass.: Harvard University Press, 1960.

Schiller, F. C. S. *Plato or Protagoras? Being a critical examination of the Protagoras speech in the Theaetetus with some remarks upon error.* Oxford: Blackwell, 1908.

Schiller, F. C. S. Article *Pragmatism* in *Encycl. Brit.,* 11th ed., 1911.

Scripture, E. W. [Autobiography] In C. Murchison (Ed.), *A history of psychology in autobiography.* Vol. III. Worcester, Mass.: Clark University Press, 1936. Pp. 231-261.

Sechenov, I. M. *Physiologische Studien ueber die Hemmungsmechanismen für die Reflexthätigkeit des Rückenmarks in Gehirne des Frosches.* Berlin, 1863.

Sechenov, I. M. *Selected works.* Ed. by A. A. Subkov, with a biography by M. N. Shaternikov. Moscow: State Publishing House for Biological and Medical Literature, 1935.

Shaternikov, M. N. Biography of Sechenov. (See Sechenov, 1935.)

Sherrington, C. S. *The integrative action of the nervous system.* New Haven: Yale University Press, 1906.

Sherrington, C. *Man on his nature.* 2nd ed. New York: Doubleday Anchor, 1953.

Shute, C. *The psychology of Aristotle.* New York: Columbia University Press, 1941.

Sigerist, H. E. *A history of medicine. Vol. I: Primitive and archaic medicine.* New York: Oxford, 1951.

Sigerist, H. E. *A history of medicine. Vol. II: Early Greek, Hindu, and Persian medicine.* New York: Oxford, 1961.

Singer, C. *Greek biology and Greek medicine.* Oxford: Clarendon Press, 1922.

Singer, C. *A history of biology.* Rev. ed. New York: Schuman, 1950. (3d ed., Abelard-Schumann, 1959.)

Singer, C. *A short history of anatomy and physiology from the Greeks to Harvey.* New York: Dover, 1957.

Singer, C. *A short history of scientific ideas to 1900.* Oxford: Clarendon Press, 1959.

Singer, C., and Underwood, E. A. *A short history of medicine.* 2nd ed. Oxford: Clarendon Press, 1962.

Sinnott, E. W. *Cell and psyche. The biology of purpose.* Chapel Hill: University of North Carolina Press, 1950.

Sinnott, E. W. *Biology of the spirit*. New York: Viking, 1960.

Skinner, B. F. *The behavior of organisms*. New York: Appleton-Century, 1938.

Skinner, B. F. "Superstition" in the pigeon. *J. exp. Psychol.*, 1948, 38, 168-172. (a)

Skinner, B. F. *Walden Two*. New York: Macmillan, 1948. (b)

Skinner, B. F. *Science and human behavior*. New York: Macmillan, 1953.

Skinner, B. F. Freedom and the control of men. *Amer. Scholar*, 1955, 25, 47-65.

Skinner, B. F. A case history in scientific method. *Amer. Psychologist*, 1956, 11, 221-233.

Skinner, B. F. *Verbal behavior*. New York: Appleton-Century-Crofts, 1957.

Skinner, B. F. The flight from the laboratory. In W. Dennis et al. *Current trends in psychological theory*. Pittsburgh: University of Pittsburgh Press, 1961. Pp. 50-69.

Smith, M. The nervous temperament. *Brit. J. medical Psychol.*, 1930, 10, 99 ff.

Smith, M. B. Some recent texts in social psychology. *Psychol. Bull.*, 1953, 50, 150-159.

Smith, S. The principles of a maze learning machine. *Psychol. Bull.*, 1936, 33, 799.

Snell, B. *The discovery of the mind*. New York: Harper, 1960.

Spence, K. W. Review of Köhler's *Dynamics in psychology*. *Psychol. Bull.*, 1941, 38, 886-889.

Spence, K. W. *Behavior theory and learning*. Englewood Cliffs, N. J.: Prentice-Hall, 1960.

Spender, S. *Engaged in writing*. New York: Farrar, Straus & Cudahy, 1958.

Sprague, J. M., Chambers, W. W., and Stellar, E. Attentive, affective, and adaptive behavior in the cat. *Science*, 1961, 133, 165-173.

St. Aubyn, G. *A Victorian eminence*. London: Barrie, 1958.

Stenzel, J. *Plato's method of dialectic*. Transl. by D. J. Allan. Oxford: Oxford University Press, 1940.

Stumpf, C. [Autobiography] in C. Murchison (Ed.), *A history of psychology in autobiography*. Vol. I. Worcester, Mass.: Clark University Press, 1930. Pp. 389-441.

Swadesh, M. On linguistic mechanism. *Science and Society*. 1948, 12, 254-259.

Swartz, P. Perspectives in psychology: V. Psychology in the historical sense. *Psychol. Rec.*, 1958, 8, 17-20.

Swets, J. A. Is there a sensory threshold? *Science*, 1961, 134, 168-177.

Taylor, A. E. *Aristotle*. New York: Dover, 1955.

Taylor, A. E. *Plato. The Sophist and the Statesman*. London: Thomas Nelson, 1961.

Thompson, D. W. *On Aristotle as a biologist*. Oxford: Clarendon Press, 1913.

Thomson, G. The two aspects of science. *Science*, 1960, 132, 996-1000.

Thorndike, E. L. Animal intelligence. *Psychol. Monogr.*, 1898, 2, No. 4.

Thorndike, E. L. *An introduction to the theory of mental and social measurements*. New York: Teachers College, Columbia University, 1904; 2nd ed., 1913.

Thorndike, E. L. *Human nature and the social order*. New York: Macmillan, 1940.

Thurstone, L. L. *The fundamentals of statistics*. New York: Macmillan, 1924.

Titchener, E. B. *Lectures on the elementary psychology of feeling and attention*. New York: Macmillan, 1908.

Tompkins, S. R. *The Russian intelligentsia*. Norman, Okla.: University of Oklahoma Press, 1957.

Triplett, N. The dynamogenic factors in pacemaking and competition. *Amer. J. Psychol.*, 1897, 9, 507-533.

Tylor, E. B. *Primitive culture.* 2 vols. New York: Holt, 1888.

Uexküll, J. v. Ueber die Stellung der vergleichenden Physiologie zur Hypothese der Tierseele. *Biologisches Centralblatt,* 1900, 20, 497-502.

Uexküll, J. v. *Umwelt und Innenwelt der Tiere.* Berlin: Springer, 1909.

Untersteiner, M. *The sophists.* Transl. by K. Freeman. New York: Philosophical Library, 1954.

Urban, W. M. *Language and reality.* London: Allen & Unwin, 1939.

Virchow, R. Scientific method and therapeutic standpoints. (1849) In Virchow, R. *Disease, life, and man.* Transl. by L. J. Rather. New York: Collier Books, 1962. Pp. 54-81.

Viteles, M. S. The new Utopia. *Science,* 1955, 122, 1167-1171.

Vlastos, G. Ethics and physics in Democritus. *Phil. Rev.,* 1945, 54, 578 ff.; 1946, 55, 53 ff.

Waddington, C. H. *How animals develop.* New York: Harper, 1962.

Wallace, D. M. *Russia.* London, 1877.

Wallace, W. Article *Empedocles in Encycl. Brit.,* 11th ed., 1910.

Walsh, C. *From utopia to nightmare.* New York: Harper & Row, 1962.

Warner, L. A second survey of psychological opinion on E.S.P. *J. Parapsychol.,* 1952, 16, 284-295.

Warren, H. C. *A history of the association psychology.* New York: Scribner's, 1921. (a)

Warren, H. C. Psychology and the central nervous system. *Psychol. Rev.,* 1921, 28, 249-269. (b)

Warren, H. C. The significance of neural adjustment. *Psychol. Rev.,* 1922, 29, 481-489.

Wasmann, E. Einige Bemerkungen zur vergleichenden Psychologie und Sinnesphysiologie. *Biologisches Centralblatt,* 1900, 20, 342-350.

Watson, J. B. *Psychology from the standpoint of a behaviorist.* 2nd ed. Philadelphia: Lippincott, 1924. (1st ed., 1919)

Watson, R. I. The history of psychology: a neglected area. *Amer. Psychologist,* 1960, 15, 251-255.

Webster's *New international dictionary of the English language.* 2nd ed. Springfield, Mass.: Merriam, 1937.

Weiss, A. P. The mind and the man-within. *Psychol. Rev.,* 1919, 26, 327-334.

Weiss, A. P. Behavior and the central nervous system. *Psychol. Rev.,* 1922, 29, 329-343.

Weiss, A. P. *A theoretical basis of human behavior.* 2nd ed. Columbus, Ohio. R. G. Adams, 1929. (a)

Weiss, A. P. Bridgman's new vision of science. *Sci. Monthly,* 1929, 29, 506-514. (b)

Wheeler, R. H. Organismic logic in the history of science. *Phil. Sci.,* 1936, 3, 26-61.

Whittemore, I. C. Influence of competition on performance: an experimental study. *J. abnorm. soc. Psychol.,* 1924, 19, 236-253.

Whorf, B. L. *Language, thought, and reality.* New York: Wiley, 1956.

Whyte, L. L. *Essays on atomism: from Democritus to 1960.* Middletown, Conn.: Wesleyan University Press, 1961.

Wightman, W. P. D. *The growth of scientific ideas.* New Haven: Yale University Press, 1953.

Windelband, W. *History of ancient philosophy.* Transl. by H. E. Cushman. New York: Dover, 1956.

Windelband, W. *A history of philosophy.* Transl. by J. H. Tufts. 2 vols. New York: Harper, 1958.

Wöhler, F. Ueber künstliche Bildung des Harnstoffs. *Ann d. Phys. u. Chem.,* 1828, 12, 253-256.

Wolf, S., and Wolff, H. G. Human gastric function; an experimental study of a man and his stomach. New York: Oxford University Press, 1943.

Wolfe, B. D. Review of R. A. Bauer's *The new man in Soviet psychology. Saturday Review,* June 14, 1952, pp. 23-24.

Wolman, B. B. *Contemporary theories and systems in psychology.* New York: Harper, 1960.

Wundt, W. *Principles of physiological psychology.* Vol. I. Transl. of 5th ed. (1902) by E. B. Titchener. New York: Macmillan, 1904.

Wundt, W. *Völkerpsychologie.* Vol. I: *Die Sprache* (Erster Teil). 3d ed. Leipzig: Engelmann, 1911.

Zeller, E. *Outlines of the history of Greek philosophy.* 13th ed. Transl. by L. R. Palmer. New York: Meridian, 1955.

Ziegler, H. E. Theoretisches zur Tierpsychologie und vergleichenden Neurophysiologie. *Biologisches Centralblatt,* 1900, 20, 1-16.

Zilboorg, G. *A history of medical psychology.* New York: Norton, 1941.

Zipf, G. K. *Selected studies of the principle of relative frequency in language.* Cambridge, Mass.: Harvard University Press, 1932.

Zipf, G. K. *The psycho-biology of language.* Boston: Houghton Mifflin, 1935.

INDEX